D1548904

The foundations of the South African cheap labour system

International Library of Sociology

Founded by Karl Mannheim

Editor: John Rex, University of Aston in Birmingham

Arbor Scientiae
Arbor Vitae

A catalogue of the books available in the **International Library of Sociology** and other series of Social Science books published by Routledge & Kegan Paul will be found at the end of this volume.

The foundations of the South African cheap labour system

Norman Levy

Routledge & Kegan Paul

London, Boston, Melbourne and Henley

First published in 1982
by Routledge & Kegan Paul Ltd
39 Store Street, London WC1E 7DD,
9 Park Street, Boston, Mass. 02108, USA,
296 Beaconsfield Parade, Middle Park,
Melbourne, 3206, Australia, and
Broadway House, Newtown Road,
Henley-on-Thames, Oxon RG9 1EN
Printed in Great Britain by
The Thetford Press Ltd, Thetford, Norfolk
© Norman Levy 1982

Library of Congress Cataloging in Publication Data

Levy, Norman, 1929–

The foundations of the South African cheap labour
system.
(International library of sociology)
Bibliography: p.
Includes index.
1. Wages — South Africa — History.   2. Labor supply —
South Africa — History.   3. Manpower policy — South
Africa — History.   I. Title   II. Series.
HD5092.L48   331.1'0968   82-7580

ISBN 0-7100-0909-7   AACR2

For Deborah, Simon, Jessica and Tim

Contents

Contents

Contents

Tables

Maps

Introduction

This work is primarily concerned with the first twenty years of gold mining. Its main burden is to establish that the foundations of the South African cheap labour system in the gold mines were laid in the first ten years of mining and successfully defended in the next decade. After 1896, with the development of deep-level mining, the industry's needs (already apparent in the early 1890s) became more urgent for a state that would identify itself unambiguously with the mining industry. It needed also a state which would enable it to effect large-scale economies in working costs and provide an extensive increase in the labour supply, based on the principles evolved in the formative years. This in effect was the consequence of the Anglo-Boer War, which led to an increase in state intervention to guarantee the conditions for the satisfaction of the complex needs of a rapidly expanding industry in the transition to the deep-level phase of production. The immediate post-war years that followed the conflict served to consolidate and defend the labour structure that was evolved in the first ten years of mining.

The historiographical treatment of the *foundations* of the cheap labour system in the gold industry – the late 1880s and early 1890s – has been less than adequate. But for the important work of S. T. van der Horst, which was written in 1938, the crucial questions which dominated the fixing of the wage rate, the mechanisms for recruitment, and the extra-economic measures to increase and retain the labour supply have until recently received little systematic historical treatment. In particular, the *early* institutional machinery for the acquisition of a large (migrant) labour supply has been given scant attention. Hence the data and sources explored by van der Horst and others have been re-examined with different criteria of relevance and, I hope, informed by the benefits of recent scholarship. Part One of this work therefore deals with the evolution of the labour structure, the phenomenon of migrant labour and the supply-price relationship. Part Two concerns the relation of mining capital to the state and the Randlords' 'revolution from above'. Part Three is concerned with the defence of that structure and the racial work restrictions that arose as a consequence of it. The state as such is not theorized, but it is intended that this first systematic documentation of the foundations of the cheap labour system in the South African gold mines will contribute to such a study, and that it will be informed to some extent by the significance attached to the historical role of the state in providing the mechanisms outlined in this work for the functioning of the labour market on the Rand.

Acknowledgments

My sincere thanks are due to the many who commented on this work at its various stages of preparation. To mention names is invidious, but special thanks must be made to Professor F. J. Fisher of the London School of Economics for his (untypical) patience in seeing this work through the PhD thesis stage (from which it grew); to Shula Marks and Harold Wolpe for their invaluable comments; to Jackie Hoogendyck, who typed many drafts and without whose initial encouragement this work would never have been completed; to Sue Dobson for her interest and brilliant secretarial skills; to Reuben Ruff for the map of Southern Africa; and last but by no means least, to Dot Lewis for typing the final manuscript. For her care over the presentation of this work and her formidable capacity to eliminate the pompous, the tautologous, and the inconsistencies that frequently creep into a work of this nature, I give my most sincere (and belated) thanks. The responsibility for the content, however, is, of course, my own. Finally, my deepest appreciation to the United Nations, whose Fellowship enabled me to undertake this study in the first place; to the Librarians at the Royal Commonwealth Society and the Official Publications section of the British Library, for their help and interest, and the assistants of Berkeley and Stanford Universities, California, for whose help I am indebted. To them all, my sincerest thanks.

Part One

The foundations

1 Calculating the wage rate

INTRODUCTION

The calculation of the African cash wage was the subject
of complicated debate in the formative years of gold
mining on the Witwatersrand. The debate was confused and
conflicting. On the one hand there was a recognition that
the African rural producer temporarily separated himself
from the land for work on the mines in order to acquire
subsistence and obtain commodities for which he was unable
to produce a sufficient surplus - a tacit recognition that
there was some structural compulsion that drew him to the
mines. On the other hand there was a belief that he (as
subject) primarily exercised a choice in which he calculated the opportunity cost of labouring on the mines.
Whilst there were several contemporary statements reflecting this position, there is none so crudely expressed
as Cartwright's recent one:

> They work hard these 'mine boys' and the slacker stands
> no chance whatever of getting the rest of the gang to
> 'carry' him.... He works much harder than he ever did
> at home. But he counts as his reward for that the
> good food, the free beer and the cash he receives.
> He also counts the club 'life' that is his when he is
> off duty. *And having weighed the amount of work he
> must do against these rewards he comes to the decision
> that this is the job for him.* (1)

Frequently the various arguments concerning the relationship between the supply and the price of the labour
force were combined to produce the view that the supply
of labour would fall if wages were raised. They reasoned
that the Africans were 'attracted' to the mines primarily
to satisfy specific wants. If wages were increased these

wants would be satisfied sooner and induce them to work shorter periods.

This perception of the problem, that high wages deflected the flow of migrant labourers from the mines and enabled them to satisfy their limited domestic needs for longer periods, was reinforced in 1893 by a comprehensive report on African labour which maintained 'that the higher the rate of wages given to the Natives, the less will be the supply because he comes to earn a certain sum; when that is gained he returns home for a spell of idleness'. (2) Later, one of the consulting engineers giving evidence to the Industrial Commission of Enquiry restated this view of the workforce: Africans are attracted to the mines only 'in order to make enough money to return to their kraals with sufficient means ... to marry and live in indolence'. (3) This view was reiterated throughout the early period of this study, wherever the African labour flow gave cause for concern. (4) Yet it will be seen that the mine-owners were to become increasingly aware of the structural constraints that both induced the rural producers to submit themselves for work on the mines and at certain times enabled them to resist the pressure of the ubiquitous activities of the recruiting agents of the Witwatersrand mines. (5) At such times (1890, 1896, 1899, 1903/4 particularly) the notion that the strength and regularity of the supply was dependent on the marginal choice of the workforce was uttered with less certainty, and resort was made to the internal re-organization of the labour-recruiting arrangements as well as contractual changes and extra-economic measures to satisfy the supply needs of the industry.

The workforce was from the outset transient and migrant rather than permanent and proletarianized. The reasons for this are complicated and relate to several factors, not the least of which were to do with the following:

(i)   the condition of African *and White* agriculture in the period between the discovery of gold in the 1880s and the Land Act of 1913 (clearly African agriculture was important during this period and Africans endeavoured persistently to retain and *increase* their land); (6)

(ii) the labour needs of the industry in the developmental stages of mining;

(iii) the industrial advantages in disciplining and controlling a part-peasant workforce housed en masse in compounds, ubiquitously overseen by mine officials;

(iv) the cost benefits to be derived by the mine-owners from this system of labour;

MAP 1 Southern Africa, 1905

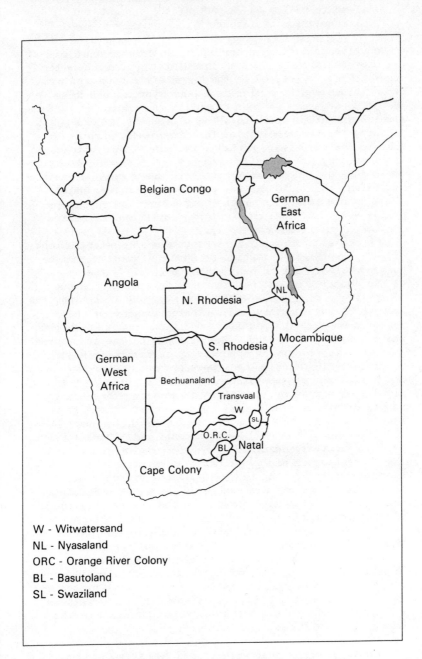

W - Witwatersand
NL - Nyasaland
ORC - Orange River Colony
BL - Basutoland
SL - Swaziland

(v) African resistance to mine labour;
(vi) state policy in respect of the control and
     regulation of labour.

Doubtless all these contributed to the emergence of
the migrant labour system as the dominant form (7) - the
one which has persisted on the South African gold mines.
Explanations that the migrant labour system was exclusively the consequence of cost calculations undertaken by the
mine-owners are ahistorical, and ultimately unsatisfactory, for they imply that the mine-owners' need gave
rise to the solution. Clearly, the mine labour system
was formed by all the circumstances under which labourers
could be acquired - at low cost - in the formative years
of mining. But this did not preclude the mine-owners'
subsequently reflecting upon their labour system or opposing alternative forms for the acquisition and reproduction of their labour supply.

The occasion for such reflection was the establishment
of the Industrial Commission of Enquiry, whose ten high-
powered members sat to hear evidence in 1897, when most
of the 'outcrop mines' had reached the producing stage and
'deep-level' mining was well under way. By this time, the
leaders of the industry had a clearer picture of their
labour needs and the peculiar conditions under which gold
was procured on the Rand. The sittings of the commission
gave the mine-owners an opportunity to air their major
needs and grievances: the impact on costs caused by
monopolist state concessions in dynamite, transport and
liquor; the past difficulties of acquiring an adequate
supply of African labourers; deficiencies in the regulation and control of the labour supply (e.g. the poor administration of the Pass Regulations). All these items
were exhaustively examined by the commission and formed
the content of carefully prepared evidence by leading
spokesmen for the industry: Hay, Albu, Fitzpatrick,
Dalrymple, Goldmann, Brakhan, H.Jennings. Significantly,
none of these witnesses questioned the efficacy of the
migrant labour system. Nor did they suggest that a
'stabilized' (urban) workforce would be preferable to
the existing migrant system. Indeed, on the occasions
that a settled labour force was discussed (under the
euphemistic heading 'locations'), it was at the instance
of the members of the commission and *not* the representatives of the mining industry. Frequently the witnesses
had to be drawn on the subject. Albu, Chairman of the
Association of Mines, for instance, was asked:

Don't you think that with regard to native labour, if

natives were allowed locations around Johannesburg it
would be a good way of getting kaffirs here? (p.23 of
the 'Evidence and Report of the Industrial Commission
of Enquiry')

The response was initially perfunctory: 'The kraal
kaffirs won't do this. Only Colonial boys will do it
perhaps' ('Evidence', p.23).
    Pressed further, he added somewhat inconsistently:

... I think if the natives had their locations here,
and had their wives and families, they would make this
place their home. ('Evidence', p.24)

There seemed to be more enthusiasm for 'locations' as a
means of replenishing the small corpus of long-term
'skilled' labourers - normally not more than 5 per cent
of the workforce on any mine (see Chapter 3). E.J.Way,
for example, giving evidence on behalf of the George Goch
mine, where he was manager, told the commission:

... We have a location upon our lower claims, and I
have boys who have their wives and families, who have
been working at the mine for the last eight years. If
locations could be established somewhere in the neighbourhood of the mines - within walking distance - so
that natives could bring down their wives and families,
I think you would have a far greater supply than you
require. ('Evidence', p.43)

But the 'skilled' component of the African workforce
was relatively small. Generally there was little interest
in 'stabilization' for the mass of the labour force. None
of the witnesses actually *asked* for 'locations' as an
alternative to the migrant labour system, and all were
very reticent about discussing the matter. S.J.Jennings,
manager at the Crown Reef Gold Mining Company ('Evidence',
p.46), and A.Brakhan, manager for South Africa of A.Goerz
and Co.Ltd ('Evidence', p.184), were, if anything, less
than enthusiastic. In both instances they treated the
matter as academic and used the occasion to ask for intensified state co-operation in the management of the
pass regulations, the liquor laws and the acquisition of
the labour supply.
    The commission's recommendation on the matter was ulti-
mately inane and irrelevant, and doubtless reflected the
lack of interest (or covert objection) to altering the
system of migrant labour upon which the gold industry had
been established. The recommendation read, according to

the 'Report of the Industrial Commission of Enquiry',
p.449:

> Much has been said about the desirability of establish-
> ing locations for kaffirs close to the Rand, but your
> commission cannot at all recommend this course. Ex-
> perience has taught that the establishment of locations
> does not improve the kaffirs in any way, but only tends
> to their deterioration. As soon as the kaffir with his
> family lives in a location, his highest aim in life is
> to see his wife and children work while he himself
> looks on.

Thus, despite the initial difficulties of acquiring an
adequate labour supply, the Chamber did not set out to
establish a large, 'stabilized' workforce, and in fact
evaded the question in 1897 when they had the earliest
official opportunity to declare their attitude on the
matter. In so doing, they were more than likely influenced by the cost factors in a technically complicated and
expensive production process wherein the price of labour
was of critical importance. (See Section iii, The
'viability' of migrant labour, below.) All the problems
already enumerated, plus the nature of the ore, the relative inflexibility of mining techniques, (8) the absence
of a need for a long period of training for the bulk of
the workforce, the fixed price of gold, the overall costs
of production - these were the determining factors in the
structuring of the industry on the basis of migrant
labour. (9) And in paring down costs and controlling and
housing this migrant, part-peasant workforce, the owners
of the Rand goldfields had the rich experience of the
Kimberley diamond fields to follow. (10)
The calculation of the wage rate and the utilization
of labour had much to do with the problems connected with
the acquisition and extraction of gold. Because the
labour strategies of the Chamber were directly related to
the cost factors determined by the geological constraints
of mining, considerable significance is therefore attached
to these particular problems.

(i)   THE PRODUCTION PROCESS: LABOUR-INTENSIVE TECHNIQUES

Geographically the Witwatersrand goldfields - a strip of
approximately fifty miles extending from the district of
Randfontein on the west of Johannesburg to Springs on the
east - were not the most conducive to mining. Despite
what was described as its 'remarkable consistency of gold

content, its climatically healthy situation, proximity to
coal fields, and the large reserve of native labour',
(11) the technical problems and relatively high costs of
appropriating the gold were frequently underplayed. Moreover the individual beds of ore varied considerably in
their incidence and economic importance. Thus while the
Witwatersrand goldfields were seen as the most extensive
deposits in the world, they were also generally of comparatively low-grade quality. Hence the significance of
the relationship attributed by the mine-owners to capital
and working costs, the problems being exacerbated among
other things by the constraints on technology that the
geological character of the gold-bearing ore imposed upon
the industry. (12)

The beds of gold-bearing conglomerate (the so-called
banket) were intercalated through a quartzite formation
bound by a siliceous cement containing iron pyrites, with
geological dislocations in the reef which caused breaks
in the continuity of the outcrop and consequently difficult technical problems and high costs in the development
stages of shaft sinking, timbering and hoisting. (13) In
addition to breaks in the reef, mining problems were made
much greater by the fact that the gold was not easy to
get at. For example, the auriferous ore was frequently
concealed under measures of coal, igneous intrusions or
dolomite formations which required to be penetrated before
a sliver of gold-bearing ore could be obtained. Indeed,
Perrings (14) is probably not too wide of the mark in his
statement that but for the low-cost system of migrant
labour, it is unlikely that the processes required to win
the gold could have been undertaken. Certainly the mine-
owners could not have undertaken them with any certainty
of a rate of profitability that would have been attractive
to investors. The difficulties of winning the gold were
recently well described by the Chamber of Mines:

Imagine a solid mass of rock tilted ... like a fat
1,200 page dictionary laying at an angle. The gold-
bearing reef would be thinner than a single page, and
the amount of gold contained therein would hardly cover
a couple of commas in the entire book. It is the
miner's job to bring out that single page - but his
job is made harder because the 'page' has been twisted
and torn by nature's forces, and pieces of it have been
thrust between other leaves of the book. (15)

The major effects of these faults were strategic and
financial, ultimately making production techniques less
flexible, increasing costs, influencing the level of

labour intensity and the utilization of the workforce in
the underground operations. Shaft sinking, and the associated development work of timbering and cutting the
lodges or sumps to collect the water and provide chambers
from which the water could be pumped, were rendered more
expensive and complex as a result of the incline of the
reef and unevenness of the geological formations. Hence
it was not always possible to sink a vertical shaft and
expect to follow the reef in the normal way. Instead
incline shafts had to be erected, which were costlier for
continuous hoisting than the vertical type and required
complex and expensive engineering techniques. To install
the incline shaft, the inclination of the reef had to be
estimated - it was at best an approximation - and the
shaft set at an angle that was likely to be only as close
to the reef as possible. (16) On some occasions the
shafts changed their inclination four or five times, com-
plicating construction and subsequent haulage still further. Indeed, in the early years of mining costly errors
occurred which had to be made good, such as on the
Robinson and Langlaate mines which were opened up with
three shallow vertical shafts which had in each case to
be abandoned for the two incline shafts. (17) For the
most part, however, once a mine had adopted a particular
development plan the cost of alteration was prohibitive,
with the consequence that mining techniques (especially
in regard to the haulage of ore) were made less flexible
and benefits of cost reductions made substantially more
difficult. (18) The greater the distance of the shaft
from the reef, the longer and more expensive and intricate
it was to hoist the broken rock. The problems became particularly complicated and costly with the development in
1893 of deep-level mines. (19) (Those mines on which the
reefs that were being worked came to the surface were
referred to as 'outcrop mines'. The 'deep-level mines'
(the so-called first row) are situated vertically over
the immediate extension of the reef, dipping from the
outcrop mines. A second row of 'deep-levels' is situated
over the reef as it extends downwards from the first row
of the deep-levels.)
    Of the three primary underground operations of shaft
sinking, ore developing and ore stoping, shaft sinking in
the deep-level mines was a much more important and distinct operation than in the outcrop mines. This was so,
according to Truscott, 'because until the reef is reached,
it proceeds alone and marks a definite stage in the history of the mine'. (20) More particularly, the development plan of the three primary operations, especially
shaft sinking, influenced the costs and arrangements for

hoisting and tramming the ore and pumping the water. The
cost of shaft sinking on deep-level mines was especially
high, since there were generally *two* shafts on each of the
deep-level properties, the deeper one being used as a main
pumping shaft and for ventilation. Moreover, the deep-
level shafts were laid out to work approximately 100
claims, that is, twice the number intended for the outcrops. (21) Hence the high cost of sinking the shafts
plus the costs of ore developing and ore stoping made the
mine-owners particularly sensitive to paring down those
costs (especially unskilled wages) which appeared to them
to be more compressible than the primary costs of mine
development. It also frequently determined the degree of
labour intensity with which the developmental processes
were undertaken. The sinking of the cheaper (vertical)
shafts were a case in point. The cost of sinking these
varied from approximately £15 per foot of shaft sunk on
the Nourse Deep mine to over £41 on the Knights Deep mine.
(22) In the first case the total depth of the operation
was 991 feet as against 716 feet in the second case. On
the Simmer and Jack East mine a depth of 1,546 feet was
reached at a cost of approximately £22 with a much larger-
sized shaft than in the first case (28 x 8 feet as against
a small excavation of less than 18 x 8 feet). (23) The
reason for this was that the operation was conducted
entirely by hand labour. Indeed (unless water interfered
with the process), whenever the intensity of labour applied to shaft sinking was high, the cost of the operations was proportionately substantially lower than when
this was not the case. (24) (See Table 1.1.)

Next in importance to the primary operations of shaft
sinking - for its impact on costs as well as its technical
complexity and effects on labour utilization - was that of
stoping. The stope is an underground working in which a
section of the reef hitherto opened up by levels is
removed. All the operations involved in the breaking of
the solid reef (including the positioning of the broken
rock to be 'trammed' away) falls under the umbrella of
stoping. (25) The cost and complexity of stoping processes varied with the angle of the dip, the width of the ore-
bore and the depth of the workings. Generally the stope
was kept as narrow as possible to minimize the waste rock
that had to be broken. (26) Once broken, the ore was
generally removed to the bottom of the stope by shovelling. The less rock to be shovelled the more economical
the operation. The amount of ore to be shovelled rested
on the techniques used as well as the dip of the reef.
Hence, where the dip was a steep one the ore could be
removed by gravity. Otherwise it had to be shovelled.

TABLE 1.1 Cost and rate of sinking vertical shafts

Name of mine	Name of number of shaft	Total depth (feet)	Size of shaft excavation	Rate of sinking (feet per month)	Cost per foot of shaft sunk			Remarks
			feet		£	s.	d.	
Rose Deep	1	911	23 x 8	-	31	1	4	
Rose Deep	2	714	18 x 8	-	26	16	5	
Nourse Deep	1	991½	Small	-	15	10	7	
Nourse Deep	2	1580	3 compartments	-	20	1	3	
Nourse Deep	3	1483	3 compartments	-	20	11	2	
Jumpers Deep	2	1057	23 x 8	65)				
				)	24	9	0	
Jumpers Deep	2	1352	23 x 8	-)				
Glen Deep	1	1005	18½ x 8	91	22	4	2	
Glen Deep	2	1017	18½ x 8	66	24	2	10	Sunk in dyke from 42 feet to bottom
Langlaagte Deep	1	1174	23 x 8	60	26	3	5	
Langlaagte Deep	2	968	23 x 8	60	22	17	7	
Durban Roodeport Deep	2	1444	18 x 8	87	19	10	5	

Robinson Deep	1	2389	22 x 8		25	14	7	Sunk entirely by hand drilling; the costs include an amount for depreciation of plant and machine used in sinking
Robinson Deep	2	1923	18½ x 8	69)	24	3	7	
Crown Deep	1	1324	22 x 8	-)	33	14	8	
Crown Deep	2	1100	22 x 8	-				
Vogelstruis Deep	East	891	18 x 7½	65	20	14	0	
Vogelstruis Deep	Central	1055	18 x 7½	89	18	12	4	
Vogelstruis Deep	West	960	18 x 7½	86	15	5	9	Sunk entirely by hand labour
West Roodeport Deep	1	734	18 x 7	67)	19	6	0	
West Roodeport Deep	2	926	18 x 7	)				
Knights Deep	Robertson	885	28 x 8	55	34	4	3	Sinking interfered with by water
Knights Deep	Connor	716	28 x 8	40	41	7	11	
Simmer and Jack East	Clement	1546	28 x 8	94	22	7	11	Sunk entirely by hand labour
Simmer and Jack East	Hammond	1518	28 x 8	96	23	3	3	Sunk entirely by hand labour
Simmer and Jack East	Lohse	961	28 x 8	70	28	12	2	Sunk entirely by hand labour

Source: S.J.Truscott, 'The Witwatersrand Gold Fields' (1898), p.190.

Approximately 20 per cent of the labourers in the stope
were required in 1897 to shovel where the dip was thirty
degrees. Where the size of the stope was relatively low
(and the timbering close) 50 per cent of the labourers
were employed in shovelling. (27) Rails were sometimes
placed in the stope where the reef was flat and the stope
sufficiently large. Trucks were then run in and the
broken ore shovelled into them. But the size and slope
of the stope did not always permit this. A very large
stope was ten feet wide and upwards, the smaller stopes
three feet wide or less. In view of the smallness of the
stopes, the amount of rock broken was therefore important.
It affected the whole range of costs that determined the
profitability of the grade of ore milled. Rock was broken
by blasting. For this, two or three holes were drilled by
hand or machine across the stope. As the labour force
became scarce - and where the stopes were large and flat
and the roof good - machine drills were seen to be as
economical as hand drilling and were consequently used
increasingly. (28) However, where the stopes were small
and the reef was at too steep a dip, the range of action
of the machine drill was limited and hand labour was more
feasible, quicker and cheaper. In certain stopes where
the amount of quartzite in the reef was high, the rock
became pulverized by the large charges used in machine-
drilled holes. Consequently the ore, when so embedded
in quartzite, could not be used when the holes were not
hand-drilled. Machine stoping under these circumstances
(where the quartzite was excessively pulverized) also
frequently brought down chunky sections (blocks) of the
reef which had to be blasted again. Hence where the
amount of waste broken was too great, and where (through
mechanization) much unsortable waste was formed, the mine-
owners found hand labour cheaper.

Under these circumstances, the extended use of machine
drills in stoping was 'often accompanied by a fall in the
grade of the ore milled'. (29) Machine stoping in an
ordinary-sized reef was in fact generally considered to
be more costly than hand stoping. With a lighter class of
drill, it seemed, the position might have been reversed.
The 'Little Giant' drill was thought to be the answer to
both the technical problems and the problems of cost when
it was introduced in the mid-1890s, but although it did
the job effectively it was found to be too costly compared
with hand labour. According to Truscott, whose work was
published in 1898, in the Jumpers mine:

> where four 'Little Giant' drills, 2¼ inches in diame-
> ter, are used in the stopes, it is found that with one

white man and five natives looking after two of them,
stoping with these machine drills costs about as much
for labour, air and explosives costs in hand drilling,
so that the cost of maintaining the drills, which is
considerable, has to be met over and above the costs
of hand labour. (30)

Where the lighter 'Little Giant' drills (about 2¼
inches in diameter and weighing less than 175 lb) were
used for stoping, they did the work of nine 'hammer boys',
who drilled 3 feet and broke 12 cwt per shift, but with
the high cost of explosives this method, especially in
the early years, was found to be more expensive. According to the evidence presented to the Industrial
Commission of Enquiry of 1897, the cost of the gelatine
that was used with machine drills was 1.63 times the cost
of that used in hand labour for each square fathom of rock
that was mined (29s. 8. 6d. and 17s. 1. 3d. respectively).
(31)

Apart from rock drilling, practically all the *underground* transport of ore from the stope-face to the shaft -
the tramming - was done by hand labour. Where a considerable amount of waste was broken, the larger pieces were
either sorted underground or trammed to other stopes already worked out. Excessive waste increased the work of
tramming, and once again the number of labourers required
for this purpose. In this early phase of underground
mining, where conditions permitted, a laborious labour-
intensive process was undertaken whereby the ore was
scraped directly into trucks which were pulled by 'end-
less' rope-haulage to the shaft. Labourers were needed
all along the line to see that the trucks did not fall
off. (32) According to Perrings, writing primarily of
the period after 1903, 'the only concession to mechanization in these areas - scraping - brought no more than
marginal reductions of the total requirements of unskilled
labour'. (33)

Generally the mine-owners kept a careful watch over the
cost of stoping and shovelling. Records of the number of
trucks of ore that were obtained by each 'hammer boy' and
'shovel boy' were scrupulously kept by the respective mine
managers. (34) The precision of the information helped
to establish the profitability of the ore and to some
extent determined the techniques to be used, as well as
the degree of hand labour to be deployed, although in the
early years hand labour was most generally in use.

Besides the relatively high costs and their effect on
labour utilization in the primary underground operations,
the techniques used in handling the rock in the confined

spaces of the stopes directly affected the cost of 'ore
dressing'. This included the *surface* processes of
screening, sorting and crushing the broken rock which was
hauled to the surface for the extraction of the gold from
the ore. (35) The cost of the sorting process was affected by the quantity of waste rock that was hauled up
with the reef. Until 1903, sorting consisted of sepa-
rating the waste rock (quartzite and sometimes slate) from
the reef matter. In addition, as reefs are on the whole
exceptionally thin and on occasion close together (and
separated only by pieces of quartzite), waste has of necessity to be mined. The effect of this was to increase
tramming and the labour force as well as the costs of
milling. Where rock drills were more extensively applied
in the stopes, the amount of waste that was mined increased - in the most extreme cases to 80 per cent of the
rock broken, and in the minimum instance not less than 10
per cent. (36) In 1898 the cost of milling and cyaniding
was 8s. per ton. (37) This, in the 1890s, represented
slightly less than a third of the average working cost
per ton of ore milled (38) - hence the importance the
mine-owners attached to cost generally, especially the
costs of mechanization relative to hand labour. The relatively inflexible high cost of winning gold - the price of
which was fixed by international agreement - was in a
large measure responsible (if optimum profits were to be
realized) for the constant wage reductions throughout the
period of this study and the significance the mine-owners
attached to the overall utilization of labour and the
migrant character of the workforce. (39)

(ii)   WORKING COSTS AND THE 'FIXED' PRICE OF GOLD

While the 'fixed' price of gold protected the commodity as
the 'money material' from market fluctuations caused,
inter alia, by changes in the supply and demand of gold,
it also had the effect of restricting the producers' rate
of profit. This was primarily due to the industry's incapacity to pass on to the consumer any increases in the
cost of production. This was true of the early years of
mining, as it was when in 1925 the mine-owners' representatives told the Economic and Wage Commission:

   (i) that the gold mines, unlike many other producers,
   cannot pass on to the consumer any increase in their
   cost of production;
   (ii) that on most, if not on every mine, an increase
   in one direction in the cost of production gives rise

to consequent increases in some other direction, with
the final result that the productive capacity and/or
life of the mine is decreased. (40)

This problem was, however, exacerbated by the growing gap
between world commodity prices and the internationally
accepted price of gold.

The declining purchasing power of gold became a serious
problem for the mine-owners in 1898, approximately eight
years after the initial Witwatersrand mines were brought
to the production stage. (41) The years coinciding with
the exploration and discovery of the Witwatersrand goldfields were occasioned by a fall in average world commodity prices - the attention of the mining companies
being consumed during the last decade of the nineteenth
century by the price problems internal to the Transvaal,
such as the inflated costs of explosives, coal and communications 'imposed' on the mines as a result of monopolist concessions granted to private individuals by the
Transvaal state. On the world stage, however, commodity
prices between 1890 and 1897 (especially the period
between 1895 and 1896) were lower than during the twenty
years between 1850 and 1873 or the subsequent years between 1896 and 1920. (42) Table 1.2 shows the output and
value of gold produced between 1887 and 1905. (43)

It was thus true to say that in the post-bellum phase,
when the index of world commodity prices fell sharply in
relation to the international price of gold, the
Witwatersrand mine-owners had already had much experience
- substantially enhanced with the expensive operations
involved in the sinking of the deep-level shafts after
1893 - in paring down costs to combat the high cost of
production. Fortunately for the mine-owners, the intervention of the British state in the 'War of Gold' and the
defeat of Kruger's government had avoided the simultaneous
conjuncture of inflation in world commodity prices and the
maintenance of monopoly costs in the essential goods and
services needed for mining. However, the high cost of
imported mining stores, (44) already 23.5 per cent of all
working costs on the Rand in 1895 (45) - and increasing
substantially with the growth of mining after 1901 -
presented a growing challenge to the mine-owners to maintain their rate of profit.

This, together with a downward movement in the average
grade of ore from the mid-1890s - caused by geological
problems and speculative investment in the ante-bellum
period and during the euphoria created by the likelihood
of a British administration replacing the existing Transvaal state - brought the industry to the crisis situation

TABLE 1.2   Annual world production of gold and index of
gold values (1887-1905)

Period	Gold (fine oz)	Value	
1887	5,117	122	
1888	5,331	118	
1889	5,974	115	
1890	5,749	115	
1891	6,320	115	
1892	7,094	122	
1893	7,619	122	
1894	8,764	132	
1895	9,615	133	
1896	9,784	135	
1897	11,420	133	
1898	13,878	128	
1899	14,838	122)	
1900	12,315	91)	war years
1901	12,626	85)	
1902	14,355	84	
1903	15,853	84	
1904	16,804	85	
1905	18,396	87	

Source: P.Villar, 'A History of Gold and Money' (1976),
p.320.

manifested in the campaign of 1903 to recruit migrant
labour from beyond the continent of Africa in order to
save the industry's labour structure. (46)   According to
Richardson, (47) the grade of ore milled 'declined from a
10-year annual average of 11.748 dwts./ton between 1890
and 1899, to 8.438 dwts. in 1903, and to 6.752 dwts. in
1910'.   This, plus the increase in working costs which
escalated from 18s. 1d. in 1899 to 23s. 8.047d. in December 1901, after seven months of crushing led the Chamber
to adopt particular strategies, especially in connection
with the recruitment of the workforce and the utilization
of labour as well as contractual changes in the terms of
service and the wage rate. (48)

In the Chamber's calculation of 'working costs' depreciation is subtracted from profits, and not considered
as a part of working costs as is usually the case. The
point is that the Chamber's statistics for working costs
should not be taken uncritically, but, whatever method of
calculation is employed, for the period under study the
costs in December 1901 had escalated substantially relative to the low figure of 1899. Thus if 'depreciation'
is added to Richardson's figure above, the working costs
would have been 21s. 9.44d. in 1899 as against
27s. 4.587d. per ton for seven months of 1901. The impact
of these increases in 'working costs' (compounded as they
were by the inclusion of what were more properly capital
charges under the item of working costs) pressed the
Chamber to exercise the greatest possible care to reduce
(through internal improvements in organization and appropriate labour strategies) those working costs which were
not subject to the same inflexibilities as those defined
above. (49) The inclusion of depreciation under the
category of working costs, and the relatively marginal
gains from technological substitution for hand labour
processes (see p. 16), tended to increase the labour-
intensive character of the industry and to induce the
Chamber to concentrate more fully on reducing the costs
of acquiring and maintaining the migrant labour force.
(50)

(iii)   THE 'VIABILITY' OF MIGRANT LABOUR

One of the advantages of the migrant system, for the mine-
owners, was therefore that it enabled them - constrained
as they were by the constant price of gold and the relative inflexibility of mining techniques - to calculate
wage rates around the level of subsistence of the *individual* miner rather than the cost of his total family
subsistence. It was evident that a single migrant could
live on a lower wage than he could if his family were with
him on the Rand and dependent on him. Instead, the small
surplus received from the land contributed to his family
welfare and helped to ensure the reproduction of the
labour supply. On this point, Meillassoux has noted in
a generalized argument:

  The agricultural self-sustaining communities, because
  of their comprehensiveness and their raison d'être are
  able to fulfil functions that capitalism prefers not
  to assume in the under-developed countries: *the
  functions of social security*. The cheap cost of labour

in these countries comes from the super-exploitation,
not only of the labour from the wage-earner himself but
also of the labour of his kin-group. (51)

The industry was accordingly organized upon a system of
migrant labour - made possible by the absence of the need
for a long or expensive period of training and the high
prevalence of hand labour techniques which, as we have
noted, the mine-owners found to be geologically and finan-
cially most conducive to the profitability of their industry. (52) Although the gold mines on the Rand were not
unique in their employment of labour-intensive techniques,
(53) they were unique in responding to cost inflation by
perfecting the recruitment and organization of the system
of migrant labour, which was the singularly central
feature of the labour structure on the Rand. (54) The
salient features of the system that so clearly appealed
to the mine-owners on the Rand have been described by,
among others, Meillassoux, Wolpe and Wilson respectively.
(55) The gist of the latter's analysis is that the
'traditional' society provides the social security for
the men who migrate to the towns. They seek the least
skill and lowest status. They 'bear the brunt' of the
risks inherent in economic growth. They demand little
in the way of employment insurance, accident compensation,
sickness benefits or old age pensions. They depend for
their security on the extended family network:

> Men know that if they are sick they will be cared for;
> if they are unemployed they will be fed; if they are
> old a roof will be provided for them by their relatives
> and friends in the community from whence they came.
> (56)

Wolpe, elaborating from Meillassoux's position, takes
the analysis further by showing that the extended family
in the non-capitalist sector 'is able to, and does, fulfil
"social security" functions necessary for the reproduction
of the migrant workforce'. (57) Furthermore, by caring
for the old, the infirm and the very young, the extended
families in these economies 'relieve the capitalist sector
and its State from the need to expend resources on these
necessary functions'. (58) To maintain the network of
reciprocal obligations between the migrant and his family,
so that the migrant worker may have access to the product
as well as the social services of the rural 'Reserves', is
therefore in this view clearly in the interest of the
capitalist sector. (59)
One alternative to this system, as the Chamber well

knew, was a stabilized urban African workforce which would
require a revision of the wage rate to include more than
payment for a single unit of labour. Wages would have to
include the upkeep of the family and certain welfare
costs, currently externalized. That the existing profitability of the mines would have been seriously threatened
by this has been attested to by many witnesses.
Cartwright, for instance, notes:

> three quarters of the mines on the Witwatersrand are
> low-grade mines that can show a profit only by crushing
> on a grand scale. At enormous expense they extract
> four to six pennyweight of gold from a ton of rock and,
> by working very much like a factory, manage to keep
> production ahead of costs. It follows that, as long
> as the price of gold remains constant, they can calcu-
> late their reserves of ore, develop them and keep
> going. *But the slightest rise in the cost of produc-
> tion, even if it adds only 6d. to the expenses of
> dealing with a ton of rock, upsets their calculations.*
> (60)

The same point (which was true of the earlier period as
of the later) was emphasized in the Chamber's evidence to
the Economic and Wage Commission of 1925. On that occasion the mine-owners noted:

> It will be clear from the foregoing that a mine con-
> taining vast quantities of normally payable ore can be
> plunged into a hopeless position by a relatively small
> increase in the cost of bringing about a reduction in
> the percentage of the payable ore contents in the
> property.... Apart from details, these remarks apply
> on broad lines and in varying degrees to most mines,
> and more specially to those with a narrow margin of
> profit.
> (61)

It will be the burden of this work to show that the
economic viability of this particular form of labour
organization led the Chamber to take active steps to
retain the migrant practice. The system was advantageous
to the mine-owners, as both Williams (62) and Wolpe (63)
though differing in interpretation, point out, because the
producer of gold will seek 'to depress the wages of labour
below its value'. (64) The system therefore was viable
because (apart from other cost-benefits of the system) the
mine-owners were able to pay less for the reproduction of
the workforce and were able to force wages below their

conventional minimum. (65) Both Sir George Farrar, on
behalf of the Chamber, and Lord Milner, the High Commissioner, recognized the consequences of the industry's
unskilled wages policies in so far as they affected the
quality of life of the labourers concerned when they
warned, during the agitation for indentured labour, that
white unskilled labourers - if employed on the mines in
great numbers - would constitute a 'pauperized' workforce.
(See pp.43, 164.) Indeed, sixty-two years after the first
mines became operative, the Chamber of Mines showed that
its attitude towards cheap (that is, migrant) labour had
not changed in the least, when it rejected a stabilized
urban African workforce and calculated that the extra cost
of stabilizing the percentage of married men in the Free
State mines would prevent them from maximizing profits.
In the Chamber's terms, it 'would make the economic survival of these mines doubtful'. (66)

(iv)   'CHEAP' LABOUR?

The notion of 'cheap' labour requires some further elaboration. As Burawoy (67) notes, the existence inter alia
of 'excessive exploitation' is not the same as demonstrating the existence of cheap labour. The questions
must be asked 'Cheap for whom?' and 'Cheap with respect
to what?' (68) In order to answer these questions with
any degree of adequacy and to avoid any simplistic treatment it is helpful to characterize in a generalized way
the migrant labour system and to pay some attention to the
mechanisms by which it can become a viable alternative to
a more conventionally situated, 'stabilized' labour force.
    Despite the view elaborated from time to time, by the
mine-owners and others, that African labourers in some way
opted to work on the mines by exercising a rational choice
to maximize their interests, it will be seen that certain
coercive institutions were (early in the history of the
Rand) found necessary to acquire, direct and contain a
continuous flow of labour to the mines. (69) Hence the
reinforcement and emergence of a tax system, the institution of the compound, the 'pass system', and subsequently the monopsonistic organization of the African labour
market, through the recruiting organization of the Chamber
of Mines, to acquire and maintain a continuous and docile
low-cost labour force. Collectively these institutions
made possible 'the system of migrant labour' and rendered
the movement of Africans from the land to the mines beyond
the personal choice of the individual migrant. (70) But
the system is not necessarily 'cheap'.

As Burawoy points out for the later period (in relation
to the question 'Cheap in respect to what?') 'a series of
costs are externalized to the "reserves", costs associated
with the residence of a large, stabilized black population
under a white supremacist state'. (71) Indeed, in the
South African context, as indicated in the following
chapters in respect of the formative years, a feature of
the migrant system is that historically the state has
intervened by legal and administrative means (72) to
assist the mine-owners to acquire labour and to perpetuate
the partial separation of the *maintenance* of the labour
force (by their employers on the gold mines) from the
renewal of the labour force (by the migrants' kin in the
rural areas). Thus the system is in the first case economically attractive to employers because the cost of reproducing the workforce is largely externalized to the
rural areas. The migrant system may be defined to some
extent by this partial separation of the two processes of
renewal and maintenance.

G.Albu, Chairman of the Association of Mines, grasped
this relationship intuitively. This may account for his
dilatory and inconsistent evidence before the Industrial
Commission of Enquiry of 1897, regarding the desirability
of a labour force, separated from the land and housed in
'locations' close to the mines on the Rand. (See above,
p. 6.) Although he clearly exaggerated the independence
of the two processes described above, he appreciated the
importance of the migrant system as a crucial factor in
reducing costs on the mines. His evidence on this theme
before the Industrial Commission of Enquiry is illumi-
nating for this reason as well as for the other, un-
questioned assumptions it makes:

The reduction of native wages is necessary for two
reasons, the one is to reduce our whole expenditure,
and the second has a very far reaching effect upon the
conditions which may prevail with regard to native
labour in the future. The native at the present moment
receives a wage which is far in excess of his existence. The native earns between fifty shillings and
sixty shillings per month, and then he pays nothing for
food or lodging, in fact he can save almost the whole
amount he receives. At the present rate of wages the
native will be enabled to save a lot of money in a
couple of years. If the native can save £20 a year, it
is almost sufficient for him to go home and live on the
fat of his land.... I think if the native gets sufficient pay to save five pounds a year, that sum is
quite enough for his requirements, and will prevent

natives from becoming rich in a short space of time.
('Evidence', pp.13,14)

The rural areas were assumed to be functional to the
mining industry: they existed to produce and reproduce
the labour force for the mines. The latter, for their
part, were there to house, feed and maintain the labourer
who could 'save almost the whole amount he receives'.
This assumption that the rural African population was
at the disposal of the mines, who needed only to mani-
pulate the wage rate in order to ensure an uninterrupted
renewal of labour, provoked a rich exchange between Albu
and the members of the commission:

> Witness: ... I would make African labour compul-
>   sory.... Why should a nigger be allowed
>   to do nothing...?
> Commission: If a man can live without work, how can
>   you force him to work?
> Witness: Tax him, then ...
> Commission: Then you would not allow the kaffir to
>   hold land in the country, but he must work
>   for the white man to enrich him?
> Witness: *He must do his part of the work of helping
>   his neighbours*. ('Evidence', p.22, empha-
>   sis added)

The merit of the migrant labour system, for the mine-
owners, was in fact the 'neighbourly help', the *subsidy*,
borne by the rural areas in bearing much of the cost of
welfare for the renewal of the mine labour force. This,
together with the economies in compound-housing and mass
feeding (and the opportunities for disciplining the workforce that the system provided), made migrant labour
viable for the mine-owners.
The cost of renewal, however, is not entirely borne by
the rural areas. Albu's intimation that this was so is
misleading - but that the rural areas *partially* subsidized
the mining industry was clearly to the latter's benefit.
Africans did not in fact 'become rich in a short space of
time', or ever. Nor did they 'save almost the whole
amount' they received. Renewal was frequently dependent
on income left over from the maintenance remitted by migrants to the rural areas - a 'service' subsequently
undertaken by the Chamber's recruiting organization. (73)
As Cartwright (1963, p.221) writes for the later period:

The letters W.N.L.A. (the initials of Witwatersrand
Native Labour Recruiting Association) have become

'Wenela' to all the tribes north of the Limpopo and
'Wenela' is now a magic word.... *Wenela delivers cash
allotments* to wives and even provides letter writers
and stamps so that absent husbands may keep in touch
with their families. (Emphasis added) (74)

Just as the migrant's kin become dependent upon the
'cash allotment' remitted by the migrant workers to the
rural areas, the latter require certain support from their
kin in the countryside in view of their impermanence and
lack of legal status in the urban situation. Thus although the processes of renewal and maintenance are technically partially separate, there is a heavy dependence by
the subsistence economy on the capitalist sector and vice
versa. (75) As the subsequent chapters will show, the
role of the state in these processes from the inception of
mining was recognized by the mine-owners to be crucial.
In the first phase of gold mining the emphasis was on
state intervention to acquire and to contain the turnover
of the labour force. In the second phase (after 1913) the
state acted more directly - at the general expense - to
secure the conditions in the rural 'reserves' necessary
for the perpetuation of the system. (76)
    Migrant labour is not necessarily always cheap. More-
over, the costs are not entirely externalized. Hence
Burawoy, for instance, notes:

We cannot ... ignore the costs associated with migrant
labour, such as high rates of turnover, recruitment
expenses and the more general sets of costs experienced
by the State and arising from the political and legal
conditions for the reproduction of a system of migrant
labour. When all these are introduced, many of them
intangible, the balance sheet becomes so somplex that
the notion of cheap labour, in practice if not in
principle, may become impossible to handle. (77)

But in calculating the costs to themselves, the mine-
owners evidently concluded before 1897 (or they would not
so complaisantly have continued the system) that migrant
labour was viable because the costs of the renewal of
labour were borne by the subsistence economy; that economies of scale and the standardization of wages, welfare,
food and accommodation in the compound system were possible directly because of the operation of the migrant
system; and that the latter was made viable because of
the high level of hand labour techniques employed and the
low grade of ore mined. Hence the significance of
Perrings's observation:

There is a direct equation to be made between the requirements of unskilled labour and requirements of
'cheap' labour. It was only because the supply price
of unskilled labour constituted no more than the cost
of maintenance of the single workers ... that such
techniques were payable. (78)

This (the predominance of relatively unskilled and
labour-intensive techniques), in addition to the above
factors, over time, made migrant labour cheap primarily
for the mine-owners, who together with the advantages of
state intervention had the capital, organization and administrative facilities to effect the cost-benefits that
might be extracted from such a system of labour. This
then was the answer to the question 'Cheap for whom?' It
is not necessarily cheap in a generalized sense, but cheap
for the mine-owners.
Historically the process by which the migrant system
was first made viable for the industry occupied two
decades of uninterrupted conflict. It is with these
twenty years that this study is primarily concerned: the
organization of the unity of the mine-owners; the creation of recruiting facilities that would acquire, centralize and regulate the supply; the creation of coercive
institutions to secure the supply; and the assumption at
first by the Transvaal state and then by the British state
of the functions of legally guaranteeing and physically
administering the system of migrant labour. In the absence of any of these institutions (in so far as the mine-
owners were concerned) it is uncertain whether the system
would have been cheap or have reproduced itself in the
long run.

(v)   COST-REDUCTION AND CO-ORDINATING INSTITUTIONS: THE
CHAMBER OF MINES AND THE GROUP SYSTEM

The cost-effectiveness of the Chamber's strategies and the
migrant system was well demonstrated even before the two
labour-recruiting and cost-reducing measures of the
reformed Pass Regulations and the Witwatersrand Native
Labour Supply Association were implemented in 1896. (79)
By 1892 the Witwatersrand was placed fourth among the
gold-producing regions of the world, and by 1895, only
seven years after the commencement of shaft-sinking on the
Witwatersrand, with an unskilled African migrant labour
force of approximately 51,000 and a capitalized par value
of £41,934,628 (plus £17,329,391 cash including permits),
(80) the Witwatersrand gold mines were the foremost gold

producers in the world. There were 130 principal producing and working companies, (81) with an issued capital
of £25,500,000, which represented (at the end of July
1895) a total value of approximately £103,000,000. (82)
    The function of co-ordinating the labour strategies and
maximizing the opportunities for the profitability of all
the mines on the Witwatersrand was assumed by the
Witwatersrand Chamber of Mines, an organization established in 1889, two years after the inception of mining
on the Rand. (83) This up-dated version of a 'gold diggers' committee' soon came to represent the initial
tenuous unity of the employers, and was crucial in
formulating common policy in relation to wages, conditions
of employment and industrial relations. (84) The organization was essential for the general reduction of costs,
and the acquisition and regulation of the migrant labour
supply, as well as the collective representation of the
requirements of employers to the Transvaal state, and subsequently to the British administration in the Transvaal
and abroad. The functions of the Chamber were broadly
outlined in the 'Constitution', (85) which (to cite the
most important objectives) enabled it

(i)   To advance, promote and protect the mining interests
      of the Transvaal....
(ii) To promote any legislative measures or petition
      Government or any Legislative Assembly or ad-
      ministrative body on any matters directly affecting
      [mining] interests.

    Any company or syndicate with limited liability which
either held mining property or was directly connected with
the industry was eligible for membership and to a single
representation at all the proceedings of the Chamber. An
Executive Committee of fifteen members (in 1906) conducted
the ordinary business of the Chamber. The members were
elected at the Annual General Meeting by ballot, two of
whom were elected as Vice-Presidents and a third as
President, the latter performing a significant role in
articulating the collective policies of the mine-owners.
In the early phase of mining, in the absence of political
representation, the Chamber frequently presented memorials
to the Transvaal government and 'through a member laid its
petitions before the Legislature'. (86) The officials in
the Transvaal state, as well as President Kruger, attached
much significance to the controlling influences in the
Chamber's Executive Committee and attributed the blame
for the 1899-1902 war to the dominance of Wernher, Beit &
Co. in the Chamber's Executive Committee. (87)   In the

post-bellum period the co-operation between the Executive
Committee of the Chamber of Mines and the members of
Milner's administration characterized the 'era of
Reconstruction'. (88)

The essential feature of this employers' institution,
however, was that it organized the unity of the various
mining companies as well as co-ordinating the labour
strategies and wages of the industry. Without this unify-
ing and cost-conscious institution, the mining companies
would not easily have maximized the profitability of their
enterprises and, if the early consequences of internecine
competition are to serve as an indication of the obstacles
to improving the labour supply and the rate of profit, the
industry would have been in a far weaker position after
two decades of mining had this specific form of employer
co-operation not been adopted. (89) The collective
strength of the Rand mining employers combined in the
Chamber with its vast recruiting mechanism, itself a
product of employer unity, to make the system of migrant
labour feasible over the long term and to extend the
system from the Transvaal and other colonies in South
Africa to East and Central Africa and to the mainland of
China as well. (90) Second only in significance to the
Chamber in respect of the reduction of the cost of mining
and its administration was the notable feature on the
Witwatersrand of the Group System of control.

The Group System enabled individual mining companies,
all of whom were organized by 1906 under some nine controlling Houses, to secure finances (91) as well as the
services of the Group for the staffs it maintained of
consulting, mechanical and electrical engineers, metal-
lurgists and other technical experts whose services would
normally not be available to them 'except at a cost much
in excess of that which prevails under the existing co-
operative system'. (92) The Group System was particularly
important in view of the geological complexity of the
Witwatersrand, which necessitated expensive and careful
research, co-ordination of practice and application of
technical improvements. Thus the costs of opening up new
mining areas, sinking shafts, installing machinery or the
undertaking of any capital expenditure programmes were
substantially minimized by the operation of this form of
financial control and co-ordination. In addition to the
'pooling' of research and technical experts, highly significant cost-benefits were obtained by the purchasing of
supplies for individual mines by the group-buying organization. Given the persistent rise in the index of world
commodity prices, which seriously affected mining stores,
the collective purchase of mining supplies was an impor-

tant factor in reducing the aggregate cost per ton of gold
mined. In respect of the cost of labour, the institution
of the Chamber, the Group System and the various factors
outlined in the preceding sections combined to make the
migrant system a viable and durable proposition for the
Witwatersrand gold mining industry. (93)

(vi)   SECURING THE MIGRANT SUPPLY

Thus the practice of migrant labour was perpetuated with
all its problems. The Chairman of the Chamber explained
the character of the system as well as one of its consequences a decade after mining began, in 1896:

> In other parts of the world when you start a mine and
> equip it you can probably go on for years and the men
> employed in the mining operation become skilled in
> their work. Here I may say, when you start a mine you
> have 25% of boys who are proficient and if you add 25%
> to them the first 25% go home. The result is you are
> continually teaching these people. (94)

Yet it was the unskilled nature of the work which made
the system possible. Moreover, the lower wage paid to
migrants relative to a stabilized workforce, together with
the welfare and subsistence available in the rural
regions, acted to make the migratory labour practice increasingly viable. Had the nature of mine labour involved
high training costs as in the Union Minière du Haute
Katanga (and the Copper Belt) the expenditure on acquiring
a larger portion of a settled labour force (provided that
the men were procurable for long periods on the mines)
(95) would conceivably have been important.
Despite the deficiencies of the system and the inadequacy of the supply, the migrant pattern was thus retained
as the alternative that was considered economically most
viable. (96) The high qualitative waste in man-hours,
transport costs and skill acquisition and the consequences
upon labour management were never enough to reverse the
migrant pattern. They formed part of the recurring costs
of gold mining. (97) Thus the response of the Chamber to
the insufficiency of the supply which was endemic to the
industry in the first stages of production was to adjust
the wage rate - which frequently meant a *reduction,* as
well as a rise in wages (98) - rather than to recast the
migratory element of its labour structure. In the circumstances the Chamber found itself under increasing pressure
from the mining managements to relieve the situation as

managers persistently complained 'of the difficulty of
securing and retaining a sufficient number of Kaffirs to
carry on the works'. In the event the Chamber was led to
explore a number of expedients to overcome its crises in
human energy, but none of them were to alter the established institution of migrant labour.

The Chamber's response was therefore not to replace but
to deal with the disadvantages of the system, which were
more numerous and complex than was initially apparent.
For given the acceptance of migrant labour, the Chamber
largely bore the onus of resolving the critical problems
consequent upon the fall in the supply due (inter alia) to
errors it might make in the calculation of the wage rate.
Hence great care had to be taken that wage and work practices were not adopted which would imperil the very practice that was being preserved. Two years after mining
started, the Chamber noted 'that the supply of Kaffirs was
at present totally inadequate' (99) and proceeded to
enumerate the serious questions consequent upon the slump
in the supply. These were diagnosed as internecine rival-
ries between mining companies manifested by attempts to
'bribe and seduce' the employees of neighbouring companies
to desert their employers. (100) The results had been:
(i) a steady rise in wages; (ii) increasing bribery of
potential recruits by competing companies; and (iii) desertion by disillusioned members of the labour force.
(101)

The Chamber therefore attributed the dearth in the
supply and rises in the price of labour to internal factors rather than to any serious deficiency in the source
in the rural areas. Convinced that the question could be
resolved by agreement on the wage rate and internal company discipline, the Chamber immediately moved to secure
some uniformity of action among the mine managements and
circulated a comprehensive questionnaire to managers with
the intention of establishing a uniform wages policy. It
linked the question of supply to the related element of
the wage rate, and asked the respective mining managements
whether they could use their collective pressure to
strengthen the regular flow of African labour to the mines
by suppressing 'improper' company practices and by promoting more uniform and economic wage policies. The
Chamber therefore asked:

In case of all the principal companies combining could
the rate of wages to natives be lowered without dis-
organizing the labour supply? (102)

The reply to the question was an overwhelming 'yes'.

Of the seventy companies who answered the questionnaire,
sixty-two replied in the affirmative and only eight said
'no'. (103) Thus only two years after the inception of
mining it appeared to the majority of the managers that,
given the presupposition that control could be centralized
and a uniform tariff of wages implemented, the supply
problem could be overcome and wages could be reduced. It
was therefore recognized early on that the essential precondition for the formation of a labour force at low cost
to the mine-owners was the internal unity and discipline
of the mine managements (upon whom rested responsibility
for the diligent observation of company agreements collectively negotiated). However, unity of action and commitment to the common mode of conduct was feasible only if
the mine managements were assured of a satisfactory supply
situation, for, willing as they were to seek collective
solutions, they were the first to admit that under
existing rivalry 'even without resort to actual attempts
to bribe [an African recruit] ... a manager finding himself short of labour has ... scarcely any other remedy
than that of raising his rates of pay'. (104)

The Chamber thus attempted to explore simultaneously
various expedients to extend the supply and to exert
tighter *control* over the labour force once the men had
been recruited. It therefore asked the managers directly,
'What means can you suggest for putting a stop to
desertion?'

The question was in fact a 'package' presentation of
the wider problems of labour control and supply, for ap-
pended to the tail of the question were contentious suggestions from the Chamber itself regarding the means by
which the labour force might be more adequately secured.
These included: (i) the fixed tariff on wages; (ii) the
'compound' or living-in system; (iii) the pass system;
(iv) the discharge ticket; (v) longer engagements; (vi)
more police supervision; and (vii) the retention of
wages. (105)

These exhibited, with few exceptions, the most prominent features associated with the migratory labour system.
They emerged in the context of a serious challenge to the
Chamber to satisfy its labour supply, and in time became
auxiliary institutions indispensable to the operation of
the migrant labour system.

Faced with these alternatives most of the company
managers opted in the first few years of mining for a pass
system and greater police supervision as the best means of
securing the labour supply. The Chamber itself felt that
'those suggestions urging a discharge ticket and more
police supervision, point probably to the only local

remedy which would be likely to have a partial effect'.
(106) It favoured the idea of a more effective pass
system by which it envisaged the issue of a free pass
(valid for ten days) to Africans seeking work and the
denial of a pass to those Africans who wished to leave
the district without a discharge ticket 'of recent date'.
(107)

However, when considering the implications of these
coercive provisions, the Chamber was aware of two major
problems: (i) the effect these measures might have on
the African labour force, which was already sensitive to
unfavourable wage, work and commuting conditions, and
(ii) the extent to which the state would be prepared to
intervene on behalf of mining capital to police the industry's labour force. In response to the first of these
problems (on the matter of labour control through the pass
system) the Chamber had second thoughts when it considered
that the proposal, if adopted, might create a bad impression on the 'Kaffir districts' about the conditions of
labour in the fields. In particular the Chamber feared
the effect this might have on labour recruitment and that
the proposal might 'retard the inflow of labour at its
source'. (108) The second problem involved an extension
of state intervention. For the large-scale policing of
the labour force even at this stage would involve a heavy
increase in the police force which would have to be mobi-
lized and maintained at the expense of the Transvaal
state. The Chamber therefore abandoned the suggestion
of tighter supervision of the labour force for the time
being, giving as reasons for its decision the fact that
it would (i) create unsupportable burdens in the increase
of the police force; (ii) provide no direct revenue for
its own funding; and (iii) in any case not be carried out
'efficiently and thoroughly' by the central authorities.
(109)

It was conceivably too early to suggest that the
Chamber had evolved a clear wages policy, but the lines
of its thinking seemed to be clear in one crucial respect.
It did not seek a workforce which would be free to enter
the industry as a stable workforce. It sought a migrant
labour force which, if not as tightly controlled as the
Chamber wished at the present, was one which would at some
time in the future be secured, if possible with state co-
operation by coercion, police supervision and bureaucratic
control. The Chamber's policy was to avoid any internal
action which might cause a depletion in the supply of
African mine labourers, and to keep the wage rate at a
level consistent with what it calculated as the cash needs
to attract rural Africans from their homes to the mines.

The Chamber therefore could be expected to pursue these
policies which would provoke little change and at the same
time satisfy the industry's insatiable need for an uninterrupted supply of unskilled black labour, oscillating
between the countryside and the city.

2 The black labour supply:
early recruitment and regulation

INTRODUCTION

The Transvaal was potentially a vast labour resource for
the mines. Five times larger in area than Natal, its
African population was twice as numerous. The rural
regions contained the promise of supply for the whole of
the gold mining industry, and their deterioration promised
a continuous movement of labour to and from the Rand. (1)
    According to Chamber of Mines statistics the total
African labour force on the mines in 1890 was 14,000, of
whom 77 per cent (or 11,000) came from the East Coast or
from the northern districts of the Transvaal. However,
the accuracy of the figures supplied to the Chamber by
the mine managers is open to some doubt due to the evasion
of Pass Regulations by the mining companies. For example,
in the first three months of 1892, 26,917 Africans passed
through the mines, but only 9,400 passes were issued. (2)
After 1890 the labour force expanded rapidly, until at the
end of the decade the number of African labourers exceeded
97,000 men.
    But although the stream of workers commuting to the
mines was substantial, the assumption that the flow of
migrants would meet the needs of the mining industry
proved erroneous. The industry's need for labour was
seldom satisfied. (3) In the first few years the mine-
owners experienced their greatest manpower shortages and
encountered serious resistance to recruitment, and a high
level of desertions by those migrants who reached the
mines.
    The ability of Africans to subsist on the land was not
considered as a major factor deterring migration to the
mines until the 1890s, when the relatively slow 'separation' of Africans from the land began to weigh heavily on
the Chamber. Not until recently, however, have studies

on the conditions of South Africa's peasantry provided
further explanation of the factors checking African entry
to the labour markets on the Rand. Although Bundy (1979)
has revised (luminously) the conventional profile of
African agriculture, much work has still to be done on
the condition of African rural production, particularly
in the Transvaal and the Orange Free State.

Nevertheless, his analysis of the conditions of the
African peasantry in the two northern provinces during
this period (Bundy, 1979, pp.204-6) is helpful in understanding African resistance to entering the Rand labour
market. Opportunities for African land purchase in the
Transvaal increased with the discovery of gold. Higher
prices were commanded by whites for farms often paid for
collectively by African tribes. By the time the Boer War
occurred, Africans owned upwards of a quarter of a million
acres of land. Demand for transport and food increased -
especially before the advent of the northern railway -
and markets for meat and maize boomed. Revenue from
these assisted Africans to buy or lease additional land,
while squatting spread throughout the 1890s. The development of African farming in the Orange Free State was less
rapid, but there was none the less a pocket of African
land ownership and - through the 1890s - much farming 'on
the halves', a system of share-cropping.

The mine-owners' response to this was to press the
state to introduce extra-economic measures such as increased taxation to force the labour supply to the mines.
The continued access of Africans to productive land occupied the attention of the mine-owners from the 1890s
until 1913, when a general solution to labour shortages
was found in the Land Act of that year (see Chapters 5
and 12, below).

Initially, however, the Chamber considered the labour
shortage to be the consequence of its recruiting strategies and the treatment of African labour on some of the
mines.

(i)   THE LABOUR SUPPLY

Conditions for migrants in transit to the mines and the
competition from white farmers for their labour combined
to restrict the supply to the mines. For one thing, distances between the rural regions and the Rand were formidable. The men travelled up to 500 miles to the mine
fields and were frequently molested en route. The Chamber
stated in a memorial to the Volksraad (2 October 1891)
'that Kaffirs could come in much more freely if they were

secured against the molestation they at present suffer'.
'Legal' interference by the police in search of the requi-
site travelling passes was common, as were arrests and
fines. Before arriving at the goldfields wet and without
food or clothing, migrants were subjected to harassment by
the white farmers over whose land they passed. If they
were without money they were compelled to work for the
farmer for a few days without payment, and on their return
journey from the mines were subjected to 'fines' for
trespassing. Reports of molestation deterred many from
working on the mines. The Chamber received frequent
reports of Africans who had been told they must work on
the farms and who consequently returned to their homes
instead of proceeding to the goldfields. Gangs of 'boys'
were frequently 'taken possession of by touts who disposed
of them at a premium'. (4)

Though concerned over the adverse effects the general
conditions of commuting were having on its labour supply,
the Chamber's alarm was centred in particular on the competition for labour. It seemed to the mine-owners that
the promise of a stream of labour oscillating between the
rural areas and the goldfields was unreasonably inhibited
by the 'selfish' actions of the white farmers, and they
resented this interference with their 'own' migrant labour
supply. The Chamber forcibly expressed these sentiments
to the Volksraad, despite some anxiety that if it protested too vigorously the landowners in the Volksraad
might introduce state controls detrimental to mining
interests. The Chamber finally attempted to pre-empt
undesirable government action which might assist the
white farmers 'now [deprived] ... of so much of their
former labour supply' by proposing the establishment of
stations or labour depots along the principal routes to
the mines and about one day's journey from the kraals,
where migrant workers could be protected from the
pressures of the farmers and obtain shelter free of charge
and at state expense. The Chamber suggested that the
depots be funded by a charge on the administration of the
Pass Laws. This would increase supply and facilitate a
reduction in wages. 'It would bring the price of Kafir
labour down to the normal rate formally paid by the
farmers who would then be free from the competition of
high wages.' (5)

At the same time as the Chamber made this proposal and
sought a common interest with farmers in keeping wages
down, its fears of preferential state assistance to white
farmers were reinforced by new government action which
bestowed extensive monopolies 'to certain persons for the
exclusive right of erecting stores within a certain dis-

tance of Kafir stations'. (6)   The Chamber feared increasingly that its labour recruits would be subjected
to the regulation and control of these government concessionaires who would dispose of their goods to African
recruits and detain or divert them to white farmers.   A
second and similar fear prompted the Chamber to urge the
government to administer 'pass' licences authorizing
African movement to the urban areas in the towns rather
than at the proposed travelling depots 'since the administration of the law at these outlying places might
be attended by abuses over which there could be no effective check'. (7)   The landowners and farmers within
the state, caught in the contradiction between further
assisting the labour flow to the mines and easing the
supply situation for the citizen-farmers, did nothing
to allay the fears of the Chamber when they granted yet
a further monopoly - for five years - to a private company
for the erection of buildings for the issue of travelling
passes closer to the mines outside the Main Reef of
Johannesburg and Boksburg. (8)   The concessionaires were
granted extensive rights which the Chamber itself had
never enjoyed, including the right to appoint officials
and policemen (funded by the Volksraad) which might be
required at each compound.   The Chamber was subsequently
advised by the government and the Mining Commissioner that
carelessness, abuse and attempts by mine managers to
defraud the revenue had led to the Volksraad taking this
step. (9)

The Chamber feared that Africans seeking a pass for
work might be forced 'to incur a liability for stores
consumed, and white men, willing to pay these debts would
have the first supply of the Natives'. (10)   In this
manner the concessionaires could both control and trade
in African labour.   Moreover, migrants would be unable to
obtain a pass to return to their homes without first
spending their money in the compound.   As a result they
would be unwilling to return to the goldfields for a subsequent term of labour.   Statements made by migrant
workers to Chief Kamangwe of the Pepeta tribe, Natal,
in November 1891 supported this conclusion. (11)

The Chamber's response to these threats to its labour
supply was to request that at the very least it should be
given facilities equal to those granted to the concessionaires for the issue of pass books.   Later the Chamber encouraged its own members 'to protect themselves by taking
out stand licences wherever it was deemed to be desirable
to allow a shop on their claims'. (12)   But these moves
did not touch the basic problems involved in improving
the flow of migrants to the mines.

The conflict was indicative of the industry's position
in the South African social formation, where it exercised
profound economic influence but lacked commensurate
political power in the institutions of the state. Ewald
Esselen, one of Kruger's political opponents, stated in
March 1892, to the delight of the Chamber, that the mine-
owners 'had raised the country's income ... and they had
the right to take part in the use of that money; they had
capital and experience, and their opinion should count in
the ... administration'. (13) Government revenue increased from £188,000 in 1883 to £4,266,000 in 1895-7
through the contribution of the mining industry. (14)
        In surveying the mechanisms for recruiting labour and
in estimating future requirements the Chamber identified
the need for greater political influence in finding the
means of acquiring and retaining its labour force. It
also revealed a huge dependency upon the state for the
satisfaction of its labour needs. In a letter of 1890
to Kruger's government the Chamber argued:

> Private enterprise has repeatedly failed in attempting
> to organise and maintain an adequate supply of Kaffirs.
> The task must be undertaken by the public authorities,
> and the Chamber trusts that the Government will lend it
> their indispensable assistance. (15)

Failing to win more direct state intervention, the
Chamber resorted to restructuring its administration and
creating its own bureaucracy to recruit the African labour
its constituent companies demanded.

(ii)   RECRUITMENT AND LABOUR CONTROL: THE INSTITUTION OF
THE LABOUR COMPOUND

In the Kimberley system workers were denied access to the
outside world for the two- or three-month period of their
contracts, and were subjected to search procedures to
eliminate theft and illicit trafficking. Control over
diamond thefts became particularly intense in the depression year of 1883, when the procedures proclaimed in
1872 were, for the first time, fully implemented.
Worsfold (1895) described the regime:

> During the term of their service, for three months or
> more, they are treated as prisoners. Every day they
> are stripped and searched on leaving the mines, and for
> a week before the conclusion of their contract they are
> isolated and subjected to a regime which makes a theft
> of diamonds a physical impossibility.

The humiliating search procedures were also proclaimed
for white workers. But when attempts were made to enforce
these in 1884 the white workers struck - with the support
of the black workers - and succeeded in escaping the
search procedures. (16)

In the early years of gold mining, the system of
control in the compounds was less rigorous than on the
diamond fields, although a clear structure was emerging.
The military-like quadrangular compound in De Beers
diamond field, with its ten-feet-high fence (soon to be
raised to twelve feet) and single large gate, encompassing
living quarters and a few stores for meat and bread, provided a model for the larger, more labour-intensive enterprises on the Rand and in Rhodesia which the mine-owners
were quick to imitate. The migrant workers coming to the
Rand were communally quartered in prison-like barracks
erected on the premises of each mine. In 1903, with the
increase in labour turnover and the particularly severe
labour shortage at the end of the Boer War, the system of
control in the Rand compounds was tightened to produce a
more centralized, coercive system of labour supervision
which 'both management and state regarded ... as a vital
institution of worker control and manipulation'. (17)

As migrant workers exchanged their rural experience
for the goldfields, and a system of rigid control, the
Chamber, it would seem, tried to project as a replacement
of the tribal system the hierarchy of mine officials whose
duties were conceived as being in some way parallel to the
roles of chief, headman and heads of homestead. According
to Cartwright:

> The task was to build up [the African's] confidence in
> all the white men who would be in charge of the com-
> pounds where he lived while he was on the Rand and to
> make him feel that the tribal authority to which he had
> been accustomed all his life would be replaced by an
> equally benevolent system of rules and customs that he
> could understand and trust. (18)

It was the mine-owners' fantasy that their African
labourers were living their tribal lives in their quarters
on the mines, and that the world outside was exclusively
the white man's world. All would be well 'if they smoked
their pipes, drank their beer and did what they were
told'. (19)

The control system was based on an elaborate structure
of 'line management' as follows:

    (i) The members of each tribe in a compound were

'represented' by a police official styled (but
not resembling) the headman of the tribe.
(ii)   Certain men were appointed by the mine management to act as 'indunas', i.e. police who were
liaison officers between the white compound
manager and the various tribal groups in the
compound. The indunas were the right-hand men
of the compound manager, and 'informed on what
was happening and [what was] said in the compound'. (20)
(iii) Each section of the compound had an 'isibonda',
who conveyed grievances and made proposals for
change to the headman. (21) The method of
selecting these officials (styled 'intermediaries between the natives and the compound
managers') varied from one mine to another.
Some compound managers allowed each tribe to
choose its own 'isibonda' - subject to veto and
discharge; others appointed them personally.
Frequently men were appointed because of their
influence in the tribe - it was hoped they would
use this to attract new recruits to the mine.
(22)

As the system evolved and controls tightened, the
various overseers of the labour force served to provide
more or less direct lines of communication to the management of the mine, and secured the control and quiescence
demanded by the white compound manager - the chief overseer of the whole system. He and his police were de facto
rulers over the compound. (23) The compound manager
wielded virtually total power over the lives of the
workers and 'set the entire working atmosphere of the
mine'. (24) The 'Report of the Native Grievances Inquiry
1913-14' (25) succinctly explained the system:

In every compound the compound manager is assisted by
a number of natives who are called police. They are
not, of course, police at all, in the proper sense,
but merely employees of the mine like the rest of the
native labourers. They are, however, in fact invested
with considerable, if rather vague powers over the
remainder of the natives; and the principal policeman,
known as 'the Induna', is a person of very great consequence indeed in the compound. (26)

The induna's job was described in the report as 'one of
the plums of the mine service', and 'in a labour structure
with relatively few chances of promotion' was thought to

provide an incentive to others to seek work in the mines -
a rather curious argument. There were other incentives
the mine-owners might have chosen to boost the labour
supply. (27) The police system was, in fact, indispensable to management as a method of supervision and control
over the unskilled, part-peasant labour force.

The compound system and the control structure prevented
communication between compounds, fragmented and divided
the labour force and fostered inter-tribal jealousies. The
rigorous application of the system served to restrict the
education, organization and unionization of the Africans
on the mines, and to defeat their efforts 'to get rid of
tribal distinctions and ... unite ... for the purpose of
obtaining better conditions from the Europeans', as para-
graph 487 of the report noted. The personal influence of
the compound manager, 'native' respect for European
authority as personified in the police, and fostering
inter-tribal jealousies were the three safeguards against
worker resistance listed in the report, although it comments that 'there are unmistakable signs that all three
of these safeguards are tending to break down'. (28)

The system was nevertheless an invaluable instrument to
the mine-owners, as Johnstone comments:

> The fragmentation, isolation and concentration of the
> African labour force in separate, dependent and prison-
> like compounds was of great advantage to the companies
> in the management of unrest and insubordination among
> African workers. (29)

The advantages of total control were manifold. In considering the transition from 'closable' to 'closed' compound, Buckle, the Chairman of the Native Grievances
Inquiry, reported:

> Theft of gold is rendered more difficult, the natives
> are better and more cheaply supplied by the Compound
> stores than by outside storekeepers; desertion is
> reduced; the curse of the illicit liquor trade is
> completely done away with ... [and] the mine native ...
> is protected from many other sources of temptation.
> (30)

The system could, however, be 'improved'. Buckle found
the 'obvious defects' of the existing compounds were 'unnecessary entrances, external windows, and walls scarcely
above the level of the lean-to roofs of the rooms built
against them'. (31) He considered desertion and confrontation likely under these circumstances, and that,

to prevent these, steps should be taken to make the compounds more easily convertible into places of detention with 'strong steelcased gates which can be locked from the outside (as at the Premier Diamond mine) and with only one entrance, and high walls with no outer windows'. (32)

The institution of the compound proved its suitability not only for controlling the labour force, but also for minimizing costs. In 1902 Pieterson reported on the living conditions of unskilled mineworkers:

> Huts usually contained 20-50 workers with double-decked bunks and turned into cabins by their occupants who nailed strips into the openings to protect themselves and their belongings.... Heating was provided by a large tin or drum of red hot coal which contributed to the respiratory disease on the mines because of smoke fumes.... Often workers slept on the floors. Some compounds had no washing facilities, others had concrete baths in the centre of the compound, for their persons and clothes. (33)

In October 1908 a report on compound management revealed 'conditions prevalent at the start of the century' in the Randfontein group of mines. The investigators listed dirty food, lack of washing facilities, no floors in the huts, no bedsteads, no stoves, no ventilation, and no lights at night amongst the features of the compounds on the West Rand. Bad drainage and overcrowding were prevalent. (34) Number One Compound on the South Randfontein General mine, the largest mine studied, was built around 1894. The rooms were made of corrugated iron, there were no floors, and drainage was poor. A further two compounds of the same age (fourteen years) on the same mine had galvanized iron roofs, no ventilation and no stoves. (35)

But for some changes introduced by the Coloured Labour Compound Commission of 1904, the appearance and conditions within the compounds changed little over the years, and it is highly unlikely that the conditions confronted by the migrant recruits in the 1890s were any better than those reported by the Randfontein Report - in all likelihood they were even more primitive. (36)

The low cost of accommodation and primitive welfare provisions were matched by the paucity of the diet. The provision of food (like accommodation and welfare) was an object for control, and the centralized character of the compound system allowed for substantial economies of scale. The 'Report of the Native Grievances Inquiry' found:

The cost of food in the mine is about 4d to 6d per
head per day. This very cheap rate is due to the
wholesale manner in which feeding is dealt with, and
if the amount of money were handed to the individual
native, he could not feed himself properly upon it.
To let the native feed himself, therefore, means either
an addition to the cost of labour or a reduction in the
net earnings of the native. (37)

In 1903 a spokesman for the Chamber of Mines stated that
the employment of white workers in unskilled capacities,
in a way comparable to the black labour force, was possible only in a 'pauperised community'. The high death
rates from nutrition deficiencies and bad sanitation bear
witness that the life of the African labourers was of a
pauperized nature from the early days of mining. Far more
than on the diamond fields, the gold-mine owners were im-
pelled to keep costs down, and there is little doubt that
few improvements were made to the compounds before 1905
and only marginal changes (to cover up the most glaring
excesses) in the years before the First World War.

(iii)   THE WORK SITUATION AND THE LABOUR SUPPLY

The men who travelled by foot or rail, often riding in
cattle trucks, to the goldfields knew virtually nothing
of the situation into which they were moving. Their new
environment was totally alien to the rural life they left
behind, and their experiences on the goldfields after
their 'separation' from the land did little to smooth
their adjustment to their new situation.

Ignorant of mining, transient, without formal instruc-
tion and unable to communicate in English, the men had to
learn as they went along. Portuguese, English and Afri-
kaans words mingled with vernacular languages to aid in
communicating the names of the implements used and
learning the rudiments of the job. (38) The men worked
in shifts from 2 pm to 6 am, or from 3 pm to 6 am, sometimes for fifteen hours without a break, although the
Chamber claimed in 1903 a norm of nine and a half hours.
(39) They were totally unaccustomed to working underground, to wearing boots, to working at a systematic pace
over long hours, to rigorous supervision. 'Bossboys' -
supervisors - hustled the men into cages and down to the
work level to await the white supervisors. In 1903 one
white miner supervised seventy-five black workers organized in sections under the charge of the bossboys. In the
process black workers suffered abuse and physical assault

by white mine captains, contractors and miners, and harassment by the bossboys. 'Violence on some mines [was] not only passively winked at but in some cases ... actively condoned.' (40)

At the end of the shift the men queued for their 'tickets' which recorded their shift work, claimed their food tickets for the day (unless they cooked their own food), and returned to the compound, where there was little lighting and where sleeping sections were scarcely maintained. (41)

In the low-grade mines profits were made only by crushing rock on a massive scale - in some mines up to three tons of rock to produce one ounce of gold. Moreover, since the price of gold was fixed by international agreement and did not vary with costs of production, profits could not be maintained by passing on any increases in costs to the 'consumer'.

The institution designed both to minimize these costs and to accelerate the process of subordinating the labour force to the discipline of industrial work was the compound system. First developed in the Kimberley diamond fields in the 1860s (as we have just seen), the compound system was a function of the employer's need to house, discipline and control a large labour force recruited from the rural regions. In addition to disciplining this labour force for work in the mines, the compound system aimed to prevent the desertions which produced a high labour turnover, and to prevent theft.

In time, despite accidents and ignorance of mining, the miners sometimes achieved an 'adequate standard of efficiency in the skilled operations', (42) but with notable exceptions (about 5 per cent of the workforce) they formed the unskilled labour force which as Horwitz notes, provided the 'low grade human energy ... that was necessary ... for the profitable exploitation of the marginal ore under conditions of low grade mechanisation'. (43) Their labour, in intensive quantities, was required on the gold mines as soon as the operative stages of production had begun. Already in 1899, as we have seen, local labour had been heavily supplemented by Portuguese East African labour.

As neither South Africa nor the Portuguese territories were able to meet the mines' demands for labour, in 1890 the Chamber was forced to take stock of the situation and the general difficulties encountered in the course of recruitment. Following previous practice the Chamber circulated eighty-five of its constituent companies, employing a total of some 10,265 Africans, in order to ascertain the extent of the shortfall. The Chamber aimed

to acquire an overview of labour needs and to consider its
labour strategy over the long range, and collectively.
Eckstein, the Chairman of the Chamber, spelt out his approach at a special meeting to discuss African wages: 'We
must have labour, but it is necessary that we have it as
cheaply as possible. We must work in unity ...' (44)

This policy was preferred to the unco-ordinated contingency arrangements previously made by individual mine
managements to relieve their supply problems. The response to the Chamber's inquiries revealed an immediate
need of 2,185 labourers, but from the information supplied
by the mine managements the Chamber formulated a number of
general assumptions pertinent to the current strains on
the supply and more relevant to *future* regulation.

In considering the antecedent factors the Chamber
noted:

(i)   There was an increase in the supply of labour in
      the off-season period - that is, in the agri-
      culturally inactive season when 2,000 men con-
      tracted to work on the mines between January and
      February every year (45) - and that the overall
      labour supply had diminished, despite the in-
      crease in the quantity of mining activity since
      1887.
(ii) Keen competition had increased wages, to a point
      which was not commensurate with the profitable
      working of the smaller and poorer companies. (46)

The first factors indicated the general problem of the
industry in regard to labour: the failure - after the
'off-season' intake - to satisfy its *regular* labour
requirements, and the difficult problem of acquiring an
adequate increase in the supply to allow for future developments. The second factor of the African wage rate
was seen to be crucial to the cost problems of the gold
industry, as has been discussed in Chapter 1. In the
early stages of mining the owners seemed to feel that
until a uniform central system of recruitment was evolved,
the wage problem was insoluble. Until then the Chamber
would have to satisfy its labour needs as energetically
as possible, and avoid any recalcitrant action by individual mine managements, whose efforts to recruit labourers had the effect of bidding up wages.

The cost of labour was relatively uncontrollable, since
each company developed its own recruiting system and ad-
justed its wage rate to attract labour. Recruiting agents
employed by each company received a per capita payment for
each labourer delivered to the mine compound and 'were

none too scrupulous in the methods they used to round up
potential mine workers'. (47)   Because of the perpetual
shortage, mines tended to bid against each other 'in the
scramble to get their quota of labour'. (48)   Until the
early 1890s, when recruitment was centralized, the cost
of labour fluctuated irremediably.

In the light of its analysis of the labour shortage,
the Chamber formulated a number of recommendations for the
future regulation of the labour supply. The proposals depended heavily on the state's intervening to retain
recruits, but as the prospect of official assistance appeared increasingly unlikely, the Chamber sought to improve its political position by providing the necessary
administrative machinery and creating its own bureaucracy.
The recommendations included:

(i)   a more rigid enforcement of the pass system; (49)
(ii) a regular increase in the supply of Africans to
      meet the 'constant demands' of the mining compa-
      nies *through intervention by the public authori-
      ties*. This would be effected 'by [making] large
      drafts for the supply of the mines available
      from the northern districts of the Transvaal,
      Zululand, tembuland and other territories - where
      there are large numbers of Kafirs very badly
      supplied with food and willing to come to the
      fields if [they were afforded] public organ-
      isation for their conveyance and protection'.
      (50)

The more positive recommendation was clearly the
decision to increase the supply by making energetic attempts to tap the labour resources in the rural areas
which had hitherto been poorly explored or had responded
negatively to the Chamber's recruiting activities.

The Chamber's proposals were communicated to the
government and initially received some support. According
to the Minister for Mining the government might consider
taking more extreme measures to increase the hut tax,
'which would put a strong pressure upon the Transvaal
natives to do a certain amount of work'. (51)   But despite
the Minister's reassuring remarks, no action was taken by
the government for the present. The supply position
deteriorated, labour requirements were not met, and the
government took none of the expected measures of relief.

(iv)   INTERNAL REORGANIZATION: THE NATIVE LABOUR
COMMITTEE

In the absence of official intervention the Chamber acted
unilaterally, although it by no means abandoned hope that
the state would give the industry the extensive assistance
it needed.   In the short term, the Chamber attempted to
rationalize the recruiting system and took energetic
measures to draft larger numbers annually to the mines
than it had previously done.   In view of the official inaction in negotiating with African chiefs in the rural
regions on the mine-owners' behalf, the Chamber entered
into contracts with the responsible African authorities
for the supply of labour.   This would be disposed of under
subcontracts to the mining companies on arrival at the
goldfields.   But the success of the scheme depended substantially upon the government's willingness to identify
itself with the Chamber's labour strategy and to provide
the necessary administrative and legal machinery for the
control of labour and enforcement of contracts.   The increased assistance of the state was indispensable.   This
support was not forthcoming, however, and in the absence
of legal provision to control labour or to ensure the
fulfilment of subcontracts, the Chamber found itself at
a considerable disadvantage.   What it required, in effect,
was that the Native Registry Department should be transferred from the government to the Chamber itself, with the
enabling powers necessary to enforce regulations.   This
official sanction did not materialize, for the farmers and
land-owning class which commanded the government of the
Transvaal were not disposed to hand over control of the
labour supply to the mining companies to this degree,
despite insistent pressure from the industry.
   The Chamber proceeded to devise its own plans to relieve the labour shortage, but continued representations
to the government.   In 1891 it addressed itself to the
Volksraad, hoping that the government 'would not allow
[another] session to go by without making some legislative
provision' either 'by raising the hut tax' or by some
other means. (52)   The Chamber had in mind the example
afforded by the government's assistance to the Railway
Company, who received regulating powers of the type sought
by the Chamber.   A further diminution in the labour supply
to the mines was attributable to the diversion of labourers for the construction of the state railway line, and
with official support still not given to the mines the
Chamber assumed a strong independent initiative.
   This gave the appearance of the establishment of administrative institutions to function parallel to the of-

ficial ones. The Chamber established its own Native
Labour Committee, which in turn (i) introduced internal
control measures for the supply-price and regulation of
the labour force; (ii) appointed 'an experienced official' to act as a labour commissioner to organize the
supply and provide official sanction for labour contracts
entered into with African headmen; (iii) endowed this
official with responsibility for the redress of grievances
of the African workforce. (53)

Hence the Chamber acted to give coherence to the requirements of the mining managements and resorted to its
own measures to increase the supply and retain its workforce, by establishing institutions such as the Labour
Commissioner and a labour committee whose designations
and functions suggested an official connection. But the
Chamber was never prepared to accept this apparent status
as the real, and continually stressed the indispensability
of more extensive intervention by the state. By adopting
the measures it did, it expected either (i) that on its
own, or with government assistance in the near future, the
supply would be increased; or (ii) that within a comparatively short time the industry would substantially
reduce its annual wage bill.

3 The wage bill:
the Agreement of 1890

INTRODUCTION

Concerted efforts to increase the labour supply and increase control over the conditions of gold production
through measures promoting internal unity of the mine-
owners gave the members of the Chamber the confidence to
enter an agreement binding them to an overall wages and
labour policy. The Agreement was the first decisive step
in the movement towards uniformity of wage practices among
each of the seventy-five mining managements previously
competing for labour. (1) This unity was to secure a
far-reaching reduction in wages, and to have major implications for the division of labour on the mines.
   Apart from the determination of the wage rate several
important principles flowed from the Agreement, the most
important of which was the demarcation of the workforce
into three categories, creating a structure for all the
mining managements. Fifty per cent of their workforce
was confined to Category III, the lowest level of the new
wage rates. More significantly still, up to 20 per cent
of the workforce in each mine could be allocated to
Class I, which gave the employers the flexibility to
exceed average wage rates and create a category of labour
which lent itself to the acquisition of skills and relative permanence in the industry. This was important later
in relation to the deployment of all mining employees, especially the white mineworkers. (2)

THE WAGE AGREEMENT OF 1890:   REDUCING THE COST OF
PRODUCTION

In the first ten years of mining, the wage bill was the
subject of much manipulation. Since the Chamber believed

the 'supply price' to be both excessive and detrimental to
the acquisition of an adequate labour force, it took
'strenuous efforts' in the latter half of 1890 to reduce
what it considered 'abnormal and excessive' labour costs.
(3) The Chamber estimated that for the first six months
of 1890 the monthly wage bill would be £45,000, with an
African workforce of 15,000. The Chamber circulated its
constituent companies in April suggesting a reduction of
wages to a maximum 'fair rate of pay' of approximately
40s. per month of twenty-eight days ('Annual Report',
1890, pp.12,66).

The 1890 Agreement, which came into operation in October, was the first of its kind, and the first of three
major attempts in the decade before 1900 to reduce production costs by cutting the price of African labour.
The Agreement provides insights into the practices of
wage paring and established the pattern of African wage
scales (and work categories) which were observed subsequently. Although rates have risen since then, they have
tended until recently to *fluctuate* around the mean between
the highest and lowest wage then established. The rate
was calculated on the basis of the cost of subsistence of
the individual miner, and the earnings essential to
recruit him to the mines. It assumed that wages earned
in the mines were supplementary to a primary economic
activity based on the land.

Initially, agreement was obtained from seventy-five
constituent companies to increase the control over supply
by introducing a monthly system of wage payments as opposed to the prevailing weekly system, and lengthening
the average period of labour service. Thereafter, in a
more farsighted attempt to secure permanency and uniformity, the Chamber secured the agreement for a reduction
in African wages from 63s. to 40s. per month exclusive of
food and shelter, for what it described as an 'ordinary
Kafir'. This 'ordinary Kafir' was an African who did not
fall into any of the classifications for 'specially
skilled' Africans, i.e. shaft developers, station men,
surface stokers, police, and office workers. (4) The 1890
Agreement made provisions for these 'specially skilled
Kaffirs' to exceed the basic nominal rate of 40s. 'Absolute freedom' was accorded to the mine managers to pay
these men 'any rate [of pay] at their discretion', provided that the total of this group did not exceed 20 per
cent of the total African workforce on the particular
mine. The freedom accorded to the managements, though
'absolute', was in fact very limited indeed.

At least half of the total workforce was to be classified under Class III of the new Agreement with a maximum

wage rate of 40s. per month. Only 30 per cent of the
total labour force could be employed in Class II, on a
maximum wage rate of 50s. per month. Rigid procedures
for enforcement were provided, including regular submissions by managements of summaries of their total workforce and the categories they occupied. Penalties not
exceeding £500 were payable on breach of any of the regulations.

In a general injunction to the companies the Chamber
declared:

> ... You are earnestly requested to pay high rates to
> as few as possible. With reference to your right to
> pay *half* your Kaffirs up to 40s. and 30% up to 50s. per
> month, this provision is only intended to apply to the
> best of these classes of Kaffirs.... *Thus the average
> rate of pay to Kaffirs will, it is hoped, be consider-
> ably less than the maximum rates agreed upon.* (Empha-
> sis added) (5)

The Chamber's admonition was demonstrably well taken.
Substantial savings in the *short* term were recorded by
December 1890, when wages aggregated around 44s. per month
- an average saving of 22s. 6d. *per man* over the three
months during which the Agreement had operated. In cash
terms this represented a saving of £15,000 per month to
the industry as a whole. (6)

There appeared to be no difficulty in enforcing the
reduced monthly payments upon the unorganized workforce.
On the contrary, the transition was a smooth one, although
the Chamber took the precaution of advising the government
of the proposed large-scale changes in wage rates and
requested assistance in the event of desertion or a
general strike consequent upon the wage reductions. (7)
A relatively small number of African labourers returned
to the rural areas, but there was no immediate slowdown
of activity and the Chamber could claim that the new rates
appeared to work successfully and to confer 'a great advantage upon general mining companies in dealing with
their Native labour'. (8) But the success was a Pyrrhic
one and the effects were short-lived for two reasons:

(i)   The revised rates checked recruitment.
(ii) The railway extensions (which the Chamber had
      pressed for) resulted in a fall in the flow of
      labour in the following year and there was now
      some competition for the workforce.

This caused the scale of rates outlined in the 1890

October Agreement to be generally exceeded. (9) As the
renewal date for the Wage Agreement approached in October
1891, the mining companies became increasingly reluctant
to continue the arrangements, many of them having already
defected from the agreed levels in the interim, and
several of them having reverted to pre-October practices,
(10) i.e. to the system of a weekly wage payment which
tended to decrease labour control and regulation, thereby
facilitating evasion of penalties for breaching the
Agreement. Under these circumstances the October Agreement was allowed to lapse, and despite efforts to sustain
a specified maximum higher wage rate, this was not observed due to the high wages now being offered by railway
contractors, and renewed problems relating to African
travel facilities. The result was an increase in the
overall average wage on the mines.
    There were many lessons for the Chamber to learn from
its recent experiences in curbing production costs and
competition for labour with a second party in an urban
enterprise. Although it had perceived the necessity for
a common wage rate, it still had much to learn in respect
of reproducing the labour supply. But of some aspects it
was certain:

> (i)   Collaboration of mine managements was possible
>   so long as the labour demand was satisfied and
>   there were no interruptions in the supply.
> (ii)   Formal arrangements tended to crumble when the
>   supply was generally scarce or subject to
>   seasonal shortages.
> (iii) At these times, internecine company rivalry for
>   labour served to raise wages well above agreed
>   levels.
> (iv)   Conditions were not yet opportune for a uniform
>   wage pattern throughout the industry.
> (v)   The failure of the 1890 Wage Agreement had de-
>   stroyed a concerted effort to provide an ac-
>   ceptable wage rate throughout the industry, and
>   this failure (marked by an unattractive wage and
>   competition for the supply) had resulted in the
>   most erratic fluctuations in the cost of labour
>   as evidenced in July and August of 1891. Mine
>   managements had allowed wages to escalate (to
>   the aggregate weekly wage level of 1889) and
>   the cost per man (inclusive of food and quar-
>   ters) had risen to 15s. (11) Indeed, in the
>   absence of formal agreement, wages had been sub-
>   ject to the greatest diversity. (12) Moreover,
>   it was clear that this situation was likely to

remain unchanged until an appropriate uniform
scale of rates was applied, and adequate provisions formulated for the control and recruitment of labour.

There was one aspect, however, that could not at this
stage be gauged. This was the *long-term* effect of drastic
wage reductions upon the supply. Would consistent cuts in
the rate seriously impair the future flow of migrants from
the rural areas to the Rand? Or would the stream of
labour stabilize itself given an 'adjusting' period of
time, statutory action, and further deterioration of the
rural economies? (13) The Chamber was to grapple with
these problems in the period following the Anglo-Boer conflict, but for the moment the urgency of the supply problem, the capacity of the rural regions to hold their
populations, and the state of inter-company competition
encouraged little flexibility of action. Since the matter
of the long-term flow was an academic one for the present,
the Chamber directed its activities towards other, more
immediate problems: the unsatisfied labour demands, the
'excessively high' weekly wage rates, and deficiencies in
the recruitment and regulation of African labour. Thus,
in the interim between the formal ending of the Agreement
in 1891 and the establishment of an effective recruiting
organization in 1896, the Chamber was left to explore
several expedients for the increase of the supply and the
control of the mine labour force. In attempting to re-
solve its problems by internal organization and wage
classification (particularly the principle of an unspeci-
fied wage for 20 per cent of the labour force) it set some
substantial precedents for the future.

4 Quasi-official control:
the state and the Chamber of Mines

INTRODUCTION

New, quasi-official, institutions were established by the
mine-owners to remedy the fall in the supply which the
Chamber claimed to be partially the consequence of the
government's 'lack of co-operation' with the industry.
Critics of the Chamber (mine managers), however, asserted
that this shortage of labour was the result of the Chamber's inflexibility in determining a viable wages policy.

The Chamber believed that with adequate organization
and effective control the 'natural' labour supply that was
embedded in the thickly populated African districts of the
Cape Colony, Zululand and Basutoland would be released for
work on the mines. Hence in the absence of effective
assistance from the state it continued to develop plans
for its own Labour Department, headed by a 'high-minded
official' designated as Native Labour Commissioner, to
help strengthen the supply. This quasi-official nominee,
who the Chamber hoped would be given official legitimation
with the title of Justice of the Peace, would, it was
hoped, promote the confidence of colonial magistrates and
inspire the Africans in the various territories to look
more favourably towards work on the mines.

The latter part of this discussion is concerned with
the criticisms of the Chamber made by the mine managers,
who felt the dearth of African labour more closely, and
who therefore were inclined to press for more immediate
and extreme remedies to raise the supply.

(i) QUASI-OFFICIAL CONTROL

Attempts to control wages and regulate the labour supply
soon became the main priorities of the industry. The

Chamber's Native Labour Committee (which, as we have noted
on p. 48, was established as a contingency arrangement
before the October Agreement in 1890) now became increasingly involved in forward planning and policy construction.   It declined to bind managements to further mutual
action, since the 1890 Agreement had palpably failed to
maintain an effective employer combination, and there
seemed little hope of securing the collaboration of the
respective managements when there was no immediate prospect of guaranteeing an uninterrupted supply.   Instead the
Chamber concentrated on creating effective arrangements
for the satisfaction of present requirements from the Cape
Colony, Basutoland and Zululand, where the new Native
Labour Committee felt 'confident' that they could procure
labour in sufficient quantities to level the 'supply-
price' and subsequently reduce wages 'by the simple
operation of the law of supply and demand'. (1)
     This view, reinforced by recent experience, became
prominent when the Native Labour Committee justifiably
concluded that the 'thickly populated native districts'
of the Cape Colony, Basutoland and Natal were 'natural'
sources of supply, and that *given the necessary co-
operation from the governments concerned* their labour
could materially relieve the industry's manpower problems.
In the latter belief that there would be a high level of
government co-operation, the Chamber was proved quite
wrong, despite some initial success such as securing a
reduction of railway fares for Africans commuting from
the Cape Colony to the Transvaal. (2)   In Natal the Chamber was most unsuccessful with its negotiations with the
authorities who, conscious of that colony's own labour
needs, were not prepared to 'do more to encourage the
emigration of natives to ... the goldfields'. (3)   In
Basutoland it made more headway and arranged for the
transport of 'one or two thousand [labourers] at [reduced]
wages of 40/- per month of four weeks for a period of 6
months', the cost of travelling expenses to be borne by
the Chamber. (4)
     These expedients - for such they were in the absence of
alternative permanent legislative or institutional arrangements - did not provide the anticipated results, and
the Chamber found 'greater stringency' in the supply of
African labour in the succeeding year. (5)   Moreover, the
attempt to acquire labour at a reduced fixed rate from the
Cape Colony proved particularly abortive, as Africans on
their arrival at the fields both demanded the current wage
rate and adamantly refused to go underground.   Others
simply absconded at the first opportunity. (6)
     The failure to tap the labour resources of the colonies

in British South Africa - the Cape, Basutoland and Natal -
led to renewed interest by the Chamber in establishing a
Native Labour Department by its own Native Labour Committee. The intention appears to have been to develop an
administrative apparatus which would act in parallel to
official government bodies and acquire quasi-official
status. The Native Labour Committee had already proved
itself to be a useful 'cabinet committee' of the Chamber
and was becoming increasingly important in the formulation
of policy. In acquiring a specific Department and a
Native Labour Commissioner the Chamber hoped to establish
controls and make recruiting arrangements on a scale which
hitherto it had failed to do. It was hoped that the provision of an official such as the Native Labour Commissioner (responsible to the Chamber's Labour Department)
would help to syphon all available African labour to the
goldfields. The appointment would also 'supply the place
which in countries where state-aided immigration obtains
is filled by a government officer'. (7) In this way a
company official would provide the liaison between the
Chamber, the mine managements, and the colonial government
officials, to sanction controls and inquire into complaints, *a task which governments might normally undertake*. This would, it was felt, assure colonial magistrates and prospective African recruits of fair treatment
lest it 'shut the Rand off' from the best source of labour
supply. The appointed official would, according to the
Chamber, organize the supply and insulate it against any
abusive practices by any of the mining companies or outside agencies. As one sanguine contemporary commentator
stated: 'This gentleman, who will be a man respected by
and of substantial influence amongst the natives, whilst
on the one hand assisting the gold mining companies to
obtain labour, will guard the interests of the natives,
from motives of expediency as well as for higher reasons.'
(8)
     Ideally, the mine-owners would have favoured a govern-
ment 'opposite number' to act in concert with the Chamber.
(9) He would have similar powers and would liaise with
the Chamber's nominee so as to 'strengthen his position
and authority'. (10) The Chamber believed moreover that
the 'power and usefulness' of its own official 'would be
augmented if his appointment were stamped by government
recognition', i.e. with the title of JP of the Republic,
but the government procrastinated. It declined to make
any appointment and gave only verbal support to the Chamber's administrative bureaucracy. In effect it acted on
its own scheme, which emanated from a Commission of the
Volksraad on the regulations and supply of African Labour,

(11) and provided for the 'united co-operation of the Captains and Heads of the locations and Kraals with the Commissioners and sub-Commissioners of Natives and employers'. In addition the missionaries were to give their assistance 'by making the Natives understand that industry is one of the most important and essential principles of civilization'. (12)

The mine-owners believed that some of the consequences of the government's refusal to reach an accommodation with the Chamber were: (i) a delay in arriving at a satisfactory solution to the supply problem; (ii) an increasing scarcity of labourers; and (iii) an escalation of the wage rates - which was a consequence both of the overall procrastination and of the scarcity of the supply.

The mine managers, however, were less prepared to attribute the cause of this failure to the state, and criticized the Chamber for its lack of policy, arguing that it had failed to arrive at a comprehensive labour strategy. Their view was effectively that the Chamber had been too influenced by the market wage likely to attract men at all times to the Rand and as a result had tended to agree to raise wages 'at every annual scarcity without any corresponding reduction in times when labour was plentiful'. (13)

On the latter point the managers drew the conclusion that 'the great law of supply and demand did not altogether apply'. (14) In this way they appreciated possibly the economic coercions - the push factors - which induced labour to leave the land. What they meant too, it would seem, was that it *should* not altogether apply, for the alternative remedies they suggested 'to correct the evil' in the labour flow were to induce Africans to seek work on the Rand irrespective of the adequacy of the wage rate. This they hoped to do by urging the government to increase the hut tax. (15) The other measures they suggested were more conventional and had at various times been demanded of the government by the Chamber - to afford protection to recruits, provide depots for the accommodation of mine workers in transit to the fields, and to help the supply by signifying recognition for the Chamber's Labour Commissioner.

One other measure suggested by the mine managers, which anticipated the central control of labour later adopted by the Chamber, urged the formation of Native Labour Bureaux for the following purposes:

(i)   sending agents to arrange supply of labour with the chiefs;

(ii) arranging central depots for their safe conduct;

(iii)   providing each company supporting the Bureaux
        with supplies of labour (pro rata to their sub-
        scription) based on their average labour force
        for the previous twelve months.

The design was such that companies were to undertake
to abstain from purchasing labourers from any tout or
agent other than those belonging to the Bureaux. Unlike
the central recruiting organization which subsequently
emerged, the Bureaux were not intended 'to fix contractual
labour periods or determine the rates of wages' (until the
supply of labour permits).

The substance of this plan was accepted by the mining
companies in 1893 - three years prior to the great agreement for rural recruitment - and put into operation for
the following twelve months. (16)

Mindful of the previous indiscipline of the mine
managements in former labour crises, however, the managers
pressed for the insertion of a penal clause in the Agreement in consequence of which the mining companies would be
required to forfeit an amount of £200 in the event of
breaching their contract. (17) Despite the appeal for
unity among the companies some of the members refused to
sign the Agreement and 'spent ⎍ousands a year in paying
touts who seized upon natives actually on their road here,
and paid 10/- or £1 per head'. (18) Although the Chamber
was optimistic of the potential for future labour supplies
and reported an inflow of 40,000 African miners in 1893
and substantially more in 1894, (19) recourse was still
made to the labour supply along the East Coast of Africa.

(ii) THE CHAMBER, THE MINE MANAGERS AND THE STATE

In summary, the Chamber's role of providing coherence and
central direction to mining policy was placed under severe
strain when the October Agreement of 1890 failed. There
was no self-criticism by the Chamber of its wage reductions, and indeed it did not admit any connection between
the lowering of the wage rate and the shortage of the
supply. Having attributed the responsibility for the
labour shortage to the lack of state co-operation, it
turned to the colonial territories of the Cape, Basutoland
and Natal, where more effective co-operation was expected.

In this the colonial governments of the Cape and
Basutoland - but not Natal - did co-operate (by reducing
the rail fares of the men in transit), but they could not
control the men themselves, especially those from the
Cape, who after a stark journey refused to labour at a

rate that had been reduced by 20 per cent. (The failure
to recruit 'colonial Africans' in any large number at a
low price when the supply was short does not appear to be
the substance of the mine managers' criticism that the
Chamber was inflexible in its wage policy. Their claim
rather was the reverse of this - that there was a refusal
to reduce the cash wage when the labour supply was plentiful. Their point was accurate to some extent in some instances, although it was not consistent with the general
policies of the Chamber.)

Whatever the cause of the labour shortage, however,
the impact of the 1890 Agreement, with its reduction in
the wage rate at a time of severe competition with the
railways for labour, did not help the Chamber to marshal
the labour resources its managements demanded. In criti-
cizing the Chamber the mine managers, who were closer to
the work situation than the members of the central body,
seemed to have had two points of contention: (i) that
not enough positive action was being taken to acquire
labour (hence the proposals for the establishment of
Labour Bureaux in the African districts); and (ii) that
the Chamber did not reduce the wage rate when the supply
was adequate. However (like the Chamber), they made no
connection between the 1890 wage reductions and the
present dearth of supply. Their solution to the problem
of supply was even more pragmatic than the Chamber's -
the creation of Labour Bureaux to increase the supply in
the belief that the labour force could be acquired since
the resources were physically there.

In establishing its Native Labour Department and a
Commissioner to negotiate with 'foreign governments', the
Chamber did not abandon the hope of more extensive state
intervention to raise the supply, but on the contrary increasingly anticipated greater support from the state.
Indeed, state co-operation seemed all the more important
as the Chamber's reconstituted labour administration was
clearly designed towards recruitment on a vast scale -
'to syphon all available labour to the goldfields'. Hence
the exasperation of the Chamber when the government announced its preference for its own machinery to marshal
labour supplies.

The state's negative approach to the Chamber's 'bureaucracy' - characterized by vague promises, occasional
verbal support and 'procrastination' - gave little boost
to the Chamber's elaborate machinery, which thereby acquired no further elevation of status outside the Chamber's perception of it. Concerned to retain their hegemony, within the Transvaal state the landlords and
farmers preferred to rely on their Commissioners and sub-

Commissioners to raise the supply generally - which did
not exclude farm labour - and leave the Chamber out of
direct negotiations. The establishment of Labour Bureaux
in the African districts by the Chamber, at the instance
of the mine managers, offset to some extent the exclusive
operation by the state in this sphere. However, notwithstanding the potential labour resources within the Transvaal and colonial territories some cynicism about raising
the supply in the immediate future led the Chamber to
direct its energies, albeit reluctantly, towards the East
Coast, where the prospects seemed greater and the supply
more readily available.

5 The East Coast labour supply: an alternative labour supply

INTRODUCTION

Here we are concerned with the Chamber's dilemma of having to turn towards the East Coast for its major labour needs when it remained convinced that the Transvaal state could (by enforcing contracts, 'protecting' the supply and revising taxation) render the need for the large-scale recruitment of long-distance labour superfluous.

Tsonga men from Maputoland, on the East Coast of Africa, had from the earliest years of mining constituted the backbone of the mine labour force on the Rand. Later, they were joined by migrants from the hinterland. In its report of 31 December 1891, the Chamber reported the presence in the previous year of approximately 7,000 Africans drawn from the Portuguese territories. These, together with 4,000 Africans from the northern Transvaal, represented 77 per cent of the African labour force. There is, however, a considerable history of recent Tsonga migration which goes back half a century.

Labour migration from the Delagoa Bay hinterland to South Africa probably began in the mid-nineteenth century when as Harries (1977, p.61) notes, numerous Tsonga accompanied Zulu 'refugees' into Natal. After 1875 Natal entered into a formal agreement with the governors of Mocambique for contract labourers who would be employed in sugar cultivation at less than half the cost of Indian labour. (1) The success of migrant labour in Natal led to their importation into the Cape as farm and railway workers, and then to Griqualand West and Barberton for work in diamond and gold mining respectively. By 1887, half the able-bodied male population of Maputo were estimated to be working at any given period in the Transvaal, Natal or Kimberley. Deteriorating soil, declining cattle-keeping, stock losses through disease, and popula-

tion pressures were among the reasons for this extensive
migration. According to Harries (1977, p.66), the reasons
are even more deep-rooted:

> The export of migrant labour by the rulers of the south
> and central Tsonga must be seen in terms of a change in
> the mode of subsistence of the area, the under mining
> of centralized pre-conquest commodity production and
> exchange, and the formation of dependency linkages.

The precise reasons for the export of labour from this
region cannot be considered here, for want of space. What
is of concern, however, is the importance of this labour
resource to the mine-owners on the Rand.

Three years after the inception of mining on the Rand,
in 1890, between one-half and three-fifths of the African
labour force came from the 'East Coast'. Moreover, many
of the labourers who were classified as 'special' employees, and whose wage rate exceeded the average, were
drawn from this source. The problem for the Chamber,
however, was that although these men served as the spine
of the workforce and acquired skills by virtue of their
longer periods of contract, they were more expensive (if
the cost of recruitment was considered) than the local
supply. Moreover, recruitment was administratively
cumbersome and costly, and in view of the presence of
what it considered a 'natural' resource of indigenous
labour, foreign labour was thought to be unnecessary in
the long term. One of the mechanisms for 'inducing' the
movement of this 'natural' supply to the Rand was thought
to be taxation.

The revision of taxation in the Transvaal is a recurring theme in this discussion. For the Chamber this was
a measure which would release the local supply and ultimately enable it to reduce wages. Hence taxation - or
force - is here seen as an expedient to raise labour in
the context of a general response to the shortage of
labour in agriculture and mining in Natal, the Cape and
the Transvaal in the 1890s.

The mine-owners did not oppose forced labour in principle, but there appears to have been some reticence about
the level of compulsion - 'the amount of force' - to be
applied. This aspect is discussed in Chapter 12 (vii)
below, but it is sufficient to note here that taxation
was (more seriously) applied in 1897 and after 1903 with
indifferent results. Albu showed some prescience in this
matter when he told the Industrial Commission in 1897:

> I as an employer of labour, say it would be a good

> thing to have forced labour, *but another question is
> whether you would get it.* You could exercise *a certain
> amount of force* amongst the natives if you impose *a
> certain tax* upon each native who does not work, or if
> he has not shown he has worked *a certain length of time*
> .... I do not know what the other countries would do.
> In the *[Cape]* Colony there is a law which compels
> natives to work. It is the Glen Grey Act. ('Evidence',
> pp.29,30, emphasis added)

Albu seems to have realized that the use of force was
problematical, and whilst he clearly approved it in principle, he was concerned to obtain a balance between the
extent of compulsion, the level of taxation and the dura-
tion a man was to be allowed to remain on his land before
he could be required to pay tax. Possibly it was because
this type of labour coercion was found to be so problematical (it involved the viability of the migrant system)
that it was not the measure used in the long run. The
instrument that was applied (and which is well beyond our
period of 'The Foundations') was one that struck at the
heart of African resistance to entering the labour markets
on the mines and white-owned farms. This was the 1913
Natives Land Act, which severed African access to further
productive land, froze existing social relations in the
declared Reserves, and undermined the African agricultural
potential. In effect it was infinitely more diabolical
than the type of forced labour contemplated earlier. However, it was not applied until after 1913, and is dealt
with in a subsequent chapter.

The substantive portion of our discussion here is concerned with the Chamber's arrangements for securing a
reliable supply from the East Coast for the vast gold
industry which had emerged. This was not attempted
before an effort was made at the eleventh hour to secure
a larger supply of local labour. The failure of this
effort to obtain local labour raised the tension between
the Chamber and the state to a high pitch, the mine-owners
accusing the state of disturbing the labour market, preventing wage reductions and undermining the security of
the mines against a scarcity of labour. A sharper confrontation was averted by a war in the African districts
of the northern Transvaal, which led the Chamber to take
up its options on the East Coast.

Dealing with the East Coast, we review the Portuguese
authorities' co-operation with the Chamber in the mining
labour traffic, and the industry's success in securing
labour for longer contractual periods at differential
rates from the remainder of the labour force - despite

competition with the railways and the continuing high
demand for recruits. Significance is also attributed to
the concentrated advantages of the Chamber over the labour
touts, and the former's capacity to acquire the supply in
greater numbers and at lower rates than the local labour
contractors in this region. The calculation of the
supply-price, however, remains an important problem if
the labour flow is to be retained.

Finally, the chapter deals with the Chamber's concern
to secure a guaranteed system for the regular flow of
African mine labour to and from the Rand. In seeking this
security the Chamber was confronted even more sharply with
the need for state support to enforce the contracts
secured at such great expense and organization. The inadequacy of the state controls over the labour turnover
had led the Chamber to place pressure on the legislature,
and to draft on behalf of the Volksraad a set of regulations for the control of the mobility of African labour,
which would draw the state (legally and administratively)
into enforcing labour contracts and protecting the mine
labour supply. Increased pressure upon the state was now
asserted to give legal effect to these regulations.

(i)   THE EAST COAST LABOUR SUPPLY

The failure of the Chamber's Labour Commissioner to acquire labour in satisfactory numbers from local resources
led him to lean more seriously on the alternative labour
market on the East Coast. The Portuguese possessions here
(particularly the area south of the Save River) were the
closest to hand, and the new Labour Commissioner soon discerned the possibility of acquiring more labour from this
source, since it differed from indigenous markets in the
Republic and the interior in four respects favourable to
the Chamber:

(i)   The official policy of the Governor General of
      Mocambique was (subject to certain reservations)
      more coercive than the Transvaal state in open-
      ing up - at 'acceptable' rates - the labour re-
      sources of that region to the mining companies.
      (2)

(ii) There was greater compulsion - structural and
      otherwise - upon 'Portuguese' Africans to mi-
      grate to the mines than local Africans in the
      South African Republic and the colonies.

(iii) Longer contractual periods could be negotiated
      than the local ones.

(iv)   Differential wage rates could be arranged not
only within the Portuguese element of the labour
force but between Portuguese migrants and the
Republic's African labour supply. (3)

The expedient of obtaining labour from other territories was regretted initially. It was expensive, administratively awkward and (the Chamber believed) *unnecessary*. If only the Transvaal authorities would wield effective *local* control, the supply would increase and
efforts could be made to reduce wages and regulate the
intake and distribution of labour. There was no reason
(it seemed) why local labour should be secured under any
less favourable conditions than East Coast labour. On the
contrary, its acquisition ought to have been easier - and
cheaper. Hence the Chairman of the Chamber 'regretted'
the need to import East Coast labour at the 'unjustifi-
able' cost of £3 per head. (4) He hoped that new Pass
Regulations (recently framed by the Chamber's Native
Labour Committee and the mines managers, and sanctioned
by the government) would 'double the labour supply' and
reduce wages and thereby effect an annual saving of
£400,000. (5) With economies of scale of this magnitude
in mind, the Chamber hoped it would not have to seek its
labour force further afield. It thus never ceased to hope
that the Transvaal government would 'find it wise to
regulate taxation so that it bears most heavily upon those
natives who live in comparative idleness'. (6)
The amendment or 'revision' of the system of taxation
was a general remedy applied in the 1890s in the Cape
Colony, Natal and the Orange Free State to increase the
flow of farm and mine labourers. Its most recent application, affecting only a small area at this time, was in
the Cape Colony, as outlined in the so-called Glen Grey
Act of 1894, which set out to remedy the supply by
creating a landless class of Africans. The Act moreover
imposed a 10s. tax on every able-bodied male who did not
go out as a labourer for three months out of the twelve.
(7)
Cecil Rhodes, the Cape Prime Minister, whose interests
in diamond and gold mining were considerable, personally
piloted the Act through the Cape Legislative Assembly in
1894. He echoed the sentiments expressed contemporarily
by the Chamber of Mines that idleness was evil and work a
virtue. Hence, in introducing the Bill, Rhodes told the
Assembly: 'You will remove from them that life of sloth
and laziness, you will teach them the dignity of labour
and make them contribute to the prosperity of the State
and make them give some return for our wise and good
government.' (8)

The Chamber hoped also that the Transvaal state would 'find it wise' to coerce on a large scale African labourers to the goldfields and the farms, provided this 'forced labour' did not threaten the continuation of the migrant system, which depended on recruiting single men when needed and returning them to their homes on the expiry of their contracts. But the Transvaal was slower to enact the necessary legislation than the Cape Colony in this respect. (Neither the unreformed Pass Regulations nor the old hut tax, which was imposed specifically to coerce African men into taking up contracts of labour in mining and agriculture, had yet provided the large quantities of labour which the industry required.) In the absence of a positive government response for a further year to increase the labour flow by revising taxation, (9) and perceiving little hope of immediately increasing the indigenous supply in this particular way, the Chamber concentrated its attention upon the extensive labour reservoirs along the East Coast of the continent.

Contrary to expectations, despite official willingness the negotiations for the East Coast labour supply proved unexpectedly protracted. First, wage rates fluctuated sharply owing to official delays, excessive per capita costs and 'exorbitant' agency fees. The mine-owners stated after much exasperation that 'at Delagoa Bay everything is done by bribery, and everybody from the highest to the lowest takes a bribe'. (10) Second, the administrative machinery was inadequate for the scale of the exercise. Progress was delayed because of lapses in the arrangements for the contracting, transport and security of the recruits procured by the Chamber's agents. Third, the market was complicated by the sharp competition for East Coast African labour between the Chamber and the railway construction company which was taking the northern railway line to Pretoria. (11)

Although the presence of competing agents for the labour force added new stresses to the Chamber's supply situation it did not induce the mine-owners to increase wages. The reverse was rather the case. In one instance a labour contractor pressed the Chamber to accept his terms on the understanding that he was under pressure from a railway contractor for a contingent of 'the cheapest native labour he had had as yet'. But the Native Labour Commissioner, C.J.Taunton, rejected the offer on the grounds 'that the proposed charges were excessive'. (12) He in turn negotiated with several alternative contractors for lower per capita costs and wage rates, and succeeded in reducing the original projection of 52s. 6d. per labourer to 35s. 'for a full grown man and 25/- per month for boys'. (13)

The diversity of charges and the competition between contractors made the Chamber wary of concluding agreements with any of the numerous contracting agencies. (14) Since it had to draw labour from further afield it aimed to secure the supply at the lowest margin of cost under the most favourable conditions. It soon became evident that the Chamber itself would have to undertake the contracting operation. This was so because there were an active number of labour contractors and touts, each trafficking in the sale of Portuguese African labour and each describing himself with varying degrees of excellence as competent to acquire labour from the coast, and each undercutting the other in important respects. Ultimately none succeeded in securing a contract with the Chamber, which declined to commit itself to any of the proposals in the belief that it could use its considerable influence to acquire the labour more cheaply itself. In adopting this course the mine-owners could only have concluded that:

   (i)   despite the extravagant claims made by foreign
          contractors the Chamber was no less competent
          to procure the foreign labour force than anyone
          else;
  (ii)   its influence (and English connection) was more
          likely to yield positive results than that of
          local touts with no standing among the Portu-
          guese officials;
 (iii)   the hazards of transporting foreign labour over
          long distances necessitated careful control,
          which experience had shown *it* was best able to
          provide;
  (iv)   its labour needs were too great to be entrusted
          to touts whose agency fees were higher than the
          Chamber was willing to pay, and this labour
          might be procured more cheaply by the Chamber;
   (v)   the recruiting methods of these labour dealers
          might antagonize the potential labour force and
          alienate it from the mining industry.

Indeed, one agency, carried away by its capacity to acquire labour, offered to 'increase the supply and effect a consequent reduction of wages paid ... so that the Native Labour Question shall no longer remain the dread of the Mining Industry'. (15) The methods to be used were unstated. So sanguine were they of their future success that they required no remuneration until 'it becomes proven that we can attain the desired end'. (16) Their objective was to raise the level of the supply so well

above demand that wage rates might be *reduced*. The Chamber, however, clearly had had sufficient experience to
realize that the contracting company's capacity to supply
unlimited labour would diminish immediately the cash wage
fell below a certain point in view of the problematical
conditions which governed the entry of Africans to the
labour market *at this stage*. These conditions concerned
access to productive land and rural poverty, as well as
physical hazards connected with mining, and problems of
communication. (17)

Thus the Chamber itself embarked upon a large-scale
exercise of importing Portuguese African labour to the
Rand. There was every reason to believe that the flow of
labour would be long-term and substantial. In the first
instance, the Chamber's agents could rely on the support
of tribal chiefs, who were willing to endorse the emigration of their tribesmen because they acquired a capitation tax of £1 from them on their return from the Rand.
Secondly, the high bride-price of £20 was an additional
stimulus to emigration. Thirdly, the condition of rural
poverty in certain areas, especially among the Inhambes,
where 'a state of semi-starvation' existed, promised an
unlimited flow of migrants to the gold mines. (18)
Fourthly, a central depot near Komatipoort on the Transvaal boundary made commuting less arduous and acted as a
central 'rendezvous' for all the East Coast Africans en
route to the Rand. This, it was hoped, would assist
transportation, prevent molestation and strengthen the
stream of the supply.

However, the difficulties of importing foreign labour
over long distances led the Chamber to make a final attempt to improve the supply from the northern districts
of the Republic and to dispatch their Native Labour Commissioner to these regions to explore the position at
first hand. The Chamber had not given up the prospect
of improving (and cheapening) the *internal* labour supply,
and this attitude was reflected in the report of the
Native Labour Commissioner when he had completed his
investigations. Basically he was optimistic about the
future, but clung to the belief that the state would come
to the assistance of the industry. For, he reported, 'all
that was required to maintain an ample supply *[was]* ...
the honest aid of the government'. (19) By this he meant
the promotion of tax and pass laws, which he did not
mention specifically by name but referred to obliquely
as 'protective and fostering measures necessary to induce
labourers to leave their homes'. (20)

The Commissioner's report, despite the past performance
of the government, was considered to be on the whole

'highly realistic', but its implementation was frustrated
by the government's delay in providing the 'requisitive
regulations' for the 'proper operation' of the labour
supply. The Chamber had reached a critical stage in its
relationship with the state, and the absence of further
measures by the Transvaal landowners in the legislature
to intervene to assist the industry brought relationships
to an impasse. The mine-owners charged the government
with disturbing the labour market, materially prejudicing
opportunities for wage reductions and undermining their
security against a scarcity of labour. (21) It had published the report of its Commissioner to speed the legislature into action, but the men in the Volksraad had done
little further to relieve the Chamber of its labour problem. A major confrontation with the state on these
matters was averted only by the sudden eruption of African
conflict with the farmers and landowners into war in the
northern districts of the Transvaal, which brought a
temporary halt to local African recruitment from the
districts and made the importation of East Coast labour
a matter of urgent necessity. (22) The Chamber now found
it necessary to make a special effort to obtain the
state's support in recruiting Portuguese African labour
and also dispatched a Special Commissioner (Duncombe) to
the East Coast to confirm 'with accuracy' the extent of
the potential labour market along the coast, and to report
on wage requirements and the cost of importation. (23)

Duncombe's report more than confirmed the prognostications of all the earlier agents in the coastal region of
Delagoa Bay. Here, within a radius of 150 miles, 'one
million souls' were 'at the disposal' of the Chamber. (24)
In addition, the Mocambique authorities had done what the
Chamber had for so long urged the South African government
to do, and imposed a hut tax on 100,000 homesteads in the
area, which helped the Chamber to secure a steady flow of
labour for the industry. (25) The prospect of a substantial number of potential recruits from this quarter was
highly rewarding to the Chamber, which nevertheless chose
to act with extreme caution, for it had observed already
that the mere existence of high concentrations of men in
a particular region did not ensure an automatic migration
of Africans from that region to the Rand. In the circumstances the Chamber's decision was to act in the closest
'co-operation with the Portuguese Authorities', the
African chiefs and the labour agents in order to secure
what it described as a regular system which would be
'welcomed by the Chiefs and Tribesmen'. In practical
terms its strategy was highly cost-effective, as was borne
out by the following:

    (i)   the low wage of each African it recruited (con-
           tracts were concluded as cheaply as 40s. per man
           per month;
    (ii)   its active co-operation with the Portuguese
           authorities, by which recruits were bound to the
           industry for a year, provided that the Chamber
           paid half their transport costs. (26) In ad-
           dition, the Portuguese authorities agreed to
           waive the more punitive and incidentally more
           lucrative of their measures against tribesmen
           who migrated to the mines without the prescribed
           travel papers. (27)

By this agreement the Portuguese, now assured of a
larger volume of trade than previously, agreed to provide
the necessary travel documents and forgo the revenue from
the heavy fines normally levied. (28) As a result of
these arrangements the total cost of recruitment per head
was calculated at 65s. to the mineowners, which the Chamber believed might still be reduced substantially once it
had established itself in the region. It was in this
respect that the Chamber believed *it* would succeed in
reducing the per capita cost of migrant workers when
labour touts were powerless. For it had already secured
the active assistance of the Portuguese government over
travel facilities and thereafter proposed to rationalize
its overheads by arranging transport of recruits by steam-
ship and rail to the Rand at cheaper rates.
These exploratory steps were followed by the dispatch
of nine gangs (704 men) on a public relations exercise to
announce to the chiefs the 'benefits of employment on the
goldfields'. The success of the plan was evident by the
recruitment of 1,560 labourers in a period of less than
three months, and the establishment of a second rest depot
at Zandfontein. (29) The Chamber obviously considered its
efforts to improve the African labour supply 'encouraging'. Their optimism was well founded. In 1894 poverty
and taxation plus an improvement in the Chamber's organization served to increase the number of recruits by
26,000 (to a total of 40,000) over the 1890 intake and
enabled the Chamber to effect an average *reduction* in the
wage rate of 4s., from £3.3s. in 1890 to 59s. in 1894.
(30) This reduction in the wage rate occurred when the
demand for labour was on the increase. The Chamber explained this phenomenon as being a result of its successful policy of widening the market for its labour force by
'tapping a greater number of sources of supply'. (31) It
made no reference to the conditions prevailing in this
region or to the economic coercion imposed by the Portu-

guese authorities. Indeed, but for the operations of
touts, the mine-owners would have attempted to reduce
wages still further. (32)

The Chamber was now in a position to establish itself
more securely along the East Coast. It managed to con-
clude an agreement with both the Transvaal state and the
Portuguese government, and extended the system of labour
rest depots along the various routes into the interior.
Its efforts were frustrated, however, by the absence of
further support from the Transvaal state to help the
mine-owners enforce labour contracts once they had been
entered into. The Chamber lamented 'this deficiency' in
labour control, declaring that 'were effective protection
afforded by law, it would be possible to introduce labour
from the Portuguese possessions to any extent that might
be required'. (33) In the event, the increase in the
turnover and demand for African labour served only to
make the Chamber more conscious of the numerous 'desertions' of East Coast Africans who could not be appre-
hended and ordered to observe their full contractual arrangements.

In its anxiety to prevent further loss to the labour
flow the Chamber pressed the state to adopt the Draft
(Pass) Regulations modelled on the Natal arrangements
concerning the registration of 'Native Servants', which
the Chamber had drawn up and submitted to the Transvaal
government. (34) These Regulations, (35) together with
the institutions that were soon to develop for the
recruitment of migrant workers, became the twin axes
around which acquisition of the labour force revolved in
the following decades for the working of the Rand gold
mines.

(ii)   THE STATE AS AGENT OF GOLD PRODUCTION

(a)   Control over mobility

The more the Chamber expanded its capacity to marshal mine
labour for distribution to its separate mining units along
the Rand, the greater its reliance on the state for the
protection of its labour force. Contracts negotiated as
far afield as the interior of the East Coast - at a relatively high cost per unit of labour recruited - required
stringent legal protection if the industry was not to
incur a net monetary loss for every man who 'deserted'
once he had reached the mine to which he had been allocated. The greater the cost of procuring mine labour,

and the higher the administrative expenses of recruitment
and the cost of food and transport from the East Coast to
the Reef, the more the Chamber required guarantees for the
retention of the labour force it had so 'expensively'
recruited.

Albu liked to think of the relationship between the
state and the mining industry as similar to that of a
twin. A few years after the Chamber had entered into
arrangements with the Portuguese for large drafts of
labour, he told the Industrial Commission of 1897:

> I can only compare ... the State and the mining indus-
> try, as twins - twins not in the ordinary sense, but
> which by some freak of nature, have grown together at
> one point. The welfare of one must necessarily affect
> the welfare of the other.... The State is supported
> by the whole of the mining industry. ('Evidence',
> pp.9,10)

Generally, the high turnover of men on the mines raised
the problem of control over the mobility of the labour
force which only the state could manage effectively. (36)
Hence the recent experience of recruiting labour in
Mocambique confirmed what was apparent to the mine-owners
from the formative years of the industry - that the relative 'stability' of the workforce depended on the ability
of the state to provide legal machinery for the enforcement of contracts. This involved the provision of administrative institutions, police and officials to deal
with infringements of the laws so framed. As the industry
grew, the mine-owners required that the state intervene
more in this way, to assure that all the mines were
brought to the operative stages and that high levels of
productivity were obtained. (There were other requirements of the state, such as cheaper communications, a
change in policy on explosives, and greater clarity on
aspects of the Gold Laws, but these need not concern us
here.)

The potential of the East Coast as a resource for mine
labour 'to any extent that might be required' attested to
the continuing significance of Mocambique labour to the
industry, and its position as the core and largest section
of the total workforce. Its acquisition and retention
rested on drawing the state increasingly into closer
working co-operation with the mines, at least in respect
of 'protecting' the supply.

(b)   Taxation

The revision of the tax system in the Transvaal remained
an important point for the Chamber, which believed that
this measure, together with the acceptance by government
of the projected Pass Regulations, would increase the
local labour supply and secure its retention. But this
was not effected by the government until 1895 and its
consequences were only felt later. In this respect the
experience of the Chamber on the East Coast, where 100,000
homesteads had been taxed with much effect upon the labour
supply, could only have reinforced the Chamber's views on
the advantages to be gained from this type of labour
coercion.

The Chamber seemed to have no doubt before the turn of
the century that the local African population would respond to increases in the hut tax by providing more labour
for mining, agriculture and communications. Although this
assumption seemed to them unproblematical at the time,
there were several significant differences between the
'foreign' and local elements of the labour force. The
former were more detachable from the land for numerous
reasons which were not examined seriously by the Chamber;
and they were contractable for longer periods of labour.
Moreover, they accepted lower rates than the local labour
force, and were reported to have displayed no resistance
to underground labour, unlike the men from the Cape in
British South Africa. These differences in resistance
to recruitment, and the rural resilience to obstacles in
the production of an adequate subsistence - or surplus -
by the respective components of the labour force, were not
considered by the Chamber, which held to the general
belief that revised taxation would release the 'natural'
labour force for service on the mines.

In the meantime, the flow of labour from the East Coast
and the absence of resistance to recruitment from that
quarter led the Chamber to seek labour at ever lower costs
per unit. Finally, the acquisition of so large a supply
of labour from Mocambique necessitated arrangements for a
regular system of labour recruitment. It was to this
task, including the priority measure of obtaining the
support of the state in the control of this labour force,
that the Chamber turned its attention.

6 Pass Regulations and the control of mobility

INTRODUCTION

The contradictory character of the Transvaal state has
already been seen to be much in evidence. On the one
hand, government policies, monopolies and concessions
acted to the disadvantage of the mining industry, while
on the other it seems to have been a slow but certain
process, by which legislation on labour, African mobility,
African taxation and certain aspects of industrial relations were enacted over a period to meet the needs of the
mining industry. (1) That this should have been so is not
exceptional, since the relationship of social classes to
the state and its various institutions is complex and
often contradictory, and is constrained by its history.
This was especially so in the Transvaal. The encroachment
of a large-scale capitalist industry upon a small white
oligarchy of landlords and farmers in a largely agrarian
economy only served to erode the latter's apparent unity
and generate new conflicts. (2)
   In view of the extensive impact of the mining industry
upon the Transvaal, the capitalists displayed a certain
rectitude in shaping the legislation they required. They
used their *informal* presence in the institutions from
which they were excluded to promote policies that were
important to them. (3) This 'presence' was manifested by
the presentation of frequent memorials to the Volksraad
by the mine-owners, and the large-scale bribery of centrally placed members within the structures of their
state. (See Chapter 9.) Their heavy contribution to the
coffers of the state, moreover, made them impatient of the
bureaucrats in Pretoria and critical of government spending. The 'Star', for instance, the newspaper of the
Chamber, reflected this discontent and wrote quite blunt-
ly, 'Pretoria, after all, is a mere parasite on the head

of the goldminer' (10 October 1898). The mine-owners,
however, were not always at loggerheads with Pretoria.
Where they had in the past been successful was in shaping,
without amendment, important regulations regarding the
republican gold-mining laws, the so-called Gold Law. The
Pass Regulations (drafted by the Chamber) were initially
subsumed under these laws.

The Gold Law of the South African Republic confined
the licence to mine the mineral wealth of the Transvaal
to white men. African, Coloured or Chinese persons could
act only in the service of whites. The relationship of
the non-white miners (Africans) to the country's gold
industry was consequently of a contractual nature, whereby
a man was separated temporarily from the land and his extended family, to labour for a determinate period (three
months or six months or longer) on the mines. Thereafter
he would return to the land, to supplement the rural
economy with some of the proceeds of the cash wage he
had acquired from mining. A man might enter into several
such contracts during his working life.

The contractual relationship entered into involved a
commitment to labour on the mines for a specified period
under certain conditions, which included a fixed rate of
wages. But the legal provisions of the Pass Regulations
imposed various constraints upon the person of the
labourer which made the contract more than an exchange
of his labour for a given wage. Whilst he was not in a
legal sense the property of his employer during this
period (although the industry was responsible for the
maintenance of his body, housing, food and medical attention, which together might be seen as a supplement to
his wage), the proscriptions on his movements outside the
work situation made him a 'wage slave' in more than the
conventional sense of the term. Having invested in his
person in recruiting him and maintaining him, the mine-
owner risked capital loss if he deserted. Hence the
measures contained in the Pass Regulations sought to give
'legal security' to any company prepared to incur the
necessary expense of 'importing Natives from a distance'
by imposing particular constraints upon all the labour
recruited. Failure to comply involved further restrictions on their persons, either a determinate sentence in
prison (with or without hard labour) or a whipping. The
function of administering these regulations was left to
the state, as were the punitive measures in case of infringements of the regulations. Bolstering these regulations was the Master and Servant Law. The organization
of the state in securing the supply therefore became a
factor, as it were, in the production of gold.

(i)   THE REGULATIONS

It was in terms of Articles 83 and 88 of the Gold Law (4)
that in 1895 the Chamber drafted a set of Pass Regulations
which in their implications involved the central government in substantial administrative, punitive and policing
activities, largely on behalf of the gold mining industry.
(5)

The regulations drafted by the Chamber were, according
to its own description, 'for the purpose of facilitating
and promoting the supply of Native Labour on the Gold
Fields ... and for the better controlling and regulating
of the Natives employed'. (6)   As such they provided the
framework of the 'pass system' subsequently adopted for
the entire labour force of the country.   It germinated
in this form at the instance of the Chamber under the
special conditions of the 1890s in order to secure maximum
control in price and supply over its developing African
labour force.   According to the regulations, an African
arriving at the goldfields was to have a travelling pass,
and was subsequently to acquire from the Mining Commissioners a district pass and then a metal badge. (7)
Failure to comply with these bureaucratic measures would
have serious consequences for the African concerned, for
in the event of his defaulting the Chamber recommended the
imposition of a fine or imprisonment for the first
offence, or 'imprisonment with lashes at the discretion
of the court'. (8)   Complex arrangements were evolved for
the issue of passes by government officials, and severe
obligations were imposed upon the mining managements to
operate the onerous system of fees, fines and payments
to the Mining Commissioner.   Failure to do so involved
heavy fines which inhibited evasion of the regulations.

These formal regulations were not accepted immediately
by the republican government, although it clearly indicated its agreement with the proposals in principle.

When the government finally set its seal on the Chamber's Pass Regulations it did so 'practically without
alteration', and the system came into operation early in
January 1896.   The object of the law was described as preventing 'the hitherto indiscriminate desertion of Natives
*which has involved so many companies in heavy money losses
and to give legal security to any company* prepared to
incur the necessary expense of importing Natives from a
distance'. (9)

The success of the new legislation was not immediately
apparent, because of two factors external to the regulations which served to frustrate the supply and turn the
excess of labour recruitments once more into a shortage.

These were: (i) a brief but abortive attempt to reduce
wages in the previous year; (10) (ii) African unrest in
the northern districts of the Republic, coupled with a
war conducted by the Portuguese authorities against the
Chief Gungunyaya. (11) The supply deteriorated in 1895
and towards December 1896, due largely (according to the
Chamber) to the exodus of labour through rumours of renewed fighting. Neither the efforts of the mining companies nor the stringent provisions of the newly enacted
Pass Laws could prevent mass desertions from the goldfields. It was therefore to ensuring the reinforcement
of the regulations that the Chamber directed its attention.

The elaborate pass legislation's failure 'to bring the
Natives under effective control and reduce the risk of
desertion' (12) led the Chamber to reflect seriously on
the efficacy of its regulations. There were undoubtedly
some serious problems to consider: (i) the low quality
of the administration; (ii) the complexity of the machinery; (iii) the need to identify the cause of the
desertions and to characterize the deficiencies in the
system of control; (iv) the need to make recommendations
to remedy the defects of the regulations, or alternatively
to consider abandoning them completely.

The Chamber rejected the view that the legislation was
either mistaken or derived from a serious miscalculation
of the market situation. On the contrary, it believed
the law to be 'in the broadest sense of the word' an
'excellent' one. (13) If the legislation were abandoned
it would be *because its administrators were inefficient*
rather than because of any inherent deficiency in the
principles. In reviewing the operation of the system,
the Chairman of the Chamber reported in 1896:

> We cannot at the present moment say that it has been
> efficiently administered. It is a complicated piece
> of machinery and it wants very careful supervision.
> If it cannot be worked in a more satisfactory manner
> ... then I'm afraid the Pass Law will have to go. (14)

The Chairman's statement that the industry might dis-
pense with the Pass Law if the quality of its administration continued to decline was not borne out. On the contrary the Chamber, having identified the defects in the
regulations, added to their complexity by increasing the
coercive character and up-dating the administrative arrangements for their 'proper' execution. In so doing it
proposed and drafted a series of amendments which would
'justify' the enactment of the new law and enable it to

serve the purpose the Chamber had in mind when it initially drafted the regulations. The amendments had two purposes: (i) to deal with the chronic problem of desertion,
and (ii) to commit the Transvaal state (and its police
force) to closer control over the Chamber's African labour
force.

The draft amendments to deal with the increasing desertions from the goldfields were severe and stemmed from
the Chamber's belief that the penalty for desertion had
been fixed too low. (15) This was especially important
to the Chamber, as touts paid the fines of the arrested
labourers and 'sold' them to the highest bidder among the
competing mine managements. The effect was that companies
had 'procured labour at considerable expense ... [and] had
simply become the medium for supplying labour for others'.
(16) The remedy resorted to by the Chamber was an extreme
one and seemed more concerned with the impact it would
have on touts than its relationship with the deserting
African labourers it was attempting to re-attract to the
mines. It persuaded the government to amend the law so
that the penalty for a first offence was increased six
times - to a fine of £3, and £5 (or five times as much as
previously) for a second offence. The intention was to
inhibit desertion by increasing its price, and at the same
time to reduce the activities of touts by making it uneconomic for them to bail men out at the former low price
and resell them. In either event the African recruit who
defaulted on his contract with his mining company was the
object of harsh fines and/or the physical and psycho-
logical hardship of corporal punishment. (17) These
changes in the Pass Law were incorporated in Articles 14
and 18 of the Amended Regulation styled as the New Pass
Law, No.31 of 1896, which the Chamber again drafted. In
addition the Chamber secured the passage of several other
amendments, of an administrative character, in order to
ensure that the authorities in Pretoria had not lost sight
of the original intention of the regulations. These too
were included in the New Pass Law, as well as other
clauses concerning the closing of various loopholes in
the administration of the Act.

As has been noted the Chamber drafted the amending
regulations, which drew the state more closely into active
promotion of the Chamber's labour-raising arrangements.
The proposals of the Chamber included the following: (18)

    (i)   that the administration of the Pass Laws be
           allowed a considerably larger staff;
    (ii) that a special body of police be appointed to
           assist the Pass Department in carrying out the
           law;

(iii)   that a new article be included in the law 'which
        shall provide for Natives leaving one district
        for another without a district pass, being ar-
        rested and immediately handed over to the
        authorities'. (19)

However, despite the enlarged scope of the New Pass
Law, within a very short time the Chamber felt that the
regulations which it had so carefully structured were
'utterly ineffective on account of the inefficient administration of the law'. (20)   In the absence of effective government control, desertions occurred on 'as
large a scale, and in as open a way as ever'.   Indeed,
expenditure on migrants was increased when, after a few
weeks, they illegally abandoned the mines for which they
had contracted for some older-established mines where conditions were reputed to be better or where kinship relations existed.   'A new mine was, therefore, a recruiting
agency for the older ones.' (21)   Under the circumstances
there was nothing for the Chamber but to consider some
alternative institutional machinery to assist the recruitment and *retention* of its large and fast-growing labour
force.   This was the central recruiting organization which
was to play so large a part in procuring recruits for the
profitable operation of the industry during the next
century.

(ii)   THE STATE AND THE LABOUR SUPPLY

From the above discussion, the following points require
particular emphasis, and a number of significant conclusions may be drawn.   The organization of the state in
securing and protecting the mine labour supply to the Rand
became increasingly a factor in the production of gold.
By the enactment of the new Pass Regulations the state was
drawn more substantially into the service of the mining
industry for the creation of labour conditions favourable
to the Chamber.   Where the administration was slack and
the machinery of control deficient, the Chamber, which was
the main beneficiary of the regulations, drafted amendments to the legislation.   It revised and updated the
regulations, dealt with infractions of contracts by pre-
scribing harsher penal provisions, and in the 1896 New
Pass Law secured a special body of police to assist the
Pass Department.
    Through the mediation of the Pass Laws, with its con-
trol over the mobility of the workforce, the Chamber
sought greater stability in the labour supply, the ac-

quisition of an effective employer combination (which
seemed attainable only with a labour demand which was
satisfied) and a reduction in the African wage rate. However, the immediate experience of the Chamber, one year
after the passage of the Pass Regulations, was that none
of these conditions had materialized. The industry had
failed to reverse the high level of labour turnover in the
gold mines, the instability of the supply situation provided inauspicious conditions for employer unity at the
constituent levels of the Chamber, and it was likely that
the decrease in the rate of wages (lowered in 1895) was an
important contributing factor in the contemporary dearth
in the labour supply.

The Chamber saw no failure in the principle of its pass
legislation and addressed itself to strengthening it in
the areas where it was deficient. It maintained its confidence in the regulations to control and protect the
labour supply and, rather than abandoning them, successfully secured important amendments to the original provisions and acquired improvements for their administration. In so far as the supply had not been satisfied and
the number of desertions had escalated, the Chamber clearly blamed the inefficiency of the administration and the
special circumstances of war in the north. But it considered both to be temporary factors and, undeterred, the
Chamber followed the original design and proceeded to
develop the necessary combination for a central recruiting
agency, primarily for the acquisition of long-distance
labour, whereafter it could direct itself to the overall
reduction of the wage rate.

7 The formation of a central recruiting organization

INTRODUCTION

The formation of a central recruiting institution formed
part of the mine-owners' general strategy for monopsony
of the labour market and was a means towards a systematic
reduction of wages from their 1896 levels.

In the year or two preceding the transition and development of some of the most important sites from outcrop
to deep-level mining, the labour shortage had presented
itself as an urgent threat to the uninterrupted growth of
the industry. Already in 1896 over two-thirds of the
Chamber's constituent companies had registered a serious
shortage of labour, and in the Roodepoort mines (one of
the earliest deep-level concerns) the scarcity had
rendered thirty-five out of a total of fifty mining stamps
inactive. War in the north and on the East Coast had affected the supply generally, and contributed to an exodus
of labour from the Rand which the Pass Regulations were
incapable of stemming. In 1895 wages had been lowered,
which did not help the supply and may have accounted for
some of the exodus from the mines. The result was the
resurgence of inter-company competition (especially evident in 1890, and again in 1895), and an escalation in the
wage rate which caused the Chamber to consider its entire
wage and work structure in danger of erosion. Here we are
concerned with the Chamber's response to these movements
in the market situation and its reaction to what it considered divisive and costly unilateral action by mining
managements to secure their full complement of labour.

The recruiting combination is seen as especially significant for its impact on wages and the labour flow to
the mines. It also marked a new stage in the unity of the
employers, demonstrating the collective strength of the
Chamber, the Association of Mines (a smaller group opposed

to the Chamber) and the Association of Mine Managers.
Their triple unity served to end the unilateral action of
individual companies and made it possible for them to
assert themselves collectively as 'masters of the market
situation' - a euphemistic phrase used by the Chamber to
describe the 'contest' between the mining companies and
the potential labourers for a regular supply of migrants
to the mines at low cost. The means to this end of control over the supply hinged upon a formal proposal to end
competition (which the Chamber believed inimical to effective employer organization) by institutionalizing the
system of labour recruitment and creating a combination
for the regulation of the supply. Two other strategies
for the reduction in the cost of production need consideration: (i) a three-pronged plan to cut production costs
by reducing wages by 20 per cent, curbing the cost and
quantity of food and making the working day underground
and overground of uniform length on all mines; (ii) a
proposal to win concessions from the Portuguese authorities for reductions in the cost of long-distance labour.
This involved the monopsony over the purchase of East
Coast labour and official sanctions against interlopers.
Each of these matters - the creation of the supply association, the reduction in wages, and the negotiations
with the Portuguese in Mocambique is treated separately
here in order to elucidate their features, although they
were clearly conceived as a unity.

The establishment of the Native Labour Supply Association was the pivot of the new strategy. Combination and
internal discipline were the employers' chief methods of
reducing the wage rate and securing the supply. The
present combination was different from previous arrangements by virtue of its unity (it was composed of all the
bodies formerly critical of the Chamber) and its carefully
articulated and extensive aims. These were (i) the
recruitment of labour both internally and externally;
(ii) control over the wages and the flow of the workforce;
(iii) securing an equitable distribution of labourers to
each mine; (iv) total control over the purchase of the
African workforce; (v) the reduction of wages by a minimum sum of £100,000; (vi) the uniting of employers by
ending the chief element of their antagonism (the competition for labour); and finally (vii) acting as a
pressure group upon the legislature for the security of
the labour supply to obtain conditions favourable to the
combination. The importance of all these interlinking
aims is considered here and significance apportioned to
those measures which, as a collective response to the
issues of labour and wages, constituted the most far-

reaching rearrangement of the supply conditions in a decade of diversity.

The measures adopted by the Chamber were interdependent and were negotiated almost simultaneously. Wages were reduced in October 1896, a central recruiting institution established in November, and an agreement with the Portuguese authorities involving a cut in the cost of long-distance labour effected in September of the same year. Significance is attributed to those measures which gave the Chamber monopsony of the market for mine labour and hence firmer control over wages.

(i) WAGES AND MONOPSONY: INTER-COMPANY COMPETITION FOR LABOUR

In 1896 the Chamber institutionalized its recruiting arrangements. In less than a decade of mining activity the gold industry had established a predictable though peculiar pattern in relation to the supply and the wage rates of its African workforce. An acute shortfall in the flow of immigrant African miners induced a vigorous re-sumption of the system of touting, which in turn en-couraged inter-company competition and an escalation in wages. (1) If anything, it was the dangers inherent in this vicious circle of practices which led the Chamber to reconsider its recruiting arrangements and end the cycle of inter-company competition and escalating wage rates. But the need for an alternative system of recruitment as-sumed an alarming urgency only after the first half of 1896, when the Chamber's Native Labour Commissioner reported an acute shortage of 1,000 men by nine mining companies due (according to the Chamber) to an exodus of labourers both to the northern Transvaal and to the East Coast because of impending war, as a result of Portuguese activities in Gazaland. (2) Soon the supply need esca-lated to 8,000 additional labourers to meet the needs of fifty-five companies (3) who pleaded that unless relief was afforded 'many mines would be compelled to suspend operations'. (4)

The Chamber responded to the crisis by urging the government to 'afford immediate relief' to the industry. (5) The government, however, promptly dispelled any im-pression that it was '*obliged* to supply native labour to the mines' (6) by directing the Chamber to discuss their labour deficiencies with the local officials (the Native Commissioners) in the African regions. These officials proved more co-operative than their seniors in the central administration in Pretoria, and were not averse to using

compulsion to increase the supply of mine labour - and
said as much.   For example, Superintendent Schiel suggested that there should be legislation to 'compel natives
to work for 3 or 4 months in the year,' (7) and Native
Commissioner Dahl formally recommended coercion to bring
the labour to the mines. (8)   However, at the top level
the government firmly declined to accept any obligation or
responsibility in this respect and expressly forbade, at
least if only for the record, the use of any coercion on
the part of its officials. (9)   The result was a vigorous
increase in the internecine rivalry between mine managements for the limited supply, accompanied by the familiar
features of touting and wage increases.   It was this competition which led the leaders of the industry to believe
that a serious market situation was developing whereby the
entire wage structure was in process of being eroded.   The
Chamber was very apprehensive of the direction the constituent companies were taking to satisfy their labour
needs, and this apprehension was shared by others.   The
Chamber's press, for instance, noted some twelve months
before that not only had the mining companies withheld
their subscriptions to the Chamber's Native Labour Department, but 'in several instances the companies actually employed touts to tamper with the gangs which were being
brought down country by the department'. (10)   This interference by the companies with the efforts of their own
department was typical of the inter-company rivalry for
labour.   All this led the Chamber to explore a collective
solution to what was patently a problem common to the
whole industry.   Its first step was to warn its members
of the consequences of unilateral action upon the African
workforce.   Hence the Native Commissioner spoke of the
demoralizing effects of recent company actions '[which]
instead of keeping [the African miners] subservient, makes
them masters of the position'. (11)   Moreover, the prevalence of competition struck at 'the roots of all sound
organization'. (12)

Believing that the situation was deteriorating beyond
repair, the representatives of the Chamber, the Association of Mine Managers and the Association of Mines met
in 1896 to retrieve the initiative and prevent the African
workforce from becoming 'master' of the market.   Their
decision struck at the heart of the industry's labour
problems and had far-reaching effects on the course of
policy in the succeeding decades.   The immediate proposals
included:

  (i)   a substantial reduction of the wage rates;
  (ii) a decision to create an association for the
        regular supply of labour;

(iii)   an attempt to win major concessions from the
        Portuguese in regard to the labour supply.

The proposals were interdependent, for unless the
labour force was centrally channelled and equitably apportioned to the various mines in proportion to their
needs, the escalation of wage rates could not be arrested
effectively. Moreover the decision to cut wages was
necessary not only to increase profits immediately but
also as a preliminary for further reducing the wage rate,
once monopsonistic methods of recruitment had been adopted. It is in this light that the three proposals above
can be considered.

(a)   Wage reduction (October 1896)

The decision drastically to reduce wages was one of the
most far-reaching decisions yet taken and is indicative
of the confidence felt by the Chamber in the efficacy of
its proposed labour arrangements. Nevertheless the step
was not taken without considerable apprehension. Earlier,
in the autumn of 1895, owners and critics alike were not
slow to point out to the Chamber's Native Labour Commissioner, who advocated a wage reduction, that 'it must
be carefully borne in mind ... that any endeavour [to
reduce rates] which either wholly or partially fails will
do far more harm than good'. (13) They obviously had in
mind the consequence of, and the confusion following the
1890 Agreement, when the demand for labour was only half
as large, and the supply fell drastically as a result of
wage reductions.
    In the event, when reductions were made the mine
managements cut wages by an average of 20 per cent. (14)
They also adopted a uniform method of reducing costs relating to food and shift work in all the compounds. (15)
The new arrangements required a minimum of nine hours of
actual labour per day for underground African labourers
and ten hours per day for the man on the surface. The
most important aspect of the new measures was the reduction of wages by 20 per cent (on average) so that the
lowest level of remuneration fell to 1s. 6d. per day for
men engaged in underground drill packing and 1s. 9d. for
shovel, timber, station and 'tram boys'. The uppermost
echelons of workers - the wet-shaft 'boys', the stope
gangers' assistants, the blacksmith's 'boys' and the
police and office store 'boys' - were not exempt from
the reductions, and received 3s. per day for their labour.
(16)

As the revised wage structure was implemented, the Chamber took the precautionary measure of informing the government of the reductions and requested it to take steps to prevent disturbances in the event of any overt discontent among the African labour force. At the same time (as a further security measure) the Chamber requested the government to provide an additional police force to maintain order and enforce the provisions of the Pass Laws. (17) In the event the only recorded reaction to the wage reductions occurred at the Crown Reef Company, where Africans struck work for two days. (18) For the rest, the unorganized workforce accepted the provisions of the revised wage rates although some 'voted with their feet' and deserted.

(b)   The Native Labour Supply Association

Having dealt with the first proposal, the Chamber could proceed to the second: the reconstruction of the arrangements for dealing with the supply of African labour. This radical restructuring of the recruiting arrangements reflected the increasing dissatisfaction amongst the companies with the existing organ of the Chamber, the Native Labour Department, in meeting supply needs or reducing or regulating African wage levels. (19) The new body they brought into existence by collective action with the Chamber took the form of a limited liability company - the Native Labour Supply Association Limited. It was capitalized by each of the mining companies, who thus constituted the new company's shareholders. (20)

In its conception the new company was to relieve the industry of all the major obstacles encountered in attracting labour to the Rand since mining began a decade earlier. If it was to meet with success when years of contingency arrangements had failed, it would need at once to guarantee the supply and contain wage rates, to procure unity where competition had inflated wages, to regulate the supply where uncertainty had made the distribution uneven, and above all to protect the wage structure by promoting monopsonistic practices to avoid the serious consequences of continuing competition on the labour market.

It was towards these ends that the new Association directed its energies. One of its essential objectives was the acquisition of African labour within the South African Republic and districts as well as countries beyond the Transvaal's borders. It aimed 'to bring large numbers of boys to the Rand and house and feed them ... and instruct them to seek work under the Pass Law Regulations'. (21)

In carrying out its brief the company was everything that
its founders had intended. It acted immediately to secure
control over wages as well as over the supply of labour,
by asserting its authority over individual company agents
whom it prevented (through agreements signed with the
managers of each operating mine) from procuring labour
in their private capacities.

Having established its monopsonistic position, the company assured the managements of an equitable share of
labour, provided that they in turn guaranteed to carry out
certain administrative actions to avoid former malpractices such as understating the size of their existing
labour force in the expectation of receiving more than
their share of labour power. (22) The Native Labour
Supply Association could then freely (23) direct the flow
of the labour which it secured to the mines where it was
most needed, thereby achieving that 'sound' organizational
structure which replaced the competition between mine
managements for labour.

As the sole purchaser of African labour the Association
sought to secure its position with the legislature in
order to entrench its monopsony. Accordingly it aimed at
the promotion of a special law by which 'any ... attempt
to obtain natives /would be/ a criminal offence punishable
by imprisonment with hard labour without the option of a
fine'. (24)

That the Association should enjoy this hegemony was
necessary, it believed, for the preservation of the wage
pattern. As a prerequisite for this ideal the Mine
Managers' Association, which drafted the constitution of
the new recruiting company, emphasized that 'unanimity of
action amongst the mines /was/ the greatest factor to be
considered'. The MMA believed 'that £100,000 so spent
with all the companies working in harmony towards one end,
viz. the reduction of Native wages, would cause a saving
to the industry of anything from £100,000 to £200,000 in
wages alone'. (25) To effect these twin objectives of
wage reduction and regulation of the supply the mine
managements recognized that employer unity was essential.
This was the most substantial lesson the Chamber could
learn from a decade of disunity.

The Supply Association, it was hoped, would engender
this unity. It would also act as a pressure group upon
the legislature to secure 'proper' measures to carry out
its work. (26) To do this it was preferable that it be
accorded some 'independent' status from the Chamber. The
founders of the Association consequently attempted to give
the new body maximum flexibility of action and financial
independence as 'an independent corporation with no of-

ficial connection with the Chamber of Mines'. (27)   But
this image, however elaborate, was not likely to, and did
not, engender credibility.   The governing body of the new
Association was composed of representatives of the sub-
scribing companies, and the executive function was vested
in an elected managing committee representing the three
powerful organizations which brought the Association into
existence - the Association of Mines, the Mine Managers'
Association and the Chamber.   The new general manager of
the Association was W.Grant, the Chamber's old Native
Labour Commissioner.   Moreover, a fortiori, the new body
assumed all the duties of the Chamber's Native Labour
Department, which it replaced completely.   Its independent
corporate structure was more formal than real, although
this should not detract *from its potential to satisfy the
supply needs of the industry and to regulate and reduce
the wage rate*.

(c)   Portuguese concessions

The third and final move in the Chamber's strategy to
secure the labour supply was to improve its external
position vis-à-vis the Portuguese authorities.   Concurrently with the reduction of wages in October 1896 and the
establishment of the Native Labour Supply Association in
November, the Chamber launched an assault on rising costs
and supply deficiencies by acquiring two substantial
privileges from the Portuguese (28) which gave it the
hegemony in the labour market which it failed to win
locally.   These concessions were acquired in September
and enabled the Chamber (i) to organize the recruitment
and immigration of African labourers from *any* part of the
Portuguese territories, and thereby to increase its
chances of acquiring the supply with no increase in costs;
and (ii) to secure the arrest of any unauthorized individual engaged in recruiting workers, and thus to preserve
the monopsonistic position of its recruiting company, to
contain the present wage rate, and to ensure the co-ordination of the supply.
    In this way, it was hoped, the Supply Association would
become effectively the sole buyer of African labour for
the gold mines.   By agreement with the existing recruiting
agencies as well as with the individual mining companies,
all internal competition for labour would be eliminated
throughout the industry, and the Chamber would be in
unique control of the wage rate, which, in theory at
least, it could keep static irrespective of the strength
or sluggishness of the supply.   These hopes were tempo-

rarily shattered by the outbreak of the Boer War, but
before that event the Chamber anticipated the benefits of
the recent restructuring of their recruiting arrangements
by effecting yet another drastic reduction in the wage
rate.

(ii)   THE IMPACT OF EMPLOYER UNITY

The formation of an employers' combination to control
wages and the supply of African labour had been the aim
of the Chamber soon after gold mining began on the Rand.
In 1890 measures to promote internal cohesion had taken
the form of the 1890 Agreement to reduce and stabilize
the wage rate as well as institutionalize the formal work
structure of the labour force. (29)   Although this Agreement had failed to secure a regular labour supply or
reduce wages, the principle of a combination for this
purpose remained the aim of the Chamber, and the formulation and passage of the Pass Regulations in 1895 and 1896
were intended to provide the necessary preconditions
(control of the workforce) for a combination which would
acquire an adequate labour supply and control wages. (30)
   Whereas the 1890 Agreement had failed because shortages
in the labour supply had forced the various managements
unilaterally to raise wages, the combination of 1896 had
the benefit of a much closer unity, born out of the experience and rivalry which followed the collapse of the
earlier Agreement.   In addition, the promise of the
monopsony of the labour force on the East Coast and concessions to extend recruiting operations to anywhere in
that territory, which the Chamber believed would guarantee
the supply, gave the new combination the likelihood of
greater success.   Adding yet greater strength to the mine-
owners' control of the labour market was the increase in
co-operation between the industry and the Transvaal state,
which at the instance of the Chamber revised the system of
taxation in 1895 and in the following year accepted the
Pass Regulations drafted by the mine-owners.
   However, despite the industry's more favourable relations with the Portuguese authorities on the East Coast
and the greater co-operation with the Transvaal state, the
combined desire to increase the labour supply and reduce
the wage rate at a time when labour was scarce necessitated the most disciplined unity and the greatest faith
in the new arrangements to secure and regulate the flow
of the workforce.   The mine-owners appear to have had this
confidence, for despite the hazards of previous experiences in 1890, 1891 and 1895, when the wage rate was re-

duced to the detriment of the supply, the employers took advantage of the 1896 combination to effect the first of two substantial cuts in the costs of production within the space of nine months. The first of these was effected in October 1896 and was considered above. The second was in 1897 and is the subject of the next chapter.

The reduction of the wage rate in October 1896 aimed, as we have noted, at saving the mine-owners between £100,000 and £200,000 per annum, and effectively decreased the wages of each labourer in the lowest stratum of the workforce by 3d. or 4d. per shift. The men in the better-paid occupations received 7d. less per shift although they retained the ratio of disparity between themselves and the lowest stratum. Neither group offered sustained opposition to the reductions, although men struck work briefly in at least one mine and the Chamber invoked the assistance of the police force under the newly amended Pass Regulations to prevent mass resistance by 'desertion' from the mines.

The existence of the Pass Regulations and the organized assistance of the state in retaining labourers in 1896 were factors which had been absent in 1890. The mine-owners hoped they would underpin their new arrangements and make them more successful than the abortive agreement of 1890.

The effects of the new combination could be gauged only in the long-term period after the Anglo-Boer War (October 1899 - May 1902) which is the subject of Part Three. Meanwhile the presence of the above factors provided the employers with the prospects of a more satisfactory labour supply and were the occasion for a further decrease in the African wage rate in the course of the following year.

8 Manipulating the wage rate

INTRODUCTION

The arrangements for securing a large 'oscillating' labour
force in a regular system of supply helped to cement the
practice of migrant labour on the Rand. The revision of
taxation, the Pass Regulations and the new employers' combination promised to relieve the mine-owners of some of
their supply problems and enabled them to treat the wage
revision effected in October 1896 as an interim one. Encouraged by an increase in the supply early in 1897, they
considered proposals for a 30 per cent decrease in wages
in the 'old' schedule, to take effect from June 1897.
Here we are concerned with these aspects of the Rand
capitalists' planning, in the light of the circumstances
above and particularly the new combination formed by the
Chamber of Mines, the Association of Mines, and the Mine
Managers' Association.

A second concern of this chapter is the renewal of
negotiations with the Portuguese for reductions in the
indirect costs of labour - the transport and other charges
imposed on traders in the East Coast supply. Although the
Portuguese authorities had conceded to the Chamber the
right to recruit labourers from all parts of their territory, the large volume of trade in African labourers had
opened their eyes to the revenue which might be expected
from that source and caused them to increase their charges
on the export of labourers by as much as 100 per cent on
the 1895/6 scale. The importance of this matter to the
Chamber is highlighted by the mine-owners' dependence on
Mocambique labour, of which at least 68,000 out of a total
African workforce of 98,000 came from the East Coast
before the Boer War.

(i)   THE REDUCED SCHEDULE OF WAGES, 1897

It was to reduce existing costs and discourage rest
periods that the new schedule of wages prepared by the
executives of the employer triumvirate, together with
their offspring the Rand Native Labour Supply Association,
was drafted. The reductions reflected the industry's confidence that it had acquired control over the migrant
labour supply. (1) The proposals were for an average
reduction of 30 per cent on the previous schedule, (2)
which was less than a year old. Not surprisingly, the
Chamber considered that the new arrangements constituted
'the most important saving in the working costs of companies effected during the past year'. (3) Indeed it was.
In effect the 'New Schedule' which was signed in 1897 represented the strength of the Chamber in the crucial context of migrant labour. It is apparent from the *relatively* small exodus of labourers after June 1897 that the combination of rural poverty and the Chamber's strategies to
recruit larger supplies of labour had begun to show results. Its hand was, moreover, probably strengthened by
the outbreak of rinderpest, which spread rapidly south-
wards from Rhodesia in 1896, decimating African cattle
herds and exacerbating rural poverty. (4) Even the most
substantial reductions, which covered thirty-seven occupational categories at meagre rates of 1s. 2d. per shift,
*did not fall below the margin of wages necessary to
'attract' labour to the mines*. It is not possible to
discern which labourers came from the rural areas af-
fording the lowest levels of subsistence, but the very
acceptance of the meagre minimum shift wage of 1s. 2d.
showed that the level of poverty in the rural areas must
have been very great indeed. Moreover, the rural conditions and the cash wage the Chamber paid clearly boosted
the supply by decreasing the rest periods.
   The wages comprised an average of 48s. 7d. per month
of thirty-two days on a scale ranging from 1s. 2d. to
2s. 6d. per shift. The maximum shift rate listed on the
schedule was 2s. 6d. Recipients of this top rate were
confined to the elite of the African labour force - the
shaft developers, station men unassisted by whites, surface stokers, head-gear men, certain categories of blacksmiths' attendants, police and office workers. Sandwiched
between these men at the top and the men on the minimum
rate were the thirty-seven categories referred to above,
who made up the majority of the labour force. Although
the new schedule allowed 7½ per cent of the African labour
force to be employed at 'special rates', this was the exception rather than the rule. (5)

Having secured its objectives of reducing and co-ordinating African wage levels, the Chamber appointed inspectors to ensure adherence to the new agreement. Together,
the Supply Association and the wage inspectorate proved
highly efficient. This was borne out in the following
year, when the Chamber reported the success of the policy
in its 'Annual Report' to its shareholders:

> despite attempts in some cases to exceed the rates laid
> down in the schedule, the moral effect of the Inspec-
> tors had been a good one [and although] the schedule
> [was] not rigidly maintained ... there is a distinct
> endeavour to abide as closely as possible by it. (6)

The Report claimed, predictably, that the net result of
the exercise was

> that the rate of wages are far lower than they would
> have been, if in the first instance the companies had
> not combined and adopted uniform rates ... and if the
> tendency to compete had not been checked by the in-
> spection system. (7)

The bureaucracy which the mine-owners had constructed
had one further important advantage for the industry. It
provided the Chamber with the negotiating authority to
conduct economies of scale which could not be undertaken
confidently until the Chamber had the assurance from its
constituent companies that they would definitely not
repeat their previous indiscipline. Thus reassured by
the new recruiting administration, the Chamber would
almost immediately turn its attention from the direct wage
payments to migrants to the *indirect* costs of importing
this labour. The Chamber sought to 'use [its] influence
with the Portuguese authorities' for the removal of heavy
passport and other charges imposed on East Coast labour.
(8) But the intractability of the Portuguese negotiators
was more than the Chamber's officials could cope with.
Despite the increasing volume of the supply, the Portuguese seemed as intent on maximizing their revenues from
the export of their human resources as the Chamber was
bent upon making optimum savings in the price of this
commodity. (9) This East Coast attitude was evidenced
in 1898 by the African Study Committee of the Portuguese
Overseas Ministry, whose ideas were incorporated in its
first article of Regulation of African labour. The Africa
Committee proclaimed it to be the duty of Europe in general to promote African advancement into civilization, and
felt that the Portuguese state in particular should 'have

no scruples in obliging and, if necessary, forcing these
rude Negroes in Africa ... to work'. (10)   However, since
the Portuguese were not prepared on this occasion to
reduce the charges on migrant labour, no new agreement
emerged.   Fortunately for the Chamber, the failure of the
industry to lower the indirect costs was partially offset
by the generally satisfactory supply of African labour.
(11)

But the problems of the supply needs of the industry
were by no means resolved at this crucial point in the
South African Republic's history.   Indeed, they were
frustrated and distorted by the temporary disturbance in
industrial production during the course of the transition
from the Boer to the British state, which was substantially the content of the Anglo-Boer conflict of 1899-1902.
(12)   However, the institutional machinery, the extra-
economic measures, and the establishment of the employers'
combination which dominated the fixing of the wage rate,
collectively provided the Chamber with the means of obtaining almost double the number of its pre-war workforce
in less than a decade after hostilities had ceased, and
twice as much again in the following decade. (13)   This
evolution of policy and practice during the first ten
years of mining, together with a new state which, as we
shall see, identified itself unambiguously with the mining
industry, provided the foundations of the South African
cheap labour system. (14)

(ii)   CONTROLLING THE LABOUR SUPPLY AND THE WAGE RATE IN
A DECADE OF WAGE MANIPULATION

The wage reductions of June 1897 were the third major
endeavour in six years to cut costs, although there were
frequent, less systematic attempts to reduce the wage
rate whenever the supply crept up significantly on the
demand.   However, the consequence of the three important
reductions of 1890, 1896 and 1897 had distinct features
and reflected different approaches to the problem of cost
reduction.

The first inter-company combination to cut costs and
systemize wage rates - the 1890 Agreement - failed owing
to the shortage in supply and the absence of legal and
administrative mechanisms to recruit and retain the workforce.   Whilst the aim of the mine-owners had been to cut
costs and unify wage and work policies, the consequence
of the action had been to provoke the direct antithesis
of this - i.e. to discourage the supply and cause crippling competition for labour and a sharp rise in the wage

rate. From the experience of 1890 the mine-owners were
induced to broaden the range of recruitment to increase
the supply, and to press for the legal enforcement of
contracts, as well as for the establishment of a disciplined combination to centralize recruitment. The subsequent decision in October 1896 to reduce the wage rate
rested on the assumptions that with a strong combination,
a guaranteed supply (through monopsony of the labour
market) and statutory control over the mobility of the
workforce the existing competition would be ended, and
the low-cost migrant labour system retained at lower cost
to the industry.

Significantly, the decision to reduce the wage rate was
taken when the supply was short and production in the
deep-level and larger outcrop mines was below capacity.
This action was intended to rectify dramatically the in-
roads that competition for labour might make upon the wage
structure and the migrant labour system. It reflected the
rural distress and the confidence the mine-owners had in
their new statutory measures and institutional arrangements for increasing the supply. The success of the
October reduction (measured by the absence of wholesale
African withdrawal from the mines) and an increase in the
supply during the first quarter of 1897 encouraged the
mine-owners to proceed with the second major revision of
African wage rates in less than nine months.

Two reductions within the space of one year require
some comment. The mine-owners had given as the *raison
d'être* for their combination of 1896 the stabilizing of
the supply and the reduction in wages. They had calculated the possibility of saving upwards of £100,000 on
labour costs *before* the combination was actually effected.
(15) Since the conditions for the October 1896 reduction
were not auspicious (the supply was the weakest it had
been for some time) the first reduction might be seen as
an interim one, although the Chamber is not explicit on
this point. The 'interim' reductions did not seriously
disrupt the supply, although there was some articulated
opposition and a two-day strike in one mine and some
'exodus' of labour when the miners literally voted with
their feet. However, the increase in the supply in the
first half of 1897 seems to have given the mine-owners
the opportunity of completing the projected saving by effecting the lowest scale in the African wage schedule
since the early stages of mining. But for a brief period
during and after the Anglo-Boer conflict, this was the
lowest rate ever paid for African mine labour. The fact
that the wage had decreased so drastically *and the supply
been maintained* gave credence to the mine-owners' view

that they had finally gained control over the supply and
the wages of migrant labour. This was important, for the
years 1896 to 1899 brought new strains on the labour
market, with the coincidence of the development of deep-
level mining and the reaching of the production stage of
the outcrop mines. The needs of deep-level mining, however, posed a new problem for the mine-owners - that of
reform or 'revolution from above'?

Part Two

The Randlords' 'revolution from above'

9 The needs of deep-level mining:

the gold industry and the state

INTRODUCTION

Mining development had reached a distinctly new phase by
1897, ten years after gold was first extracted systematic-
ally from the Rand. Not only had the phenomenon of deep-
level mining begun, but over 40 per cent of the outcrop
mines had reached the producing stage. The significance
of this development lay in the increased labour needs of
the industry, fresh demands for capital and a scramble
to secure the 'proclaimed land' for the operation of deep-
level mining. All these placed strains on the mine-
owners' relationship with the landowners, farmers and
small non-mining capitalists in the Transvaal.

The demand for labour in this new phase had assumed
altogether new proportions. In the three years between
1896 and 1899 the labour force had increased by 43 per
cent and showed every potential for further accelerated
growth. In the five years between 1907 and 1912 the total
supply more than doubled that of 1899, the peak year for
African labour in the ante-bellum period. The mine-owners
had foreseen this growth two years before the war and had,
for this and other reasons, cemented the combination of
mining companies, improved their recruiting mechanism and
tightened loopholes in the Pass Regulations by which the
state helped to secure the labour force through imposing
legal penalties on 'deserting' labourers. But despite
these measures the Chamber was still greedy for labour for
the proper working of those mines which had reached the
producing stage, as well as for the development of deep-
level mining from which the future optimum profits were
anticipated. Already in 1899 eight deep-level mines produced 23 per cent of the total gold output.

The capital requirements of the deep-levels were corre-
spondingly greater than those required by the outcrop

99

mines because of the difference in costs of the two techniques of mining. In addition most of the deep-level
mines had not yet entered the production stage. Economies
of scale, especially in the cost of explosives, fuel and
labour, were therefore required by the mine-owners in
order to cut costs of production and recover the capital
expended in sinking shafts and building mills for the new
mines. This brought them into increasing conflict with
the other classes in the state. Despite the antagonism
between the landed class and the representatives of mining
capital, Kruger's government was not in all respects
greatly unfavourable to the mine-owners. The Gold Law was
generous, taxation was relatively low and the Pass Regulations had drawn the state into heavy policing and administrative expenditure, largely on behalf of the mines. However, the political exclusion of the mine-owners from the
legislature, the overly bureaucratic regime, difficulties
in raising an adequate labour supply and the high cost of
dynamite and coal led the mine-owners to consider that
their position could be improved if their control of the
administration was more in keeping with the proportion of
their contribution to the revenue of the state.

H.Jennings, a consulting engineer for Eckstein & Co.,
put the matter succinctly for the mine-owners to the 1897
Industrial Commission:

The government must take us into its confidence. It
must allow our trained ability to bear upon the serious
problems before us. We must be made partly responsible
for the administration of this government, and to be
made responsible we must have representation. ('Evidence', p.224)

The precise nature of the Chamber's thinking on this
matter, however, is still a matter of historical debate.
The conflict expressed itself in the campaign against
(what the mine-owners referred to as) the inefficiency
of the administration, notably in matters which touched
on the liquor laws and Pass Regulations, since they affected productivity and the labour supply respectively.
But the charge of 'inefficiency' masked more deep-seated
conflicts over labour, monopolies and political control.
Frequently, state inaction was a matter of policy rather
than ineptitude. The mine-owners' charges, though often
warranted, should therefore be considered with necessary
caution. In this context, it should be noted (with some
hindsight) that the above grievances became not just
routine complaints against an 'inept' administration of
'three dozen families' in an enfranchised Boer community

MAP 2 Sketch map of the Transvaal showing the Mining
Inspectors' Districts of Johannesburg, Germiston,
Krugersdorp and Pretoria, also the sub-districts of
Barberton and Pietersburg (dotted lines indicate
boundaries of magisterial districts).

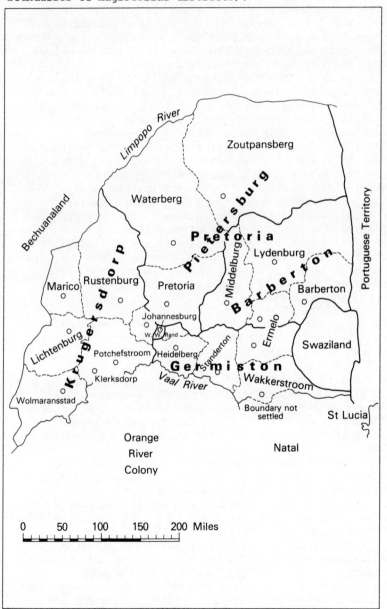

of 30,000, but the occasion and *casus belli* of a war waged
by the British Empire against Paul Kruger's government, in
consequence of which the mine-owners would reduce the cost
of explosives, fuel and wages and secure vast increases in
the labour supply necessary for the exploitation of the
deep-level and outcrop mines along the gold reef in the
Transvaal. The imperial Cabinet may have had additional
motives for ousting the Boer government, but these were
not overtly evident from the content of the ante-bellum
confrontation with Kruger's government.

J.A.Hobson ('The War in South Africa') links the attempt to secure political control of the state to the advantages to be gained from cheapening the cost of gold
production, and directly attributes blame for the war to
the Randlords. This view, still highly contentious, was
compatible with the official view of Kruger's government
that the mine-owners' exclusion from political power left
them 'lessees' of the national wealth rather than its
owners. It was for political control of the state, Kruger
believed, that the mine-owners pushed the imperial government into war. This matter is more extensively explored
in Chapter 10, but the needs of deep-level mining and the
political status of this fraction of mining capital (relative to that of the other social classes within the Transvaal state) need to be examined before the problematical
questions concerning the causes of the Boer War can be
considered adequately.

(i)   THE LABOUR SUPPLY AND COST MINIMIZATION: THE PHASE
OF DEEP-LEVEL MINING

As the industry entered the phase of deep-level mining,
its labour needs assumed new quantitative proportions.
Whereas the African labour force had risen from 14,000 to
70,000 between 1890 and 1897, (1) the supply needs rose
to 100,000 men (or by 43 per cent) *within the next three
years*. (2)   Moreover, the need to extend the level of
labour recruitment had become progressively more serious
with the greater demand placed on the industry by those
deep-level companies which had already entered the list
of gold producers. Generally the labour position had
become very strained once again. In 1897 there were 106
non-producing gold companies. In 1898 this number was
reduced to forty as a result of concentration on current
development activity, and the effect was to increase substantially the demand for labour. (3) The position became
more serious the following year when five more deep-levels
came into operation, making a total of eleven in 1899, al-

though only an average of 8.6 deep-level companies were
at work throughout that year. They produced 961,194 oz.,
of a value of £3,376,497, or *23 per cent of the total
output*. (4)
   The Chamber's anxiety over the supply situation was
clearly not merely another category in the long list of
agitational complaints against the landowners and relatively small capitalists in the Transvaal state. The
industry now depended on the recruitment of labour on a
far larger scale than before, and it required much more
intervention from the state than hitherto to fulfil its
supply needs. The mine-owners' gluttonous appetite for
labour may be illustrated by reference to the actual
recruitment of unskilled labourers between 1899 and 1912
(Table 9.1) when the impact of deep-level mining was
becoming more apparent. (5)   (The labour supply in 1904-7
was, of course, augmented by a Chinese component of over
50,000 labourers.) (6)

TABLE 9.1   Labour recruitment, 1899-1912

Year	Recruits	
1899	96,709	
1899-1903	-	years of war
1904	63,438)	
1905	91,816	) years of indentured) Chinese labour*
1906	85,538)	
1907	106,232	
1908	140,304	
1909	162,439	
1910	183,613	
1911	189,912	
1912	192,575	

* The Chinese labour component was 53,828. Repatriation
  was phased between 1906 and 1910.

Source: Annual Reports Chamber of Mines, 1899-1912.

   To some extent the Chamber had anticipated this rate of
development three years before the outbreak of the war and
had streamlined its administration accordingly. (7) But
despite initial satisfaction in 1897 (8) it was not opti-

mistic over the long-term prospects and was concerned for
the future of the gold industry, whose success had hitherto rested on its ability (i) to marshal (albeit with some
difficulty) large supplies of labour; and (ii) to mobi-
lize recurring sums of new capital in Britain and Europe
despite the very high risk and relative uncertainty associated with a speculative industry in a remote situation. (9)

The two items of capital and labour were interlinked,
for the labour factor was crucial if the industry was to
sustain the confidence of investors and maintain the high
level of investment of £93.1 million which had accompanied
its growth between 1887 and 1903. (10) The profitable exploitation of the mines was clearly connected with the
industry's capacity to secure an adequate labour supply at
the lowest possible cost and to minimize the other, less
flexible costs of production. The amount available for
distribution in dividends depended on the mine-owners'
success in balancing these costs against the gold produced
for the market. In the first sixteen years of mining, the
average *internal* return on capital amounted to 8.5 per
cent and during this time £18.7 million was distributed
in dividends. (11) Undoubtedly the Chamber attributed
this success to its ability to marshal labour supplies in
more or less the required numbers, and to maintain an uninterrupted flow of gold production at the minimum cost.
(12) But this position had to some extent been secured
before the industry was established on the basis of deep-
level mines, and when production was centred predominantly upon the outcrop ore. (13) Whether the industry could
sustain this level of investment and profitability depended on meeting labour requirements and the degree of
cost minimization which could be effected in this new
phase of gold production.

It was generally acknowledged both internally and
abroad that the future of the Rand depended upon the
growth of the gold mines. Hobson noted in 1900:

In all human probability for some decades the persons
who control the Rand gold mines hold the economic
future of South Africa in the hollow of their hands.
(14)

If he had been more precise and had taken note of the
prognostications of the various mining engineers - Hatch
and Chalmers, Hays Hammond, and Hamilton Smith, for example - he would have foreseen more clearly the emergence
of the powerful fraction of mining capital involved in
deep-level mining, and have distinguished between their

needs and those of the owners of the outcrop mines. The
former sector was represented primarily by the firms of
Wernher, Beit & Co., Cecil Rhodes's Consolidated Goldfields of South Africa, and the developing deep-level
enterprises of Farrar, Goerz and Albu. It was this fraction of mining capital which challenged more specifically
the politically dominant landowning class in the Transvaal
state, both in 1896 during the Jameson Raid, and in 1899
before the South African war broke out. (See Chapter 10
(i).)

(ii)   THE GROWTH OF THE 'DEEP-LEVEL FRACTION'

In the early years on the Rand the question of deep-level
mining activity was scarcely considered. Indeed, it was
a matter for speculation whether the Main Reef series -
the outcrop mines - would be payable at all. Before long,
however, despite some of the more speculative ventures
which had the effect of lowering the average grade of ore
mined on the Rand in the next decade, (15) the Main Reef
had gained for itself a reputation for 'gold continuity
... which established great confidence in the Rand, and
induced capitalists to sink enormous sums of money in
development and equipment before a single ounce of gold
was extracted'. (16) In the event, it was not the outcrop
mines which were to absorb the most capital or, in the
long run, to prove the most profitable.
    In 1895 the two mining engineers F.A.Hatch and J.A.
Chalmers reported that 'it was to the development of the
Deep Level areas that the Witwatersrand district must look
for the most important augmentation of its life'. (17)
What they were saying was not anything new to the Randlords, however. Hamilton Smith, one of the engineers
retained by Rothschild's, had predicted earlier (in 1892)
that the mines of the central Witwatersrand would reach a
depth of 3,500 feet and would yield gold to the value of
£325 million in thirty years. The German Commissioner
Schmeisser confirmed this and increased Smith's calculation to £349 million over forty years. (18)
    Among the first to appreciate the potential of the
'deep ground' were the Eckstein's representatives of the
London-based firm of Wernher, Beit & Co., who secretly
(and cheaply) acquired blocks of deep-level claims on the
dip of the most favourable outcrop properties - later
(1893) to be formed into Rand Mines Ltd in order to exploit its deep-level mining operations. (19) Unlike
Consolidated Goldfields of South Africa, which was almost
exclusively a deep-level concern, the local firm of Eck-

stein maintained vast holdings in outcrop companies. (20)
The representatives of this group were the most politically articulate and the most implacable opponents of the
Kruger regime. Otto Beit, Lionel Phillips, Georges
Rouliot and Percy Fitzpatrick were all representatives of
the giant firm of Wernher, Beit & Co. and were at various
times prominent representatives of the Chamber and important spokesmen of the deep-level fraction of mining
capital. They were also plotters in the 1895 attempt to
seize direct control of the Transvaal state.

Almost simultaneously with the formation of Rand Mines,
Consolidated Goldfields of South Africa, the mining house
created largely by Cecil Rhodes (though more actively
operated by his business partner John Rudd) had taken
advantage of the new techniques to extract gold-bearing
ore from sulphide reef and had absorbed a large part of
the assets of three companies with deep-level holdings.
The company was reconstructed in 1892 and again in 1894
and new capital raised. After 1892 Consolidated Goldfields sold its holdings in outcrop operations and invested exclusively in deep-level properties. In 1893,
at the same time that Rand Mines was formed, Rhodes and
Rudd established a subsidiary finance company, Goldfields
Deep, to promote a number of deep-level mines. (21) Of
all the antagonists of the Transvaal state, Rhodes and
Alfred Beit were the most overtly involved in the unsuccessful coup of 1895 to upset the state.

By 1895 the scramble for mining rights south of the
Main Reef was practically over. Hatch and Chambers observed at the time that 'there is scarcely a piece of
proclaimed ground south of the outcrop ... for which the
mining rights have not been secured, and claims are even
held at as much as three miles from the outcrop'. (22)
In particular, the firms of Barnato and Farrar had each
acquired extensive deep-level properties on the East and
Central Rand in 1894 and 1895. The former firm, Johannesburg Consolidated Investment, floated Barnato's Consolidated Mines to exploit the deep-level operations, and the
latter, George Farrar's Anglo French Exploration, owned
the East Rand Proprietary Mines, which held both outcrop
and (largely undeveloped) deep-level properties on the
East Rand. (23) Neither Barnato's nor Farrar's group
had adequate capital resources, although the latter was
the stronger of the two. Farrar, like most of the representatives of the deep-levels, was a co-plotter in the
Jameson Raid, and subsequently went on to campaign for
the indenture of Chinese labour, the bulk of which was
employed on the deep-level mines. (24)

The development of deep-level mining exacerbated the

tensions which already existed between mining capital and
the farmers and landlords in the Transvaal state. This
was because the labour needs of the deep-level companies
were vastly greater than those of the outcrop mines, and
their capital requirements were ten times higher. (25)
Government policies were considered unhelpful in securing
adequate supplies of unskilled labour, and the dynamite,
railway and liquor monopolies were thought, quite correctly, to have inflated the cost of production, lowered
productivity and diminished profits. (See Chapter 10
(ii), p.131.) Average working costs per ton were consequently much higher: 28s. 1.4d. in 1898 on the outcrops,
34s. 6d. per ton on the deep-levels. The high rate of
the latter was due partly to the Chamber's method of calculating the cost of production by including the payment
of debts and the completing of equipment out of profits.
(26) The impact of both the higher cost of production
and the mine-owners' practice of setting off the above
items as capital charges were to place even greater
pressure on the mine managements to reduce their working
costs, especially the cost of unskilled labour.

In these respects the deep-level companies were prone
to cost problems which were not experienced by the outcrop
mines. Apart from the technical problems of working at
increased depths and at very high temperatures, there was
the problem of increased capital expenditure for equipment
and development while the mine was in the non-production
stage. In addition, the deeper the mine went, the higher
the costs rose. The Geldenhuis 'deep-level' for example,
a small mine whose depth was only 1,000 feet, required a
working capital sum of £328,000 by March 1896 and was
still incomplete. (27) Where the shafts had to be sunk
to a depth of 3,000 feet the estimated cost was more than
double this sum. (28) Cartwright, (29) following Hatch
and Chalmers, estimated the cost of establishing a mine
to the depth of 3,000 feet as £650,000. He broke down
the costs as shown in Table 9.2.

According to Blainey the cost of preparing four 'first-
row' mines for production would be the equivalent of the
entire Transvaal gold dividends for 1894. (30) Once the
capital had been acquired, however, the profit potential
of the deep-levels was substantial. One estimate of a
200-stamp mill with a total yield of 350,000 tons per
annum was evaluated at an annual net return of 24 per
cent for a period of sixteen years. (31) However, in
order to recover the cost of building the mills and sinking the shafts, and to maximize profits later, the deep-
levels (more urgently than the outcrop companies) sought
to cut the cost of production in the specific areas of

TABLE 9.2   Cost of establishing deep-level mine to 3,000 feet

Sinking and equipping two shafts to a depth of 3,000 feet	£300,000
Pumps (two sets)	£100,000
Mine development	£100,000
Mill, cyanide works, etc.	£150,000
Total	£650,000

explosives, railway, and the various items connected with labour costs. This is where the conflict between the Chamber and the state was felt most acutely.

(iii)   CONFLICT: THE STATE AND THE 'DEEP-LEVEL FRACTION'

One of the main grievances of the deep-level mine-owners was the high cost of dynamite, especially since the rock in these mines required 35 per cent more explosives than the outcrop mines. (32)   Explosives cost from 12 to 20 per cent of working expenses. (33)   The dynamite monopoly under Kruger's regime, which inflated the cost of explosives, seriously affected the profits of the industry as a whole, and especially the deep-level mines, which together with the outcrop mines were using approximately 200,000 cases of dynamite a year (34) between 1894 and 1899.   In addition to the inflated price of explosives, the high cost of coal (estimated at 10 per cent of the working costs) and the high expenditure on labour constituted the main grievances of the Chamber.   As Blainey points out for the year 1896:

> The deep level capitalists and technical advisers argued that, with efficient government in the Transvaal, the cost of native labour and explosives and coal and imported supplies could be so sliced that the costs of production on the Rand could quickly fall by maybe fifteen or twenty per cent. (35)

By 1899 the need of the deep-level owners to reduce costs was even greater.   Since Kruger's policies made the economies they desired impossible, the main deep-level concerns in particular accused the state of plundering the industry.   One of the consequences of this tension between the state and this fraction of capital was the

Jameson Raid in 1895. It is not possible to deal adequately with this abortive attempt to remove the Transvaal
landowning class from the control of the state, but as
noted above (p.106) the agents most directly involved were
the personnel of Consolidated Goldfields, Rand Mines and
the Farrar Group. All three of these, and Consolidated
Goldfields exclusively, were heavily committed to deep-
level mining. They had the most to gain from the attempted coup, but all the mining companies would benefit if it
were successful. (36)

The state's support of the smaller capitalists in the
dynamite and other monopoly industries did not mean that
the government's policies were unfavourable to the mine-
owners in all respects. On the contrary, as we have seen
the Gold Law was eminently liberal, and the state appro-
priated no more than 5 per cent of the admitted profits
of mining. If one looked at the gold production of 1898,
the government took only one-seventieth of the total value
of gold produced in that year. (37) Moreover the law compared very favourably with its counterpart in Rhodesia,
where the Chartered Company was accorded the right to
appropriate as much as 50 per cent of the net profits of
any prospector who acquired a purchaser for his claim.
As Hobson commented: 'In Rhodesia the Shareholders of a
company yield a taxing power for the private benefit
vastly in excess of the power that the Transvaal Government exercised for the public good.' (38) Whether in fact
that revenue was wielded for the 'public good' is open to
question and will be considered below, but this is not to
detract from the benefits the Gold Law offered the mine-
owners. Nor was this law the only advantage secured by
the industry. (39)

The Pass Regulations implicated the state in expensive
policing activities on the Chamber's behalf, and government agents collaborated with the mine-owners in the
coercion of labour recruits. (40) However, in the phase
of deep-level mining neither this law nor any other advantages compensated certain of the mine-owners for their
effective exclusion from more direct control of the institutions of the state. They attempted to seize power in
1895/6 and failed, and were to make a further, more so-
phisticated bid in 1899 to raise themselves to the political dominance in the state that the condition of their industry seemed to them to demand. (41)

In their campaign against the Transvaal state the Chamber and its allies harped on the inaction and the high
cost of the bureaucracy, in particular the expense suffered by the industry as a result of the dynamite and
transportation monopolies. Chamberlain, possibly briefed

by the Randlords, took up the cudgels for the mine-owners
(he had been shown the Report of the 1897 Industrial Commission, which, as Marais (1951, p.190) notes, was the
work of the mining industry) when he wrote to Milner:

> Whatever force there may be in complaints in regard to
> the legislation of the Republic, the general ineffi-
> ciency of the Administration, which is clearly shown
> in the Report of the Industrial Commission and conti-
> nues to be demonstrated by debates in the Volksraad on
> alleged scandals, probably contributes as much to cause
> discontent as the legislation itself. (42)

In her memoirs, 'Some South African Recollections'
(1899), Mrs Lionel Phillips, wife of the local representative of Wernher, Beit & Co., wrote:

> the liquor laws were so badly administered; their
> provisions are good, but the police are most inadequate
> and corrupt, and allow the illicit traffic in liquor to
> be carried on under their eyes, it is even said to
> their profit. (43)

There was more official evidence for lethargic administration of the law. A member of the Transvaal Volksraad
noted in the debate of 8/9 July 1898 on the recommendations of the Government Industrial Commission:

> it could not be denied that [the] laws were badly ad-
> ministered. The Liquor Law was good, but its adminis-
> tration was bad. Even so in regard to the Pass Law.
> So lax was the administration of this law that touts
> enticed Kaffirs away from one company to another, get-
> ting 2/- per head. (44)

The official view was that the Randlords, foiled in
their attempt to subvert the Republic in 1896, now paid
agitators 'to lash the populace into frenzy against the
government as being the root of all local woes'. (45) In
the war pamphlet 'A Century of Injustice' serialized in
the 'Standard and Diggers News', Johannesburg, in 1899,
the writer rejected the charges of inefficiency and incompetence:

> we no longer hear of gold thefts; and the representa-
> tives of the mining industry have repeatedly expressed
> their satisfaction with the administration of the Pass
> Law, and more specially the Liquor Law ... the accusa-
> tions of incompetent administration so often brought

against the government of the S.A.R. is devoid of all
truth and is only intended to calumniate and injure it.
(46)

The point the Chamber stressed, however, was that it
was the administration which was ineffective, not the
legislation. It was not necessarily that the state failed
to secure beneficial legislation for the Chamber, but that
on many occasions its administration was too weak and
procrastinating to give adequate effect to its statutes.
The complaints against the government (which carried the
implication that the Chamber wanted not only reform but
also inclusion in the Executive) pressed the point that
the Transvaal landowners and small, non-mining capitalists
were too parochial and self-interested to satisfy the industry's ample needs. This view was adopted by J.A.
Hobson, who had no illusions about 'the Rand Magnates'.
He construed the conflict as one between the needs of a
fast-growing industry and a government of farmers:

The Government offices at Pretoria, the Netherlands
Railway, the Regulations of the Natives, the administration of the Gold, Pass and Liquor Laws in the Rand,
the provision of municipal government for the quick-
growing towns with their heterogeneous population *could
not be properly undertaken by this small community of
farmers*. The old semi-military system under comman-
dants and field cornets could not be adapted to fit
the new circumstances of a large industrial population.
There was no proper means of training officers or of
even securing for them a decent business education,
since the Boers took no direct part whatever in the
development of the gold fields and the subsidiary industrial life. (47)

Hobson's contention, paradoxically, echoed the mine-
owners, when he wrote that the state would have been
strengthened in its 'capacity for legislation and administration' if the bureaucracy were widened to embrace both
white groups. *The 'rude methods' hitherto employed were
tolerable for a simple population of farmers but totally
inadequate for a complex industrial society, working the
largest goldfields in the world*. 'Good government' demanded 'wider and keener business ability'. (48) This
interpretation is still the subject of historical debate.
Simons and Simons, for instance, possibly oversimplify the
matter by characterizing the industry's problems as
'originating in government policy [and] not in a backward
social structure'. (49) As such, the mine-owners' posi-

tion was neither 'irremediable nor so grave as to warrant
the use of force'. (50) Hobson and the spokesmen for the
industry, on the other hand pointed to the economic dominance of the mines in the social formation, the weak contribution of the landed classes to the revenue of the
state, and the incompetence of the bureaucracy. Fitzpatrick claimed that the heads of the auditing departments
were not specially competent to supervise the state's
finances and that there was 'the gravest reason to believe' that funds were wastefully spent'. (51) Hobson
claimed that it was through the gold industry that the exchequer had increased its revenue from £177,876 in 1885 to
£4,480,000 twelve years later, (52) and that the bureaucracy should therefore 'embrace' the more business-like
population. De Kiewiet (accepting the contemporary
campaign against Kruger in the manner presented by the
mine-owners) noted in a similar way:

> For every reluctant pound which the Transvaal had to
> spend in 1882 it had £25 in 1895, gathered from stamp
> duties, land transfers, concessions, property and
> claims licences and customs payments.... The fairy
> godmother was clearly gold. (53)

The mine-owners' case, as presented at the time and
as it appears in retrospect, was that since the economy
was centred on gold, the industry ought to have a proportionate influence in the institutions of the state,
the more so because its economic contribution strengthened
the existing regime without any reduction of the cost of
gold production. Indeed, the contemporary analyses of the
direct mining contribution to the revenue of the state
emphasized the paramount position of the gold industry in
an otherwise pre-industrial, largely agricultural society.
The strong economic influence which the industry wielded
in an economy largely founded on gold was emphasized by
the mine-owners to underline their weak political position
in the state. The extent of the industry's contribution
to the Republic's revenue (Table 9.3) was presented at the
time in a manner which stressed this inconsistency.
The statistics were produced to show that in the five
years preceding the Anglo-Boer War 30 per cent of gross
profits was paid to the Transvaal government while investment in production absorbed 45 per cent and 25 per cent
went to shareholders. The protagonists for the Chamber
were not slow to point out that during the first four
years of this period (1894-7) the amount paid directly to
the Transvaal exchequer exceeded the shareholders' dividends. When in 1898 for the first time dividends exceeded

TABLE 9.3 The distribution of profits of gold production, 1894-8

Year	Gross profits	Dividends to shareholders	Paid Boer government
1894	£7,930,481	£1,595,963	£2,247,728
1895	£8,768,942	£2,329,941	£2,923,648
1896	£8,742,811	£1,918,631	£3,912,095
1897	£11,514,016	£2,923,574	£3,956,402
1898	£15,942,573	£4,999,489	£3,329,958
Total	£52,898,823	£13,767,598	£16,370,387

Source: Supplement to the 'Critic', 8 July 1899 (cited by Y.Guyot, 'Boer Politics' (1900), p.56).

the exchequer's share 'the government of Pretoria determined to put the matter right'. (54)

The debate revolved around the transport and explosives monopolies and the administration of the liquor laws, as well as the virtually chronic need for labour. The Chamber's position was put in 1896 by J.P.Fitzpatrick, Secretary of the Reform Committee, but his observations were equally relevant in 1899:

> If you want the real grievances [against the government] they are: The Netherland Railway Concession, the dynamite monopoly, the liquor traffic and *native labour which together constitute an unwarrantable burden of indirect taxation on the Industry* and two and a half million sterling annually. (55)

The contradictions between the Chamber and the state, plus the mine-owners' belief that the proportion of direct and indirect taxation was 'unwarrantedly' burdensome, led them to push their campaign against Kruger by scrutinizing the details of state expenditure (which they substantially funded), particularly those items concerning the cost of the administration. (56) The list of official salaries was singled out for particular attack, since the bureaucracy was charged not only with incompetence but also with personal corruption - at the expense of the industry. According to Fitzpatrick (57) the abuse of the state revenue (see list of fixed salaries in Table 9.4) had reached alarming proportions by 1899. He noted bitterly:

The salary list is now twenty-four times what it was
when the Uitlanders began to come in numbers. It
amounts to nearly five times as much as the total
revenue amounted to then. It is now sufficient if
equally distributed to pay £40 per head per annum to
the total male Boer population. (58)

TABLE 9.4   Transvaal fixed salaries

1894	£419,775
1895	£570,047
1896	£813,029
1897	£996,959
1898	£1,080,382
1899 (Budget)	£1,216,394

Source: J.P.Fitzpatrick, 'The Transvaal from Within'
(1900), p.256.

The point was finally driven home by Y.Guyot, one of
the Chamber's most articulate protagonists:

These 30,000 Boers who represent the electoral portion
of the community, do not pay one-tenth of the revenue
of the State. They represent, however, a budget of
over 4 million of pounds or 133 per head.... The
Burghers are thus fund-holders in receipt per head of
a yearly income of £133 from the Uitlanders. Never has
there been an oligarchy so favoured. It is true that
all do not profit in the same proportion.... The
Transvaal Republic is administered in the interests of
a clique of some three dozen families. (59)

The campaign against the government monopolies, the ap-
propriation of so large a proportion of state revenue in
fixed salaries, and 'the burden of indirect' taxation was
furthered by charges - which extended from the President
to the entire Executive - of incompetence, corruption,
nepotism and theft. None of the allegations against the
Executive was formally proven before the war, although
the high cost of the bureaucracy was a matter of public
record. (60)
    As far as the Chamber was concerned, the faults of the
administration were due to the political exclusion of the
'English sector' from the government. The Chamber resented disbursing its profits to the landowners in the Trans-

vaal state without substantial representation, if not
control, of the state, particularly when it believed the
bureaucracy to be inefficient and too parochial and self-
interested to cut costs and facilitate adequate labour
supplies to enable the industry to sustain profits in the
transition from outcrop to deep-level production. The increased needs of the industry required an unrestricted
African labour market 'from the Cape to Cairo' which the
Transvaal Republic, preoccupied with its survival and the
acquisition of labour for its citizen-farmers, was unable
adequately to promote. (61) The motives of the mine-
owners were well publicized at the time. The deep-level
fraction was not differentiated, but the Rand financiers
cited were those of the deep-level firm associated with
Cecil Rhodes:

> The Rand financiers have told us very plainly what they
> mean to do when, at the price of gallant lives and
> broken hearts, they rule as absolutely in Johannesburg
> as they do in Kimberly. At a meeting of the Consoli-
> dated Goldfields Company of South Africa held in the
> City on 14 Nov., the consulting engineer (Hays Hammond)
> boldly announced that under English rule he hoped to
> be able to cut down the wages of the Kaffirs by one
> half, and a director (Rudd) who followed him declared
> that they would *compel* the natives to work for them.
> (62)

There were thus 'urgent reasons' why the mine-owners
sought political control of the Transvaal, not the least
of which was a reduction of working costs. As Hobson
(confusing Eckstein's firm with the deep-level concern
of Rand Mines - both controlled by Wernher, Beit & Co.)
noted:

> Eckstein and his fellows intend by new economies in the
> working of the mines ... and by the more effective
> control of the labour market, to keep to themselves as
> far as possible the economic gains of the new order....
> *These considerations make it evident that a small group*
> *of financial capitalists had large and definite ad-*
> *vantages to gain by upsetting the government of the*
> *Transvaal*. (63)

This view was not very different from the official one,
which in no mean way accused the mining houses of wishing
to upset the Kruger regime:

> The only fly in the ointment of the multi-millionaires

controlling mining destinies is the existence of a
government at Pretoria which they cannot influence.
When they first appreciated the enormous riches of the
Rand they also recognized that there was only this one
thing which stood between them and actual, entire, absolute possession of the coveted mineral area. So they
thought to remove that obstacle by force and failed.
What does the continued existence of the Republican
government really mean to the millionaires? So long
as the present form of government remains paramount,
the nominal owners of Rand mines are but trustees and
custodians - lessees so to speak - of the national
wealth. (64)

In the event the mine-owners gained ascendancy in the
Rand. The part played by the representatives of the deep-
level companies in precipitating this is explored in the
next chapter, which examines the relationship of the
Chamber to the new state and assesses the benefits the
mine-owners hoped to gain in the transition from the Boer
to the British state.

10 The transition from Boer to British administration:
the impact of state intervention

INTRODUCTION

In an *ex post facto* statement in 1902 on the causes of the
war the Chairman of the Chamber blamed the 'dynamite
monopolists, liquor sellers and various classes of ad-
venturers' who 'corrupted, bribed and poisoned the mind
of the Boers' against the 'capitalists' in order to preserve their positions. (1) Their efforts, he believed,
intensified after their success in preventing acceptance
by the late government in 1897 of the 'Report of the
Industrial Commission of Enquiry', which was favourable
to the industry and unflattering to the dynamite monopolists. The notion that the war had been promoted by the
capitalists 'to secure a reduction in the cost of working
the mines' was rejected as 'absurd'. (2) The Chairman's
statement, which aimed at absolving the Chamber of responsibility for the war bears quoting at length, since
this view was subsequently adopted by most South African
historians:

  Granted that with a sound, honest administration some
  reduction may be effected. Still the amount is problematical, and, considering the vast sums that had already been sunk in machinery and works, would it have
  been sane reasoning to risk the loss of all that ...
  for the doubtful prospect of obtaining cheaper dynamite
  or lower railway tariffs.... Would it have been in
  their best interest to spread mistrust, frighten capital and possibly run the risk of all that had already
  been done? ... I have never heard of a capitalist,
  unless he is mad, that would spend all his time and
  energies in trying to surely damage nine-tenths of what
  he owns so that he may or may not pull off a doubtful
  coup on the remaining tenth. (3)

There is little evidence to support the Chamber's dis-
claimer, although most historical accounts of the period
refrain from blaming the mine-owners for the war. Since
the interpretation that follows is a departure from traditional historiography, a brief critique of the more
influential works in the English language would help to
elucidate the matter. An exhaustive critique of the
literature is not contemplated and would be beyond the
scope of this study.

(i)   THE HISTORIOGRAPHY OF THE WAR

It seems fair to say that for the most part the mine-
owners' interest in the war is underplayed. G.H. Le May,
(4) for instance, maintains:

> The explanation of the war as a capitalists' conspiracy
> must be discarded.... One cannot ignore the direct and
> indirect effect of South African stock among the in-
> vesting public in London; but to say that is to say
> that the mines were of international interest. It is
> true [that it was publicly estimated] that the ad-
> ditional profit which the mines could make once they
> were emancipated would be £2½ million a year ... but
> whatever the ambitions of some of the magnates may have
> been ... what they wanted, in the main, was not war,
> which would certainly disrupt their operations and
> might lead to the destruction of their shafts ... but
> the coercion of Kruger in their interests. (5)

Le May's interpretation is consistent with the post-war
statements by representatives of the Chamber and, like
much of the literature, assumes that it was not 'revolution from above' - through war - that the mine-owners
wanted most, but urgent reform from the government. However, if the capitalists wanted to 'coerce' Kruger rather
than overthrow him, why were they silent when Milner
refused to compromise? Marais (6) maintains that they
were divided, but Le May does not use this argument. He
places the initiative with the Colonial Office and implies
that the mining interest subordinated itself to imperial
aims. He is not concerned with the post-war arguments by
the Chamber that the 'coup' would be a 'doubtful' one, or
that it would involve maximum destruction or that the
interruption of mining operations would be lengthy. He
does not use these arguments to absolve the mine-owners:
they were, at best, willing spectators of Milner's imperial strategy:

It was essential to Milner's plans that the war should be quick, decisive and limited. It should do the maximum of damage to Boer morale. (7)

The whole exercise required 'a thunderclap of victory'. It would seem that this was essential to maintain the acquiescence of the representatives of mining capital. In the event the length and cost of the war were greater than anticipated.

Le May notes that the effect of South African stock cannot be ignored - and then proceeds to do just that. It is illogical to highlight the significance of South African stock on the London market and dismiss the effect that high costs and labour shortages might have on investment. Nor is it helpful to remark on the anticipated saving of £2½ million in the costs of production and to ignore the impact the failure to secure this would have on dividends. There is concrete evidence for the economic argument, but only speculation in regard to the political potential relative to the shift in the balance of power.

De Kiewiet (8) also identifies the importance of the gold industry in the war, but places the emphasis on the British government's 'lengthy quest for a united South Africa'. (9) According to De Kiewiet:

The Boer War was caused by two broad sets of circumstances.... The first quite clearly, was the existence of the gold mines and the powerful financial and commercial interests whose focus was the Witwatersrand ... a second set of circumstances, more creditable than the first, and an authentic expression of British policy in South Africa and the rest of the Empire, must be placed beside the first. The Boer War was also the culmination of the British Government's lengthy quest for a united South Africa. (10)

De Kiewiet's principal error seems to be to characterize the gold mines as *South African*:

By what means fair or foul, soon or late, bloody or peaceful, would the Transvaal and the states by which it was surrounded recognize that the gold mines were South African gold mines, that its white and black labourers came from every corner of South Africa, that the Balkan mentality of Natal politicians, the superiority complex of the Cape, and the hothouse patriotism of Transvaal politicians were making the land rank with intrigue.... By what means they could be led to recognize that the gold and diamonds, railways and tariffs,

race and language about which men quarrelled ... were
all the most cogent reasons for not quarrelling. (11)

Whilst the Chamber was concerned to see the resources
of the country placed at the disposal of its industry, it
did not see the mineral wealth as belonging to South
Africa as a whole. On the contrary, the Chamber claimed
consistently that it was the trustee of the shareholders.
This, at the very least, was always respected by the imperial administration. De Kiewiet dignifies the war with
an idealism for which there is very dubious and contradictory evidence. (12)
    Robinson, Gallagher and Denny (13) also associate the
war with grand imperial strategy. It was an attempt 'to
keep up their supreme influence against a nationalist
threat.... they were drawn at last into reconquering
paramountcy by occupation'. (14) The economic cause was
the threat to imperial hegemony:

    South Africa was a case of colonial society receding
    beyond imperial control. It was also a case of econom-
    ic development raising the enemies of the imperial con-
    nection to political preponderance over the colonial
    collaborators.... The new found commercial supremacy
    of the Transvaal was sustaining republicanism and
    threatening to draw the colonies into a United States
    of South Africa. (15)

Their explanation of the imperial action is largely
conjecture and they are silent on the crucial part played
by mining capital. Similarly, other influential historical studies (Walker, 'A History of Southern Africa';
Marquard, 'The Story of South Africa') (16) neglect the
needs of the mining industry, especially the deep-level
mines, and confuse the superficial *occasion* for the war
with its cause. Few explore the needs of the industry in
the phase of deep-level mining.
    J.S.Marais, in 'The Fall of Kruger's Republic', (17)
takes a different view, and his historiography is impressive. The antecedents of the war are traced carefully
through the interaction of the mine-owners, the Boer administration and the imperial government, as represented
by Chamberlain and Milner. There is no monolithic opposition to Kruger. The Chamber of Mines and the Association of Mines in particular are divided in their attitude
to the Kruger government. J.B.Robinson and Barney
Barnato, 'each endeavouring to secure his own ends', are
anxious to make a separate approach to the government.
(18) Only in 1897 is this disunity checked by some public

rapprochement between the rivals, but they continue to
differ privately among themselves. Wernher, Beit remains
'uncompromisingly hostile to Kruger', but this antagonism
is not shared by some of the leaders of other big enterprises. Eventually the Colonial Office, itself ambivalent, steps in. According to Marais:

> In January 1899 Milner took the important step of ar-
> ranging joint action between themselves and the Chamber
> of Mines in opposition to the dynamite monopoly. They
> were making a bid for the support of the 'Capitalists'.
> ... But ... even at this juncture, the 'Capitalists'
> were not unanimous. They could not agree to the de-
> mands to be made on Kruger. It was not only 'foreign'
> firms like those of Goerz and Albu that were unwilling
> to ask too much, but also a 'British' firm like the
> Consolidated Goldfields.... When the [British Govern-
> ment] took over, the Capitalists retired into the
> background. Those of them who did not agree with the
> British Government's policy were prepared to acquiesce
> under the combined pressure of the Colonial Office and
> Wernher, Beit and Co. (19)

The significance of Marais's work is that he not only
notes the ambivalence of the imperial government on the
subject of intervention on behalf of the Randlords but
also places an equally divided Chamber of Mines (rather
than the undifferentiated Uitlanders) at the centre of
events. But in the process the mine-owners become the
instrument of the Colonial Office rather than the reverse:

> In the prolonged crisis that culminated in the war, the
> roles were reversed. In 1895 Rhodes and a number of
> Rand capitalists took the lead, but counted on the sup-
> port of the British government at the critical moment.
> The mess they made of their enterprise taught the
> capitalists their lesson.... They withdrew into their
> shell ... and left the political initiative to the
> British government. As the crisis deepened they
> emerged out of their shell once more, this time as
> instruments of British policy. They acted now as men
> under orders, relying on the superior political wisdom
> of the professional statesmen. (20)

It is improbable that the articulate mine-owners, with
their strong influence and substantial resources, would
silently 'act under orders' if the British government
pursued a policy with which they were not in substantial
agreement, especially in so vital a matter as the poten-

tial destruction of their equipment and mining shafts.
The issue, however, is not whether the British government
sought war and silenced the mine-owners with the promise
of future benefits, but whether the dominant fraction of
the Randlords, through the offices of Milner and Chamberlain, provoked Britain into war against the Boer state.
It is this proposition 'that they engineered the war for
the sake of dividends' that Marais rejects. Yet according
to his own evidence a section of the 'capitalists' were
prepared to pay that price, particularly those supporting
Wernher, Beit & Co., who (according to Marais) combined
with the Colonial Office to put 'pressure' on the imperial
government. (21)

It is the deeper relationship of Wernher, Beit & Co. to
the Chamber and the special needs of the deep-level mining
houses, and the contradictions between these and the
Transvaal state, which Marais neglects to consider, although this would have provided the deepest insights into
the causes of the war. Of all the deep-level mines, the
nine most advanced were owned by Rand Mines or Consolidated Goldfields. (22) Rand Mines was exclusively a deep-
level mining company, its owners being Wernher, Beit & Co.
represented locally by the House of Eckstein. (23) The
government identified the House of Eckstein and Consolidated Goldfields as its main antagonists, maintaining
that these giant enterprises had 'mapped out the possible
mining areas' and now dominated the scene:

> With the riding roughshod over the majority - whose
> wishes and desires formerly had to be considered - the
> voice of a section of the Chamber is stifled. (24)

More specifically, in a significant reference to the
relationship of Wernher, Beit to the rest of the industry,
the government press noted:

> As the Chamber of Mines is now constituted we are
> justified in considering it merely a new branch of
> Messrs. Wernher Beit and Co. Let us hope that as they
> have obtained a giant's strength, they will not use it
> like a giant.... We must look with grave suspicion on
> controlling power being centralized and consolidated
> in the hands of an already powerful group, thus prac-
> tically securing its complete ascendancy. (25)

Since capital and labour needs were greatest in the
deep-levels, the owners of these mines were more anxious
than others to effect cuts in the cost of production and
procure labour supplies from far afield. Although the

contradictions between the deep-level companies and the
Transvaal state were greater than between the state and
the outcrop companies, (26) the whole industry clearly
stood to benefit from a change of regime that would effect
substantial cuts in the costs of production. In addition
the deep-level mines, with their higher costs and greater
demand for labour, stood to gain considerably more. (27)
Through their control of the Chamber and their links with
the outcrop concerns the deep-level companies, especially
Wernher, Beit, took the lead (together with the Colonial
Office) in pressing for change. (28) It was not a simple
case of these firms 'riding roughshod over the majority'
as their critics suggested (see p.122 above), but that
given their vast capital resources and their greater need
for a reduction in costs Wernher, Beit and Consolidated
Goldfields were more vocal and influential than the other
firms. Moreover, their hand was strengthened by the
financial interest that many of the outcrop companies had
in the deep-level operations on the Rand. (29)

The situation before the outbreak of the war was, it
would seem, to some extent analogous to the position in
1895. In that year the deep-level companies were concerned to shape a united front against Kruger, and
preached 'that his overthrow would benefit all'. (30)
The evidence would suggest that three years later the
major deep-level interests 'representing the future of
gold mining' once again took the lead in the interests
of all the large mine-owners, but on this occasion involved the imperial government in the proceedings. The
Kruger government, through its press, warned of the threat
of the deep-level firms, especially Wernher, Beit, to the
Transvaal state:

> Secretly, slowly, but very surely, the consolidation
> of mining interests goes on towards monopoly - probably
> the greatest in the world, rivalling even the monster
> oil trust of America.... It has been long known that
> practically all the companies in the Witwatersrand are
> controlled by nine distinct financial groups, but the
> knowledge is not so general that - three millionaire
> interests govern the whole. One of the trinity is the
> House of Eckstein. (31)

Earlier in 1899 the government press warned that the
'forces which failed to shatter Transvaal independence in
1896 ... were forming a fresh plan of attack'. (32)
Noting the strength of their antagonists the papers observed that the aim of the 'new campaign' was to direct
public opinion through the press 'and steadily push for

the complete ascendancy of capitalistic influences in politics'. (33) They believed that the first part of their enterprise - securing nearly all the leading papers in South Africa and acquiring interests in influential organs of opinion in London and elsewhere - had been carried out. The second stage - political supremacy - was already being launched;

> Try to hide the truth as we may, the capitalist is almost already supreme in the land, and it may not take too long to change the 'almost' into 'altogether'. (34)

The opposition of the deep-level companies to the state and the ascendancy of Wernher, Beit and Consolidated Goldfields were clearly recognized by the government of the Republic, which explicitly identified these firms as the major threats to its supremacy. Marais correctly notes the belligerence of Wernher, Beit & Co. towards the government, but underplays the importance of this and of the interest of the other deep-level concerns in removing the landowners from the control of the state. The war can be understood only through considering the needs of the deep-level mines and their links with *all* mining on the Rand. The contemporary sources did not attribute the war to causes other than the machinations of the mining giants, and in the search to establish wider causes of the conflict, to attempt to relegate the Randlords to the role of innocent bystanders, or, as Marais maintains, as 'men under orders', seems to be to ignore the evidence.

The assumption that the 'capitalists' desired to achieve 'certain well understood reforms' rather than to attack the republican government also requires very careful investigation. Marais - uniquely in the historiography of the period - identifies the needs and grievances of the mining industry in their proper magnitude: the high cost of the dynamite from the state monopoly; the 'scarcity and expensiveness of Native labour'; the high cost of coal due to the inflated rates of the Netherlands railway company; excessive import duties which inflated the cost of white mineworkers. When each of these is considered separately, particularly the high cost of the turnover of African labour and the need for increased recruitment to the mines, it is evident that more than institutional reform was required. A greater degree of state intervention was needed, which, for a variety of reasons, the landlords and small capitalists of the Transvaal were unprepared to consider: Marais makes the industry's need for public assistance clear:

The mining companies declared that with *the government
cooperation* a great reduction in the cost of Native
labour could be effected.... *The government* should,
for example, enforce more the liquor law of the
Republic.... It should also encourage the flow of
labour to the mines.... Wages could be reduced /from
60s. to 30s.] *if the government* was prepared to help.
... The industry expected *the government* to play an
active part in the recruitment of labour ... at the
very least it should remove obstacles which impeded
the flow of labour to the mines. (35)

Clearly the mine-owners wanted at the very least to
share political power - i.e. to establish a state that
reflected the co-operation of the small capitalists and
landed interests with mining capital. The opposition of
the representatives of the former classes to the Chamber
stemmed from the belief that the expansion of the influence of mine-owners and the consequent influx of 'uitlanders' would involve 'the ultimate absorption of /the
Transvaal's] independence'. (36) 'Reform' of the type
required by the mine-owners was thought to be antithetical
to the interests of those classes who dominated the Transvaal state. The alternatives facing the predominant
mining interests were to accept the political domination
of the 'Boer' state while pressing for 'reform', or to
establish their own position by force of British arms.
(37) Pushed by the deep-level fraction which had the most
to gain from a rapid transference of power, and encouraged
by the support of Milner and his men in the Colonial and
War Offices (see Pakenham, 1979, p.57), they chose the
latter.
  Marais is well aware of the conflicts between the representatives of mining capital and the Transvaal state
(although he does not adequately separate the respective
fractions of mining capital), but he falls short of
placing 'the responsibility for the war at the door of
the mining magnates'. (38) Instead he sees their demands
as 'instruments' in a vague colonial design for 'paramountcy' in which the gold mines which had been at the
centre of the controversy slip away into an impressionistic imperial background. Marais's explanation is ultimately unsatisfactory, as at least a section of mining
capital required a rapid and far-reaching change in the
Transvaal state. Their dilemma was whether this was attainable without the political and military presence of
the imperial power. (39)
  Unlike Marais, H.J. and R.E.Simons (40) partially
accept (albeit cautiously) the Hobsonian view that 'the

one all-important object [of the mine-owners] was to
secure a full and cheap regular supply of Kaffir and white
labour' and that 'this concisely ... was Britain's war
aim'. According to these authors '[this] judgment now
seems harsh and intemperate but gains credibility from
the content of the agitation preceding the war and the
policies it followed afterwards'. (41) They gloss over
the mine-owners' difficulties and seem somewhat ambivalent
about laying the blame exclusively at the door of the
Randlords:

> The wasted costs were exaggerated and the grievances
> trivial. They originated in government policy, not in
> a backward social structure, and were neither irremedi-
> able nor so grave as to warrant the use of force. (42)

Broader imperial interests were raised:

> Britain did not ... make war only to benefit share-
> holders.... Gold mining was changing the Transvaal
> into Africa's most advanced economic region. It was
> likely to become the centre of a vigorous Afrikaner
> nationalism ... challenging Britain's presence in all
> South Africa. (43)

Chamberlain and Milner 'decided to prevent the growth
of a rival imperialism ... demanded franchise reforms ...
asserted rights of a Suzerain and when these strategies
failed, provoked the war'. The latter, however, is seen
as 'a political interpretation' which 'serves as far as
it goes, but does not account for all the facts'. (44)
In the end the authors accept the best of both worlds and
acknowledge that 'economic and political motives have
seldom blended so nakedly as in the capitalists and
politicians who conspired ... to bring about the downfall
of the Transvaal'. This was a 'classic example of im-
perialist aggression prompted by capitalist greed'. (45)
   Despite their identification of the war with 'capitalist greed', nowhere in the Simons' account are the needs
of the deep-level mines considered, although this section
of the industry in particular had by 1896 reached a critical phase in the need to secure labour and minimize costs.
The authors stress the (generalized) interests of the
mine-owners but then partially withdraw these 'claims'
for the 'imperial view' - for which no evidence is
brought.
   In 'The Oxford History of South Africa' (46) the blame
for the war is centred on the deficiencies of Joseph
Chamberlain. He was impressionable and weak and allowed

himself to be 'misled by the jingo rhetoric from the South
African League', with the result that he 'greatly exaggerated the extent of the threat to British interests'. (47)
His gullibility led him to believe (erroneously) 'that
there was a pan-Afrikaner conspiracy to eliminate British
influence'. The 'threat' was not that of a rival imperialism or a shift in the balance of power, but a racial
conspiracy to eliminate British influence altogether, and
in the final analysis even this had no objective reality,
but rested upon 'exaggerated' fears in the mind of the
Colonial Secretary. According to the 'Oxford History'
the Transvaal government 'was capable of accommodating
the Uitlanders' - given 'time and absence of external
threats'. (48) The conflict was more or less a constitutional one concerning the 'Uitlanders' or the South
African League on the one hand and the Kruger regime on
the other. The mine-owners are not separately identified,
nor are the divisions among them.

Apart from being 'misled', the Colonial Secretary also
miscalculated, according to the 'Oxford History'. His
strategy had been based on the understanding that
'pressure would make Kruger yield rather than go to war',
but this was a false assumption made (presumably) because
he had been ill-advised or had misjudged 'the Boer psychology'. Whatever the reason, the 'explanation' for the
war does not encompass conflict with the mine-owners per
se and assumes that the interests of the undifferentiated
'Uitlanders' and the republican administration were, given
time and the absence of provocation, easily reconciled.
Finally, Chamberlain had not only erred, but had also
chosen his Commissioners badly and was unduly influenced
by Milner, for whom 'there was no intermediate positions'
in relation to the imperial theme. 'Milner had [had] the
stronger will' of the two men and Chamberlain had suc-
cumbed to the pressure of his rhetoric.

In the 'Oxford History', where human frailty has
precedence over economic factors there is no place for
the needs of deep-level mining or for the benefits which
the Chamber or a section of the mine-owners might hope to
derive from the war. There is no doubt, however, that the
benefits of the war were substantial and in many instances
anticipated by the Chamber. It is in this light that the
following discussion should be seen, rather than as an
attempt to prove the causes of the war by reference to
its consequences.

(ii) WAR AND ITS BENEFITS

With the end of hostilities in sight, the Chamber of Mines
endeavoured to recover its pre-war position as rapidly as
possible. It had made contingency arrangements before the
war, and in September 1899 transferred its offices and
administrative personnel to the Cape Colony in the belief
'that there was little prospect of a pacific settlement of
the differences between ... the South African Republic and
the British Government'. (49) It thus provided for the
continuation of its work in Cape Town, and mining resumed,
albeit tentatively, eighteen months before peace was negotiated. By the end of 1901 twelve mines were in operation, running 653 stamps and producing 52,897 fine ounces
of gold valued at £224,698, although the Chamber formally
returned to Johannesburg only in 1902, to deal with the
problems arising from the resumption of mining, and the
return of refugees, and to consider projected legislation
affecting mining interests 'representing which the Chamber
[had] been allowed to make suggestions'. Only five months
after peace was declared forty-five mines were in operation with 1,970 stamps. Gold production was valued at
nearly three times the previous year's output at £823,338.
(50)

The labour resources for resuming full production were
drawn from some 10,000 African labourers who had remained
on the mines instead of returning to the rural areas, as
nine-tenths of the workers had done at the outset of the
war. (51) Average wages were 26s. in the second half of
1901 and 26s. 8d. for the first six months of 1902, as
compared to *47s. 1d. in 1897*. (52) The average wage increased to approximately 35s. in 1902, but exceeded the
pre-war levels only in April 1903 after a serious crisis
in the labour supply. (53)

Between May and December the labour force was supplemented by Africans recruited in the Transvaal, Basutoland
and the Cape Colony. After December 1901 Mocambique
labour was acquired after agreement had been negotiated
between Milner and the governor of that territory. (54)

The immediate wartime situation which confronted the
'exiled' Chamber was the security of the mines, shafts and
equipment. To deal with this it recruited its former employees into the Mine Guard to police the property, where
some minor damage had been done in the early stages of the
war but no 'wanton damage', despite the alarm caused by
the uncovering of a plot to damage twenty-five of the
Witwatersrand mines. (55) It is notable that apart from
the peripheral damage referred to above, equipment was
unharmed and production was not interrupted for long, al-

though concerted efforts to protect property had to be
taken, and the mines opened later than expected, twelve
months after Pretoria was occupied and nineteen months
after war broke out. Fears for the loss of 'machinery and
works' were proved groundless, and between October 1899
and June 1900 six mines were exploited directly by the
Kruger dovernment and another six mines in operation were
required to turn their production over to the state.   The
extent of the loss suffered by the mine-owners was estimated at £6,667,442, which included the gold production
commandeered by the Transvaal government valued at
£2,697,173, (56) although this was not all lost to the
Chamber as it successfully negotiated an arrangement with
Milner and Duncan (the new Colonial Treasurer) for the tax
deduction of defence costs incurred during the war. (57)
Lost profits during the war were estimated at £24 million.
(58)

The move to resume work had been prompted in 1901 by
the continued movement of the labour force from the Rand
to their homes in the rural areas, which if not checked
might have serious consequences for the early revival of
the industry. The confidence of investors also needed
to be restored. Milner, the High Commissioner, was 'ex-
ceedingly anxious that the mines should start without
delay' (59) since 'the news that the mines were about
to restart had been sent to Europe (not by him, he insisted, but through other channels) and had produced a
good effect'. (60) He was afraid that 'if there was a
delay there would be a harmful counter effect'.

The mine-owners were indeed very keen to resume production. During its 'exile' in Cape Town the Chamber,
aware of the prospects of operating at lower cost once
the destruction of the Transvaal state had been achieved,
concerned itself with reducing the future cost of production and retrieving the labour supply. It revised the
schedule of African wage rates, reducing average rates
from 47s. in 1897 to 26s. 4d. in 1901 and 26s. 8d. in
1902, and reconstituted 'on a wider basis' the organization for large-scale recruiting, the Native Supply Association, renaming it the Witwatersrand Native Labour
Association (WNLA). (61) The decision to revise the wage
rate turned out to be a disastrous miscalculation of the
market situation and of the willingness of Africans in
South Africa and Portuguese East Africa to be recruited
to the mines under post-war conditions. (62)

Milner (despite his rejection of the 'absurd and most
damaging charge of being under the influence of Capitalists') unambiguously identified himself with the cause of
the gold mining industry. (63) A rapid recovery of the

mines would encourage the inflow of capital and satisfy
shareholders as well as helping provide the funds for
reconstruction. In a memorandum to Chamberlain in November 1901 Milner envisaged 'the certainty of a vast and
immediate expansion of mining and other enterprises after
the war', to support inter alia an expanded population of
British workmen. (64) By coupling the expansion of mining
with aiding British workmen, Milner both expressed his
vision of a 'thoroughly British Transvaal' and justified
his highly favourable treatment of the mining industry.

The mine-owners also linked the development of their
industry with British prosperity: (65)

Every £ sterling spent in the mines for machinery made
in Britain provided 1.1/4 days employment for an
English workman. Similarly 5/8ths of a day's employment was gained for the supplies that were manufactured
in Britain for the mines.... If we suppose that the
industry attains to double the dimensions of August
1899, the number directly maintained in England would
be over 59,000. (66)

Similarly the Chamber quantified the numbers of local
white workers and their families dependent on the mines:

The number of persons that were directly dependent upon
the mines was 30,000 in 1899. With double these dimensions the white population directly dependent on the
industry would be 60,000 or if the present ratio of 1:5
white mining men to African labourers is retained the
number would be 103,000. (67)

This projection referred to the local whites only, not the
African workforce. Nor did the Chamber extend its projections to the rest of the territories of British South
Africa and their populations, black or white, though all
were affected by the mines. But by making explicit what
was well known to the imperial government and the High
Commissioner, the Chamber very probably provided a rationale for Milner's favourable treatment of mining and en-
sured that policies detrimental to working profits or investment in the mines would not be followed.

This was in keeping with the pre-war expectations of
the Chamber. Hays Hammond had anticipated large reductions in working costs when the war was over, and publicly
claimed that:

With good government there should be an abundance of
labour, and with an abundance of labour *there will be*

>*no difficulty in cutting down wages.* [The labourer]
>... would be quite as well satisfied - in fact he would
>work longer - if you gave him half the amount. (68)

Apart from the proposed wage cut, the mine-owners estimated savings approximating £2.5 million. (69) As soon
as Kruger was ousted wages were reduced by almost half and
the new state intervened to cheapen the cost of explosives
and railway rates and to end the liquor monopoly. In September 1901 (during the war) it appointed a commission to
inquire into the dynamite, liquor and railway concessions
granted by the South African Republic, which resulted in
the cancellation of the contentious dynamite concession
and the expropriation of the Netherlands Railways Concession.

The Chamber had made frequent and unsuccessful representations to the Volksraad of the old regime on these
issues. (70) It had objected to the existence of the
dynamite monopoly on the grounds that it inflated prices,
prevented free importation of explosives, discouraged invention and caused profits to accrue to private individuals with inequitable and disproportionate benefits to the
state. The effect of this policy had been the imposition
of a direct annual tax on the mines. (71) The ending of
the monopoly as soon as the Boer administration was removed boosted the confidence of investors and assured an
effective reduction in the costs of production. This was
borne out in 1903 when the price of explosives was halved
and 9d. or 10d. saved per ton of ore milled. (72) As
F.A.Johnstone has pointed out:

>Profits were absolutely dependent on low production
>costs, because of the very low average grade of the
>ore and because of the fixed price of gold.... The
>realization of profits thus implied intensive cost
>minimization.... The Transvaal Chamber of Mines cal-
>culated that a difference in working costs of only 1/-
>per ton meant a difference in profits of about £1.5
>million. (73)

Of the other burdens which pressed heavily on the industry before the war the republican rail and liquor concessions were all-important. (74) The former was the most
pressing although the debilitating effects of liquor took
a heavy toll of the workforce. (75) In regard to the
railway rates the high tariff on goods over the main lines
and especially the high cost of coal transportation inflated the costs of production. Under the Republic the
costs of goods tariffs and coal rates were substantially

higher than those charged in Natal, the Cape or what was
now the Orange River Colony. The abolition of the railway
concession and reduction of rail rates were, like the dis-
solution of the dynamite monopoly, direct benefits of the
war. Another gain was the dismantling of the monopoly
grants given by the Kruger government to the National
Bank. The Chamber successfully challenged its retention
by the new administration on the grounds that it ought to
be in the hands of the state 'or allow the privileges
equally to all other banking institutions in the country'.
(76)

The crucial question, however, was the Gold Law (No.15
of 1898), under which the industry enjoyed title to much
of the mineral wealth extracted. In the year of its
passage one of the Rand magnates claimed that the Gold Law
placed in the hands of the mine-owners 'probably a higher
percentage of the ... extracted mineral, than ... the
mining laws of any other country'. (77) Four years later,
in 1902, the Attorney General for the Transvaal described
the Gold Law as 'the most capitalist law in the world',
and added, 'the mineowners ... would like it to be left
alone'. (78) In this respect he was not strictly correct,
as the owners pressed for some minor concessions as well
as the principle that 'mineral rights did not (and should
not) belong to the State'. (79) Chamberlain, however,
insisted that the state did in fact own mineral rights,
and accordingly entrusted Milner with finding a suitable
formulation for this aspect of the law. (80)

The new administration established a Commission to
inquire into the working of the old law and 'abstained
from any extensive interference with the fundamental
principles of the existing Gold Law', (81) although three
members of the Commission refused to sign the final
report. In a minority report they called for the protection (from prospecting) of homesteads and lands under cultivation, a guarantee to farmers for damages to the surface of their land or their stock, and the reservation of
extensive rights by the Crown to withdraw areas from
prospecting. (82) But like the minority members of the
Transvaal Labour Commission of 1903 who commented also on
the Gold Law, the Commission's Report made no such recommendations, did not upset the Chamber, and the mining law
of 1898 remained unchanged until 1908.

There was also the important question of taxation. The
Chamber accepted the 5 per cent increase (to 10 per cent)
in taxation on the profits of the industry as the necessary cost of the 'benefit which we derive from British
institutions in the Transvaal'. (83) This magnanimity
was made possible by two main factors: the 10 per cent

profits tax announced in June 1902 was not to be retrospective, and the new system, which was one of direct
rather than indirect taxation, benefited the deep-levels
by spreading the burden more evenly on deep-level and outcrop mines. (84) In the previous regime the unreformed
taxation system (a new system was mooted but not put into
operation because of the war) was largely indirect and was
especially detrimental to the deep-level mine-owners, who
were liable to taxa\ n before they reached the producing
stage. In addition\ the Treasury's agreement to allow tax
deduction for defence costs incurred during the war, as
well as generous amortization allowances and beneficial
tax arrangements in respect of reconstituted companies,
gave the Chamber reason to acknowledge 'the benefits [of]
British institutions in the Transvaal'. (85) It would
seem that although some members of the Chamber, especially
the President, Fitzpatrick, thought the new tax move 'a
thoroughly bad departure', and some would have preferred
to see the tax either remain at 5 per cent or even be reduced below that, (86) the *overall* tax arrangements and
the abolition of the monopolies were accepted and welcomed
by the mine-owners as beneficial results directly of the
war.

The increase in the profits tax was offset immediately
(as we have seen) by savings secured by the abolition of
the dynamite monopoly to the extent of 9d. and 10d. per
ton of ore mined. (During 1903, 5,105,016 tons were
mined. The price paid for explosives in 1903 was 50 per
cent less than in the early part of 1899.) (87) Given
that the tax concessions, deductions of defence costs,
and the fact that the new measures were not retrospective,
were not the only benefits enjoyed by the industry, the
evidence affirms the Chamber's view that 'it is a matter
of satisfaction to all of us that the general conditions
under which our gold industry is today being carried on
... compared with pre-war days [has] certainly changed
for the better'. (88) By all accounts it was the Chamber's victory as much as it was the mine-owner's and
'Milner's' war. Having acquired the tax concessions and
the abolition of the monopolies which (especially the
dynamite monopoly) 'relieved [the mines] of an incubus
which in the past had constituted a heavy tax on the industry', enormous drive was still needed to restore the
mines to their pre-war level of production, which had declined to a value of £823,338 in December 1902 when the
Milner administration assumed control, (89) as Table 10.1
shows.

Milner's explicit dedication to the cause of the mining
industry was perhaps the most significant benefit of the

TABLE 10.1   Pre- and post-war gold production

Year		Producing companies	Stamps	Output in oz	Value
August	1899	83	6,340	408,324	£1,709,760
December	1901	12	653	52,897	£224,698
December	1902	45	2,970	193,830	£823,338

African wages for six months ending 31 December 1901	26s. 4d.
African wages for six months ending 30 June 1902	26s. 10d.
average during year 1902	26s. 8d.
average monthly pay 1902	47s. 1d.

Cf. Report of Government Mining Engineer for the statistical year ended 30 June 1902.

war. (90)   State co-operation with the industry extended to all levels - not only in fiscal matters but also in measures to facilitate African labour recruitment and retention through the extension of the Pass Department, the creation of a system of courts to deal with breaches of the Masters and Servants legislation, and the active encouragement of mine labour by the Native Commissioners as well as direct negotiations in British Africa to supplement the migrant workforce. (91)   Least of all did Milner disturb the wage and work pattern of the republican era. Early in 1901, in what was described as an 'excellent despatch' to the Colonial Office, both 'in substance and tone', Milner expressed the view that 'mineowners were entitled to combine in order to depress the level of wages; while the role of the Government was to ensure, and enforce, labour contracts resulting from such combination of employers and disorganisation of employees'. (92)   He particularly appreciated the potential of the mining industry to raise revenue for post-war reconstruction, and told the Inter-Colonial Council that the more rapidly gold could be extracted 'the greater would be the overspill ... [i.e. the excess over profits required to remunerate the capital invested] and it is the overspill which benefits the local community and fills the coffers of the State'. (93)   A prosperous mining industry was to be the basis for building up other resources.   The Chamber in turn was quite ready to give Milner and his administration its full support, (94) subject to the reminder that

the mines were not the property of the state and that
intervention in favoured areas was the just reward of
the industry:

> We cannot forget that we represent millions of capital,
> and we are bound to see that the interests of those who
> trusted us ... are duly protected.... We ask for no
> specially favoured treatment but only justice. (95)

If in 1899 the provocation of the war was detrimental
to the mining industry, as the Chairman of the Chamber had
ex post facto suggested, there was now nothing but 'confidence' in the 'judgment' and the 'impartiality' of the
High Commissioner, who, ironically, had done most to prepare the 'moral field' for the war. (96)   The Chamber's
approval of Milner was quite explicit:

> Fortunately, the destinies of this part of the African
> Continent are placed in the able hands of Lord Milner.
> ... We have every confidence in his judgement and im-
> partiality and feel sure that the various interests
> entrusted to his care will be treated with every con-
> sideration. (97)

Initially Milner intended to attract thousands of
British workmen to the Rand in order to 'counterbalance
the Boers'. He envisaged an increase from 100,000 to
250,000 members of the white population in five years.
(98)   According to Denoon:

> what he required was nothing less than a demographic
> revolution: the mechanism he counted upon was 'the
> certainty of a vast and immediate expansion of mining
> and other enterprises after the war' which would enable
> the economy to support a vastly increased population of
> British workmen. (99)

But the Chamber was more interested in unskilled black
labour and ignored Milner's plans (except for civil
servants). The Chamber's aim was 'first to employ native
labour from the Transvaal', where from all accounts the
resources of the northern Transvaal were very great, and
when once the country was properly opened up 'a very large
percentage of [the] labour supply would be drawn from
these districts'. (100)   The Chamber derived much benefit
from the transition to the British state in pursuing this
aim.
Earlier we noted that the ultimate success of the industry's policies depended on official action and sanction

of its policies. (101)   The Chamber had never reconciled
itself to accepting any alternative position, and the use
of the state's institutions was indispensable for the
successful operation of the industry's low-cost labour
system.   In 1902, when the republican regime had been
removed by the force of British arms, the Chamber was
able to record the gains mining capital had made at the
political level:

> The chief gain that we must recognize in comparing our
> position today with our position before the war is that
> we now have a pure and sympathetic government in the
> place of one which was, I fear, neither the one nor the
> other.   Moreover, we have a certain amount of repre-
> sentation which we could never say we had before. (102)

In saying this the Chamber was in part recording what
Legassick (103) has called the social transformation that
occurred in South Africa as a result of war and annex-
ation:

> [It was a] capitalist revolution from above and without
> in a situation where internal capitalist forces could
> not achieve such a change.   More specifically it was
> sparked off by the needs of the deep level gold mines
> for a drastic reduction in working costs which could
> be ensured ... only by a ruling class with wider geo-
> graphic powers and greater efficiency than the Trans-
> vaal landowners. (104)

From the mine-owners' point of view it was not essential that the executive personnel should be chosen from
the Chamber. (105)   The Milner administration acknowledged
the paramountcy of the mining interest explicitly not only
in guaranteeing the pre-war laws which served the industry
but also in passing new ones (106) and effecting immediate
and substantial reductions in the cost of gold production.
The new administration also reflected the dominance of
mining capital in the creation of close working relations
between the new institutions and the Chamber of Mines.
This was especially true in the crucial field of 'Native
Policy' with the appointment of Sir Godfrey Lagden, a
favourite of the Chamber, who was given responsibility
for the administration of African affairs in the Transvaal
Colony.   The relationship between the office of the Secretary for Native Affairs and the Chamber was promising from
the start, and the Chamber noted on the occasion of his
appointment:

With the efficient organisation established by Sir
Godfrey Lagden, the laws will be duly enforced and the
evils from which we have suffered so much in the past
will no longer exist. (107)

Lagden did not disappoint the Chamber. Jeeves (108)
notes 'that it would be easy to make a case that Lagden
and his officials answered rather to the Chamber and WNLA
than to their superiors in government'. There was a free
flow of correspondence between the Secretary for Native
Affairs and the Chamber, while the monthly reports of the
Chamber's executive were sent to Lagden, and the bi-
monthly reports of WNLA sent to the board of management.
Officials of the Chamber and WNLA often conferred and
Lagden was frequently 'briefed' on policy changes. (109)
This close link between the Native Affairs Department
and the Chamber was paralleled by officials at all levels
of Lagden's hierarchy, particularly the mining inspectors,
who were 'rarely critical of the compound managers'. (110)
Generally the officials of the NAD used their positions to
encourage the flow of African labour to the mines and to
intervene on behalf of the mining managements during industrial disputes. (111)
In addition to the intervention of the new post-war
state at the administrative level, there were legal
guarantees providing for the maintenance and reproduction
of the African mine labour force. In the republican
period the landowning class had guaranteed the maintenance
of the labour supply to farms and mines by the adoption of
rigorous Pass Regulations as well as the Master and
Servants Law protecting employers against breaches of
contract (see Chapter 6). After the war, when mining
capital came to the fore politically, the state approved
many of the pre-war laws favourable to the industry and
added some significant new ones. (112)
Lagden also approved much of the pre-war legislation
concerning African policy, and advised Milner that 'many
of the Laws and Regulations in force under the late Transvaal government of the natives were sound in principle'.
(113) His objection to the 'late' republican administration echoed the view of the Chamber, that the Boer state
was 'notoriously defective' rather than that its legislation was inept. Thus Lagden issued proclamations which
partly amended old laws and partly created new ones.
Notable among these were the regulations concerning the
Pass Laws which were made more rigorous, and which were
re-enacted by proclamation. (114)
The Master and Servant Law - one of the earliest enact-
ments of the Transvaal Republic (Law 13 of 1880), which

defined contractual relations between employers and employed - was similarly taken over (under Proclamation
No.37) by the new regime in 1901. The essential feature
of this law was that it exerted legal control over the
mobility and conduct of African labour and made breach
of contract by the labourer, as well as 'insubordination'
towards employers and 'making a disturbance on the
master's property', a criminal offence. White workers
were not subject to the same penal provisions as Africans,
and breach of contract on their part was a civil not a
criminal offence. (115) The incorporation into the new
state of the Master and Servant Law and the Pass Laws
(updated between 1903 and 1905 with a finger impression
section) helped the mine-owners to retain and improve
their system of labour control and coercion. These laws,
together with some pressure for reform of the mine compounds (to improve recruitment and avert desertions, as
well as to avoid censure from the home government, which
was keeping a 'close watch on mine labour conditions')
did much to preserve and improve the pre-war practices
of the mine-owners to sustain their low-cost labour
system. (116) In these, as in other matters, the Chamber
worked with the administration, offering suggestions
'which so far as possible, were followed'. (117)

If one of the negative features of the republican state
was its creaking administration, the mine-owners could now
look forward to a restructuring of the civil service in a
way that served the best interests of their industry.
(118) According to Denoon:

> By 1904 it becomes difficult to distinguish government
> from Chamber, and increasingly pointless to try ... a
> senior civil servant who had to deal with mining
> questions was entirely untenable unless he had the
> support of the mining companies. (119)

Jeeves offers a more cautious view, however, and notes
that the alliance between the industry and the state was
'more complex and variable than a relationship of simple
domination of one by the other'. (120) There was none the
less much liaison between government officials and the
Chamber, as well as some interchange of personnel.

Irrespective of the cross-flow of correspondence,
personnel and advice between Milner's officials and representatives of the mining industry, it is not necessary to
prove 'collusion' between the agents of the state and the
Chamber to show that the post-war state expressed the predominance of mining interests in the Transvaal. The combination of the plethora of laws supporting mining capital

and the accelerated intervention of state institutions on
the mine-owners' behalf was sufficient to establish the
nature of the transition in the so-called 'period of reconstruction'. This is not to say that the mine-owners
eschewed the opportunity of selecting officials of their
own choice. Politically and ideologically the civil
service, the police and the executive all bore the impression of the new supremacy. The regime encouraged a
stream of English immigrants so that the personnel of
government expanded to 600 employees, the vast majority
of them English. It was important to the Chamber that
the high officials of government and the technical ad-
visers 'of all the numerous departments ... will be drawn
from Great Britain or other parts of the Empire'. (121)
These officials, the Chamber thought, were more likely to
be sympathetic to the 'mines' than local employees. Similarly the ordinary police force, on whom the mine-owners
relied in an emergency, should consist of 5,000 men in the
South African constabulary, 'nearly all of whom are new
settlers in this country'. (122)

If the Chamber disclaimed any responsibility for the
provocation of the war, it certainly reaped the benefits
of the result. In January 1903, on the occasion of
Chamberlain's visit to South Africa, the mine-owners
acknowledged their debt to the imperial government for
what Legassick referred to as the Rand's 'revolution from
above' and agreed to arrangements for a war indemnity -
funded largely by themselves. The negotiations were effected privately between Chamberlain and the directors of
the companies (123) when, after some persuasion, the mine-
owners agreed to subscribe £10 million as the first stage
of a £30 million loan. (124)

According to Cartwright, Chamberlain's 'persuasive'
theme was 'that the wealthy firms of the Transvaal had a
patriotic duty to ... contribute to the cost of reconstruction.... It was to be a magnificent contribution to
wiping out the debts of the past.' (125) The Chamber accepted their 'patriotic duty', told Chamberlain that the
loan 'fulfilled' their obligations to the imperial government, and acknowledged that the 'burden' (of the war and
costs of reconstruction, presumably) had been largely for
the benefit of the mining industry:

> The settlement commended itself to [the Chamber] as
> fulfilling the essential conditions and spontaneous
> acceptance of the obligations which we all recognise
> and admit; it was the expression of our willingness
> to share the burdens which had been undertaken by
> others to so large an extent *on our behalf*. (126)

In the event, the loan was never floated and the companies were not called upon to subscribe the sums they had underwritten, but the circumstances in which the loan was negotiated generated the allegation that 'Chamberlain purchased the war tribute and the friendship of the magnates, in exchange for a promise of Chinese labour for the mines'. (127) Evidence for this is inconclusive and seems to rest upon (i) the fact that the loan was negotiated when crucial decisions were being made in respect of Chinese indentured labour and (ii) the mine-owners' strong opposition to the loan. (128) It would seem that if Chamberlain wished to use the Chinese labour question as a counter for bargaining with the owners, he was forced to let the industry off very lightly for what had turned out to be a very costly war and offer them a rate of interest on the loan of a gilt-edged 'four percent or more' which was highly unfavourable to the exchequer. (129) If a deal was struck, the mine-owners appear to have driven an exceptionally hard bargain. In practice, while the loan was never floated, the question of Chinese labour continued to receive the greatest attention from the Chamber and the administration - both when they came to review the post-war labour market and when the mine-owners needed to defend their labour structure.

Part Three

The defence of the labour structure (1902-6)

11 The post-war labour market

The post-war labour shortages were complicated by changes
in rural conditions as a result of the war; post-war
changes in the labour market and new demands for unskilled
labour outside the mining industry. The Chamber also miscalculated the market response to decreased wage rates and
was beset by problems in its attempt to preserve the two
tiers of the labour structure which it had established
so assiduously during the first decade of mining.

In view of Milner's commitment to mining capital to
increase gold production, raise the confidence of investors and also fund the reconstruction of the country
from the 'overspill' of the gold industry, the Chamber's
problems were taken very seriously by the new administration. The end of the war saw a feverish demand for
labour at all levels of the economy, not only in the
mining industry as it moved into post-war expansion, and
the boom led to a mushrooming of new companies which
exacerbated the dearth in the labour supply. (1) The new
state gave priority to the requirements of the Chamber in
dealing with its labour shortage, the major resource in
short supply.

(i) THE POST-WAR LABOUR MARKET

The impact of the war temporarily hardened the resistance
of rural Africans to the recruiting agents of the Chamber
of Mines and channelled a certain proportion of the labour
force into the more remunerative and less arduous occupations on the roads, railways and reconstruction projects
which now provided an alternative form of employment. (2)
Generally, there was confusion about the precise impact

143

the war had had upon the African rural population. Moreover, the Chamber made a prolonged bid to cut its average
African wage bill by slightly more than one-third - which
exacerbated its supply problem and complicated its assessment of the labour market. There have been few
studies on this aspect of the post-war period, and our
information about the condition of African farming remains
to some extent inadequate and 'Chamber-centred'. Bundy
(1979, pp.207-10) has attempted a brief reconstruction of
the northern provinces after the war. According to his
account, possibly 100,000 Africans settled on land vacated
by whites during the war. High prices for sales of
produce offset the decrease in mine wages, and enabled
some to resist entering the Rand labour market. This
process was bolstered by increased opportunities for
squatting - a consequence of greater mobility under the
new conditions of state. More significantly, social relations on the land changed marginally: there was a move
from labour tenancies to rent paying and co-ownership of
land. There were also more tenancies by Africans of individual or company owned land, largely of absentee white
landlords who preferred the quality of African farming to
white. Generally, by 1904, nearly half the African population in the Transvaal rented privately owned land;
over a quarter of a million either leased crown lands or
farmed their own lands. In total, three-quarters of a
million Transvaal peasants had access to land on terms
more favourable than the 123,000 Africans in government
locations or those in official employment (Bundy, 1979,
p.209). Generally, African farming was more effective
than the official reports suggested, although this should
not imply that there was affluence. On the contrary, as
indicated below (pp.147-50), there was enough rural
poverty to make one cautious of generalized accounts.

Another set of factors affecting the urban and rural
labour markets was state policy, which allowed increased
African access to crown lands, where squatting at £1 per
annum was preferred by African farmers to labouring 'on
the halves' on white farms. A pertinent point, in this
respect, was that rent collection from squatters on crown
lands was lethargic during this period. Apart from the
latter fact, rent was lower for these squatters than the
annual rent paid to white farm landlords. Over and above
these benefits was state policy in regard to delaying tax
collection (see below) - which also seemed to check migration to the mines. These were not all the problems the
industry had to deal with. A major problem was the withdrawal of the spine of its workforce in response to
rumours of war in September and October 1889. Only 10,000

of the pre-war workforce of 96,000 remained in their jobs,
spread thinly over the various mines, during the course
of hostilities.

One of the factors to emerge from the Chamber's post-
war analysis of the labour supply was that the mine labour
force was the product of twelve years of recruiting efforts, during which a 'standing army' of men remained at
work 'continuously for very long periods, forming a sort
of stock-in-hand' which the monthly recruiting brought
up more or less to the requirements of each mine. (3)
What had remained of the pre-war supply was the rump of
this 'army', consisting of men who regularly renewed their
contracts, accepted an urban life-style and only oc-
casionally returned to the rural regions. The diminution
of this 'settled' workforce was significant since by
virtue of its continuity and accumulated training this
'stock-in-hand' had become the most skilled section of
the African workforce. The industry depended on this core
and was seriously weakened by its wartime exodus. What
was required was to recover this pre-war labour force and
to overcome the 'retarding influences' restricting its
recruitment. Of these influences the reduction of the
wage rate in 1902 was the most important. (4) This was
not immediately admitted by the Chamber, although in 1903,
when the WNLA was obliged to defend itself against its
critics, it conceded that 'the most important cause of
all' was the reduction in wages, which effectively closed
the supply from the Cape Colony and Basutoland and 'no
doubt ... very gravely' affected the Transvaal itself. (5)

The bold decision to reduce the wage rate at a time of
intensified competition for labour probably failed because
the Chamber did not appreciate the full impact of the war
on the rural African populations. Dogmatically, they
carried out one of their pre-war aims - reducing wages,
if possible by half - and were prepared to 'sit it out'
in the hope that in the long term they would succeed. (6)

This reduction of the wage rate was, it would seem, not
only due to adherence to pre-war aims but the result of a
serious need to reduce costs in the wake of the war and a
firm belief that 'new areas of supply would be thrown
open' as a result of the change of state power. Under
these circumstances, the previous labour shortages would
be a phenomenon of the past. (7) The Chamber therefore
sought to recoup on its wartime losses in production and
profits by (i) reducing wages in anticipation of an extended labour market; (ii) effective administrative
measures to curb the high turnover of African labour
(through the streamlining of the Pass Regulations); and
(iii) taking advantage of the enlarged recruiting associ-

ation to syphon a steady supply of labour from British and
Portuguese Africa to the Witwatersrand. (8)

The Chamber failed in miscalculating the effects of war
and intensified competition in the post-war labour market,
and now it erred in its assumption that reduced wages
would (given time and patience for the 'experiment' to
take effect) increase rather than decrease the movement
of migrant labour to the mines. (9)

There was also competition between the mines and the
towns for African labour. The Chamber defended its post-
war rate of 35s. as against 60s. and 100s. paid in other
industries on the grounds that if it increased wages the
urban employers and contractors would outbid it. (10) The
Chamber's position was made explicit by its President:

> We have a ... partnership with the whole population.
> In our schedule of wages we, to a great extent, fix the
> standard of cost. The townspeople have to outbid us
> to attract the natives to them [to work] in the smaller
> industries. (11)

The truth was that the higher the wage costs in the
towns, the more expensive the cost of subsistence for
white labour and consequently their wages, as well as the
cost of African labour and stores for the mines. (12) The
mine-owners were aware that irrespective of mining policy
(i) the towns attracted workers who preferred urban life
to the mines or the rural areas and (ii) workers were
drawn to the towns from the mines by higher wages and
less arduous employment. (13) The problem was not a new
one for the mine-owners, but its dimension increased in
the post-war period. (14) The Chamber's response was to
suggest that all wages in the non-mining sector, especially in the central railway and public works, be standard-
ized according to the mining pattern, and to offer the use
of its recruiting agency WNLA to acquire labour for the
municipality and railway *before* it met the demands of the
Chamber. (15) Having met its own and other industries'
requirements, the Chamber would then rely on the Transvaal
administration to protect the labour force on the mines by
rigorously enforcing contracts and preventing desertion
through the rigorous operation of the Pass Regulations.

Apart from the attraction of African labour to the
relatively small non-mining sector, the WNLA belatedly
identified the following reasons for the resistance to
recruitment in its 1903 post-mortem: (i) during the war
the labour force had the opportunity of earning high wages
on military works and transport which employed 'many
thousands' of men - hence the ability to resist recruit-

ment to the mines;   (ii) no taxes had been collected for
two years - which was another reason why men did not immediately enter the cash economy; (16)   (iii) stores in
the countryside had been closed, hence there was little
inducement to earn money;   (iv) there was a dearth of
livestock owing to slaughter and loss during the war,
which made the purchase of cattle difficult. Money was
therefore available to supplement subsistence, and migration to the mines was delayed. The significance of this
analysis seems to have centred around this last point -
that the conditions militating against recruitment were
temporary and they would only delay rather than permanently rule out large-scale migration to the mines. (17)

The reports of rural destitution in the immediate post-
war years may account for the Chamber's tenacity in cling-
ing to its first post-war wage reduction. The official
accounts of African conditions are ambiguous. They suggest on the one hand an African population 'full of money
and very independent', and on the other hand men whose
minds were 'a good deal unhinged' by war and 'whose homes
had been destroyed'. (18) Most reports agree that 'they
were on all sides bewildered'. Many were 'demoralized',
and it was thought that provision for 'a great deal of
hunger' might have to be made. (19) Many Africans were
left much poorer by the war and were eventually to become
destitute, although they might have earned relatively high
wages from the military during hostilities. Those who
were already destitute were resettled in 'locations' acquired in the Colony by Lagden for the landless and destitute. Many of these had lost their stock and their land,
which had either been sold, seized, stolen or commandeered
by the Boers during the war. (20)

The general position was not improved by the payment of
compensation for war losses. An interim sum of £85,090
was distributed directly to African claimants by 1902, and
a further £17,000 was 'awaiting settlement'. In all a sum
of £200,000 was granted for compensation, but a portion of
this was withdrawn for the settlement of claims in the
Orange River Colony, Swaziland, and districts ceded to
Natal. (21) Milner told Chamberlain at the close of the
war:

> Compensation to natives must needs be a very rough and
> ready affair. Great thing is to give something quickly
> to restart them as they are fearfully destitute. If
> the Army was to pay for all it has taken from natives
> I do not think they would want anything else. (22)

In this last sentiment Milner revealed the fears of the

Chamber and others that if compensation awards were consistent with the losses sustained there would be serious
consequences for the immediate renewal of the labour force
on the mines. In the event, however, the level of compensation that the Central Judicial Commission agreed to
pay was minimal and neither arrested rural poverty nor
reduced resistance to recruitment. Compensation was assessed at £661,106, towards which the Commission agreed
to pay £114,000. (23) There is thus no support for the
claim that 'many [Africans] received considerable sums in
consideration for losses of stock and other property',
(24) or that Africans had for any length of time 'all the
money they wanted' and no means of spending it. (25) Many
Africans 'were in a more or less destitute condition' at
the end of the war. Those in the camps were the worst
off. In June 1902 there were thirty-eight camps, comprising 55,910 people, of whom roughly one-quarter were
men. At most 8,000 were employed either by the government
or privately at 1s. per day. (26) The death rate was approximately 10 per cent, representing 6,345 deaths during
the seventeen months in which the camps were in existence.
(27) Two outstanding problems therefore confronted the
population at the end of the war: land shortage and the
question of compensation for losses of stock and other
property. (28)

The somewhat affluent image of the post-war African
population which the Chamber and the WNLA on occasions
projected was contradicted by the various Native Commissioners appointed by Lagden for the rural areas of
the Transvaal. Lagden himself reported that 'It is perfectly true that [Africans] have lost their ... cattle
[but] the compensation they are likely to receive can
never buy their equivalent back at the prices now ruling.'
Similarly the Native Commissioner for the Waterberg District concluded:

> there is no doubt that many cattle were taken by the
> Boers.... For every receipt produced [for cattle
> commandeered or killed by the military] three other
> receipts were due.... Cattle have so appreciated on
> the market that the price paid for cattle to natives
> on commandeering note will not replace those cattle.
> (29)

Once his money was spent the African farmer was deprived of his stock and of any possibility of recovering
his previous position. The Native Commissioner for the
Lichtenberg District described one of the effects of this
poverty:

At first the Dutch farmers had a good deal of difficulty in getting farm labour. A large number of the
younger natives had a good deal of money they had
earned with British columns and were not inclined to
work. As the money gets spent, however, the difficulty
rights itself. (30)

It was for this reason that the Chamber believed that
the resistance to mine work could only be temporary. (31)
Indeed, rural destitution was the significant consequence
of the war. In the long term it would serve to weaken
resistance to recruitment to the Rand, but until that
point had been reached the labour shortage threatened to
be serious. (32)

The problems of rural poverty had a number of important
dimensions. Poverty could (ideally) be ameliorated by
grants of land, food, stock, improvements in land and
marketing, and provision of technology. In addition the
authorities might suspend the collection of taxes as they
had done between 1900 and 1903. But land was largely the
preserve of whites, and stock was scarce and expensive.
Rural destitution was therefore chronic. Yet it was important to check the poverty, not only to relieve the obvious distress, but also because the African economies
were ancillary to the industrial economy of the towns and
their collapse would threaten the migrant system and make
African labour costly. In the normal process of industrialization, rural reorganization and poverty would accelerate the establishment of an urban working class independent of the land, but this is what the mine-owners
hoped to avoid. The Chamber seemed to seek the retention
of the rural African areas in a condition short of destitution but not wholly self-sufficient. (33)

The mine-owners' ideas could be systematized in the
following way:

  (i) the ruination of the rural African economy would
      affect the cost of production, for without this in-
      direct contribution of the African economy to the
      industry the mine-owners would have to consider an
      alternative to the migrant system and thereby forgo
      one of the pillars upon which the ultra-profitable
      exploitation of the industry rested;
 (ii) the viability of the rural areas was essential for
      the regular replenishment of the migrant labour
      force, for they provided the basic subsistence for
      the potential recruit and his family; and
(iii) to maintain the existing profitability of the mines
      it was important that the kinsmen of the recruited

labourers should continue to furnish welfare in the
form of accommodation during the periods between
contracts, for shelter during old age, or convales-
cence in ill-health - the latter being particularly
relevant given the hazardous character of mining
occupations.

Hence the strategy was to preserve these rural economies from disintegration, and for this Milner's assistance
was essential. (34) Help along the High Commissioner's
lines of preserving traditional structures was provided
by Sir Godfrey Lagden. The approach he adopted was to
avoid any disturbance of tribal custom or erosion of land
tenure by directing the five commissioners he had appointed -

  (i) to study the existing laws and procedure and to
       pursue a common policy;
 (ii) to deal at once with any tribal questions requiring
       immediate treatment, but not to sanction without
       reference any changes of succession that had taken
       place during violent disorder;
(iii) to facilitate return to the farms of those natives
       who formerly lived there and wished to return. (35)

The increasing separation of Africans from their land
indicated in (iii) above threatened the whole structure
and became a cause of concern to Lagden's administration.
The rural communities threatened by landlessness were
either former tenants of Boer farmers or had been displaced by war, or were required to leave the land because
the farm population exceeded the numbers of Africans allowed by law to be on any one white-owned farm. There was
also a category of people 'who were otherwise derelict and
had no homes whatever to go to'. Lagden sought to acquire
'locations' into which these men might 'wander and squat'.
Potentially these areas were an important source of
labour, but for the present, despite the loss of land
and cattle and the absence of immediate compensation,
there was an overall resistance to the Chamber's recruiting agents. To explain this resistance the mine-owners
were forced to review their recent reduction of the wage
rate and to admit that their wage policy had been a
failure, and that they had miscalculated the market response to the wage cuts.

(ii)   THE MISCALCULATION OF THE MARKET RESPONSE TO WAGE
DECREASES

On the resumption of mining after the war the Chamber
successfully reconstructed the two pillars of its recruiting structure: (i) the centralized recruiting association;   and (ii) the agreement with the Portuguese for
imported labour.   The latter was essential, as East Coast
labour constituted the largest component of the pre-war
African workforce. (36)   The first consequence of the
Chamber's work (which started 'unofficially' immediately
the conventional war ceased in 1902) was the emergence of
the Witwatersrand Native Labour Association, and the
second consequence the modus vivendi with the Portuguese.
The anticipation of a large demand for labour and the need
to recoup its workforce at low cost led the Chamber to
abandon its old supply association and create one 'with
larger power and wider scope'.   According to F.Perry, who
became the Chairman of the new association, the WNLA and
the modus vivendi with the Portuguese were linked, since
the latter insisted on the establishment of a single
organization 'which would have the weight of the Chamber
of Mines behind it and which would be absolutely responsible for all its agents in Portuguese territory'. (37)   The
new organization was similar in structure to the former
one, and like its predecessor restricted its constituent
companies from engaging black labour except that distributed to them by the Association. (38)
    As a prerequisite to its arrangements with the Portu-
guese, the Chamber entered into negotiations with the
Labour Board of Southern Rhodesia for a division of the
African labour market.   The Rhodesian Board agreed to
recognize the new Association and withdraw its agents
from Portuguese East Africa.   The Board would employ
labour from this territory only if supplied by the WNLA.
In return the WNLA would deliver 12.5 per cent or one-
eighth of all labour recruited there to the Board, or
failing that recruits from the northern Transvaal.   The
agreement is significant only as an indication of the
Chamber's complete misjudgment of the Africans' response
to post-war mining.   The efficacy of the centralized administration would have been greater had the post-war
conditions not persisted, but in the event the agreement
was terminated at the end of 1902 when the WNLA admitted
that it could not fulfil its undertakings. (39)
    More important was the agreement with the Portuguese
on the modus vivendi.   Here Milner was urged to intervene
(since well over two-thirds of the labour supply was
formerly recruited in Mocambique) to formalize arrange-

ments between the new British colony of the Transvaal and
the administration of the Mocambique province. (40) The
Chamber had briefed Milner in 1900 when the first tenta-
tive steps towards resuming mining had been taken, and
advised the High Commissioner that the matter of labour
from Mocambique was urgent if the mines were to start
without serious shortages of labour. He was told that,
subject to minor alterations, the old regulations of 1897
would provide a 'reasonable working arrangement'. (41)
The negotiations extended over a year when the High Commissioner concluded an agreement with the Governor General
of Mocambique for a modus vivendi on matters of common
interest to the two territories. (42) The agreement allowed the Chamber's authorized agents to recruit in Portuguese African territory, subject to local laws and regulations. Essentially similar to the 1897 agreement, the
Portuguese received a 'consolidation fee' of 13s. for each
man recruited. The new agreement enabled the Chamber to
recruit Portuguese Africans for periods of twelve months
at a time (longer than for local recruits), after which
the labourer was free to exercise an option to remain on
the mines or return to his homestead. (43) The intention
was to recoup as quickly as possible the 'standing army'
of labourers which had provided the pre-war backbone of
each mine's labour force. In effect recruitment proved
disappointing throughout 1902. (44)

The poor response was ascribed by the WNLA to resistance to underground labour. The reluctance to work on the
mines, the WNLA believed, was provoked by adverse reports
of the physical effects of mining by Africans returning
to their homes from the mines. (45) But a more important
reason was the reduction of wages and the fact that higher
wages and less arduous work attracted the migrants to
other sectors of employment. (46) It would seem that the
WNLA was less willing to concede that the reduction in
wages in 1901 was the most important factor in keeping
labour away from the mines, than to shed the belief that
the industry needed time to gauge the effect of its wage
experiments. Having begun the experiment the Chamber felt
disposed to carry it on: 'You may say for too long, but
you cannot look for success or failure to be settled in a
month, or six months, in a matter of this sort.' (47)

Reports from the Native Commissioners in the five
districts into which the Transvaal had been divided consistently reported, however, that the reduction in wage
rates and the relatively high wages paid by the military
during the war were the reasons for African reluctance to
work on the mines. The Commissioner for the vast area of
Lydenburg, Middleburg, Barberton, Carolina and Ermelo, for
instance, was quite sure:

Undoubtedly the reduction of wages on the mines kept the Natives for a time from seeking work there, and they got better wages and more congenial work under military repatriation and public works. (48)

Many others identified the problem similarly. Grant, the former Labour Commissioner for the Chamber, told the Transvaal Labour Commission in 1903:

The effect of this illjudged action was to comparatively stop the return of natives and to alienate them from the field of labour where they were pressingly required. (49)

Lagden, the Secretary for Native Affairs in the Transvaal, also affirmed:

circumstances proved that ... the reduced rate of wages has been the means of deterring many from going to the mines and has not had the effect of keeping the rate down throughout the country. (50)

Thus the Chamber was made well aware that the wage reduction had been ill-conceived. But it would be naive to assume that it had not considered the likely short-term consequences of its action. Perry, the Chairman of the WNLA, had in the discussion on the labour shortage after the wage cuts admitted that the experiment required time and boldness and could not be abandoned before it had been given a chance to yield results. The Chamber's confidence seems to have been bolstered by the weakening of the rural economies during the war, and by the new opportunities for securing government co-operation. (51)   Had the Chamber succeeded in obtaining labour much would have been gained. The revised maximum wage rate was 35s. for thirty days' work and a minimum of 30s., (52) an average reduction of 14s. on the 1899 average of 48s. 7d. per month of thirty-two days. (53)   'Flexibility arrangements' permitted mine managements to pay above the new maximum rate, and non-producing mines in the shaft-sinking stages could pay 50s. per month or 1s. 8d. per day. A ceiling of 40s. per month or 1s. 4d. per day was imposed on producing mines. (54)   As in later agreements, the flexibility arrangement was allowed, provided that this overall maximum average rate was maintained. The new rates were lower than any other rates available on either railways, roads or harbours. The one exception was agricultural labour, where the wages were lower but accommodation and food more acceptable. (55)

Clearly the Chamber resisted any revision of the new wage rates in the hope that its labour force would trickle back when subsistence and tax needs forced men once more into the labour market. In the interim it looked to the rest of Africa to restore the pre-war labour force which it failed to acquire locally or on the East Coast. The Chamber's strategy was described somewhat grandly as being 'to extend the area of recruiting as widely as possible in order to leave no source of ... supply in Africa un-tapped'. (56) The Chamber's recruiting agents explored (with little success) market conditions in British Central Africa, British East Africa, the Congo Free State, the Province of Uganda, and Portuguese and German West Africa. (57) It was still hopeful that it might control the labour market 'when the territories of the chartered com-panies and British Central and East Africa were thrown open'. (58) In this the Chamber was encouraged by Sir H.H.Johnson, former Governor of the Protectorate, who believed there was 'an inexhaustible supply' in Nyasa and Uganda for which all that was needed was 'a careful organ-isation and good management'. (59)

The extensive efforts of the WNLA did not yield results to justify the optimism. Sixteen months after the re-sumption of milling, the African labour force on the mines comprised 42,218 men, compared to 97,800 in June 1899. (60) One of the rare comments about the Chamber from the South African Native Congress, in 1903, provided a partial explanation for this state of affairs:

No serious attempt has been made to encourage or regu-late the supply of labour on right lines by any of our statesmen. The whole question has been left with the mines and the farming community, and the terrible re-sults of the absence of administrative control in the scandalous irregularities under the old regime at the Rand made such a deep impression on the Native mind, that there has been no surprise at the scarcity of labour. The sudden depression of wages before the effects of the war or the impressions formed of the evil conditions of the old regime had time to subside, was a masterstroke of bad diplomacy by whomsoever in-vented. It also reveals the attitude of the mine-owners - a cold, hard, unsympathetic calculating de-termination to reduce native wages at any cost. (61)

Ultimately the Chamber did order a review of its schedule of wages and an inquiry into the extent, nature and possibility of changes in the composition of the labour force. The Special Committee of the Chamber it

appointed was composed of a representative number of consulting engineers and the powerful Association of Mine
Managers. The Committee considered three options to raise
the level of productivity and profitability of the mines
in the aftermath of the war. These were:

(i) the restoration of the African labour force to its
     pre-war dimensions;
(ii) the substitution of white unskilled labour for
     African labour;
(iii) the indenture of coloured labour from outside
      Africa. (62)

The first option concerned the Chamber's policy of ex-
ploring extensively in Africa for recruits. In dealing
with the 'restoration of the African labour supply to its
pre-war dimensions' the Special Committee does not appear
to have considered the question whether labour was required in the same numbers as in 1899, or its equivalent
in terms of efficiency and productivity. (63)
  Suggesting the substitution of African labour by white
indicated a major departure from prevailing practice which
the Chamber was reluctant to entertain, and about which
the Committee made far-reaching recommendations, including
a contingency plan should 'the supply fall far short of
the present'. Whites were to be used extensively in
underground occupations hitherto designated as unskilled,
especially in the Schedule I categories of rock-drillers,
plate-layers, pipemen's helpers and station loaders. (64)
On the surface of the mine unskilled whites were to be
employed as cleaners, as assistants to the engineers, and
also do work in the mills and sorting tables and in the
crusher stations. (65) An 'apprenticeship system' in-
denturing whites without skills for work hitherto undertaken by Africans, as attendants to carpenters, fitters
and blacksmiths, was also mooted. (66) With the exception
of the apprenticeship scheme, however, the Chamber rejected the Committee's proposals, and although the number
of whites employed in productive and non-supervisory 'unskilled' occupations listed under Schedule I above steadily increased from 1901/2 until 1906/7, (67) the number of
black employees in the categories of clerks, and especially rock-drillers, increased from fifty-seven in 1901/2 to
335 in 1903/4. (After that date rock-drilling was reserved for whites under Schedule I of the Transvaal Labour
Ordinance of 1904 and no further figures were given.) (68)
  This trend towards an increase in the employment of
whites in occupations which were unambiguously productive,
non-supervisory and non-coercive was a phenomenon perti-

nent to this stage of the industry's development. It was
occasioned by a moderate change in the division of labour
in an attempt by the mine-owners, during a period of experimentation, to secure higher profits than hitherto.
But the general principle that unskilled whites should
replace blacks in these and other categories of work was
not accepted by the Chamber, which therefore rejected the
Committee's recommendation. (69)

The third option discussed by the Committee, that of
importing labour from beyond the African continent, fore-
shadowed the debate six months later on the question of
importing indentured labour from Asia for unskilled work
on the mines. On this point it seemed that the Chamber
was inclined to delay a decision - either because it was
itself divided on the desirability of the policy, or was
uncertain of the political wisdom of requesting permission
from the imperial government to indenture Asian labour
before the labour market on the continent of Africa had
been fully tested. (70) According to Mawby, (71) the
deep-level firm of Farrar's, through its representative
W.Dalrymple, advocated Chinese labour to the mines in
July 1902, but met with opposition from the representatives of the House of Eckstein. The substance of this
objection (according to Mawby) was not one of principle,
but concerned the timing of the scheme. The Eckstein
group appears to have been convinced that the indenture
of Chinese labour 'would never be sanctioned by the
[imperial] government', and that it was desirable only
if African labour proved insufficient. (72) Whatever the
causes of the division - which has been variously described as a conflict between deep-level and outcrop
interests, and as an internecine dispute between Eckstein
representatives and the parent body, Wernher, Beit & Co. -
opposition to the scheme was silenced between May and July
1903. (73)

But before it embarked upon what proved to be a highly
contentious matter, the Chamber decided to accept the
first proposal of its Special Committee, which was to
intensify efforts to recruit local and East African
labour. It stated publicly that the reduced post-war
schedule of wages had been responsible for the dearth in
supply, especially when 'other conditions exist which
render it necessary to make the wages more attractive than
they now are to natives from the northern Transvaal,
Basutoland, Zululand and the Cape Colony'. (74) The
'other' conditions were clearly the marked post-war phenomenon of a competitive labour market in which the wages
of the 'secondary' sector were more attractive than those
of mining. (75)

Hence the Chamber acted to 'restore' its workforce by accepting the recommendations of the Committee that it (i) intensify recruitment and pursue its efforts with Lord Milner to 'assist in throwing open new areas of supply'; (ii) strengthen further the central recruiting organization; (iii) increase the wage rates. (76) The latter remedy was introduced immediately, and average wages for Africans were increased above the pre-war level for the first time.

(iii)   RAISING THE WAGE RATE (APRIL 1903) AND REINFORCING THE TWO-TIERED STRUCTURE

The revised schedule of wages was implemented in April 1903. The former schedule was abandoned and a standard rate adopted of 45s. to 50s. per month for surface labourers and 60s. for underground workers 'subject to certain modifications in respect of inexperienced natives'. (77) As in the previous agreement, mine managers were accorded some flexibility by the WNLA to pay higher wages to the more skilled of the labour force. Thus while 7.5 per cent of the total employed on the mine were to be paid the standard rate of 45s. per month, 5 per cent could be paid 'any wage [that the management] might deem desirable'. (78)   Managements had discretion to extend the piece-rates system, task work and contract work. The one crucial constraint was that the average African wage on any one mine was not to exceed 50s. per thirty shifts. (79)

The labour supply did not, however, immediately increase, although the effect of piece and contract rates was to increase productivity and efficiency. (80)   This increase could have had an important bearing on the rate and extent of recruitment, but the Chamber found it politic to emphasize the need to recoup and exceed the quantity of the pre-war labour force. There is strong evidence (see p.207) (81) for the view that it was unnecessary to restore the total number of the pre-war labour force in view of the increasing labour efficiency, improvements in the labour process, more stringent control over liquor consumption, and more effective prevention of desertion, after 1902. (82)   While it is not disputed that there was a serious labour shortage in the first few years after the war, it seems that the Chamber exaggerated its labour needs in order to maintain pressure on the authorities for the importation of Asian labour. This will be discussed later in the context of Chinese labour.

In the interim there remained the problem of meeting the serious labour shortage, given that there was no im-

mediate response to the rise in wage rates, although there
was some movement back to the mines from other urban employment. More needed to be done if the overall flow of
labour was to improve, for low wages, adverse physical
conditions, and inadequate commuting facilities to the
mines had raised the resistance of the rural population
to the recruiting agents of the WNLA. The Chamber had
recognized this problem and had accepted the Special Committee's recommendation to couple the revision of the wage
rates with the strengthening of the WNLA, which would in
the long run steady wages and counteract the legacy of
antipathy in the rural areas.

It is highly speculative to assume, as Denoon does,
that if recruitment had been more adequate the scheme
advanced by the chief engineer of the Consolidated Goldfields Group might have been adopted and the high salaries
of expensive white miners decreased by the use of Africans
in skilled and semi-skilled occupations. (83) It was not
necessarily cheaper to replace expensive white labour with
cheap black labour as the Consolidated Goldfields men suggested. Their scheme seemed reasonable because of (i) the
increasing skill and efficiency of African workers; (ii)
the absence of a comprehensive statutory colour bar at
this stage; (iii) the fact that the salaries of white
miners constituted the largest item in the costs of production. (84)

There is, however, no evidence that the Chamber wished
to alter fundamentally the two-tier system in which (according to Denoon, whose figures are more or less consistent with those of the Industrial Commission of 1897)
the white miners earned 34.5 per cent of the total wage
bill, and over five times as many Africans only 24.5 per
cent. (85) The following explanation for the retention
of this arrangement may be offered, the reasons being
economic and historical. The emphasis of the argument,
though, rests on point (iii) of this explanation.

   (i) The original demand for skilled labour necessitated
       the importation of English technicians, who were
       supplemented by members of the local white popu-
       lation whom they trained and unionized and who thus
       could not be easily replaced. (86)
  (ii) Over 30,000 members of the local white community had
       as a consequence become dependent upon the mining
       industry, and their replacement by African labour
       would undoubtedly create substantial conflict as
       well as the need for a comparable stable black work-
       force. The unwritten job and wage bars might be
       seen as part of the cost to the mine-owners of the

partnership they enjoyed with the white community,
wherein the highly remunerated white segment of the
labour force partly assumed the overall functions
of supervision, management and coercion - 'the
global functions of capital' (87) - and assisted in
the retention of a cheap and essentially repressive
labour system. Paradoxically, the system was not
entirely to the benefit of the whites, although they
had much to gain, for the two tiers of the labour
force were mutually reinforcing. While the white
employees served to discipline, supervise and frequently coerce the black labour force, the blacks
served as 'intermediaries' between white employer
and white employee, restraining the full bargaining
power of the latter. (88)

(iii) Although there was a sharp differential in skills
between the two tiers of the labour force, there was
a developing stratification within the African
labour force, in which a section of the men had
become increasingly skilled, efficient and prized
by the mining managements. (89) Historically this
significant proportion of workers consisted of the
Portuguese East Africans, who constituted three-
quarters of the total labour force between 1889 and
1904. They were characterized by the managements as
'naturally better miners than the others', and as
'long-service men' they became more skilled than the
short-service recruits. (90)

According to Perry:

It is not too much to say that in efficiency they represented four-fifths of the whole native labour on the
mines before the war. They were the backbone of the
industry. The cost of the labour force was unimportant
by comparison. (91)

It was this group of 5 per cent of the total workforce
(92) that the Chamber released from the constraints of its
wage schedule and allowed managements to remunerate at
'any wage they deemed desirable', provided that the overall labour average of 50s. per thirty shifts was not exceeded. (93) In my view the Chamber did not wish to replace whites by blacks for the reasons outlined. It
preferred to deal with the matter informally as the flexibility arrangement suggested, by paying the more skilled
black miners higher rates than the less experienced Africans. In that way it preserved the labour structure and
kept down the costs of production, simultaneously uti-

lizing in skilled capacities a proportion of men who constituted the long-service component of the workforce while
retaining the system of migrant labour. This policy was
economically rational and rested on the social and economic traditions of the country. The controversial Consolidated Goldfields alternative was consequently rejected
at the time, and continues to be eschewed to the present
day in favour of the practices described here.

The Chamber's reliance on an expensive white skilled
labour force in the midst of a vast low-cost black labour
force seems at first paradoxical. But, apart from historical constraints, it would probably have been very
difficult for the Chamber to abandon the white workforce
and replace it with migrants as well as a contingent component of stabilized black labour. A skilled workforce
was generally incompatible with a high turnover of migrant
labour in view of the time, training and costs involved,
plus the need to replenish the workforce if production was
to be consistent and uninterrupted. (94) If a large proportion of the black workforce were stabilized, the whole
contract labour system would be jeopardized as pressure
for the narrowing of wage differentials between the two
tiers of an exclusively black labour force developed and
demands for increased stabilization mounted. Combinations
and industrial action to press for these and other radical
demands might follow, with the possibility of a total
collapse of the low-cost labour system and the high
profitability of the industry. (95)

Historically, skilled workers in England and the rest
of Europe have organized to erect barriers to exclude
semi- and unskilled workers from their (protected) occupations. The phenomenon is not necessarily racial. There
is therefore no reason why an exclusively black, stabilized workforce should not seek to protect its position
in order to maintain a wage differential from which it
benefited. But in South Africa, the employers had much
to gain from a labour structure divided on racial lines.
The industry required this division to maximize profits,
and the white workforce was utilized in such a way as to
perpetuate the system of low-cost black labour. This
system enabled the mine-owners to effect savings in work
organization, accommodation, food, welfare and workmen's
compensation as well as securing the maximum social control over the workforce. Unionization among blacks was
prohibited, and the mine 'police' frequently quelled
worker protest. (96)

The legal guarantees acquired by the white workers to
entrench their privileged status served in the long run
to perpetuate the differences between the two tiers of the

workforce and to guarantee the low-cost system for the
employers. Conflict between the Chamber and its white
workforce was never concerned with the total replacement
of white labour by black, therefore, but only with a
relatively minor reduction of the white-black ratio.

A high wage rate for the white labour force and strict
demarcation of occupations for the black labour force were
therefore necessary costs to the mine-owners if the rate
of profit was to remain high, irrespective of the historical association of whites as skilled workers with the
power to vote and combine in trade unions. Hence the
Chamber fixed the relatively stabilized proportion of
African workmen at a maximum of 5 per cent (97) early on
in the history of the industry, and spokesmen for the
mine-owners reiterated 'that the white workers should form
a superior group of workers, supported by a large mass of
unskilled non-white workers'. (98)

(iv)   THE CHAMBER'S RESPONSE TO THE LABOUR SHORTAGE

The revision of the wage schedule by the Chamber was the
least radical of the alternatives before it in 1902, and
left open the more contentious issue of the relationship
between the two tiers of the labour structure and the
effect any alteration of it might have on the costs of
production. The Chamber was loath to upset the institutional arrangements of the industry, and its recent experience when it decreased wage rates after the war led
it, for the time being, to test the market response to
the new increases and to acquire 'consensus' in respect
of the importation of indentured labour.

12 The first defence of the labour structure:

the Transvaal Labour Commission and the unskilled labour supply

(i) THE WHITE UNSKILLED LABOUR PROBLEM

The pressure to deploy white miners in unskilled occupations placed the Chamber on the defensive to preserve and reinforce its existing cost structure. The debates which ensued over both white unskilled work and Asian indentured labour were therefore linked by the need to satisfy the labour demand without altering the structure or increasing labour costs.

The Chamber was adamant that unskilled white labour was not wanted. The reasons were economic, but often carried with them racial overtones to the effect that the capacity of whites for heavy unskilled labour was less than that of blacks, or that the tasks were too menial for 'civilized' men. The Chamber appealed to Chamberlain, and told him on the occasion of his visit to the Transvaal in December 1902: 'With the grade of ore worked there is at the present time a large proportion of work which cannot possibly be done by white labour.' (1) The appeal to Chamberlain was made on the grounds that the erosion of the pre-war labour structure was increasing the costs of production of low-grade ore at a time of falling production levels and thereby decreasing profitability and the attractiveness of mining to investors. The fall in the level of production was in fact due primarily to two factors: (i) the war and supply shortages which had combined to reduce annual output from 4,295,608 fine ounces in 1898 to 1,690 in 1902; (2) (ii) speculative ventures undertaken in the early stages which lowered the *average* grade of ore mined on the Witwatersrand. (3) In dealing with Chamberlain the mine-owners emphasized the first factor. The Chamber argued that the black-white ratio had been reduced as a consequence of shortages from 8:1 before the war to 5:1 after the war, and that this was

as far as it should go. In December 1902 there were
49,500 Africans and 10,000 whites, (4) and if the
pressures for the employment of unskilled white labour
succeeded, the ratio would undergo a further decline
with drastic effects on the costs of production and on
profitability. It seems that when the Chamber approached
Chamberlain it hoped that the government would not impose
any rigid constraints on its labour structure, and that
the Colonial Secretary would deter the new administration
in South Africa from too close an identification with
those whites who wished to widen the scope of mining employment to absorb unemployed whites in unskilled capacities at the expense of the shareholders.

The downturn in the labour ratio was in fact not intended by the Chamber, but was the product of two independent phenomena: the overall shortage of African labour
and the (temporary) employment of workless white labourers. This latter was a post-war expedient and not a new
departure in the industry's labour policy. The whites
were remunerated at 5s. per day 'until they could find
other and more profitable employment'. (5) Their temporary employment in the mines provided the occasion for
various experiments and cost-benefit analyses on the use
of white labour in unskilled capacities, although the
Chamber continually insisted that it was fundamentally
unprepared to accept any experimental substitution of
white for black workers. (6) This was because it believed
such experimentation to be largely irrelevant, for the various comparisons in the relative muscular efficiency of
one section of the labour force compared to another did
not deal with the important items in the costs of production. Far more important was the incomparably higher cost
of the wages necessary to maintain the white work force
and the greater expenditure required on such items as
living quarters, furniture, medical attention, diet, and
accident and life insurance. (7)

The campaign mounted by the Chamber in defence of its
labour arrangements drew it into more active intervention
in the country's political life, in particular the 'agitation debates' over Asian labour, and in the colony's
Legislative Council. The Chamber financed and made much
use of the Asian Labour Importation Association, from
which it launched a persuasive political offensive. (8)
It made its position particularly clear in October 1902,
when its recruiting attempts were blocked in Mombasa. On
that occasion the Chamber addressed itself to the Secretary for Native Affairs and through him to Milner and the
Colonial Secretary. The statement carried the impact of
a declaration on 'white' labour.

The efforts on the part of employers of labour to find
employment for the 'unskilled' whites have been misre-
presented in two directions: First, as an attempt to
force down white wages; secondly, as the commencement
of a great design to substitute white labour for black.
   We are bound to represent with the utmost emphasis
of which we are capable that these two courses are the
extreme, and are not in any way contemplated by the
Chamber. We would regard it as a calamity of the worst
description that a pauperized white population should
be introduced here and the country flooded with white
men who could not fairly be employed except at a rate
of wage upon which they and their families could not
properly exist. As to the substitution of white for
black, it is an economic impossibility.... There are
certain classes and there is a certain proportion of
work which cannot possibly be done and never will be
done except by means of labour cheaper than it is
possible or proper that white labour shall descend to.
(9)

In declaring its attitude so forcefully the Chamber
(despite its reference to the 'proper work' for white
labour) was merely reiterating its position that its
labour structure was based on migrant labour, and it had
no wish to contemplate the substitution of white workers
for black, or to create a stabilized African workforce,
whether 'pauperized' or not.
   Initially, therefore, the Chamber's strategy was to
deflect the pressure on its labour structure and maintain
the status quo. It suggested that its competitors for
labour, especially the railways and public works, should
experiment with white unskilled workers as navvies. This
would ease the demand on the African labour market and at
the same time 'cause the government rather than the mines
to pay' for the experimentation. (10) Milner told a
deputation in June 1903, six months before the Draft
Ordinance to import labour:

The railway difficulty is a good object lesson....
[There] we as you know [are] making an experiment with
British navvies. We have got 500 and although they are
very costly, I would gladly employ 5,000. I have had
the figures taken out, and though the navvy individually does much more work than the native, his wages, food
and accommodation cost so much more.... The work is
fully twice as dear as if done by natives. The government, no doubt, can afford for a great public object
and the relief of the strain [on the] labour market at
present is such an object to get. (11)

The Chamber turned on its critics who advocated an extension of unskilled work in the mines to whites by illus-
trating the advantages to the whites of the migrant practice over the alternative of a large white unskilled workforce. It had received many offers of white labour,
'quite efficient and much cheaper', from Italy, Hungary,
Portugal and Greece, which might eventually acquire skills
and compete with the local and immigrant whites presently
on the mines, but the Chamber had declined these offers,
including one of some 10,000 Italian peasants, 'men used
to the spade and pick and thoroughly reliable hard
workers'. (12) Although these men were not deterred by
strenuous physical work and would give their labour for
low wages, the Chamber rejected them because they would
require 'healthy and substantial quarters; furniture,
blankets, medical attendance, accident or death insurance
and an adequate diet'. (13) It was these costs which made
white labour unacceptable, not any inability to work as
cheaply and productively as the African labour force. To
employ these men on the mines would, in the words of the
owners, be to employ a 'pauperized' population unable to
maintain adequately either 'themselves or their families'.
    The black labour force, it would seem, escaped this
description because of what the mine-owners called a difference in cultural expectations. But in reality the
African workforce could be provided with what the Chamber
knew were unhealthy quarters and inadequate food, clothing
and no security against accident because of the migrant
system which maintained the labourers' connection with the
land and thereby relieved the Chamber of the direct responsibility of providing for the family sustenance or
welfare necessary to care for the sick or aged - or to
reproduce the workforce. The mine-owners therefore preferred intensive recruitment of African migrants rather
than of white labour, and this remained the Chamber's
policy.
    Migrant labour was, however, to be obtained not from
the continent of Africa alone, though either the Chamber
or fractions within it were not yet agreed upon a course
of acquiring indentured labour from beyond Africa. (14)
The statements of the Chamber were somewhat confused on
this subject, reflecting to some extent this indecision.
Hence the note of uncertainty when the Chamber protested -
perhaps too much - that it should not be 'persuaded to
relay the foundations of the industry' or pursue 'unsound'
policies. What was required was

    a patient and exhaustive trial [of labour recruitment
    on the continent] because the premature abandonment of

any serious attempt ... may afterwards be regarded as
a shortcut to a pre-determined conclusion, as an effort
to show but not prove that the first and natural field
for our recruiting exertions - Africa - has been exhausted. (15)

(ii)   THE SEARCH FOR AFRICAN LABOUR

Geographically speaking, the 'first and natural field' for
the Chamber's recruiting activity was the continent of
Africa. But given the post-war need to increase the
profitability of the low-grade ore and to satisfy the
overall demand for low-cost labour, the Chamber may have
considered that, under careful conditions of recruiting,
relatively long-term contracts and low-cost labour policies, Asian labour might be cheaper. Thus the search for
labour on the African continent in the early months of
1903 might be seen in one or more of the following ways:

  (i) as an interim measure before embarking upon the
       scheme for indentured Asian labour;
 (ii) as an interim measure before all members of the
       Chamber were united on the importation of Asian
       labour;
(iii) as a genuine attempt to gauge the response of po-
       tential recruits to the recent increase in wage
       rates;
 (iv) as a political strategy to silence the opposition
       and win consensus for the scheme.

   Both the 'Minority commissioners' of the subsequent
Transvaal Labour Commission (Quinn and Whiteside) and the
dissident members of the Transvaal Legislative Council
(Raitt and Hull) very much doubted the sincerity of the
Chamber's efforts to secure the labour it required from
the African continent during 1903. According to Raitt,
who opposed the Asian labour scheme, the Chamber had
decided as early as 1902 on importing a workforce from
Asia:

   After the declaration of peace it must have been evident to everyone that the question which would arise
   was how the natives were to be brought back to the
   mines, and it was equally evident that before the
   mining authorities knew whether the natives could be
   brought back or not they had already determined on the
   importation of Asiatic labour. (16)

As evidence of this contention, and proof that the Chamber had little intention of attracting its pre-war workforce, Raitt cited the 1902 reduction of 50 per cent in African wages, as well as subsequent statements by the Chamber's protagonists in March 1903 'that the time was fast approaching when the government should be approached with a definite request to formulate an Ordinance under which the importation of Asian labour should be permitted'. (17)   According to the same source (Raitt, 'Debates of the Transvaal Legislative Council', p.110):

The position at the time was that the natives had been driven back to their kraals on account of the war, and after a lapse of three years it was impossible to say when and where these natives could be recovered, and yet in spite of that, the Chamber of Mines determined in order to tempt them back and put every inducement in their way, to reduce their wages 50%.   Everyone knew this was the most foolish policy.   The wages were raised in February, but immediately after, in March, Sir G.Farrar began the propaganda of Chinese labour. How could it possibly have been determined (after so short a time) whether the rise in wages would bring the native back or not. (18)

There is no evidence available to show that the Chamber reduced wages in 1902 in order to pave the way for Asian labour, although it is clear (see Chapter 11, p.155) that the subject was discussed by its Special Committee in 1902.   It was not publicly accepted as the Chamber's policy, either because of a lack of agreement among the members of the Chamber (as Mawby suggests) or in order to test the market on the African continent prior to any change in the 'natural field' of recruitment. (19)   Whatever the reasons, the mine-owners did conduct a search throughout a substantial area of Africa for the restoration of its labour force.

The Chamber looked principally to the vast African population in the subcontinent, which it estimated as 1,060,000 in the Cape Colony, 900,000 in Natal, 700,000 in the Transvaal, and 510,000 in Mashonaland and Matabeleland. (20)   Two tactics for recruitment were considered: (i) strengthening the centralized recruiting associations; (ii) extra-economic measures such as taxation to release the potential supply.   However, only the first of these strategies was followed, (21) although the expedient of taxation was not overlooked.   In a cryptic description of Chamberlain's secret meeting with the Chamber of Mines, the President reported:

I do not think anything connected with [the country]
is more important to Africa generally than his pro-
nouncement on the Native question. He made no discovery. He told us nothing which we did not know ...
for among the works of the great Chief who lay dying
this time last year ... will be one little beginning
called the 'Glen Grey' Act and I will pay this tribute
to Cecil John Rhodes - 'He tried while others talked'.
(22)

The idea of coercion through increased taxation was not
actualized, however, although it remained a potential
strategy for use in the future.

The labour supply failed to materialize in Africa, despite the Chamber's statements that extensive efforts had
been made by the WNLA in British South Africa and Central
and East Africa. (23) According to the Chamber's critics,
particularly Hull and Raitt, both of them prominent
spokesmen in the Chinese debate in the Transvaal Legislative Council, the WNLA 'had not taken the best means of
inducing the natives to come to the mines'. (24) They
contended that the 'methods of the WNLA were doomed to
failure' and that there was 'overwhelming' evidence to
show the 'utter inadequacy' of the Association, which was
'as far as the public were concerned, a secret body'. (25)
In their view they were not yet certain that the WNLA had
'exhausted the labour supply of South Africa'. (26)

These criticisms of the Chamber and its recruiting Association were made in December 1903, but during the
period between February and December of that year there
was considerable WNLA activity. According to the Chamber
the territories of British South Africa and East and
Central Africa held promise but did not relieve the present supply needs. It was thought that at some time in
the future they might prove important sources of labour,
but 'a certain breathing space' was still needed. (27)
Nevertheless, the presence of this vast population appeared to be a source of optimism for the Chamber, which
believed that, with the co-operation of Milner and the
British administrations throughout Africa, sufficient
labour would be available for the mines and for the
'collaterial industries' (28) to develop. This labour
force would be acquired by the 'application throughout
Africa of a uniform national and just native law policy'.
(29)

During this period of recruiting activity Milner, who
adopted the Chamber's problems as his own, obtained permission from the Foreign Office to recruit 1,000 Africans
from British Central Africa, but although 931 men were

successfully recruited 'they were unable to endure the
climactic conditions of the Witwatersrand'. On the west
coast of the continent, in Nigeria and Liberia, the
Chamber was totally unsuccessful. Permission to recruit
labour was refused 'owing to recent slavery and internal
dissensions'. Similarly, recruiting in Portuguese West
Africa was not possible, as the Portuguese claimed that
there was only sufficient labour there for the requirements of public works. South of Portuguese West Africa,
in German South West Africa, only 620 of the 1,000 men
for whom negotiations were made were recruited, and the
mine-owners considered these labourers to be 50 per cent
less efficient in drilling work than the local and Portuguese East African workers. (30) As for the labour of the
Cape Colony, these men had a 'rooted disinclination to go
underground' and only about 6,897 men were recruited from
this quarter during the whole of 1903. In Natal, Zululand
and Amatongaland the recruiting Association remained excluded from operating, despite efforts by the Chamber to
encourage the Natal authorities to repeal the 1901 Act
prohibiting recruitment for service in the Transvaal.

Little that was positive had emerged from the Chamber's
recruiting activities by the first quarter of 1903, therefore, and the position did not improve later on. The
monthly wastage of workers throughout 1903 exceeded even
the most pessimistic projections, and the resistance to
the WNLA's recruiting agents was described as 'disastrous'. 'No less than 55,509 ... left the service of the
companies as against 75,406 [who were] distributed through
the agency of WNLA.' (31) Recruiting agents had been
dispatched to Central, East, and South West Africa and to
other regions with very limited success. In 1903 the
monthly average of recruitment during January to April was
8,000, of whom over half came from Portuguese East Africa.
Numbers declined steadily during June, July and August of
that year and reached a trough period in December with
only 5,865 recruits. (32)

This decline occurred despite the penetration by the
Chamber of two out of the three extensive Portuguese
African territories under private charter. (33) The
Chamber believed the reason for the poor response in the
newly opened up areas of Portuguese East Africa and other
parts of the continent to be due to (i) lack of time and
organization; (ii) the fact that this very large population was as yet unaccustomed to wage labour. (34) If
the Chamber's drive towards recruitment was more than a
token attempt to satisfy its critics that African labour
was not available in sufficient numbers, the significance
of this diagnosis was that the mine-owners perceived the

shortage as temporary and remediable over time, rather
than the product of a fundamental resistance to work on
the mines. In general, however, the evidence would support Richardson's conclusion that

> Even making allowances for exaggeration of aims, and
> deliberate under-recruiting in 1903 to accentuate the
> claims for the Chinese, all figures indicate a serious
> labour supply situation. (35)

It seems unlikely that the WNLA's recruiting exertions
were merely for the record, i.e. that the Chamber was
simply going through the motions of 'scouring the continent' to satisfy its local critics and the Colonial
Secretary that 'the African population South of the
Zambesi did not comprise a sufficient number of adult
males ... to furnish an adequate amount of labour for the
mining companies' (see p.186). The monthly wastage of
workers throughout 1903 created great strains for managements and this, together with the general shortfall, must
have produced a sense of great urgency for an *immediate*
increase in the supply. It was this which had prompted
the Chamber, albeit reluctantly, to raise wages in 1903,
although this too was an interim measure. Wages were
reduced in June 1904 and again in December 1905. (36)
   The prolonged reduction of the wage rate between mid-
1901 and the latter part of 1903 was a determined exercise
by the Chamber to secure labour on its own terms and conditions in spite of the large unmet demands for labour by
the various managements: 'You cannot look for success or
failure to be settled in a month, or six months, in a
matter of this sort.' (37) What the Chamber failed to
achieve in 1903 it won in the year following the indenture
of Asian labour. By 1905 the impact of Chinese labour
plus the incidence of severe drought had served to break
Africans' resistance to work on the mines. In that year
the Chamber's labour demands were over-subscribed and men
flowed to the Rand on the Chamber's terms and conditions.
(38)
   The 1901-3 manipulation of the wage rate may therefore
be seen as the first step in the Chamber's post-war strategy for the defence of low-cost labour, and the importation of Chinese labour as the second move to the same end.
The merits of indentured labour as a means of increasing
the supply by '[driving] the Kaffir out to work at lower
rates of wages' was part of the debate in the turmoil of
1903. (39)
   When eighteen months after the war the Chamber moved
into action to reduce costs, it had in mind Asian inden-

tured labour and cast all its energies towards winning
support for that contentious proposal. In March 1903 it
raised the matter formally at the South African Customs
Union Conference in Bloemfontein, and obtained a resolution that left the way open for the extention of the
migrant system beyond the continent of Africa.

(iii)   THE CHAMBER AND THE TRANSVAAL LABOUR COMMISSION,
1903

The South African Customs Union Conference at Bloemfontein
concluded, on the Chamber's evidence, that

> the African population South of the Zambesi did not
> comprise a sufficient number of males capable of work
> to satisfy the normal requirement of the several colo-
> nies, and at the same time furnish an adequate amount
> of labour for the large industrial and mining compa-
> nies. (40)

Although the implication of the resolution was that indentured labour would be required if there were insufficient
resources in Southern and Central Africa, there was no
explicit approval for Asian migrants. According to Milner
the Bloemfontein Conference merely declared the introduction of Asiatics to be 'permissible'. 'Nobody present',
he told Chamberlain somewhat hypocritically, 'wanted
Asiatics, but everybody felt that in his own individual
case they might become necessary.' (41)
    The Chamber did not embark immediately on a scheme to
acquire this labour, but in view of the contentiousness of
the matter and Chamberlain's reservations it sought wider
support for its views. (42) The Transvaal Labour Commission, which was established in October 1903, might be
seen as part of this strategy, although the Commission
concerned itself with the labour shortage in all sectors
of the economy and not specifically with the mining industry, although the latter was the most important. The Commission's findings were, however, crucial to the Chamber
since, if favourable, they would give official sanction
to the mine-owners' labour policies and protect them from
their critics.
    Milner assisted the mine-owners in securing a favour-
able report by appointing (in the words of Hull in the
Transvaal Legislative Council) 'a vast majority of the
Commissioners [who] were in favour of the importation of
Chinese labour, and a small minority ... opposed to it'.
(43) Hull noted that

if the Government had been sincerely desirous of having
an independent and impartial enquiry, some arrangements
could have been made by which some of the Judges in
this country could have been appointed, or, if they
were too busy they could have obtained Judges from
England. (44)

Loveday, one of the four opponents of the Transvaal
Labour Ordinance, told the Legislative Council that 'it
was a great mistake that partisans should have been appointed to the commission'. (45) Of the twelve men invited to serve on the Commission, he cited George Farrar,
who had already publicly advocated the importation of
Asiatics, and Goch, Tainton and Phillips, who were members
of the Foreign Labour Association. In addition Loveday
noted Dodd and Farrow, both of whom had asked to address
a meeting in support of importing Chinese labour, and
Brink and Sam Evans, whose 'pro-Chinese proclivities were
well-known'. (46) The two other members of the Commission, Quinn and Whiteside, were outspokenly against
importation.
  The Chamber's critics claimed that the terms of reference of the Commission were also set up to suit the mine-
owners' case. Since the Commission was established after
the WNLA's negative recruiting campaign, there seems to
be much point in the accusation, especially since the
commissioners were required to inquire into what amount
of labour is necessary for the requirements of the agricultural, mining and other industries of the Transvaal
and to ascertain how far it is possible to obtain an
adequate supply of labour to meet such requirements from
Central and Southern Africa. (47)
  As the Chamber's recruiting agents had scoured the subcontinent and Central Africa before the Commission com-
menced proceedings, it knew that there was little likelihood of acquiring an adequate supply from these sources.
According to Loveday the Commission consisted of 'gentlemen who really had made up their minds that there was no
labour in South Africa, and that the introduction of
Chinese labour was the only solution'. (48) Notwithstanding the composition of the Commission and the fact
that the terms of reference were clearly favourable to
the Chamber, the mine-owners prepared a persuasive case
to be brought before the Commission, and the Executive
Committee of the Chamber presented an exhaustive statement
which became part of the evidence of the Commission's proceedings and, as we shall see, substantially influenced
its outcome.

(iv)   THE TRANSVAAL LABOUR COMMISSION: MAJORITY REPORT

The question of imported unskilled Asian labour loomed in
the background of the inquiry. The main challenge to the
Chamber (over which the Commission split into two groups)
(49) was the debate on the use of unskilled white labour
on the mines, a policy which the Chamber rejected and
wished to refute before it could embark on any serious
proposals for what had become its 'Chinese' alternative.
As 'eight or nine of the twelve commissioners, prior to
the commission's appointment, had expressed themselves in
favour of Chinese labour' (50) it is not surprising that
the Majority Report bore the stamp of the Chamber's evidence.
    The introduction to the Report cast the framework for
indentured labour by noting a spurious historical continuity with slavery in the country's labour shortages. It
linked the need for labour in the era of the mineral
revolution with the use of slaves and the Natal Colony's
indenture of Asian labour in 1860: 'the labour trouble
in its present form is a growth of the past half century.
... Up to 1835 slave labour was extensively employed in
South Africa and the labour difficulty ... has arisen
since that date.' (51) In general the Majority Report
emphasized the need for the development of 'new spheres
of recruiting operations', (52) which endorsed the Chamber's view that there was no 'adequate supply of labour
in central and southern Africa', (53) thus providing the
Chamber with the official sanction it needed.
    The reasons given for the dearth of labour in the mines
were cultural and economic and related to communications
to the mines from various parts of Africa. (54) The
Report concluded that these areas, especially Central
Africa, had never produced 'any large supply of labour
except in the form of slave labour', and several of the
states of this region had had to import men from outside
South Africa. As for Africa south of latitude 22, there
were, in the Commission's view, not more than 10,000
labourers who could be procured at any one time from the
Transkeian territories or Basutoland and Swaziland, and
even then 'their recruitment would [deprive] other territories of labour which they need'. (55) As for Portuguese
East Africa, which in the pre-war period had yielded
80,000 of the 110,000 African mineworkers, it was unlikely
that the previous record of 8,000 men per annum would be
maintained. (56) The reason for this was deemed to be
inherent in the migrant movement rather than due to any
organizational deficiency in the WNLA search for labour
or the African resistance to mining: 'any district whose

labour resources have been exploited for a number of years must tend after a certain maximum is reached, gradually to decrease until the flow and ebb to and from the labour markets equalize each other'. (57) Thus once again the conclusion pointed towards 'exhaustion' of the market available - albeit a temporary phenomenon, but carrying the strong implication that the development of new resources, outside Africa, was required. This is in fact what the Chamber itself had said.

Relying heavily on the evidence of the mine-owners, the Commission rejected the charge made against the Chamber that the labour shortage had been 'the outcome of design' or that it was due to 'superficial and non-essential causes which could have been readily obviated by well-directed efforts'. (58) On the contrary, the Commission found the causes of scarcity to be 'deep-seated' and numerous but not necessarily permanent.

(i) Africans were for the most part from 'primitive, pastoral or agricultural communities, who possess exceptional facilities for the regular and full supply of their animal wants and whose standard of economic needs is extremely low'. (59)

(ii) The rise of industries in South Africa had created the need for industrial workers. The resources to fulfil these needs were to be acquired from 'among nomadic or pastoral peoples who (until recently) were ignorant of the uses of money' and who could not suddenly be drawn into the industrial labour market. (60) 'The only pressing needs of a savage are those of food and sex, and the conditions of native life in Africa are such that these are as a rule easily supplied.' (61)

(iii) The labour dearth prevailed because of the nature of the tribal land system of South and Central Africa, which made the African 'independent of wages' and placed him 'outside the industry'.

(iv) Despite these unfavourable conditions the labour market should not be seen as permanently inadequate, for Africans were becoming consumer conscious. They were not static in their wants, for contact with whites had caused them to 'acquire habits and wants which will increase that demand for money, and will, therefore, impel them to labour more continuously than at present'. (62)

(v) So-called non-economic causes of the deficiency in the supply were to be found in the customs and characters of the various peoples.

In respect of the first of these causes, it should be
noted that the 'low standard of economic need' was the
factor which made this labour force attractive to the
Chamber. The high wants of Greek, Italian, Hungarian -
or Afrikaner - labour would inflate the costs of production. (63) But this is not what the commissioners wished
to stress. By referring to the easy satisfaction of
'animal wants', it seems, they were in an oblique way
trying to emphasize the tenacity of Africans in the rural
areas in providing for their own subsistence rather than
seeking a cash wage on the mines. The commissioners'
formulation of the problem compares with what Meillassoux
has described as attributing problems in development 'to
the sexual incontinence of the natives or to their devious
mentality'. (64)

Meillassoux's point is that such an analysis generally
conceals, or reveals, a failure to perceive the real situation and leads towards a contradictory conception of undeveloped countries as separate from the developed economies, yet blending into them: '[The undeveloped countries
are seen] as dual economies consisting of two different
and non-communicating sectors and that the primitive
sector is slowly blending into the capitalist one.' (65)

The Transvaal Labour Commission was careful to draw attention to the dynamic character of the impact of the
developed sectors on the 'traditional' African economies
(where 'contact with whites' - i.e. with the capitalist
sector - had caused the inhabitants to 'acquire habits
and wants which will increase that demand for money, and
will, therefore, impel them to labour more continuously
than at present'), but was somewhat inconsistent (in
Meillassoux's sense) in describing the tribal land system
as placing Africans 'outside the industry' and 'independent of wages'. (66) This statement was especially
misleading as close on 100,000 Africans had actually been
engaged in the industry in 1899, and many times that
number had passed through the mines between 1887 and 1903,
the year of the Commission's Report. It would seem that
in arguing   was in essence the Chamber's case, the
commissioners were anxious not to discourage the flow of
capital to the mines or give any untoward impression that
an adequate supply of labour was not strictly speaking on
tap in Africa, and yet were also anxious to make a special
plea for indentured labour. Hence Africans were referred
to rather curiously more as potential labourers than as
the present mainstay of the industry, and their 'reluctance' to enter the labour market was one more reason for
the indenture of Asian labour. Furthermore, the 'extremely low' standard of economic need and continued access to

land would, in the Commission's view, prolong their entry
in sufficient numbers into the labour market.

The Commission was, in fact, ambivalent about the attention paid by witnesses to suggested modifications of
the system of land tenure, (67) and eventually agreed that
no changes should be recommended in the industrial habits
of African peasant communities 'until a great modification
of [their] conditions had been brought about'. (68) This
view was consistent with the Chamber's, i.e. that 'until
the African economy progressed, the labour surplus to be
drawn on must be on the whole small and subject to season-
al variations in crops or changes in the pastoral wealth
of the tribe'. (69) The word 'progressed' is ambiguous.
The Commission seems to have meant both an increase in the
demand for manufactured commodities and a decreasing capacity of African economies to provide a sufficient surplus to satisfy these wants. Both factors would ultimately increase the labour supply to be drawn to the mines.
The fourth point made by the Commission amplified this
point as well as pointing to the corrosive effect of the
capitalist sector on the African economies: Africans were
becoming increasingly 'consumer conscious'. This was sub-
stantiated by official reports from Natal and Basutoland.
The evidence showed that in the case of Natal the importation of manufactured goods rose from £140,082 in 1894 to
£271,450 in 1902. In the case of Basutoland, which was
an important area for the Rand, since labour was sought
from this area, the population was equally consumer-
oriented. Here the importation of manufactured goods had
fluctuated between £93,615 and £135,560 between 1893 and
1899, indicating great possibilities for increases in the
numbers entering the labour market. (70) Elsewhere the
demand for manufactured articles was smaller, but would
doubtless expand. The greater the demand, the Chamber
believed, the greater would be the economic compulsion
on Africans to enter the labour market. But, for the
present, the needs of the mines could not be met wholly
in Africa, and further extra-economic measures would at
this stage be counter-productive of the supply. (71)

Vast unsubstantiated claims were made on the fifth
point, regarding culture: e.g. that (i) industry was
regarded with aversion and thought to be degrading among
the warlike; (ii) other types of Africans avoided certain
classes of labour, mining being one such class (exempt
from this generalization were the Portuguese East Africans, who proved the exception to the rule); (iii) some
tribes in Central Africa 'refused to perform any kind of
work at all', and where cattle was an element it was a
further disturbing factor; (iv) custom prevented men over

forty and boys under fifteen years from working, which
restricted employment 'to one half of the native male
population'. (72) In fact, although there may have been
some substance to these statements, many of these claims
masked the much wider question, structural and otherwise,
of the continued accessibility to land; and on the mines
to the wages, the nature of the work, conditions, health,
diet, compound control and labour relations. All these
determined the response of potential recruits to urban
work and especially work on the mines. (73)
   This review of the labour market, which seems to have
been intended to clear the Chamber of the accusation that
it had 'designed' the shortage, also gave pointed support
to the promotion of Asian labour and consequently the
extension of the migrant system. Basically, the Commission sought the principal causes of the supply problem in
what it described as the conditions affecting 'the home
and the kraal' (74) rather than the rate of wages, working
conditions, industrial relations, means of communication,
compound management, and health and sanitation on the
mines, although it certainly believed these factors to
influence the supply. (75) The latter approach was taken
to some extent by the two members of the Commission who
submitted a Minority Report with alternative proposals.
(76) They objected to the reliance placed by the Commission on the extensive evidence submitted by the Chamber,

> an institution whose functions are to watch over the
> shareholders in mining companies.... It is therefore
> obvious that in carrying out their duties as guardians
> of the financial interests of people living outside
> this Colony the function of the Chamber is to see that
> the mines under their control pay the largest dividends
> possible to their absentee principals and this without
> any regard to any local feeling and opinion. (77)

(v)   THE MINORITY REPORT: THE WHITE UNSKILLED LABOUR
DEBATE

(a) The supply

Although the opponents of the Chamber's Asian labour
scheme confronted the mine-owners with intricate economic
evidence to support their case for the extended use of
white unskilled labour, they also used arguments of an
ideological (racial) character. In the view of Quinn and

Whiteside, who prepared the Minority Report, the policy
of the Chamber was to perpetuate 'the inferior race labour
system by the importation of Asiatics' rather than to
develop 'the growth of a large working population'. (78)

Yet despite this ideological emphasis, there was an
acute consciousness of the cost and profit factors which
led the Chamber to establish its particular type of labour
structure. It became the practice during the crisis
period of 1903-4, and later, for various interested persons to offer alternative combinations of the division of
labour on the mines that would provide for the profitable
organization of the labour process. They were primarily
plans to accommodate a substantial number of unskilled
whites in the industry's labour structure. It was with
these economic calculations that the Minority commissioners concerned themselves.

They attached much importance to the evidence of
W.Wybergh (a member of the Chamber's Executive Committee)
and W.Grant (Native Labour Commissioner to the Chamber
from 1895 to 1899), whose testimonies were given, they
believed, only 'casual' attention by the Majority commissioners. Their contention was that the Chamber had
deliberately exaggerated the labour shortage to strengthen
their case for the importation of Asians. It had over-
stated by 50 per cent the number of Africans required to
work per stamp on the mines, and had also ignored the
evidence 'that mines in other countries are worked with
less than half the number of labourers with greater economy', suggesting instead that it was only with cheap
coloured labour that they could be worked profitably at
all. (79)

Quinn and Whiteside's Report disputed the basis of the
Chamber's case and charged the mine-owners with intransi-
gence in their attitude towards lessening their dependence
on African labourers. (80) They felt that 'given the
desire' there were good prospects (i) for decreasing the
mine-owners' dependence on these labourers; (ii) for improving methods and machinery; and (iii) for extending
the use of white labour to satisfy the demand for workers
in unskilled categories. (81) Their statements were supported, on the whole, by evidence from three separate
sources:

  (i) from three important witnesses to the Commission:
       Price, Spencer and Skinner;
 (ii) from certain expert witnesses of the Chamber before
       the late Republic's Industrial Commission of 1897;
(iii) from independent (i.e. not the Chamber's) witnesses
       such as Stuart, Ingle and Creswell. All of these

gave statements which ran counter to the Chamber's
submissions.

The urgency of the supply situation was also disputed,
and the Minority commissioners rejected the alarmist conclusions of their peers, stating: 'we should prefer to
put it that a rapidly increasing supply from time to time
lagged behind a rapidly increasing demand.' They maintained that the mine-owners had previously overcome their
labour shortages and at times - in 1895 and 1897 - enjoyed
a surplus, while in 1892 and 1897 'reductions were successfully effected'. (82) The implication was that the
Chamber had emphasized the shortages and glossed over the
brief pre-war occasions when supply was satisfied in order
to strengthen its case in defending its labour structure
and gaining support for the importation of Asian labour.
In their own way the Minority commissioners were equally guilty of exaggeration, since they were committed to
emphasizing the Chamber's successes in labour recruitment
in order to narrow the dimension of the shortfall between
supply and demand and to promote the case for the use of
white labour. In general the Majority Report was correct
when it stated that shortages were chronic 'except at one
or two rare intervals'. (83)
The problem was, to some extent, one of numbers. Both
Reports accepted that labour was in short supply, and the
question revolved around the extent to which the situation
demanded an infusion of indentured labourers. The Minority members queried the dimension of the shortfall and opposed the Majority belief that the importation of labour
would increase the supply by '[driving] the Kaffir out to
work at lower rates of wages'. (84) They believed this
to be a miscalculation of the market situation and cited
the case of Natal, where the importation of Asian labour
had not increased the supply of African labour for agriculture. Indeed, they believed that 'the most effective
inducement [to enter the labour market] is a high rate of
wage'. (85) But the way to alleviate the labour problem
was by the employment of whites in unskilled capacities.
In 1904 approximately 1,000 whites carried out work performed only by Africans before the war, mainly in the
'rough timbering' jobs. This process had begun at the
end of 1901 and was a function of the shortage of black
unskilled labour. What the Minority commissioners wanted
was an extension of this ad hoc 'temporary' solution to a
position of principle. (86)

(b) The case for and against white unskilled labour

The Minority disputed the Chamber's contention that the
grade of ore in some mines was too low to be worked
profitably other than 'by the agency of cheap coloured
labour'. The Chamber, they averred (correctly), had presented two inconsistent views - one in 1897 before the
late Republic's Industrial Commission and the other before
the present inquiry. The reason for this discrepancy was,
they felt, the mine-owners' desire to emphasize their
Asian alternative to the use of white men in the unskilled
occupations. With this aim in view the Chamber told the
Commission:

   (i) 'that the grade of ore in the Rand mines was so low
       that they did not bear comparison with other mines,
       the problem being "how to extract that value at a
       cost which will leave a significant margin of
       profit"'. (87)
  (ii) that if white labour was employed at 12s. per day
       and each white worker performed double the amount
       of work done by an unskilled African labourer, the
       cost of production would still be increased by
       10s. 1d. per ton; (88)
 (iii) that there were 79 crushing companies treating low-
       grade yields. If whites replaced black labourers
       in any of these companies, 48 would be working at
       a loss 'and the profits of the remaining 31 would
       be very materially reduced'. (89)
  (iv) that the notion that the white mining men could
       perform twice the labour of black miners was
       'entirely erroneous', since 'as a muscular machine,
       the best developed native - (when he had remained
       long enough at the mines to be thoroughly trained)
       is the equal of the white man'. (90)

   The credibility of this evidence was strongly con-
tested, since it conflicted with the Chamber's testimony
before the Industrial Commission, when it had taken the
opposite view and emphasized the common elements in mining
on the Rand and in America. On that occasion the Chamber
had stated:

   The natural conditions and circumstances under which
   this mining is prosecuted may well be compared with
   those surrounding and affecting the cost of working
   auriferous lodes, veins or ledges in the Rocky Moun-
   tains and Pacific Slope States of America. The methods
   of mining and reducing the banket ores here are practi-

cally the same as those followed in American quartz
mining. (91)

In 1903 the Chamber refused to entertain any comparisons.
According to the earlier evidence the Californian mines
were manned by white labourers and employed between six
and eight men per stamp. (92) The wages paid to them were
slightly half the average paid to white labour in South
Africa, and considerably less than half for work comparable to that done by Africans on the Rand. As a result
'mines which would just about pay operating expenses on
the Rand are made to yield a large profit in California'.
(93)
    The Chamber's rejection of any comparison with other
mining experience - both in its Statement and in its
Evidence to the Labour Commission - was treated with the
utmost suspicion by Quinn and Whiteside, who saw it as a
deliberate attempt to mislead the Commission. The mine-
owners handled the issue of white unskilled labour with
little subtlety, and the General Manager of East Rand
Proprietory Mines expressed almost exclusively racial
reasons for the incomparability of white and black labour
when he presented the Chamber's views on the subject.
When wishing to be evasive the Chamber could easily be as
racialistic in attitude as its opponents. When asked why
white labour could not be employed on the mines in South
Africa as economically as in the USA, Canada or Australia,
the following explanations were offered:

  (i) the white worker in South Africa 'is entirely de-
      moralized by the presence of the Kaffir'. Because
      whites are given African men to work with them,
      their efficiency 'is unquestioningly very much lower
      than in the corresponding trades in other coun-
      tries'.
 (ii) the white man 'expects the Kaffir to do work to
      which he is not accustomed and of course he does it
      very slowly, the result is that neither does very
      much'.
(iii) South Africa has no large number of labourers who
      are 'accustomed to toil with their hands and to work
      hard'.
 (iv) the cost of living is too high. 'The average wage
      earned per month by an unskilled worker has been
      (over 13 months) £15 or 9/10 per day. In order to
      keep costs where they are on the basis of Kaffir
      labour, the white man must do the work of 3.145
      Kaffirs. Men who can do that will not come here for
      10/- per day as long as [the cost of living] is so
      high.' (94)

This last statement had some realistic bearing on the situation, especially in view of the experimentation currently being undertaken. The greatest factor, relative to wages, was the difference between those items concerned with the cost of subsistence of the white unskilled miner - which, unlike the practice with the black miner, included the cost of family, more expensive quartering, and welfare. Not only did the migrant system reduce the cost of these items, but the contract system plus control in the compound and in the work situation made Africans 'ultra-exploitable' compared to unskilled white labour. (95) Hence the Chamber's reference to high 'white' expectations and '[white] demoralization by the presence of the Kaffir' served only to mystify and explained very little of the true nature of the mine-owners' labour strategies.

The Minority commissioners were also suspicious of the experiments conducted by the Chamber in 1902 and 1903 in which the muscular efficiency of white unskilled workers was compared - unfavourably - with that of Africans. (96) The experiments were performed in order to ascertain whether whites could perform at the same intensity as the blacks, but the Minority was suspicious of the Chamber's sincerity in this respect. They quoted the testimony of one of the mining engineers:

> the question as to whether white labour could be employed or whether local coloured labour would be employed or whether it would be obtained elsewhere, depends entirely upon the wishes of mine owners. Primarily they have their say and if they say to their engineers 'we wish you to make a very great effort to have white labour on the mines, and the man who can show us how to use white labour will be well rewarded', then I think very good efforts would be made to use white labour and that it might be successful. (97)

The mine-owners were not, in fact, disposed to extensive experimentation with white unskilled labour, because they believed that as a general principle the replacement of African labour by white would mean the 'cessation of profitable work in most of the mines on the Witwatersrand'. (98)   This had been their view in 1902 when the Special Committee considered the post-war labour shortages, and their view remained unchanged when experimentation took place less than a year later. The Special Committee had noted:

> the policy of replacing unskilled African workers by

whites was to be deprecated as a 'universal' principle but might be applied on the assumption that [African labour] procurable falls far short of the present. Native labour ... is much the cheapest and most profitable. (99)

In effect the type of experimentation that was undertaken was irrelevant, as the factors which increased the costs of production had so little to do with labour efficiency, since the major concern was rent, housing and welfare. But the Chamber was prepared for the less sympathetic evidence of F.H.P.Creswell, manager of the Village Main Reef mine, who favoured extending the employment of white labour 'throughout all the gold mines' on the Witwatersrand. (100)

Creswell's experiments largely ignored such cost factors as rent, housing and welfare (101) and concentrated on the cost per tonnage of ore mined by the white unskilled labourers during an experimental period underground at the Village Main Reef mine. According to these experiments, with one white worker receiving a wage of 12s. per day and doing the work of two Africans, the cost of ore mined was 3s. 9.5d. per ton, compared to the pre-war figure of 7s. 0.6d. (102) Since the latter figure did not take into account the lower costs of dynamite and the lower pre-war African wage rate, Creswell estimated that the *African* pre-war rate would have been 6s. 4.4d. per ton of ore mined, i.e. 5.1d. less than the cost of unskilled *white* labourers. But with an improvement in organization, differences would, he thought, be negligible and white labour would be shown to be as profitable as African unskilled labour. (103) However, the cost analysis was highly unscientific. The calculations of the work of one unskilled labourer to two Africans were made by the Chamber's consulting engineers and were theoretical and arbitrary. According to the general manager of East Rand Proprietary Mines, basing his evidence on post-war costs, an African unskilled worker earned an average of 9s. 10d. per day and an equivalence of 3.145 whites were required to replace him. (104) Generally speaking the exercise in comparative muscle-power produced highly impressionistic calculations. (105)

The main objection to Creswell's experimentation, however, is that it was deficient in the most crucial aspect. It failed to acknowledge that the rate of wages was determined not by productivity but by 'rent costs and conditions of living' - factors which the Majority commissioners were quick to point out:

The evidence of the past is 'overwhelmingly and conclusively against the contention that white labourers
can successfully compete with black in the lower fields
of manual industry'. According to the Commissioners,
the only evidence in support of white unskilled labour
was submitted by Creswell, whose 'figures were disputed
by competent witnesses' and his experiment was not
carried out under test conditions. *More specially the
rate of wages was determined by 'rents, costs and conditions of living - variations which completely alter
all the factors of the experiment'.* (106)

He also made use of experimental conditions which un-
realistically inflated the intensity of white supervisory
labour. (107)

There were several other anomalies which diminished any
universal value Creswell's experiments might have had. Of
these, the most glaring was a short-circuiting of the
sorting process, and the selection of the most easily
worked stopes along the richer South Reef portion of the
mine. (108) Since the Village Main Reef mine was among
the six most advantaged mines, yielding 50s. per ton on
the most easily worked stopes, the experiments there were
not helpful in establishing the cost of extensive white
employment on the less favourable mines. After examining
the details of Creswell's experiments, Jennings, the
Chamber's chief consulting engineer, concluded that he
had incurred a loss of £7,840 over the nine months ending
December 1902. This was in line with the general experience of the five other mines besides Creswell's in which
labour experiments had been conducted. (109)

The mines concerned were the Crown Reef, East Rand
Group, George Goch, Lancaster, and Geduld Proprietary
Mines. The comments of the experimenters were significantly different from Creswell's on these mines. The
manager of the Central Geduld Mining Co. Ltd, for example,
noted that for pick and shovel work whites were more efficient, but 'as soon as ordinary sinking or mining conditions occur they are not more than equal to the work of
one Kaffir who would be more reliable and under better
control, and I would certainly prefer the Kaffir'. (110)
The latter point is important for, whatever the comparative rate of efficiency in the performance of white unskilled labourers, under these particular conditions of
experimentation white workers were not subject to the same
measure of discipline and coercion as the Africans, which
in work of this nature must have had an important long-
term bearing on output. Indeed, it is more than likely
that the results of the muscle-power exerted by whites in

all Creswell's experiments were heavily inflated. At best
there was always the chance of an unskilled man being
elevated to a skilled position if he satisfied his superiors during the experiment, and at the least there was the
opportunity of retaining a temporary livelihood. (111)   In
addition, one other factor that was totally misleading
about the experiments - on both sides - was that comparisons on efficiency were being made with African performance before the war, when liquor seriously decreased
the general level of efficiency. (112)

In general the Chamber made full use of the experiments
to thwart the threat that the extensive use of unskilled
white labour might pose to its carefully balanced distribution of labour costs. There was, to say the least,
clearly no great incentive on the part of those involved
in the Chamber's experiments to prove a high quality in
white labour. As we noted above: 'the question as to
whether white labour could be employed or whether local
coloured labour would be employed or ... obtained elsewhere, depends entirely upon the wishes of mine owners'.
(113)

The mine-owners, however, had acted on certain aspects
of the recommendations of its Special Committee to extend
opportunities of employment to a proportion of unskilled
white workers in certain categories of work. (114)   The
aim was a limited one to reduce costs and replenish the
skilled white miners from local sources by training local
unskilled white labourers as apprentices to 'learn while
they earned' - at unskilled rates. These men were little
different from, and possibly less experienced than, the
African attendants they were able to 'release ... on the
carpenters', fitters' and blacksmiths' shops'. (115)   This
extension of unskilled work to white miners served (to use
Hay's phrase) to provide 'a fund of unskilled labour' to
increase the quantity of skilled labour power on the Rand.
(116)   It was not a move to replace Africans by white unskilled labourers as a general rule. In this respect the
Chamber shared the view of its Special Committee that such
replacement was to be 'deprecated as a "universal" principle'. (117)

However, although this committee emphasized its rejection in principle of the substitution of white for black
workers, it produced a contingency plan should 'the supply
fall far short of the present'. Notwithstanding the rejection of these proposals in principle by the Chamber,
the Minority commissioners seized upon the 'contingency'
plans as a realistic scheme for the employment of an extended number of white unskilled labour on the mines. The
contingency plan formulated by the Special Committee pro-

vided for the extensive use of white labour in unskilled
occupations, especially in rock drilling, where there was
a steady demand, and as, for example, plate-layers, pipemen's helpers and station loaders. (118) White men were
also recommended for work on the surface of the mine as
engineers' assistants and cleaners, or in the mills. They
might also be employed at a low initial wage around
crusher stations and at sorting tables. (119) The recommendations went on to suggest that properly indentured
white apprentices might also 'release to a certain extent
the native attendants on the carpenters', fitters' and
blacksmiths' shops', (120) while mechanical labour-saving
devices could considerably reduce 'the present high estimate of the needs of the industry as regards native
labour'. (121)

The Minority commissioners made much use of this plan.
They were also anxious to utilize the evidence given by
the Chamber to the Industrial Commission of Enquiry in
1897, and somewhat paradoxically based their conclusions
on the Chamber's evidence before that Commission rather
than the Labour Commission. This was because the evidence
to the Industrial Commission supported their aim of employing an additional 3,750 whites (122) who, they maintained, would derive 'an immense benefit [from] such employment', especially 'when so much is heard of the number
of white men who are in want of work'. (123) They assessed the 'actual legitimate requirements' of the gold-
mining industry in 1903 at 75,000, which estimate con-
trasted sharply with the official figure, in the Majority
Report, of 129,000. Quinn and Whiteside attributed this
disparity in the evidence to the overwhelming influence
of the Chamber upon the Commission. Indeed, it was their
contention that it was on the evidence of the Chamber of
Mines that the Bloemfontein Conference in March 1903 had
resolved that 'the number of native male adults south of
the Zambesi is insufficient to satisfy normal requirements', (124) and that it was this resolution that had
dictated the terms of the present Commission. They
believed that there was a dearth in the supply, but for
very different reasons than those given by the Chamber.
These were:

   (i) 'that the present so-called shortage in the Trans-
        vaal is largely due to temporary and preventable
        causes';
  (ii) 'that there is sufficient labour in central and
        southern Africa for present requirements' although
        efforts will be required to obtain this labour;
 (iii) '... that there is ... sufficient labour in the
        territories for future requirements';

(iv) 'that in many ways the supply of native labour can
be supplemented and superseded by white labour'.
(125)

Paradoxically, it was largely because the Chamber appears to have shared three out of the four conclusions of
the Minority Report that it did not wish to adopt the last
conclusion, which involved an extensive alteration in the
existing labour arrangements.

(vi)   THE OFFICIAL REJECTION OF WHITE UNSKILLED LABOUR

The Majority commissioners (not unexpectedly) supported
the status quo in the labour structure and rejected in
principle the employment of white labour in unskilled
capacities on the following grounds, all of which were
based on their total confidence in the rationality of
the Chamber's past policies: (126)

(i) White men had not been used for the 'rougher classes
of manual work' during the period of mining or industrial activity on the Rand. As whites had not
been used it was to be concluded that such employment was uneconomical.
(ii) Had white labour been desirable there would have
been 'a gradual displacement of black by white
labour'. The facts showed that 'a contrary displacement of white by black' had occurred. (127)
(iii) The evidence of the past was 'overwhelmingly and
conclusively against the contention that white
labour can successfully compete with black'; more
specially the rate of wages was determined by
'rents, costs and conditions of living ... variations which completely alter all the factors of
[Creswell's] experiment'. (128)

The acceptance of the Chamber's evidence was reflected
unambiguously in the Commission's conclusions. These
were, briefly, as follows:

(i) The demand for African labour in agriculture,
mining, the railways and Transvaal industries was
greatly in excess of supply - and demand would increase with the advancement of mining and agriculture;
(ii) 'whilst no complete data of the future requirements
of the whole of the industry are obtainable, it is
estimated that the mines of the Witwatersrand alone

will require, within the next five years, an additional supply of 196,000 labourers'. (129)
(iii) there was no 'adequate supply of labour in central
and southern Africa' to meet these requirements.
(130)

These findings were thoroughly consistent with points i,
iv and v of the Chamber's 'conclusions':

  (i) a large number of unskilled labourers were required
for the mineral fields and to develop future industries;
(iv) the existing recruiting fields were 'almost or quite
exhausted' and new or other fields were either not
open or could not be developed for a number of years;
  (v) the use of (white) unskilled labour was 'economically
impossible'. (131)

    Thus the Commission made the Chamber's view official.
This measure of state co-operation in securing the industry's labour supply from abroad (in the numbers determined
by the Chamber) was to have far-reaching consequences for
the African labour force. For the moment, however, the
Chamber assessed its short- and long-term labour needs in
the light of its current situation. It calculated the
industry's immediate needs for unskilled labourers at
129,588 and projected that a further 368,637 men would be
required in the following five years. (132) The Chamber
probably believed it would eventually acquire this workforce from various areas in southern Africa which it saw
as the mines' 'principal and natural' labour market with
a potential labour force of over 6 million men. But until
such time as this workforce could be released in the
numbers required and on the contract terms set out by the
mine-owners, an 'extra-territorial' migrant labour force
from Asia would have to 'fill the gap'. The merit of
Asian labour was that it would augment the weak supply in
1903, make wage cuts possible, and in the long run weaken
the African's 'commanding' position in the labour market.
(133) The African labour markets the Chamber had in mind
are listed in Table 12.1.
    This resource of 13.5 million potential labourers
should have been a cause for optimism for the mine-owners,
who were looking towards a sizeable workforce which was
procurable not only at an 'economic wage' but also close
at hand. The question, however, was how soon this low-
cost labour force would be available to industry. In its
evidence to the Labour Commission the Chamber (avoiding
the issue of the condition of African agriculture) noted

TABLE 12.1 Principal labour markets in South and Central
Africa (134)

Area	Number	Source
Cape Colony	1,652,036	Govt 30.6.1903
Natal	791,010	'Blue Book 1902'
Orange River Colony	129,787	Colonial Secretary 2.8.1903
Southern Rhodesia	563,271	Native Comm. 1903
German South West Africa	300,000	Consul General
Bechuanaland Protectorate	147,000	Resident Comm. 11.8.1903
Swaziland	60,000	Sir G.Lagden
Basutoland	262,561	Sir G.Lagden
Transvaal	605,666	Sir G.Lagden
Portuguese East Africa (Southern provinces)	1,815,180	Breyner and Wirth official figures
Total	6,326,511	
Northern Rhodesia	556,000	Maj. Croydon and 'Statesman's Year Book'
British Central Africa	± 900,000	'State Year Book 1903'
Uganda Protectorate	4,000,000	'State Year Book 1903'
Portuguese East Africa (Northern Province)	1,815,180	
Total	7,271,180	
GRAND TOTAL		13,597,691

Source: 'Transvaal Labour Commission Minority Report',
para. 60.

that Africans in South Africa were more likely to respond
to the prospect of industrial labour than those in Central
Africa, since they had come into contact with whites, had
acquired new habits, tasks, and wants, and had become ac-
customed to regarding industrial labour as the means by
which these wants might be met. (135)   The position was
quite different in Central Africa, where the inhabitants
had as yet no notion of the meaning of industrial work.
Until they had 'acquired wants beyond bare subsistence and
the habit of working in order to supply them, they would
not form an important source of labour'. (136)   In the
event, speculation of this sort could be abandoned, for
the impact of Chinese labour served to restore the supply
and fulfil the labour demand on the mines within a few
years of the scheme's introduction. (See Chapter 15, pp.
242-3.)   In this respect Arrighi's cautionary remarks
about the importance of considering political mechanisms
to increase the pace of the development of the African
wage labour force are highly significant. (137)   In the
present instance the state not only intervened to 'expand
the supply of labour to match demand at [the] customary
level of wages', but (as we shall see) also considered
land and tax measures to secure the labour requirements
at the 'customary wage'.

(vii)   LAND, TAX AND THE LABOUR SUPPLY

The witnesses who appeared before the Labour Commission
mainly recommended schemes of 'compulsion, either direct
or indirect' (138) to improve the labour supply. Not
least of these schemes were 'modifications' of the African
tribal system and changes in African land tenure.   Evidence was presented which favoured 'measures which would
compel the native to work', either by requiring from him
a certain measure of labour annually, or by such drastic
changes in his condition as would have the same effect.
(139)   The Commission totally rejected these particular
remedies, however, stating (without explanation) that the
consequences of compulsory labour were prejudicial to employer and employee and created huge social problems.   Although it did not specify what these social problems would
be, more than likely the Commission had in mind the effects compulsion might have on the traditional sectors of
the economy which supported the system of migrant labour.
    The Commission also discussed a proposition for the
imposition of higher taxes.   Basically, it seems, it
believed the value of taxation at that stage to be over-
estimated. (140)   The commissioners had arrived at this

conclusion as a result of the observation by witnesses
that Africans responded to pressures of taxation by
raising their output of agricultural produce, i.e. they
rented arable land from private landowners in order to
meet their tax commitments by increasing output. (141)
The additional rent, therefore, was effectively a voluntary tax which Africans found preferable to migration.
(142) Thus the Commission's view was that at least for
Transvaal Africans the taxes of £2 per head, and £2 (for
polygamists) on each wife, were ineffective as means of
drawing men into the industry as long as they remained in
possession 'of what is practically an unlimited amount of
land'. (143)

The policy adopted was therefore a cautious one, for an
increase in taxation might not produce an increase in the
supply of labour. As taxes were applied indiscriminately,
the system might either lead to an extension of the
acreage under cultivation or serve in certain circumstances to weaken the traditional economies' capacities
to reproduce the workforce or provide the required welfare. (144) It was a risky measure. Moreover, the effects of the existing tax system had still to be gauged.
In the event, the Commission addressed itself to the continued access of Africans to productive land and considered the introduction of legislation to modify the system of
African land tenure. In the Commission's view, so long as
an African 'could meet his wants and his small money-need
by the sale of the produce of his land, industry would
continue to experience a shortfall in its labour force'.
(145) Whilst changes in land tenure were important, they
would take time to yield results, and should be applied
generally throughout South Africa. (146) The proposed
modifications which the Commission anticipated, would substantially change the relative capacity of Africans to
resist recruitment to the farms, mines and the collateral
concerns, and would therefore have to await the political
union of the territories of British South Africa before
they could be introduced. (147)

The idea of expropriating African land and handing it
over to whites for settlement was eschewed by the Commission. This would have been tantamount to what was described at the time as 'abrogating the African tribal
system' (148) - possibly meaning that it would interfere
with the ability of the extended family in the traditional
economies to provide the social security functions which
the mine-owners themselves preferred not to assume. (149)
The Commission opposed any measures which would 'weaken or
destroy the existing bases of native security'. Hence it
did nothing to tamper with the system, recommending

measures to conserve rather than destroy it. In the view
of the Commission 'communal responsibility was an advantage which should be strengthened rather than weakened'. (150) As we saw in Chapter 11 (p.150), this was the
policy which had already been followed by Lagden immediately he assumed office, and was the subject of his
instructions to the five native commissioners under his
authority. Under Lagden's administration, existing laws
and procedure were to be followed and no changes in succession to land were to be sanctioned without reference
to him. (151) African law and custom were therefore afforded official recognition, as were the various territories of African occupation and to some extent the
authority and powers of the chiefs within those territories.

The Commission also opposed the creation of stable
urban African communities (as suggested by the Bloemfontein Conference) for the reason that 'its consequent
evils would outweigh its advantageous effect on the labour
supply'. (152) The evils were not spelt out, but both
these proposals (on the abrogation of the tribal system
and the creation of an African urban community) were antithetical to the wage and labour structure of the mining
industry - and the commissioners promptly rejected them.
They noted cautiously on the former that 'marriage and
family ties, native laws of succession, inheritance,
ownership are bound up indissolubly with the existing
tenure of land and native tribal system, and to weaken or
destroy the existing bases of native society involves
social consequences of the gravest and most far reaching
character'. (153)

The reluctance at that time to deal decisively with the
source of the industry's labour shortage - the continuing
access of Africans to productive land - reflected the
over-riding importance that the mine-owners' spokesmen
attached to preventing the weakening of 'the existing
bases of native society' lest this should undermine their
low-cost labour system. One 'strategic problem' arising
from this policy of conservation, as Wolpe points out for
the later period, was 'the necessity to maintain production in the Reserves at a level which, while not too low
to contribute to the reproduction of migrant workers as a
class, is yet not high enough to remove the economic im-
peratives of migration'. (154)

The response of the Labour Commission, in the specific
conditions of 1903, was to avoid the adoption of any
measures which would intensify this dilemma. It therefore
did not recommend any far-reaching transformation of African economies, and rejected any formidable changes in

favour of 'minor remedies' such as the prevention of
squatting, improving the means of communication to and
from the Rand, increasing the quality of food on the
mines, and introducing yet shorter periods of service.
(155) Together it was thought all these measures might
have a 'beneficent effect on the supply'.

It was not until the next decade, seven years after the
ending of Asian labour importation, that the state intervened to provide a structure for the African areas that
would maintain a level of production which would not
impair the African contribution to the social security of
migrant workers, and at the same time would not be so high
as to reduce the 'push' factors which sent men to the
mines for a cash wage to pay their taxes and buy those
wants for which the African economies produced an insufficient surplus.

The instrument subsequently adopted to maintain the
African economies, release more labour, and (ideally)
achieve a level of production adequate to meet the social
security needs of a continuously flowing migrant workforce, was the Native Lands Act of 1913. (156) This Act
(which is beyond the chronological scale of this study)
created certain areas (largely those already populated by
Africans) as black Reserves, and precluded Africans from
owning or occupying land outside these areas. The Act
simultaneously prohibited whites from owning or occupying
land within the Reserves. By defining the landed area
available to Africans, the Act sought to inhibit any increase in the agricultural product within the traditional
economies which would slow down the rate of migration. At
the same time it made no change in the capacity of these
areas to provide the social security needed to replenish
the migrant labour force. The result was (to cite Wolpe)
(157) that the balance between 'production, distribution
and social obligation in the Reserves ... was inherently
fragile and subject to irresistible pressures'. In order
to guarantee the purpose of the Act, prevent landlessness,
and ensure an even distribution of land (as well as the
production of agricultural products), measures were
adopted to prevent any concentration of land within the
African areas by African landowners. (158) A complex
scheme was thus devised which conserved and transformed
but did not destroy those elements of the 'traditional'
economies which were crucial to the continuation of the
migrant labour system.

The reluctance of the Chamber and the Transvaal Labour
Commission to deal as decisively with this matter in 1903
was probably due to the immediate post-war condition of
'white' agriculture, the need for such legislation to be

applied generally throughout South Africa, (159) and also
to the plans afoot for the importation of an auxiliary
migrant workforce from Asia to cut costs and overcome
African resistance to mine labour. The strategy was to
provide arrangements for securing Asian labour rather than
to introduce any far-reaching reconstruction of the system
of land tenure.

13 The Asian labour alternative

INTRODUCTION

It is helpful to consider the Chamber's claim for imported
labour in the context of its need to secure its wage
structure during a period of rising costs, declining
yields and serious resistance to recruitment as well as
some competition for the workforce from railways, roads,
harbours and farms. (1) Not least, Asian labour was an
alternative to the employment of white unskilled workers
which the Chamber believed should be avoided at all costs.
Here we shall (i) explain the Chamber's policy of acquiring an alternative source of labour from Asia and
consider the consequences of this policy, particularly the
accommodation the Chamber was required to make with the
white miners in return for their 'incorporation'; (ii)
show that the reasons for racial work restrictions were
economic in origin despite the racial overtones with which
they were presented; and (iii) indicate the 'symbiosis'
between the Milner administration and the mine-owners.
    This is a departure from the traditional approach,
which accepts the Chamber's statements and Milner's acquiescence at face value. For example, one typical account states:

> The shortage continued and Milner proposed the importa-
> tion of indentured labourers from Asia. Despite con-
> siderable 'white labour' opposition, it was agreed at
> the Customs Conference of 1903 that as labour was not
> available nearer home, 'recourse must be had temporari-
> ly to indentured unskilled labourers from Asia.' (2)

This type of formulation is highly favourable to the
Chamber, since it plays down the influence of mining capital on this issue. Indeed, this simplistic acceptance of

195

the 'Asian proposal' represents a trend in the historiography of the period. An exception is van der Horst's 'Native Labour in South Africa'. Whilst she does not examine the need to cut costs so as to preserve the labour structure, she does make the significant point that the South African Customs Conference failed to satisfy any criteria of what constituted an 'adequate' supply. She correctly points out that estimates of labour requirements 'have frequently been made in South Africa, but they have tended to overlook the fact that any such calculation is simply based on an estimate of the number it would pay to employ at a particular rate of wages'. Arrighi makes the same point in connection with the Rhodesian mining industry: 'when they spoke of plenty in connection with supply, they had in mind not only quantity but also price'. In dealing with the labour supply on the Rand, the remarks of van der Horst and Arrighi need to be borne in mind. (3)

(i)   THE ASIAN LABOUR DECISION

The final decision to employ Asian labour seems to have been made between May and July 1903, twelve months after the proposal had been discussed (and, as it turned out, temporarily rejected) by the Special Committee of the Chamber. (4)   The decision was prompted by the threat to the industry's greater profitability and its labour structure, both of which were challenged by the twin effects of inflation and labour shortages in the period immediately after the ending of the war. (5)
   The 'Asian alternative' to increase the unskilled labour supply at low cost seems to have been the Chamber's ultimate option in a situation where (i) the mining of low-grade ore on the Rand was seen at the time to require a labour-intensive, migrant-type labour structure to maintain the existing rate of profit; (6) (ii) the supply was inadequate;   (iii) wages had been forced up and the cost of stores increased;   and (iv) the commodity price of gold was fixed. In these conditions, and given the nature of gold as the commodity produced for its capacity to serve as the 'money material', the item of expenses which seemed most compressible to improve the industry's profitability was the African wage bill. (7)
   It was, however, clear that the Chamber seriously considered the importation of Asian labour even before it decided to improve the supply by increasing African wages in April 1903. The decision to indenture labour seems to have been taken after several months of internal debate.

(8) The matter had been raised in 1896 (9) but not acted
on. It was discussed again by the Special Committee
within months of the formal peace treaty, in the context
of the immediate post-war labour shortage. (10) On that
occasion (September 1902) the Chamber had rejected the
proposal of 'an indentured Coloured labour force from
outside the African continent' in favour of the Committee's proposals to test the supply by increasing the
existing schedule of wage rates, strengthening its central
recruiting organization and intensifying its recruitment,
and pursuing its efforts with Lord Milner to 'assist in
throwing open new areas of supply'. (11) This alternative
was followed, partly in view of the sharp resistance to
recruitment that followed the immediate post-war wage
cuts; and (if Mawby's evidence is to be accepted) because
of the opposition of the partners of the Eckstein group to
the proposals. (12) According to this view, the substance
of the opposition within the Chamber was political: that
is that the imperial government would never sanction the
indenture of Chinese labour 'before their necessity was
convincingly shown' and that Chinese labour was desirable
only if African labour proved insufficient. (13)

Whatever the basis of what appeared to be the Chamber's
(temporary) abandonment of the 1902 proposal, the mine-
owners did in fact increase the wage schedule in April
1903 to improve the labour supply, and made some extensive
efforts to scour the African continent to augment the unskilled labour force. (14) However, subsequent criticisms
of the Chamber's efforts, and the remarks of the Minority
members of the Transvaal Labour Commission, suggest that
these were interim measures to avoid any further disloca-
tion in production, and that the 'Chinese alternative' had
not been ruled out by the Chamber. According to the
evidence already quoted, the 1902 reduction in wages by
50 per cent was seen as 'proof' that the Chamber had
little intention of re-attracting its pre-war African
workforce and 'had made up [its] mind that [it] would
have Chinese labour'. (15)

The Chamber's attitude, however, may not have been as
unequivocal on this matter as its critics suggested, but
as the pressure mounted for the augmentation of the unskilled workforce by white workers, the Chamber seemed to
become firmer in its intention to indenture labour from
China as a means of reducing costs, increasing yields and
protecting its two-tier labour structure. The preliminary
moves it made were cautious. Having scoured the African
continent for labour, it then opened the way to Chinese
indenture by securing a resolution at the Customs Conference which, in Milner's words, did not make importation

certain but rendered it 'permissible' if the supply from
Africa was found to be inadequate. (16) The Chamber also
dispatched one of its mining engineers to China and elsewhere to report on the experiences of those who had employed foreign migrant labour. (17)   Thus, before the
Bloemfontein Conference concluded in March 1903 that 'the
African population south of the Zambesi did not comprise
a sufficient number of adult males capable of work to
satisfy the normal requirements', and prior to the conclusion of the Transvaal Labour Commission in November
1903 'that there was no "adequate" supply of labour in
central and Southern Africa', the Chamber had the inden-
turing of Chinese labour in mind as the course it would
follow. (18)

     In dispatching its agent, H.R.Skinner, to explore the
'extra-territorial' market for labour in Asia, the Chamber
gave instructions to inquire into the costs, class,
habits, wants, food and work of these potential labourers.
The survey was an essential prerequisite for securing a
migrant-type workforce, for if the cultural and welfare
requirements of the men were too high they would be 'uneconomical' to employ and the exercise would be self-
defeating. (19) The search was confined therefore to a
particular class of migrant who corresponded in two important respects to the African workforce. These were
(i) that the workmen should have a relatively low level
of cultural wants and (ii) that their families would not
be dependent for their basic subsistence on the cash wage
the men would earn in the mines. (20) Skinner's preliminary inquiries were therefore important.

(ii) PRECONDITIONS FOR INDENTURE

As well as initiating these inquiries in Asia the Chamber
gave its attention to reducing the white employees' fear
that Chinese immigrants would compete with them in the
work situation. In its earlier stages the problem arose
in the form of finding a formula to restrict the economic
activity of this auxiliary workforce through measures
which were superficially described as 'confining the
yellow evil'. (21) The 'evil' in this respect was not
specifically racial but concerned certain fears of the
consequences of importing Chinese workers: (i) white
mining men feared the Chinese labourers' capacity to sup-
plant them in the skilled occupations; (ii) white farmers
feared that the Chinese would compete with them in agriculture.

     Thus, long before the first Asian arrived, a number of

preconditions were agreed in order to secure the labour
structure and reassure the white miners that (i) 'Free
Chinamen' would be debarred from remaining in the country
on expiry of their contracts;   (ii) their conditions of
indenture would confine them to 'absolutely unskilled
work';   and (iii) they would be precluded from the right
to own or lease land or pursue trade, practise handi-
crafts, garden or take up agriculture. (22) These informal statements for the control of Asian labour were
subsequently embodied in legislation to ensure that
'Chinese labour if introduced, should be employed as
unskilled workmen only'. (23)

It may not actually have been the Chamber's original
intention to institutionalize these constraints on Chinese
labour, for initially it seemed content to draw little
distinction between the Asian component of its migrant
workforce and its African resource. It would probably
have preferred to operate a flexible de facto bar for the
Asians, just as it did with its African workforce, but for
the need to secure the acquiescence and allay the apprehensions of its white workers. The conditions under which
Asian labour was imported were very specially shaped by
the compromises the Chamber felt it necessary to make in
order to preserve the two tiers of its labour structure.

The Chamber aimed to provoke as little disruption as
possible in the production of gold by simply extending the
migrant labour system beyond Africa. The important priority was to ensure that this venture would be 'economically
rational'. This meant that the labour force was to be
'docile' and acquired at the lowest possible cost, so as
to enable the mine-owners to avoid any alteration in the
labour structure, or - as Richardson puts it more problem-
atically - to cause the mine-owners not to 'alter the
degree of capital intensity in the practice of winning
gold'. (24)   Hence the close attention paid to the reports
sent by the Chamber's agent from California, British
Columbia, the Federated Malay States and Japan, (25) and
the various areas where Chinese labour was used. The
'better class of Chinese coolie' (located in South China)
was recommended as suitable to supplement the unskilled
labour force on the mines. Their special recommendations
were that they exhibited qualities which the Chamber
thought were consistent with the African component of the
workforce, i.e. they were 'docile, law-abiding and indus-
trious people' who would go underground 'without much
trouble'. They were also obtainable in sufficient numbers
to meet both present and future demands and were contractable for more than three times the average period of
African labour, although they would not necessarily be
cheaper. (26)

According to a contemporary source the southern provinces of China, in particular Kwang Tung (to which the Chamber's agents proceeded), were wretchedly poverty-stricken:

> It is not easy to imagine a lower standard of human existence than is met with in the mud villages of the worst districts. In ordinary years there is always a longer or shorter interval between the exhaustion of the old supply and the ingathering of the new crop of rice, when the farming folk subsist for the most part on vegetable refuse. In famine years women and children are sold quite openly.... To these poverty-stricken areas the agents of the Director of Emigration proceed. (27)

But before the men arrived on the Rand the scheme to indenture this type of labour was preceded by an open conflict between the Chamber, supported by the Milner administration, on the one hand, and critics of the scheme on the other. The debate was significant for several reasons:

  (i) the degree of opposition the Chamber's policy engendered amongst the white community and the consequence of this antagonism in so far as it led to the establishment of a statutory colour bar in the mines;

 (ii) the extent of the Chamber's commitment to the migrant system, and the tenacity of its defence of its labour structure;

(iii) the insights into the labour policy of the mines which could be gained during the course of the 'agitation';

 (iv) the influence of mining capital in the South African social formation.

The process by which the Chamber attempted to 'incorporate' the white community in the working of its cheap labour policies was extremely arduous during the agitation period, when the mine-owners did their best to assuage the anxiety of white miners and assure them that their jobs would not be undermined in the event of an influx of large numbers of unskilled Asian labourers.

(iii)   THE ASIAN LABOUR LOBBIES

For the most part the Chamber did not itself formally
prosecute this political campaign, but rather promoted
the Labour Importation Association to win widespread support for its policy. (28)   The 'agitation' evoked a vigorous response from opposition groups, namely the White
League, the African Labour League, the National Democratic
Federation, and 'Boer' groups. (29)   The most significant
lobbies were therefore:

  (i)   the Chamber itself;
 (ii)   the Labour Importation Association, (30) which was
        sponsored by the Chamber;
(iii)   the African Labour League, which was promoted by the
        'anti-Asian' group of the Chamber of Commerce;   and
 (iv)   the White League, which enjoyed trade union support.

The various 'interest groups' attempted to win the ear of
the High Commissioner and the Colonial Secretary, and took
their views to the white public to gain publicity and support for their respective positions.

(a) The Chamber of Mines

Sir George Farrar generally put the position of the
Chamber, although the main burden of the agitation was
undertaken by the Labour Importation Association.
Farrar's contribution was significant for what it revealed
of the type of accommodation the mine-owners were prepared
to make with the white mineworkers in return for their approval of the 'Asian policy'. He addressed himself to the
fears of the white miners when he told a meeting in
Boksburg:

   What are your special objections to bringing in unskilled Asian labour? They are these: that he might
   remain in the country, become a tradesman and compete
   against you, in which case you are afraid that you see
   Asiatic carpenters, fitters etc., in fact Asiatics in
   all branches of skilled trade. Now what's my answer
   to this.... They must come here absolutely as unskilled labourers only, and, therefore in order that
   your position may be absolutely secure, I would guarantee never to consent to any legislation on this question unless [mining, trading, landholding] restrictions
   are embodied in that legislation. (31)

Two other persuasive arguments which were soon to help
the mine-owners' case against white unskilled labour
(though Farrar did not mention them on this occasion)
were:

(i) that white labour, if imported, would rapidly become
    skilled and would in turn compete against other white
    miners; and
(ii) that if sufficient unskilled (Asian) labour was
    secured 'it would mean an increase in jobs for about
    15,000 skilled white men'. (32)

The latter point was a powerful inducement to the white
miners to support the Chamber's labour strategy. (33) The
converse was that failure to support the Chamber would en-
danger employment prospects.

(b) The African Labour League

The most articulate opposition to the Chamber's policy was
mounted by the African Labour League, founded in June 1903
by a section of the Rand's commercial leaders. This body
of businessmen, supported by some prominent labour leaders, was committed to the extension of whites to unskilled
labour in mining, building and public works. It is unlikely that their opposition to Asian labourers was exclusively racial. The employment of a large number of
local and immigrant white workmen with their families
might have secured a more adequate consumer market for
the commercial sector - hence the intensity of their campaign. It is also likely that their opposition to Asian
labour might have been defensive in order (i) to prevent
the undermining of the existing consumer market through
the substitution of well-paid whites for low-paid migrants; (ii) to protect white employment; (iii) to protect the economic privileges of the white labour force;
and (iv) to prevent competition from Asian shopkeepers -
a phenomenon which could not be ruled out. (34) Whatever
the reasons, the content of their opposition to the Chamber's labour policy struck at the centre of the claims of
the mine-owners.
    The African Labour League contended that there was in
fact sufficient African labour for mining and other work,
and that the Chamber should reduce its black labour force
and provide incentives for mechanical invention to extract
'the last ounce of gold from the Reefs of the Transvaal'.
(35) It challenged the Chamber's and the WNLA's claims
that Chinese labour was necessary, and accused these

bodies of misrepresentation and ineptitude in regard to
procuring that portion of the African supply which was
available. Their arguments contained the following criticisms of the Chamber: (36)

   (i) 'the steady and substantial increase in [African]
       labour since the higher tariff of wages' showed that
       the Chamber had not previously offered a sufficient
       cash inducement to potential labourers. Hence the
       resistance to recruitment was not fundamental or
       psychological but economic and remediable;
  (ii) available African labour had not 'by any means' been
       exploited by the recruiting agency;
 (iii) the months of May, June and July were 'the worst
       time for recruiting' (37) and thereby invalidated
       the Chamber's conclusions in respect of the general
       weakness of the supply;
  (iv) mechanical invention would make possible the employ-
       ment of a large number of whites and 'add to the
       stability of the country';
   (v) the Chamber had 'exaggerated the present depression'
       in order to urge the importation of Asian labour.

The attack provoked a strong response from the WNLA but
no cogent defence from the Chamber on points iv and v.
That there was a serious argument to be met in respect of
iv concerning mechanical innovation seems to be borne out
by the evidence available.
   Despite the fact that the mine-owners had been dragging
their feet on the matter of technological innovation, the
technology employed on the mines by 1902 was by no means
insignificant. Machines were required for a variety of
operations, e.g. crushing the ore, treating the finely
crushed pulp, compressing air to work underground mechanisms, ventilating the working area, hauling the rock from
the workface to the shaft, hoisting the rock to the surface, and conveying it to the mill. (38) In addition to
all this, mechanization was needed for pumping, lighting
and various other 'minor' operations as well as metal-
lurgical treatment. (39) Between 1890 and 1898 mechanical
innovation (given the technical problems discussed in
Chapter 1) had proceeded 'very notably', so that by 1898,
to cite a single instance, the state mining engineer then
estimated that there were 1,350 air drills representing
the work of 55,000 labourers. (40) According to Cartwright, the average working costs on the mines in 1894-5
were approximately 29s. 6d. or 30s. per ton, which figure
was reduced by 1904 to 19s. as a result of technological
innovation. (41)

Cartwright's calculations partly took into account improvements introduced after 1903 for handling the ore underground. (42) However, despite these improvements, the Chamber had been largely disinclined to increase the capital intensity of the industry. In the words of the mine-owners, mechanical innovation was 'somewhat overshadowed' by labour shortages. (43) This is not to say that mechanical innovations such as the 1903 rock drill were negligible between 1898 and 1904, (44) but (according to the Chamber) 'the recognition of inventions and their introduction had been somewhat tardy in some cases'. (45) This tardiness, especially in the case of ore removal, was due not to negligence but to the fact that the very narrow stope-widths on the Rand mines inhibited mechanization. An example of this was the rock drill. The significance of this machine was marred by the increased stoping widths that it required, and consequently it caused a *rise* in working costs.

As noted in Chapter 1, the general narrowness of the stopes necessitated the greater use of unskilled labour, since the physical removal of waste ores could, for the most part, be best and most economically accomplished by hand. Where labour shortages prompted the use of mechanical drills, and where conveyor belts were used to shovel the greater quantity of the waste ore produced by these drills in the thin reefs, the net gains were marginal, and these innovations contributed to a decrease in the rate of return on investment. (46)

That the Chamber had not in recent times pressed the matter of technological innovation was borne out by the evidence of the African Labour League, which drew attention to a reference by F.Eckstein to a new mechanical drill which would 'enable 10,000 or 15,000 White miners ... to work in place of 50,000 or 60,000 natives'. (47) The drill never materialized. It is not clear what precisely was being referred to, but the Chamber's admission that it had been 'somewhat tardy' in its attention to mechanical innovation was sufficient to give support to the League's contention that, if the Chamber wished, mechanical innovation could help to solve the industry's manpower problem. When it suited them, the mine-owners' critics were not particularly mindful of the Chamber's cost problems - i.e. that technological substitution of labour, where the geological conformations allowed it, might produce only the most marginal gains in short-term liquidity and profitability. (48)

Indeed, in the case of Eckstein's reported reference to the rock drill, it would seem that the incentive to innovate was likely to have been blunted by the knowledge

that an increase of 10,000 white labourers would not only
increase the direct costs of labour but would add contingent costs of housing, welfare, compensation and other
contributions which the mine-owners normally offered their
skilled workforce. Under these conditions, unskilled
labour was seen to be cheaper, given the fixed price of
gold, the inflexibility of mining techniques (which were
determined by the initial investment pattern of mining)
and the low-grade ore. Hence the Chamber's emphasis on
rigorous cost-control and the acquisition of a large
(migrant) labour force at what was (to use Arrighi's
phrase) calculated as the 'traditional price'.

The attitude to innovation at this time must therefore
have been coloured by the view that although the mechanical revolution would solve the unskilled labour problem,
it would do so at the expense of dividends. Changes in
the degree of capital intensity that allowed only marginal
gains, and were likely over the long term to lower the
profitability of a mine, gave little satisfaction to the
Chamber.

Thus although the white/black ratio had narrowed from
9:1 before the war to 4:1 in 1903, and despite the fact
that the supply of labour was 60 per cent of the pre-war
labour force, and 45 per cent of the stated requirements
for 1903, (49) the Chamber focused on acquiring labour at
the lowest possible cost rather than on encouraging technological innovation.

The preliminary solution to the unskilled labour
shortage and the problem of high working costs, in the
context of 1903, was seen, it appears, as the acquisition
of a low-cost (Chinese) labour supply. This workforce
began to arrive on the Rand in large shiploads in 1904
and the two years following. After 1904, the average
costs per ton of ore retrieved were reduced as a result
of this importation, together with a certain amount of
internal reorganization (see Chapter 15) and some mechanical innovation. Under these circumstances, it would
appear that the mine-owners could attain some benefit
from mechanical innovation provided (i) that it released
a significant amount of labour for other productive work;
(ii) that it suited the geological conformations of the
mines, i.e. did not produce high adventitious costs; and
(iii) that it did not interfere grossly with the established labour structure. Hence Consolidated Goldfields
was able to report the reduction of average costs by
4s. 6d. per ton in 1907 and the Robinson Deep mine could
report (one year after the introduction of a tube mill in
1904) that it had increased the tonnage of ore treated to
2,000 tons per annum, and that it had improved its gold

recovery by 3 per cent as well as raised its profits by
4s. 9d. per ton. (50)

The light rock drill which 'eluded' the industry in
1903 appeared in 1910 - as a result of a £5,000 prize offered in 1906 by the Chamber and the government - and
preceded the innovation of the hammer drill, which was
introduced in the 1920s. (51)   In the period immediately
after the war, however, from 1903 to 1908, the acquisition
of the low-cost Chinese labour force and the encouragement
of some technological innovation rescued the industry from
the trough it experienced one year after the war, and allowed it to retain the system of production and labour
structure that enabled it to maximize profits.

In retrospect it would seem that the use of Chinese
labour, rather than the mechanical inventions, was the
more beneficial remedy for the mine-owners.   Moreover,
the mechanical drills introduced in 1902-3 for stoping,
and the belt conveyors used to shovel the ore where the
stopes were narrow, tended to cause an increase in working
expenditure rather than a saving, compared to labour-
intensive methods. (52)   Thus - to return to the argument
of the African Labour League - in the period from the re-
sumption of mining to the height of the campaign to secure
Chinese labourers, little further innovation had taken
place on the mines, and the Chamber could not contradict
the view of its critics that the labour shortage *as such*
could be reduced significantly by mechanical invention.
This, however, would not improve the cost-efficiency of
the industry or increase its rate of capital accumulation.

The thrust of points i, ii and iii of the League's argument was that the Chamber had exaggerated the labour
shortage to strengthen its case for Asian labour.   The
League's argument was that although the African mine
labour force was numerically less than in the pre-war
period, it was 'rapidly approaching its former effective
value'. (53)   There was much evidence for this contention.
Whilst the WNLA claimed the presence on the mines of
68,222 labourers in May 1903, as compared to 96,704 in
February 1899, no allowance was made for improvements in
productivity.   Milner himself had referred 'with unmiti-
gated satisfaction' to the increase in African efficiency:

> In old times a large deduction had to be made from the
> labour power of the mines for natives incapacitated by
> drink.   This deduction amounted at times to as much as
> 30%. (54)

Adopting a more cautious approach than Milner, the League
argued from a reduction of 20 per cent to show that the

pre-war labour force of 96,704 represented an actual efficiency force of 77,363, which total gave the stated
shortage a much smaller dimension. (55)

Two further factors regarding the quality of the workforce added to the strength of the League's case. These
were that African efficiency had increased owing to the
system of piece work, and that productivity had also increased as a result of fewer 'desertions'. In the first
respect the Colonial Secretary had been informed in 1902
that 'in some instances the work obtained per native is
double and on the average ... [has] increased 10% to 14%'.
(56) In the second instance, productivity had risen
through greater administrative control of the workforce.
Between 1898 and 1899 so-called desertions amounted to
over 30 per cent of the total number of contracts. During
the eleven months ending 13 January 1903 the number of
desertions had been reduced to 4 per cent of the number
recruited. (57) In wielding these arguments the League
was content to show that since the present labour contingent of the Chamber was in their view valued at an efficiency force of 77,363, there was a relatively small deficiency in the current supply situation which could be
made up within the next three months by recruiting activity. The impact of this argument was that it undermined
the urgency of the Chamber's case for Asian labour and
opened the way for greater pressure for the employment
of white unskilled workers.

The League also challenged the Chamber on their statistical evidence of lower output. It believed that this
had nothing to do with the labour shortage and much to do
with the deployment of the African workforce. It acknowledged that the current output was lower than before the
war, but disputed that the decrease was exclusively a
function of the shortage of labour as the mining groups
were 'making provision for the future by distributing
numbers of natives to non-producing mines which will
shortly emerge as producers'. (58) The League was supported in this by the Chamber's own newspaper, the 'Star',
which commented:

> The mining groups cannot both eat their cake and have
> it too. They cannot employ their available labour to
> broaden the basis of the industry and at the same time,
> because immediate results are not visible, complain
> that the industry is stagnant. (59)

In the same issue of the newspaper, the Chamber was criticized for diverting its personnel into the non-producing
mines. The article noted that 'if the Chamber's present

supply was concentrated on the producing mines we should
have approximately our old industry'. (60) The League
claimed that in the light of their investigations the
labour demand would have been met by the Chamber had it
recruited more vigorously.

   The implications of the League's criticisms were serious for the WNLA. Either the agency was inefficient or
it deliberately restricted its recruiting activity to
exacerbate the shortage. (61) The League evidently accepted the latter position. In attacking the mine-owners,
it drew upon the discrepancy between the optimistic statements of the Chamber about the availability of the supply,
and the poor performance of the WNLA in recruiting labour.
For example, it quoted the President of the Chamber, Sir
Percy Fitzpatrick, who noted in February 1903 (three
months before the formal commencement of the Chamber's
'Asian campaign') that 'short cuts to the solution of the
labour problem were attractive but unsound', (62) and that
the supply was available in Africa:

   I deprecate the grasping of straws, the abandoning of
   experiments entered upon.... I deprecate the reckless
   aversion to the old Order, which appears to me to be
   only manufacturing evidence that we have done our best
   and that we have tried every expedient, and that Africa
   is exhausted.... I am equally sure that our omniscient
   critics, who from week to week propose hasty and radical changes, are driving towards that condition of
   things in which people will believe that Africa is exhausted and that there is nothing for it but the introduction of the Asiatic. (63)

What seemed inconsistent to the League was the repeated
optimism that labour on the continent of Africa was available (and that recourse to Asian labour would not be
necessary) and the WNLA's failure to recruit the required
labour force. The reason given for the WNLA's failure was
that there was a paradox in the Chamber's position - i.e.
that the labour force was potentially available but not
immediately on supply, and that the Chamber did not wish
to undermine its wage structure by employing unskilled
whites in the interim period. (See p.168.) A 'breathing
space' was repeatedly emphasized. For instance, Gordon
J.Sprigg, the Cape Prime Minister, told the Colonial
Secretary in August 1903 that 'what is required above
all is the exercise of patience ... if the continent south
of the equator be explored, sufficient labour is available, not only for working the mines in the Transvaal but
for all other requirements'. (64) Various statements re-

iterated this view, e.g. the citation of Sir H.H.Johnson
in 'The Times': 'properly controlled the recruitment of
the natives of tropical Africa will solve the South African labour problem'; (65)   and the speech by Dr Jameson
declaring that 'there is sufficient labour in the country
to meet all requirements especially when Uganda and West
Africa have been tapped'. (66)   These statements were not
intrinsically false or necessarily over-optimistic, but
they were unhelpful to the Chamber in view of the WNLA's
failure to acquire the labour at the time.

The League seized on the statements of the spokesmen
for the mine-owners to discredit the Chamber's claims for
Chinese labour. In particular it fell upon the highly
sanguine statement by Sir Godfrey Lagden:

> It may be that there are 5 million natives south of the
> Zambezi, of which 800,000 might be sturdy men. If
> every man took his fair turn of labour there can be
> little doubt that South Africa has sufficient for all
> purposes. (67)

Such remarks made nonsense of the Chamber's arguments for
Asian labour. Basically, the League ignored the notion
that a 'breathing space' was required before the supply
would be available in the numbers required (68) and at the
wage the industry was prepared to pay. On the contrary
the League appears to have seen that there was a relationship between the supply and the price, and to have believed that the expansion of the industry could be expected
with adequate wage inducements, reasonable care of the
health and comfort of recruits, and protection from drink.
(69)   The Chamber's preoccupation with an 'ultra' low-cost
labour policy, it would seem, meant very little indeed to
the League.

(c) The Labour Importation Association

The task of providing a rejoinder to the African Labour
League was assumed by the Labour Importation Association
(LIA), an organization 'established by the Chamber of
Mines to press its viewpoint on Chinese labour'. (70)
The Association argued that:

> whatsoever the opinions held in different quarters as
> to the possibility of an increase in native labour in
> the future, it is an obvious fact that at the present
> time the supply is wholly inadequate. (71)

The extent of that inadequacy was quantified by the WNLA in the early stages of the 'agitation' as (i) 4,000 short-service labourers per month 'for the next six months [April-October 1903] and the need to maintain that average number afterwards'; and (ii) a certain number of long-service labourers from Portuguese East Africa to bring the supply up to the old number of 75,000 and to add to that a further 30,000. (72)   Immediate overall needs were esti-mated at a total presence on the mines of 145,000 men. This did not allow for the opening up of new properties and deep-levels, which required a total of 200,000 or 300,000 men 'in the next two or three years'. (73)   The Labour Importation Association claimed that despite all diplomatic and other efforts 'the rate of increase in the native supply is so small that a considerable period must ... elapse before the mines return to their pre-war ac-tivity'. (74)

It is noteworthy that the Association ignored the com-ments of its critics on the increased productivity of the workforce and the deployment of labour in the non-produc-tive mines, and continued to refer to the need for the recovery of the pre-war labour force.   In effect it dis-missed the arguments of the opponents of Asian importation and called upon them to abandon their 'inveterate preju-dice' against what they feared might become an 'Asiatic invasion'. (75)

Paradoxically, while exhorting the white community to abandon their prejudice, the Association appealed to them on what appeared to be a racial basis, and identified itself with those 'whose aim it was to make South Africa a "White man's country"'. (76)   This aim, it stated, could not be met by encouraging the importation of 'lower class unskilled white labour' - 'remembering what is really meant by a "White man's country".... The unskilled labour must be left to those alone who are best fitted by race and the conditions of life to undertake it'. (77)

It was clearly important to the Chamber, if it wanted to obtain official sanction from the British state for its policies, that it produce evidence that the white popula-tion in the Transvaal either supported its policy of Asian labour importation or at least was not hostile to it. (78) Moreover, it required a favourable international press to bolster the confidence of investors who doubtless felt some anxiety during the agitation.   According to Kubicek, (79) the mining houses of Wernher, Beit & Co., Consoli-dated Goldfields, the Farrar interests, Sigismund Neumann and the Albu groups together arranged through Baron Jacques de Guinzberg (a financier and director of the Compagnie Française) to give stock options to 'twenty two

of the most important French papers on the understanding
that they must write in favour of the importation of unskilled Asian labour ... in the Transvaal ... and more or
less write in favour of the Witwatersrand generally'. (80)

In addition to seeking a favourable press, the Chamber-
LIA increased the pressure on the local and metropolitan
authorities to support its campaign by placing the onus
for the prevailing economic depression in South Africa
'on the enforced inactivity of our vital industry,
crippled as it is through lack of motive power which can
only be supplied by unskilled labour'. (81)

At the local level both the Labour Importation Association and the African Labour League communicated their
attitudes to the High Commissioner (and via his office
to the imperial government) through the form of resolutions adopted at mass meetings held amongst the white
mining men. The Association in particular held a large
number of meetings with the white workforce, in which it
secured (it would seem through the coercion of the
workers) 'overwhelming' majorities for its Asian policy
and promptly dispatched the resolutions so adopted to the
High Commission and Colonial Office. (82)   The pattern was
followed by all the lobbies.

The main resolution passed at meetings of the Labour
Importation Association (which were held throughout August
and September 1903) depended for its success on the impending Report of the Transvaal Labour Commission. (The
Commission sat from 21 July 1903 to 6 October, and reported on 19 November 1903.) The intention of the Chamber to
find 'consensus' for its policies was clearly in order to
satisfy the critics of the imperial government that there
was support in South Africa for the importation of Asian
labour, and to avoid any impression that the government
was blindly agreeing to policies exclusively supported by
the Chamber. The resolutions passed at the meetings of
the LIA read:

> That providing the finding of the Labour Commission is
> that there are not sufficient natives in the country
> to provide unskilled labour for the requirements of the
> mines, this meeting pledges itself to support the im-
> portation of Chinese labour under stringent restric-
> tions. (83)

There was little doubt that the Commission would find
in favour of the Chamber, and many of the Commission's
critics fully expected the outcome. An executive member
of the National Democratic Federation, for example, wrote
to John X.Merriman:

> The main report, of course, is exactly what everyone
> knew it would be from the first. I don't think a more
> disgraceful and barefooted 'put-up job' has ever been
> fixed onto a wretched Community than this. (84)

Indeed, the High Commissioner anticipated the Report in
his remarks to the Colonial Secretary, who in turn suggested a strategy to be adopted once the Report was made
public, namely that a mining representative should introduce in the Legislative Council 'a resolution which can
be fully debated, official members being given a free hand
to speak and vote'. (85) Thus it was one of the features
of the 'Asian debate' that the Colonial Secretary and the
High Commissioner were privately in support of the mine-
owners but anxious to avoid any accusation of open identification with the Chamber of Mines. Notwithstanding this
intention to appear impartial, however, the evidence shows
clearly that the imperial government and the South African
administration not only accepted privately the position of
the Chamber but on occasions publicly defended its cost
structure. This relationship between the administration
and the Chamber was especially apparent when Milner put
the Chamber's case to the third of the anti-importation
lobbies, the White Labour League.

(d) The White Labour League

The White Labour League was formed 'to win the Transvaal
for the white man'. Although its arguments against Asian
labour were frequently racist in language, its opposition
was undoubtedly economic in character. Its spokesman,
Hutchison, told Milner:

> it was absurd to say that the Chinese would only be
> employed in unskilled labour. Once they were imported
> they would be employed in skilled labour if they became
> proficient ... at the end of the first twelve months
> there would probably not be a single white man employed
> underground. The sealed compounds would become China-
> towns. (86)

While the African Labour League substantially represented a section of the Chamber of Commerce, the White
League enjoyed the support of the white Trade Union Con-
federation and the Witwatersrand Trades and Labour
Council. The latter registered its 'complete accord and
sympathy [with the white activists] against the threatened
invasion of Asiatics in this Colony'. (87) The Pretoria

Trades and Labour Council, representing 2,000 artisans,
similarly allied itself with the White League, entering
a 'most emphatic protest against the importation of Asian
labour'. (88) It believed that Asian labour would be
'detrimental both morally, socially and physically' to the
country. (89) According to David Tiktin: 'Organized
labour never wavered in its opposition to Chinese labour
and its leaders were prominent in assisting the White
League's anti-Chinese campaign.' (90) Organized labour's
opposition to Chinese labour ranged from fears that the
introduction of the Chinese 'would cut up trade unionism
in the mining industry by the roots', (91) to the belief
that the labourers would not remain confined to unskilled
work and would replace the white workers. (92)

The campaign mounted by the White League was vigorous
and sometimes violent, and attracted whites both on the
mines and in the non-mining sectors in Pretoria and on
the Witwatersrand. The League pledged:

> to prevent by every means ... the carrying into effect
> of the proposal for the introduction of Asiatics to
> work in the mines and other industries in the Trans-
> vaal. (93)

The case they put to Milner was significant because of the
fears it revealed for job security. Since the White
League's attack on the mine-owners was sharper than that
made by the African Labour League, and likely to receive
sympathetic support among liberals 'at home', Milner
listened to them carefully, and dispatched a report of
his interview to the imperial government. In effect,
Milner's response to the White Labour League was the reply
of the British administration in South Africa to the fears
of organized labour on the Rand in respect of the employment of Chinese labour. The complaints by organized
labour were as follows:

(i) The 'capitalists' had asked for Chinese labour on
     the ground that they could not afford to pay higher
     wages, yet in their view 'any business concern which
     was making 33.1/3% on gross turnover could afford to
     pay fairly high wages'. They pointed out, in proof
     of their point, that in 1898 gross production on the
     mines was £15 million, of which £5 million was dis-
     tributed in dividends. (94)
(ii) They considered that the real effect of the importa-
     tion of Chinese labour was that there would be a
     reduction in the number of white men employed on the
     mines. They believed this likely because of the

contradictory statements of the Chairman on what
precisely was to be the dividing line between
skilled and unskilled labour. According to the
League's estimates 7,600 whites would be dismissed
out of every 10,000. (95)

(iii) Whilst the mineral wealth belonged to the country,
most of the benefits were exported. For example,
85 per cent of the shares in the mines were held
outside the country, so that the dividends of only
15 per cent of the shares remained in South Africa.
'In addition to this vast sum of money (which left
the country every year) the Chinese, if introduced,
would take away probably all their wages with them.'
(96)

In his response the High Commissioner repeated the
Chamber's assurances that 'white jobs' would be protected
by legislation, and emphasized that the British government
would not agree to the introduction of Asiatic labour if
it thought that 'the mass of the European population were
dead against it'. (97) He attempted to reassure the White
League that the Asian immigrants were not to be settled
'in the midst of and mixed up' with the white population.
They were not wanted to compete for work 'which white men
perfectly well perform themselves'. They were wanted

in considerable numbers for temporary purposes and
under control which will ensure their return to their
own country, in order to do work for which it was
economically impossible to pay wages on which a European can live in this country. (98)

Milner seemed to have no doubt that the imperial
government would approve statutory constraints on Asian
labourers and thereby guarantee that the assurance the
mine-owners were making to the white employees would be
honoured by his administration. In regard to the League's
fear of a settled Chinese population, he told the delega-
tion that he considered it fallacious to assume that Asian
indentured labour, once imported, must necessarily remain
in the country. It was not a satisfactory argument, in
his view, to suggest that because Asians remained in other
countries 'where the danger of their so remaining was not
foreseen and therefore not guarded against', that should
be the position in the Transvaal Colony'. (99) Nor should
neighbouring colonies feel in the least disturbed by the
matter. On the contrary:

they have much more cause for uneasiness in the pros-

pect of the Transvaal making constantly increasing
demands on their labour supply, already none too
abundant, and forcing up their current rates of native
wages to a crippling figure. (100)

Since Milner's remarks were directed at the deputation
as much as the 'home' public and the shareholders, he proceeded to 'reply' in some depth to the substantive complaints by the League. He noted that the critics of the
Chamber opposed Asian importation on three grounds: (i)
that South African labour was sufficient in quantity for
the mines; (ii) that if necessary other (African) labour
might be recruited; and (iii) that white labour could
solve the supply problem and be used in unskilled categories. But what were the facts? He prefaced his remarks
with the statement:

To some of the extreme advocates of Asiatic labour you
would think this place is on the verge of total ruin.
What is really the case? The production of gold even
now is greater than in 1895 or 1896. (101)

It was at this point that Milner inadvertently gave
substance to the view of the African Labour League rather
than the White League that the Chamber had not taken into
account the improvements in the efficiency of its labour
force and that the flow of labour from the rural regions
to the Rand was increasing. He showed both that the rate
of production was steadily improving and that despite
'enormous difficulties' African recruitment was increasing. He defended the Chamber's policies and praised the
WNLA for the vigorous upturn in African recruitment,
thereby disposing of the charges made by other critics
of the inefficiency of the recruiting Association. Moreover, Milner endorsed the Chamber's argument that a
'breathing space' was required before the labour resources
of Africa would be released for the mines. His statement
showed lucid identification of the Chamber's position:

For several months there has been a net gain of at
least 3,000 a month. This is a considerable increase
and a notable achievement ... but [it] has only been
obtained by a great rise in wages, by greatly increased
expenditure in every direction and by immense and
ubiquitous activity in recruiting. The pace is hardly
likely to increase, yet at this pace it looks as if it
would take a considerable number of years to obtain
labour sufficient for our actual present requirements.
... At the present rate, it would, I say, take years

to get the labour in South Africa, assuming it is there
to be got. (102)

The High Commissioner eschewed the use of white unskilled labour on the mines. Rather he looked to the acquisition of unskilled Asian or African labour for the development of the industry. (103) 'This was the only way
South Africa could be made a white man's country in the
only sense South Africa can become one - but one in which
a largely increased white population can live in decency
and comfort.' (104)

It will be noted that the arguments Milner used on this
occasion were those of the Chamber itself, and were expressed in the Manifesto of the Labour Importation Association. (105) It is noteworthy too that neither Milner nor
the Chamber wished to foster a politically powerful
'aristocracy' of the labour force. The latter was a consequence of the Chamber's wage structure with its reliance
on migrant labour and 'economic partnership' with the rest
of the white community. (106) Hence Milner projected a
view of the future of South Africa which would be founded
on a white labour force differing in 'accommodation and
comfort' from the rest of the workforce, but in no way
wielding political control as a white labour aristocracy.
He foresaw the development of agriculture and industry enabling the cost of living to 'fall of itself' and so cause

a great increase in the white population without any
diminution in the status of the individual white, for
though he might not receive the same amount of money as
he does today, a less amount ... would represent a
greater amount of accommodation and comfort and many
enterprises could flourish which have no chance today.
(107)

Thus for Milner the future of the economy lay basically
in the extension of the migrant labour system, which effectively perpetuated the features which then and later
characterized the entire South African labour structure.
These were a relatively highly paid skilled (white) component, many of them performing largely supervisory functions, and a low-cost unskilled and semi-skilled (black)
labour force constituting the core of the country's workforce. In the conditions of 1903, Milner's policy also
required (for the foreseeable future) the importation of
Asian labour to maintain the Chamber's labour structure.
This was indeed the purpose of Milner's exercise before
the White Labour League.

(iv)   STATE INTERVENTION: THE LABOUR COMMISSION AND WHITE
INCORPORATION

The degree to which the state intervened directly to
assist the mine-owners in the early years of the transition from Boer to British rule has already been discussed
(in Chapter 10 (ii) and Chapter 11).   In the context of
the Chinese labour question (or more pertinently the
Chamber's initiative in 1903 to defend its labour structure and reduce the costs of production) state intervention was essential.   Firstly, the formal acceptance of
the mine-owners' case by the Transvaal Labour Commission
was necessary to provide local sanction for the Chamber's
controversial policies, and secondly the seal of official
approval was required for the introduction of an enabling
ordinance in the Transvaal legislature to acquire Chinese
labour.   Following on from this, a third and crucial
reason for state intervention was the Chamber's need to
involve the imperial government in the actual importation
of Chinese labour.
      The close identification which existed between the
Chamber and the High Commissioner's office undoubtedly
facilitated the swift passage of the legislation through
the Transvaal legislature.   A strategy was prepared in
which the Colonial Secretary, who had seen a preliminary
draft of the Chamber's proposal, urged the placing of a
resolution for the indenture of Asian labour before the
Transvaal Legislative Council. (108)   The mine-owners in
turn went through the formal motions of calling a special
meeting of the Chamber upon the publication of the Report
of the Labour Commission and in accordance with the
Colonial Secretary's suggestion, resolved that

      [As] there is no adequate supply of labour in central
      and southern Africa a draft law be published for the
      information of the people.   They must have time to
      consider it. (109)

      The object of this strategy was partly to ensure that
'consensus' was seen to be observed.   More especially, the
Chamber was concerned about the 'considerable opposition
which had to be faced and which had to be converted if
possible into support'. (110)   In order to secure this
support and to ensure co-operation from the imperial
government in the expensive and risky venture of inden-
turing 'long-distance' labour, (111) it took the critical
decision to put a motion to the Transvaal Legislative
Council, asking for Asian labour and accepting certain
restrictions to be included in the Bill 'in such a way

that the position of the white workman of today would be
in no way jeopardized, nor any loophole left by which this
coloured labour could compete with them'. (112)
    The motion was formally introduced into the Council by
Sir George Farrar, the spokesman for the mine-owners.
(113) The motion read:

> that the attention of the Government be called to the
> Report of the Transvaal Labour Commission and that the
> Government be requested to introduce a Draft Ordinance
> providing for the purpose of supplementing the supply
> of labour on the mines ... under such restrictions as
> will ensure their return to their native country on the
> completion of their contracts.

The opposition in the Council to the Chamber's motion
reflected in microcosm the respective positions adopted
during the 'agitation'. Milner was probably correct in
his assessment that a strong minority of the white working
class (114) - by which he meant practically the whole of
the organized labour movement - plus traders and a few
score of professional and commercial men constituted, the
opposition to Asian labour. (115) But whilst many of the
Chamber's claims of public support for their policy were
made to impress the colonial authorities, there is no
doubt that the mine-owners secured some success in ap-
peasing labour's opposition to its proposals. (116) By
January 1904 Milner responded with some exaggeration that
'the British population of the Transvaal had for the most
part veered round to accepting Chinese labour, albeit very
reluctantly'. (117) At best, it would seem the opposition
of the white population of the Rand had been made less
militant, although organized labour, as we have seen, consistently opposed the 'horrible nightmare of the yellow
agony' and continued to do so after the formal acceptance
of the Transvaal Labour Ordinance. (118) But the number
of organized workers was relatively small, and the Chamber's direct pressure on its white workers, plus its
promise of statutory inclusion of restrictive measures on
the occupation which the Asians might follow, must at
least have neutralized opposition if it did not secure adherence to the Asian labour policy.
    The support the Chamber received from a section of the
white population might be ascribed to three factors. The
first was a certain degree of coercion by the mining
managements to persuade workers to vote in favour of pro-
Chinese resolutions at the various meetings called by the
LIA. According to Kneebone, the Organizing Secretary of
the Johannesburg District Committee of the Amalgamated

Society of Engineers, the mine-owners '[stumped] the whole
line of reef, seeking by all and every means - mine captains at the chair at mine meetings, mine officials acting
as scrutineers of the voting etc - to manufacture ...
public opinion to be cabled home and elsewhere as a true
reflex of the feelings of this community'. (119)

The Transvaal Mineworkers' Association protested,
throughout the Chamber's campaign, against the coercion
of its members by the mine managements, their protests
reaching a peak on 9 August 1903 when the Association held
six different meetings and passed resolutions against the
'unmanly action of the management of various mines in attempting to coerce employees into signing for importation'. (120)   Raitt, one of the four opponents in the
Legislative Council of the Labour Ordinance, confirmed
the 'considerable pressure brought to bear upon the mining
employees to induce them to change their minds.... At the
mine meetings ... the mine manager was in the chair and
... when a vote was taken, the tellers were frequently or
nearly always "shift bosses".' (121)

A second reason for the support given to the Chamber
by a section of the white labour force was the threat of
unemployment in a 'crippled industry' if the Asian importation scheme was rejected. In view of the worsening
industrial and commercial depression, this threat may well
have been an important contribution to the 'shift in
public feeling' that Milner referred to at the end of
1903. (122)   The Chamber certainly made use of these fears
of unemployment. Hence a third reason for white support
of its scheme was the promise of future gain in the event
of a satisfactory influx of unskilled labour, and 'catas-
trophy' in the event of 'delay or rejection of Asian importation'. The spokesman for the mines told the white
mining men: 'There were 3,000 stamps on the Rand, which
if they were all working, would result in £450,000 being
disbursed among the white community.' (123)   In the same
vein, the Chamber showed that in the case of a particular
company an additional sum of £1,985,463 would be paid per
year in salaries and wages to white men if the 'present
stagnation' was overcome. In addition, 'a further sum of
£2,191,536 sterling per annum would be paid to the mer-
cantile community and the coal companies in the form of
trade accounts'. (124)   On the other hand, if the scheme
were delayed or rejected 'incalculable harm' or 'catastro-
phy' would ensue.

The catastrophe the Chamber referred to was the prospect of unemployment as a result of the cessation of
mining activity in the low-grade mines. This had been
said before, but the present threat of unemployment was

an important inducement to the white mining men and all other members of the white community who were dependent upon the mines in 1903 to silence their criticisms of the Chamber. It seems clear, however, that possibly the most significant step in securing white support for Chinese labour was the compromise taken by the Chamber to institutionalize work and wage constraints for Asian immigrants. It was this which evidently allayed the fears and apprehensions of the whites and assured them that the Asians would not take their jobs from them.

Hence the aptness of the accusation by the African Labour League that the Chamber was promising 'restrictions on the movements of Asiatics to catch votes'. Moreover, the League claimed that the Chamber had introduced 'with indecent haste' a resolution into the Legislative Council 'before the people had a chance of voting on it' - that is, before a referendum could decide the issue. (125)

The official view of the administration and the public statements by the Chamber combined during the closing stages of the agitation to convey to the imperial government an impression of increasing agreement on Asian labour. What was apparent, however, were the deep cleavages the various reports concealed. For example, Milner's report to the Colonial Secretary in 1904, which provided the imperial government with the 'consensus' news it required to give its sanction to the scheme, drew attention to what Milner considered to be a 'shift in public feeling' as the LIA 'made its impact' upon the public. He reported to the Colonial Secretary:

On 1st April /1903/ a great mass meeting which was held in Johannesburg, condemned Asiatic labour with hardly a dissident vote. A similar meeting held on 14th December 1903 was a complete fiasco and the opponents of Asiatic labour were obliged to fall back on a ticket meeting of 200 people in a small hall. (126)

The actual circumstances of the meeting referred to by the High Commissioner were not so unambiguously favourable to the Chamber. (127) On that occasion, on 14 December, the African Labour League called a meeting to urge upon the government 'the holding of a Referendum on the question of importation of Asiatics'. This meeting was 'packed' by the Chamber's supporters, who were exhorted to attend the gathering on the grounds that the meeting was being held to 'stop the absolutely necessary importation of indentured coloured labour' (Cd. 1895, 1904, p. 184). Failure to attend the meeting, it said, would result in the country's being 'ruined'. The consequent

attendance of 10,000 members of the white community was
an indication of the extent of coercion as well as of the
degree to which the matter excited the mining and commercial community. In the event, however, the gathering
was disrupted by the Chamber's supporters and the organ-
izers were prevented from presenting their resolution for
a referendum. (128)

There is no indication of the extent of the support the
ALL would have acquired for a referendum, (129) but it is
evident that the Chamber was anxious to prevent the
passage of a motion calling for one, (130) and took advantage of the chaos of the time to move a resolution
which was more consistent with the wishes of the mine-
owners, namely for the publication of a draft ordinance
as soon as possible to provide for the introduction of
'unskilled Coloured labour under proper restrictions as
to employment and repatriation'. (131)

It now remained for the Legislative Council to give
effect to the Chamber's scheme as well as to the first
statutory racist legislation since the war.

14 Racist legislation and the introduction of Chinese labour

INTRODUCTION

The interdependence of the mine-owners, the state, and the social classes that made up the 'white community' in the Transvaal was emphasized in the mine-owners' campaign in 1903 to preserve their wage structure. This interdependence was both a hindrance and a source of strength to the owners: a hindrance in that the Chamber could not act unilaterally but had to seek the support of the other two 'partners' for the stability of its policies; a source of strength in that once 'consensus' had been gained there was a degree of certainty that conflicts would be minimized.

In the campaign to secure Asian labour, the mine-owners who were at the centre of the three-way relationship needed the support of the local administration, the imperial government, and the various fractions of the white 'community' in the Transvaal Colony. For instance, they required the support of the imperial government to approve legislation and authorize the importation of Chinese labour, (1) and they needed the assistance of the local administration to approve and co-operate, providing legal sanctions against desertions or breaches of contract by the labourers whose indenture was obtained at such great effort and expense. (2) The mine-owners also needed the support of the different elements of the white community to minimize conflicts between white and Chinese mine-workers and appease the agricultural and commercial classes who feared competition and loss of trade, respectively, as a result of the importation of Chinese labour. (3) Support from these sources was also needed since the imperial government was prepared to import Asian workers on the Chamber's behalf only on the understanding that 'white opinion' was not seen to be hostile. (4) It

was primarily the latter precondition for state intervention which led the Chamber to embark upon the period
of 'agitation' and closer 'partnership' in which statutory
concessions were promised to the white mineworkers and
restrictions placed on Chinese migrants in respect of
farming and trading. (5)

In practical terms, all that now remained was for the
administration to set its seal to the details of the proposed arrangements. This it was prepared to do for the
following reasons: (i) its ties with the mining industry
(the Chamber had noted in 1903 that, if anything, 'the
chief gain that we must recognize in comparing our position today with our position before the war is that we
have now a pure and sympathetic government'); (6) and
(ii) the fact that it was to a large extent beholden to
the mining industry, since its public debt had increased
from £14 million in 1898 to £61.5 million in 1903. (7)
Since Milner's development plans were dependent on the
buoyancy of the gold industry, the Chamber was quick to
point out that 'all these optimistic estimates [new railways, municipal tramways, sewerage, lighting] are not
worth the paper they are written on, unless the mining
industry expands and prospers'. (8) The conditions for
'expansion' and 'prosperity' were in the Chamber's view
dependent upon a minimum cost structure which did not
admit of white unskilled labour. The administration supported this argument and saw the Chamber's campaign to
defend its labour structure as a guarantee of the future
profitability of the mines and of continued European
investment - which cause the state was keen to do its
share to encourage. Milner had publicly recognized by
July 1903 'that the domination of the Transvaal economy
by the Capitalist mining industry had in the end tied the
State as irreversibly to its demands for cheap unskilled
labour as it had the leaders of the industry'. (9)

Thus Milner's administration supported the introduction
in the Transvaal legislature of an ordinance which accepted in principle the indenture of Asian labour and
provided the specific constraints which inter alia relieved white fears for their jobs and which explicitly
excluded Chinese workers from any of the skilled mining
operations. (10)

(i) RACIST LEGISLATION: MINES, WORKS AND MACHINERY
ORDINANCE (1903); TRANSVAAL LABOUR IMPORTATION ORDINANCE
(1904)

These constraints and restrictions were provided in two

separate statutes: the Mines, Works and Machinery
Ordinance of 1903, and the Transvaal Labour Importation
Ordinance No.17 of 1904. (11)   The latter statute clari-
fied the ambiguity of the work category of 'unskilled
labour' by providing a comprehensive schedule of fifty-six
occupations from which Asian migrants were excluded. (12)
It also provided for the labourer's return to his country
of origin on the completion of his three-year contract and
thereby satisfied the apprehensions of miners and agriculturalists alike. (13)   These regulations were reinforced by the controlling provisions of the Transvaal
Labour Importation Ordinance, which prevented labourers,
so long as they resided in the Transvaal, from acquiring
licences to deal in liquor, mining, trading, hawking,
building and fixed property, which thereby extended the
co-operative partnership of the Chamber to the non-mining
sector of the economy. These constraints were introduced
specifically to reduce the fears among the white commercial and agricultural sectors which surfaced during
the 'agitation'.   Sir George Farrar best articulated the
nature of the alliance the Chamber was seeking with its
former critics when he addressed an audience of white
miners on the Reef.   His remarks were directed towards all
opponents of the Asian labour proposals, not specifically
the white miners:

> You in Boksburg are agitating against [Asians] coming
> into the country, and against them trading and holding
> land.   I am absolutely one with you.... If Asian
> labourers unfortunately have to be brought into this
> country, they can only be brought in under Government
> control, and only as unskilled labourers, prohibited
> to trade, prohibited to hold land or compete with any
> white man. (14)

Thus the Ordinance gave relief to a wide range of
economic fears which the Chamber found it essential to
assuage through racially discriminatory legislation to
reduce the hostility towards and secure support for Asian
indentured labour. There were several consequences that
emerged from this statutory action. One effect was to
provide heavy restrictions on the mobility of Chinese
labourers, who consequently became effectively prisoners
of the Chamber of Mines. (15) They were confined to the
premises on which they were employed and required a permit
to leave them - and even then could not absent themselves
for longer than forty-eight hours at any one time. (16)
In addition, and of major long-lasting significance, was
the impact of the legislation on the African workforce.

For the long list of restrictions on occupational practices intended for the Chinese were absorbed (under
government Notices) into the Mines, Works and Machinery
Ordinance of 1903 which militated against the occupational
mobility of Africans. (17) An enduring feature of the
'Asian exercise' was that the legislation initially introduced to allay white anxieties served subsequently to entrench a permanent racial wage and work bar in the country. The legislation served to secure and institutionalize the Chamber's labour structure. From the mine-owners'
point of view this was the most important implication of
all. Effectively the Mines, Works and Machinery Ordinance
removed the colour bar legislation of the old republican
laws (18) and cemented the Chamber's wage structure by
enabling the government to frame regulations where necessary under the Ordinance. This provided a modus operandi
for the unscrutinized enactment by Whitehall of racially
restrictive regulations through government notices. (19)
This was an oblique method of enacting legislation and
invited less attention in Britain. (20) Indeed, had the
Milner administration acted less obliquely and legislated
directly for a statutory colour bar, the matter would
doubtless have been the subject of closer scrutiny by the
Secretary of State in Whitehall. As it was, by 1906,
three years after the passage of the Act, the list of
'white-reserved' occupations had grown, without challenge,
from the category of mine managers to an extended range
which included onsetters, banksmen, engine drivers, boiler
attendants, lift operators and shift bosses. (21) The new
regulations either reserved for whites occupations previously carried out by a small number of Africans (for
example, banksmen and onsetters) or served to entrench the
'traditional' occupations of the white miners.
    It is significant that as a result of the Asian im-
portation scheme some of the inconsistencies in the Chamber's labour structure were ironed out, particularly those
involving supervisory functions. Banksmen and onsetters
were two cases in point, where no particular skill or
lengthy training was required, but each of these workers
gave instructions to the winding-engine drivers at the
top and bottom of the mine shaft and supervised the
loading of men and material into the skip. (22) Whereas
the Chamber had successfully made special representations
to the Volksraad in 1896, when the republican government
introduced the colour bar for these occupations, the
reverse was the case in regard to the 1903 regulations.
By that time these supervisory functions were undertaken
mostly by whites, and the jobs were listed (by the government mining engineer in 1902) as occupations reserved for

whites. (23)   The 1903 Mining Regulations simply institutionalized these arrangements.

The process by which these discriminatory regulations
developed serves to illustrate an interpretation of the
genesis of the industrial colour bar in South Africa,
namely that the discriminatory work and wage barriers were
not the result of 'racial beliefs, prejudices, or ideolo-
gies stemming from outside the economy' (24) but rather a
force emerging within the economy to preserve the wage and
work structure of the mining industry. This is borne out
by the point that the acquisition of Asian labour preserved the mines' labour structure and minimized costs.
(See Chapter 15.) This was possible because the relax-
ation of pressure on demand helped to avert any escalation
in wages which might otherwise have occurred. Indeed, the
flow of African labour that fulfilled the demand in the
following year - at no increase in wage rates - serves to
confirm the view that 'the presence of Chinese labour
helped to break African bargaining power'. (25)   The
matter is discussed fully in Chapter 15, and its significance for all those concerned in the production of gold -
management and labour - cannot be over-emphasized. Undoubtedly the scheme provided the Chamber with the
'breathing space' it needed to maintain its structure,
and justified its expenditure and effort on importing the
new migrants who arrived from Hong Kong and (contrary to
earlier expectations) North China after June 1904.

(ii)   ORGANIZATION AND ARRIVAL OF CHINESE INDENTURED
LABOUR

The large-scale organization made necessary by the Chamber's scheme of long-distance recruitment proved complicated and costly. It was an extensive undertaking and,
administratively, appeared to be an extension of the local
organization for African migrant labour in which the
Chamber's monopoly was all-important. Depots and recep-
tion units were established in various parts of China with
a manager and staff with headquarters in Tientsin. The
administrative unit responsible for the exercise was
similar in structure to the WNLA. It was called the
Chamber of Mines Labour Importation Agency (CMLIA), with
the executive of the Chamber of Mines composing the Board
of the Agency. (26)   Recruiting fees were naturally higher
than for African migrants. The cost per recruit was £17,
which covered the passage, railway rates from the coast,
subsistence depots en route from China, medical fees and
'incidental' expenses. The 'blanket fee' also covered the

cost of repatriation, and a capitation fee to the Chinese
government. (27)   Only an institution with experience in
the large-scale mobilization and recruitment of labourers,
and the resources of the Chamber, could conduct so extensive an exercise.   As Richardson points out:

> Only the pooled resources of the mining companies could
> hope to meet these requirements satisfactorily enough
> to maintain State support without hopelessly escalating
> recruiting and shipping costs. Diverse and dispersed
> activities could easily weaken the industry's bargain-
> ing position in relation to the various contractors
> connected to the whole process of emigration and expose
> the mining houses to expensive local difficulties.
> Strong centralized control over importation [was] ...
> imperative. (28)

The first contingent of labourers consisted of approximately 1,055 men who were settled - in separate quarters -
on the East Rand Proprietary mine. (29)   By December 1904
thirteen shipments had arrived and some 10,918 Chinese
migrants were employed on sixteen selected mines along
the Rand. (30)   Whilst the first shipload brought men from
Hong Kong, almost all the others were recruited in the
northern provinces bordering on the gulf of Chili, and
inquiries were afoot for further supplies in the Yangtze
Kiang valley. (31)
    In all, approximately 63,000 Chinese labourers came to
the Transvaal between 1904 and 1906. (32)   The men were
used largely (but not exclusively) by those mining groups
with deep-level interests.   Hence the three groups Farrar/
Anglo French (not exclusively deep-level companies), Rand
Mines and Consolidated Goldfields had Chinese labourers as
48.95 per cent, 42.71 per cent and 35.48 per cent respectively of their overall labour force. (33)   Other
groups with substantial deep-level interests - A.Goerz &
Co., Neumann & Co., and H.Eckstein & Co. (through its connection with Rand Mines) were also dependent on Chinese
labour for roughly one-quarter of their labour supply.
General Mining had 34.5 per cent Chinese, and Johannesburg
Consolidated Investment Co. 24.8 per cent.   J.B.Robinson
(whose interests were not deep-level) had only 10.55 per
cent. (34)   The men were treated as so many units of
labour. They were largely unmarried, and were housed in
compounds according to a small specified cubic air space
for each labourer. (35)   The living conditions were overcrowded and unhygienic, and there was evidence of bubonic
plague. (36)
    The wage paid to the Chinese labourers was the subject

of contention between the Chamber and the government Mines
Department. The latter claimed that the average Chinese
wage was 33s. 6d. per calendar month, as opposed to 53s.
paid to Africans. The Chamber claimed that the Chinese
were paid 52s. 10d. for thirty shifts, as opposed to
56s. 6d. for Africans. But these figures did not reflect
actual wages, for they included compound, recruiting and
repatriation expenses. According to the Ordinance a
minimum of 50s. should be paid to the Chinese recruits.
The mine-owners claimed that they exceeded this (52s. in
1904 and 53s. 9d. in 1905), (37) but the Economic Commission disputed this. According to the Commission wages
were 6d. or 1s. less than that paid to the African workforce, but fell within the Chamber's scheduled margin of
1s. to 2s. 6d. per shift. (38) But more significant than
the wage disparity between the Chinese and African members
of the unskilled labour force was the fact that the
Chinese presence on the mines enabled the Chamber system-
atically to reduce African wages, bringing them down close
to the level of Chinese wages. In January 1905 the
Average African wage rate was 56s. 7d. per month. It
declined to 55s. 6d. in February, 55s. 1d. in March,
54s. 5d. in April, 53s. 11d. in May, 53s. 6d. in June,
with sharper falls towards the end of the year, causing
the average wage to be 51s. 9d. in 1905. (39) This reduction, together with the decline in the engagement of
African labour (described in the next chapter), were the
two most obvious and immediate consequences of the Chinese
presence on the mines. The statutory colour bar and the
institutional arrangements which developed from the importation of Chinese labour were other dimensions of the
'Chinese alternative'.

Thus Chinese labour both preserved the labour structure
and reduced costs. (40) In the long run the latter was
the most significant; but the cost reduction is also important, for the action taken by the Chamber to revise
contracts and reduce wages caused some decrease in the
African labour force after March 1905 as workers were not
prepared to accept the revised contract conditions. (41)
When they returned to the mines, they did so largely on
the Chamber's new terms. (See Chapter 15, pp.234,241.)

On the administrative side, and intrinsic to the question of costs, tighter controls were exercised in 1905 by
the Chamber over its Chinese workmen to increase productivity. These were effected through amendments to the
Labour Importation Ordinance and allowed (i) summary
trials by resident magistrates at the place of work;
(ii) the infliction of collective fines for crimes committed by any one member of the work section; and (iii)

'any White man to arrest without warrant any Chinese labourer found outside the Witwatersrand district'. (42) The drive to reduce costs and increase productivity inevitably provoked criticism abroad. Predictably the Chamber rejected 'the taint of slavery which ... Campbell Bannerman and his friends [felt sure] pervaded the whole question of Chinese labour'. (43)

Eventually, at the end of 1905, in response to liberal protest, the imperial government decided to halt further recruitment pending the granting of responsible government to the Transvaal. The provision for a constitution of government for that Colony was made in Letters Patent dated 6 December 1906, and a clause in that document stated that no further licences would be issued for the introduction of Chinese labourers into the Colony. The overt reasons for this action were twofold. The first noted (rather belatedly) that the employment of Asians was an experiment which should not be extended until the opinion of the elected representatives of the Colony had been obtained. The second stated significantly that the danger of financial crisis had disappeared since the pre-war African labour force had been exceeded, and the scheme was no longer essential. (44) This was true, but it was due not so much to the 'breathing space' the mine-owners had enjoyed as to the direct effects of the indenture of Chinese labourers. Indeed, as the Transvaal Legislative Council prepared to repeal the Transvaal Labour Ordinance African labour was reported to be 'plentiful' and recruiting continued apace with no increase in the wage rate and on contractual terms more favourable to the Chamber than previously. (45)

The important legacy of the Transvaal Labour Ordinance was that it got the Chamber 'over the hump' (46) and that its occupational provisions were adopted by the discriminatory Mines, Works and Machinery Ordinance and made applicable to the rest of the migrant workforce. The cancellation of the scheme and the withdrawal of the Chinese labour force ought not to be seen as a measure of its failure. On the contrary, the Chamber's three-sided strategy had succeeded impressively. It had maintained its low wage levels for the migrant workforce, and even reduced the costs of production. The pressure for the employment of whites in unskilled jobs had been resisted, and the labour structure had been kept intact. The cost of the Chinese venture, undertaken in the defence of the labour structure, was £1,013,000, representing a total of between £16 and £18 per indentured labourer. (47) But it would have cost the industry a great deal more if the 'Chinese experiment' had not been adopted.

15 The restoration of the labour supply

(i) INCREASE IN THE SUPPLY, 1904-6: SELECTIVE RECRUITING

The significant increase in African recruitment in the
months after the passage of the Transvaal Labour Ordinance
in 1904 would lead one to assume that the case for importing Asian labour was not as desperate as the Chamber had
suggested. But the matter was more complicated than this.

The large-scale entry of Africans into the labour
market after 1904 was due to a conjunction of circumstances, only one of which was the impact of Chinese
labour, which cumulatively enabled the Chamber to
strengthen and surpass its pre-war workforce within two
years of the passing of the Ordinance. Recruiting activities - albeit of a selective kind - were extended into
areas where the WNLA had not previously enjoyed facilities
and had recently negotiated recruiting rights. (1) More
money was spent on recruitment, with expenditure mounting
as the work of the WNLA increased. Between 1901 and 1905
the Association spent £952,278, of which over half was
spent in 1904 and 1905. (2) The result was a presence
of 85,377 Africans on the Witwatersrand in 1903, increasing to 87,891 in 1904 and again to 101,524 in 1905.
(3) If the African workforce employed by contractors was
included, the numbers given of Africans on the mines would
be still higher. (4)

In addition to the stepping-up of recruiting activities, new liquor arrangements and the passage of more
rigorous Pass Regulations combined to increase productivity and to steady the labour supply by curbing turnover,
although 'desertions' were still high in 1905 and 1906,
when the number of men who withdrew their labour in breach
of their contracts was upwards of 10 per cent of the total
workforce. Numerically this was recorded as 10,223 and
11,973 for 1905 and 1906 respectively. (5)

231 Chapter 15

Despite the relatively high turnover of labour, however, there seemed to be a steady and 'gradual augmentation of the supply'. (6) The increase in the wage rate
introduced in April 1903 slowly began to have its effect
on the market, especially after 1904, although in that
year the supply from Portuguese East Africa was the lowest
it had been for some time, for reasons discussed below.
Recruitment throughout the African labour market, particularly in areas outside British South Africa, was
buoyant, especially in 1905, despite the fact that recruiting activity was selective in character. This selectivity continued until 1906, by which time Chinese indentured labour outnumbered the 'Portuguese African component
of the workforce by more than 10,000 men. The general
policy appears to have been the recruitment, in the ratio
of approximately 1:2, of the more skilled and experienced
men who had previously worked on the mines. (7) Table
15.1 provides some indication of this 'trend' which began
in December 1903. It is noteworthy that the Chamber's
policy of selective recruitment, despite the much-publi-
cized shortage, anticipated the arrival of Chinese labour
and continued in operation after they were deployed in
the mines. The effects of this selectivity on the African
workforce is noted below.
The rate of recruitment was maintained in 1905, despite
the fact that in that year 50 per cent of the 38,409
labourers (8) recruited from Portuguese East Africa were
men who had already served one or more contracts on the
mines. (9) (See Table 15.1.)
An additional reason for the improvement in the labour
supply (according to the Chamber) was the effect of unemployment on the commercial sector in 1904, caused, it
claimed, by the relative 'stagnation' of this sector as
a result of the labour shortage on the mines. But this
argument on its own is circuitous and 'Chamber-centred'
and omits the effects of a serious harvest failure which
coincided with the depression of 1904. This is not to
dismiss the effects of the depression, but to indicate
that there were several reasons for the improvement in
the supply. (10) Generally the increase might be attributed to all the factors outlined here, in addition to the
effect of the slump which had begun in 1903 and continued
into 1904, when 'widespread retrenchment in public and
private enterprise' took place and Africans found ordinary
jobs closed to them at a time when they had 'simultaneously to face the consequence of bad harvests'. (11)
For the first three months of 1905 the demand for
labour was fully satisfied, and even a small surplus
emerged. The numbers recruited in these months 'were

TABLE 15.1   Proportion of 'Old Mine Africans' employed from 1 December 1903 to April 1904

Month	No. re-cruited East Coast	'Old Mine boys'	%	No. re-cruited Pieters-berg	'Old Mine boys'	%
December 1903	2,084	1,164	55.84	635	326	51.33
January 1904	1,585	905	37.09	848	487	57.42
February 1904	1,472	824	55.97	1,083	630	58.17
March 1904	1,915	1,142	56.93	996	531	53.31
April 1904	1,510	982	64.77	713	451	63.25

Source: WNLA, Schedule E 1904. Cited 'TCM 15th Annual Report 1904', p.49.

much larger even than ... in the last three months of 1904 which in turn surpassed all previous records'. (12) Lower mortality and some improvements in health helped to make the supply firmer, and there were fewer reported cases of sickness, although pneumonia and respiratory diseases were still important causes of death on the mines. If one in-cludes accidents and diseases, the death rate for 1903 was 80.92 per thousand, declining to 48.2 per thousand in 1904. (Diseases alone accounted for 43.97 per thousand in that year.) (13) Although mortality was still very high, the decreasing rates and the net increase in recruitment generally strengthened the supply. The rate of mortality was highest amongst Africans from the Portuguese East African possessions, where serious poverty was reported. (See below.)

Relative to the total supply the Portuguese East African contingent was falling. In 1903 the number of recruits from the areas of Gaza, Inhambane and Lourenco Marques Districts was 43,625, or 51.09 per cent of the grand total recruited for the mines. In 1904 the numbers from these areas fell to 27,633 or (at the most generous of the Chamber's calculations) 40.5 per cent of the total, and in 1905 the proportion was still lower, although actual numbers had risen to 38,469 recruits, comprising 36.2 per cent of the total. (14) No increase was recorded

in 1904 from the traditional sources in Portuguese East
Africa (those south of latitude 22°), the main areas of
increase on the East Coast being the newly tapped districts of Tete and Quilimane.

(ii)   FLUCTUATIONS IN THE 'PORTUGUESE' AFRICAN LABOUR
SUPPLY

The overall increase in the labour force in the early
months of 1905, which reduced the 'Portuguese' African
proportion of the total, was due to an improvement in the
Chamber's recruiting activity in the Transvaal, Cape and
Rhodesia, where most significant, though temporary, increases were made; (15) and, of course, to the indentured
Chinese labourers, who soon replaced the East African
labour force as the largest single component of unskilled
workers on the mines. (16) The downturn in recruitment
from the East Coast in 1904, the first year of the arrival
of the relatively long-term Chinese workers, appears to be
the consequence of several factors. The first of these
was the selective recruitment of 'old hands' who had already served one or more terms on the mines. During April
1904 the percentage of Africans in the category of 'old
mine boys' was 64 per cent from the East Coast. (17) The
ratio of new to 'old' hands fell to 46 per cent in August,
when the supply from the traditional areas of Gaza,
Inhambane and Lourenco Marques greatly improved. (18) The
Chamber, however, conceded that this selectivity was a
cause of the decrease in the supply from the 'traditional'
areas in this region, but attributed the 'delay' in recruitment of the men 'who otherwise would be leaving home'
to the high rainfall in March and April which prevented
the gathering of crops. Other reasons for the 'small
output' of African labourers were given to the WNLA by
the Governor-General of Lourenco Marques. According to
this official the decrease in the supply was 'chiefly due
to abnormally plentiful crops ... the accumulation of cash
by the returning natives [who] had not had the same opportunity as formerly of spending their earnings in the
Transvaal ... [and] that the natives were becoming more
and more agriculturalists, and were finding out that they
could provide themselves with what they wanted by the sale
of the produce they grew'. (19)
    Despite these apparently deep-seated reasons, the flow
of labour from the 'traditional' districts of Portuguese
East Africa soon began to improve, as did the supply from
the districts north of latitude 22° - except in 1905,
where recruiting ceased for a short period owing to the

high mortality rate of recruits on the mines from these districts. In general, however, the supply of labour from the traditional areas rose substantially in 1905 and virtually maintained its buoyancy in 1906, as indicated in Table 15.2. (20)

TABLE 15.2   Portuguese East African recruitment, 1901-6 (excluding Quilamane and Tete)

District	1901	1902	1903	1904	1905	1906
Provinces of Mocambique: Lourenco Marques, Gaza, Inhambane	-	38,111	43,625	27,633	38,469	36,401
Mocambique District	-	494	1,086	1,308	1,568	2,073
Total		38,605	44,711	28,941	40,037	38,474

Sources: 'TCM 15th Annual Report 1904', pp.412-13; 'WNLA Annual Report 1905', p.362; 'WNLA Annual Report 1906', p.583.

Thus with the help of its Chinese labour force the Chamber had held on to its wage structure, and when the Portuguese labourers entered the mines in great numbers they did so without the Chamber having to make any compromises in its current wage and work terms.

Tables 15.3 and 15.4 afford a comparison of recruitment between the 'Portuguese' Africans and those in British Africa during 1903 and 1905. Table 15.5 gives the figures for the Province of Mocambique and includes the recruiting regions of Quilimane and Tete - new areas of recruitment in which there was much rural distress. Here 1,938 Africans were recruited in 1904 as against 447 in the previous year. (21) Poverty may provide one of the chief explanations for the increase in the overall number of recruits. Destitution was chronic, and spread from Quilimane and Tete to the coastal districts of Mocambique. The whole of this territory, which was carefully covered by the recruiting agents, was prone to serious distress. In all, three crowded administrative districts were formed to recruit labourers, namely Lourenco Marques, Gaza and Inhambane. Of the 50,000 miles the territory covered, over half was barren, waterless and scant of population.

TABLE 15.3   Recruitment during 1903

		Percentage of total
Cape Colony	7,082	8.29
Bechuanaland	2,730	3.19
Basutoland	2,008	2.35
Transvaal	11,775	13.79
Swaziland	273	0.31
Orange River Colony	50	0.05
Province of Mocambique –		
South of latitude 22°	43,625	51.09
No.2 District	1,086	1.22
Quilimane District	447	0.52
Beira	84	0.09
British Central Africa Protectorate	941	1.10
German South West Africa	620	0.72
Local	14,656	17.16
Total	85,377	

Source: WNLA cited in 'TCM 15th Annual Report 1904', p.100.

TABLE 15.4   Recruitment during 1905

British South Africa	
Transvaal	14,199
Swaziland	39
Bechuanaland	2,352
Cape Colony	10,580
Basutoland	2,382
Rhodesia	4,005
British Central Africa	
Central African Protectorate	1,398
North East Rhodesia	482
Port Jameson	130
Portuguese East Africa	
Gaza, Inhambane and Lourenco Marques Districts: South of latitude 22°	38,469
Quilimane and Tete Districts	587
Mocambique District	1,568
Nyasa	94
Beira and Chinde	177
German West Africa	40
Local	24,482
Total	101,524

Source: 'TCM 16th Annual Report 1905', p.11.

TABLE 15.5   Portuguese East African recruitment, 1901-6

District	1901	1902	1903	1904	1905	1906
Provinces of Mocambique: Lourenco Marques, Gaza, Inhambane	-	38,111	43,625	27,633	38,469	36,401
Quilimane and Tete	-	-	447	1,938	587	1,359
Mocambique District	-	494	1,086	1,308	1,568	2,073
Total		38,605	45,158	30,879	40,624	39,833

Sources: 'TCM Fifteenth Annual Report 1904', pp.412-13;
'WNLA Annual Report 1905', and 'Annual Report 1906', p.
583.

Hence the people were concentrated in the habitable parts
south of latitude 22°. Here, in 1903, 100,000 lived in
Lourenco Marques, 180,000 in the Gaza districts and
360,000 in Inhambane. (22) Moreover, the Portuguese
believed an extra 25 per cent could be added to the
640,000 they had estimated initially, making for a population of 800,000 concentrated in a ratio of thirty inhabitants to the square mile in the habitable regions.
    When there was rural distress, therefore, it was con-
centrated in a highly populated area and the exodus to the
mines increased. Between 1902 and 1905 over 148,358 men
from this territory were recruited, an average of 37,000
per annum. The men worked on the mines for a year or
more: 'More than half the males of working age ... [were]
constantly at work for European employers.' (23) Recruiting agents, pressed to maximize recruiting, frequently
signed on men whose 'poor standard of efficiency and
physique' were quickly evident to the mine managements.
(24) An indication of the extent of physical weakness
amongst these recruits can be gauged from the WNLA's establishment in 1904 of a hospital 'for the temporary detention of incoming natives not quite fit for mine work'.
(25) According to the Medical Officer of the WNLA, the
mortality rate in these areas could 'reasonably be in-
ferred to have been very great because owing to the
failure of crops, famine prevailed in the districts from
which the natives came.... The natives who came here were
emaciated, weak and scorbutic, but according to all ac-

counts those who remained were in a still worse condition.' (26)   The mortality rate of Africans from
Quilimane and Tete was as high as 140.97 per thousand in
1905, and though it decreased quite substantially to 37.82
in 1906, it was still excessively high. (27)   Recruits
from the Mocambique District were equally susceptible -
90.95 per thousand in 1905, and 59.45 in 1906. (28)   Nyasa
men were also highly prone to death in the mines, with a
rate of 80.36 per thousand in 1906 showing little improvement on the previous year. (29)

(iii)   LOCAL, CENTRAL AND WEST AFRICAN LABOUR

Generally, the British Foreign Office rallied to the needs
of the Chamber and authorized the emigration of 5,000
Africans from the geographically elevated districts of
British Central Africa. (30)   Some recruitment was also
negotiated from German West Africa, and the WNLA recruited
1,000 from this area for part of 1904.   Approximately
2,362 Africans were forwarded by 'the Rhodesian Labour
Bureau to the Witwatersrand' in 1904, and a further 4,005
in 1905. (31)   At the local level, the WNLA recruited
10,405 Africans from the Cape Colony in 1904, and a further 10,580 the following year for short periods for surface work.   (The Cape men consistently refused to undertake underground work.) (32)   Finally, 10,597 men were
recruited from the Transvaal's northern districts in 1904,
and a further 14,109 in 1905.   Some small numbers were
also acquired from the eastern part of the Transvaal. (33)
In addition to these, in 1904 a large number of men,
totalling 26,924 in all, either transferred their service
from one mine to another, or came to the mines from the
African areas independently of the WNLA.   In 1905, 24,482
men were re-engaged, (34) and the number increased in 1906
to 36,564. (35)
   It would seem that a significant inducement to work in
the Transvaal was the collection of taxes.   Under Ordinance No.20 of 1902 every adult male resident there was
required to pay a consolidated tax of £2.   Tax collection
had been postponed in view of post-war rural hardship, but
it was enforced in 1904 to relieve the labout shortage.
Its imposition was coincidental with the payment of war
loss compensation.   According to one source 'the result
of enacting the provisions of the ordinance ... in this
district has been that the prison here is full to over-
flowing'. (36)

(iv)   IMPACT OF CHINESE LABOUR ON AFRICAN RECRUITMENT

In effect, from 1904 onwards, the number of Africans employed on the mines increased steadily from between approximately 76,000-78,000 in 1904 (37) to more than three
times that number in the two years preceding the outbreak
of the First World War. The total number of Africans engaged in both producing and non-producing mines during the
latter six months of 1904 and after must have given great
satisfaction to the mine-owners, especially since work on
the non-producing mines was made possible by the employment of Chinese labour. Table 15.6 illustrates the improving position for the mine-owners.

TABLE 15.6   Labour recruitment, 1904-12

Year	African recruitment	
1904	68,438*)	In addition 53,828
1905	91,816)	Chinese migrant labourers
1906	85,538)	were employed
1907	106,232	
1908	140,304	
1909	162,439	
1910	183,613	
1911	189,912	
1912	192,575	

Source: 'TCM 23rd Annual Report 1912', p.77.

*   The figures for 1904 differ in the Chamber's records.
    In the 'TCM 15th Annual Report 1904', p.xxv, 'the dis-
    position of natives received during the year by the
    WNLA' was 78,121. In the WNLA's table of actual re-
    cruits the number is listed as 60,967. The latter
    figure seems the most probable.

The total supply situation had unquestionably turned in
favour of the mine-owners, and there seems no doubt that
the main reason for this was the importation of Chinese
labour.

As the resident magistrate for Baberton reported in
June 1905 ('Transvaal Administration Reports', 30 June
1905, p.L166):

I have been informed native labour is more plentiful
now than it has been for the past seven years. There
are several contributing causes, but the chief is
without doubt the importation of Chinese labour to the
Rand. The exhaustion of the money earned during the
war, taxes, locusts and bad seasons have all had their
effect in producing more native labour.

Similarly, the magistrate for Krugersdorp noted ('Tvl.
Admin. Rep.' 30.6.1905, p.LN9):

Throughout the latter portion of the year native labour
has been fairly plentiful, and is now more plentiful
than at any time since the war. This is principally
due to the introduction of Chinese labour for mining
work, which has rendered a much larger number of
natives available for farm work. Wages have fallen
slightly since June 1902.

The improvement in the total supply situation as well
as the declining number of African employees relative to
Chinese continued in 1906, the year that indentured licences ended. During that year 13,067 fewer African miners
were employed in the Witwatersrand area compared to the
previous year, although there was an overall increase in
the employment of unskilled labour. The position is illustrated in Tables 15.7 and 15.8 respectively.

The most general indicator of the extent to which the
labour strategies of the mine-owners had proved successful
during the early post-war years is the change in the ratio
of 'coloured' (including Chinese) to white labour between
1899 and 1906, as the figures in Table 15.9 show.

Table 15.6 illustrates the success of the Chamber in
recruiting labour on a minimum cost basis in the decade
after the South African War. But the satisfaction of need
is relative, and no sooner had supply moved closer to
demand than the existing norms became outdated and new
norms were created. (38) What was significant about all
this, however, was not only the relative increase in
numbers but also the fact that the supply was obtained on
the basis of the Chamber's selective wage and work policies.

With the augmentation of the unskilled workforce by
Chinese labour and the steady increase in African recruits, the 1903 shortage was turned into a surplus. In
February 1905 it was reported in Johannesburg that 'generally speaking every mine under supervision has its full
complement of surface boys, numbers being turned away
daily'. (39) It was now possible for the mines to select

TABLE 15.7 Number of Africans and Chinese employed by the gold mines on the last working day of each month during the year 1905-6

Month	Coloured (African)	Chinese
1905		
July	103,623	43,191
August	100,081	44,609
September	97,721	44,538
October	96,392	45,956
November	96,283	45,856
December	93,831	47,267
1906		
January	93,933	47,166
February	93,843	50,000
March	94,277	49,922
April	93,739	49,832
May	92,576	50,974
June	90,882	52,352
June 1905	104,902	41,340

Source: Report of Government Mining Engineer 1905-6.

TABLE 15.8 Decrease in employment of African workers relative to Chinese, 1905-6

Date	Producing Mines		Non-producing Mines	
	African	Chinese	African	Chinese
30 June 1905	84,318	36,320	10,991	5,020
30 June 1906	74,556	49,541	7,686	2,811
Increase	-	13,221	-	-
Decrease	9,762	-	3,305	2,209

Source: Report of Government Mining Engineer, 30 June 1906, p.3.

TABLE 15.9   Ratio of white to coloured labour, 1899-1906

Date	Whites	Coloured and Chinese
July 1899*	1	8.578
June 1902	1	4.343
June 1903	1	5.383
June 1904	1	5.434 (including Chinese)
June 1905	1	8.457 (including Chinese)
June 1906	1	7.822

*   June figures not available

Source: Report of Government Mining Engineer 1905-6, p.3.

the sort of employees they most ideally wanted: 'good
workers or old mine hands'.   According to one official
source the Inspector at Boksburg reported: 'Many natives
are seeking work.   I estimate 75% are [Cape] Colony
natives sent by bad crops and the closing of the Cookhouse
railway.' (40)   By 1906 the total African supply was again
buoyant, though less than in 1905.   The Chinese component
increased, however.

A further effect of the indenture of Chinese labour was
therefore to reduce the employment opportunities for the
black workforce and enable mine managements to select recruits under conditions very favourable to themselves.
Hence in 1905, as the supply situation improved, short-
term contracts were rejected in favour of contracts with
those labourers willing to serve for a year.   Men wishing
to work on the surface were turned down in favour of those
willing to work underground. (41)   For what was a brief
first time in the industry's history, conditions of employment could be dictated with confidence by the owners.
It could be said, in Denoon's words, that the period ended
the short phase when black labour 'held the whiphand'.
(42)   Wages accordingly declined steadily in the months
of 1905, (43) as Table 15.10 shows.

The effect of these wage reductions, as well as worsening labour and compound conditions in 1905 and 1906, were
a relatively high withdrawal of labour and a rise in the
number of complaints registered. (44)   According to the
'Transvaal Administration Reports' for the years 1905 and
1906, the total number of men prosecuted, accused and con-
victed under the Pass Laws had more than doubled.   (This
is shown in Table 15.12.)   As most of the 'criminal cases'
occurred in the principal mining areas of Johannesburg,

TABLE 15.10   African wage levels, January-July 1905

January	56s. 7d.
February	55s. 6d.
June	53s. 6d.
July	53s. 11d.

Source: Denoon, The Transvaal Labour Crisis 1901-6,
'Journal of African History', vol.III, no.3, 1967, p.493.

Krugersdorp, Germiston, Florida and Roodepoort (see Table
15.11), it would be correct to assume that the majority of
those involved were African mineworkers.

TABLE 15.11   Criminal cases in principal mining areas of
Johannesburg, Krugersdorp, Germiston, Florida, Roodepoort,
year ending 30 June 1905

Prosecutions	Accused	Convictions
4,485	7,815	7,587

Source: 'Tvl. Admin. Report', 30 June 1905, p.M7.

TABLE 15.12   Return of all criminal cases dealt with and
disposed of in courts of the chief magistrate and resident
magistrates,1905-6 (Pass Laws)

Date	Prosecuted	Accused	Convicted
30 June 1906	12,936	20,128	17,483
30 June 1905	5,638	8,718	8,124

Sources: 'Tvl. Admin. Report 1904-5', pp.A9-10;   'Tvl.
Admin. Report 1905-6', pp.A15,16.

Despite infringements of the Pass Laws and the withdrawal of labour, however, the demand for labour was
satisfied for the moment, and just as all mining labour
needs were met in 1905, the supply of unskilled labour in
1906 was said to be 'plentiful', and, depending on such
circumstances as 'good crops, or their failure', the
Chamber now felt the labour problem was under control.
   Indeed, the Chairman of the Chamber, careful to state
that the present satisfactory supply had much to do with
the presence of over 53,000 Chinese labourers, noted that

'the figures ... show that during the year 1906 the fluctuations have been lower than usual, and at present native
labour may be said to be plentiful'. (45) There were
regular net monthly increases in the recruitment of Africans during 1905, and, as we noted, an adequate supply for
1906, although there was an overall decline in recruitment
for that year. (46) It must be assumed, given the Chamber's statements in 1906 (see below), that the mine
managements had as much labour as they wanted and were in
a position to adjust the supply as they wished and to
withstand the desertions which followed the new contract
conditions. (47)

It would seem that the workers most affected by the
combined size of the African and Chinese labour supplies
were the migrant workers from the Cape Colony, who reacted
sharply to wage reductions and consistently showed a
definite preference for short-term contracts and surface
work. (48) As the Chamber reported 10,580 employees (49)
from the Cape in 1905 and 4,055 for 1906, (50) the decline
must have had much to do with the WNLA's selective recruiting policies. (51) Indeed, the selectivity of the
mine-owners and their strategy of employing the 'best'
African labour available led to their rejection of 'a
large proportion' of the vast number of African labourers
recruited in 1905 as 'constituting ... classes unadapted
to, and unsuitable for underground mine work'. Nevertheless - despite this - for part of the year the Chamber
experienced some difficulty in 'finding employment for
all labour coming forward'. (52) With virtually half the
number of Africans engaged in 1905 being placed on twelve-
month contracts, and recruitment being well ahead of any
previous years since the war, the Board of Management of
the WNLA now ceased to refer to recruits as an undifferentiated quantity of muscle-power. They became instead
'labourers of varying grades'.

(v) IMPACT OF CHINESE LABOUR ON 'WHITE' EMPLOYMENT

The 'unexpected and almost phenomenal recruiting of Native
labour' in the early months of 1905 (see Appendix 3) also
affected the employment of white miners, whose numbers had
increased from a total of 14,346 in December 1904 to
17,696 in 1906 in the producing and non-producing mines.
(53) With the influx of Chinese labour and the more
vigorous recruiting of Africans, the mine-owners' strategy
appears to have been to use white labour on a growing
scale in the producing and non-producing mines. (54)

With the imperial government's announcement at the end

of 1905 that no further licences for the importation of
Chinese would be granted, the Chamber anticipated a re-
striction in the supply of new capital and undertook
little new work.   Construction work currently in progress
was completed, but no further new work in the developing
mines (which financed such development from new capital)
was undertaken.   The immediate impact on the white miners
was that the number employed on these non-producing mines
fell from 3,657 in January 1906 to 1,958 in December. (55)
There was, moreover, a direct threat to white employment
in the producing mines, where the surfeit of unskilled
labourers made the use of machine rock-drills - supervised
by white labour - uneconomic.   The problem was well stated
by Sir Lionel Phillips, the Johannesburg representative of
the Rand Mines group:

> The necessity to [consider further work] ... has arisen
> rather suddenly owing to the unexpected ... recruiting
> of Native labour which during last month added 11,000
> to the supply.   In view of the rapidly rising number of
> Chinese and Natives available, the condition of affairs
> which we had anticipated to arise in time seems likely
> to be upon us ... so much so, that they tell me they
> are thinking of placing hand drillers in stopes where
> rock drills had to be used owing to the scarcity of
> manual labour....   About 2,500 White men could upon
> this ground alone be dispensed with in time, but it
> is, of course, out of the question to dismiss them.
> It would at once be said that White men were being dis-
> placed by Chinamen....   The increasing Native labour
> supply will very soon necessitate extra work to find
> occupation for them. (56)

The livelihood of white artisans as well as other
workers on the mines, and 'numerous residents whose living
is indirectly derived from the mining industry', (57) thus
became linked with the Chamber's campaign to reverse the
imperial government's decision to authorize licences for
the indenture of Chinese labour.   For the moment, however,
the supply of unskilled labour was deemed 'plentiful',
(58) and white labour would not (as Phillips feared) be
seen to be 'displaced by Chinamen', (59) although the
continued employment of whites on the developing mines
in the existing high numbers was in some doubt.   Table
15.13 shows their decreasing employment on the non-
producing mines after January 1906.

TABLE 15.13 Whites employed on producing and non-producing mines, 1903-6

Date		Producing mines	Non-producing mines	Total
December	1903	9,153	2,891	12,044
December	1904	12,124	2,222	14,346
December	1905	13,679	3,569	17,248
January	1906	14,039	3,657	17,696
February	1906	14,120	3,550	17,670
March	1906	14,423	3,345	17,768
April	1906	14,417	2,816	17,233
May	1906	14,806	2,685	17,491
June	1906	15,023	2,185	17,208
July	1906	14,946	2,041	16,987
August	1906	14,927	1,985	16,912
September	1906	14,826	1,969	16,796
October	1906	15,053	1,950	17,003
November	1906	15,026	1,910	16,936
December	1906	14,860	1,958	16,818

Source: 'TCM 17th Annual Report 1906', p.xxviii.

(vi)   IMPACT ON RECRUITING PATTERNS

The increasing efficiency of Chinese labourers, whose contracts were often for periods three times longer than those of African workers, was a subject of increasing interest to the Chamber. The extent to which this factor influenced the recruitment of Africans at the end of 1905 and in 1906 is unclear, although important cost analyses undertaken by the Chamber produced results highly favourable to the Chinese. (60) There were, however, other problems connected with recruitment which were not necessarily linked to the Chinese labour supply. As Jeeves pointed out:

one of the difficulties of anticipating labour needs was that an increase in recruitment levels in one month would inevitably produce an accelerated outflow six to

twelve months later as the contracts of these workers
expired. Any sudden change in recruiting methods was
likely to catch the industry unawares. (61)

In this respect a case in point was the Tete District,
where high recruitment in 1904 and changes in recruiting
strategies in 1905 seriously affected the numbers acquired
in 1905 and 1906. (See p.236.) The system of recruitment
seems to have got out of hand in the first nine months of
1906, coinciding with Robinson's withdrawal from the WNLA
and with an increase in the local (non-recruited) supply
of African labour. Migrants either evaded the WNLA and
entered the labour market independently or were acquired
clandestinely by certain mine managements. (62) Between
January and October 1906, 16,756 of the total of 26,256
men (63) entered the labour force independently of the
WNLA. (64) Indeed, the situation was such that 'management was able to rely on its Chinese labour and continued
to regulate its unskilled labour content by making contract improvements when black labour was needed. When in
late 1907 and early 1908 the black labour content began
to increase at a rate greater than a decrease in Chinese
labour, management again enforced less favourable contract
conditions.' (65)
The WNLA's recruiting patterns underwent a change which
became descernible from the year in which Chinese indentured labour began. In 1904, 53.95 per cent of the WNLA's
recruits came from outside British South Africa. In the
year 1907 the figure was 75.55 per cent. (66) Inside
British South Africa the supply was relatively abundant
until after the end of our period, but since much recruitment was independent of the WNLA it lacked the earlier
control and co-ordination. This led Lagden to comment
in a manner reminiscent of the earlier years:

'the government could never counteract the dishonest
and disloyal action of certain mines who betrayed the
confidence they ought to have in each other and stole
each other's labourers as they did before the war.'
(67)

But despite the problems, the mine-owners felt that
there was much cause for optimism. This is expressed in
Table 15.14 and reflected in a statement by the President
of the Chamber when, at the end of 1906, he reviewed the
progress of the industry over the whole decade:

If you will permit me to make a comparison with the
year 1896, embracing a period of 11 years, you will

find that though a long and devastating war has intervened, the progress of the gold mining industry has
indeed been remarkable. (68)

TABLE 15.14   Comparison of production and labour employment between 1896 and 1906

Year	No. of stamps in use	Gold production	No. of unskilled labourers	No. of white labourers
1896	5502	£8,603,821	54,012	9,375
1906	8497	£24,616,704	151,073*	17,495

*   Includes Chinese labourers.

Source: 'TCM 17th Annual Report 1906', p.xliii.   The
introduction of Chinese indentured labour had clearly
contributed substantially to this optimistic mood, production having surpassed the pre-war levels only in 1905 with
4,706,433 fine ounces as against 4,295,608 in 1898.   Cf.
P.Richardson, 'Journal of African History', vol.XVIII,
p.87.

Undoubtedly the indenture of Chinese labour was the
most substantial cause of the improvement in the Chamber's
general position.   That, together with the other factors
noted above, served to save its labour structure, so that
even after the Asian labour force had returned to China,
the Chamber was able, with some subtle variations between
1918 and 1922, to maintain the work and wage patterns it
had established in the early years of mining.

Appendices

Appendix 1

Names of companies classified under groups
(Source: 'TCM 13th Annual Report 1902', Annex)

Names of companies classified under groups with the name of the representative of the group on the Committee of Consulting Engineers

Committee of Consulting Engineers

Mr Hennen-Jennings (Chairman)
Mr H.H.Webb
Mr Sidney J.Jennings
Mr F.H.Hellmann
Mr G.A.Denny
Mr G.J.Hoffmann
Mr J.H.Johns
Mr S.C.Thomson
Mr G.E.Webber
Mr Pope Yeatman
Mr H.R.Skinner
Mr W.L.Honnold
Mr R.N.Kotze
Dr F.H.Hatch
F.J.Carpenter (Secretary)

Consolidated Goldfields of South Africa — Representative – Mr H.H.Webb		H.Eckstein & Co. — Representative – Mr Sidney J.Jennings		Farrar and Anglo-French — Representative – Mr Hellmann per Mr W.G.Holford		General Mining and Finance — Representative – Mr G.A.Denny	
Producing mines	Non-producing mines	Producing mines	Non-producing mines	Producing mines	Non-producing mines	Producing mines	Non-producing mines
Robinson Deep	Central Nigel Deep	Bonanza	Modderfontein-Extension	Angelo	Angelo Deep	Meyer & Charlton	Cinderella Deep
Simmer & Jack Propy.	Jupiter	City & Suburban	Robinson Cent. Deep	Driefontein	Benoni	New Goch	New Steyn Estate
Luipaards Vlei	Knights Deep	Crown Reef	Village Deep	New Klein-fontein	Boksburg	Roodepoort Un.	
Nigel Deep	Rand Victoria East	Ferreira		New Comet	Chimes West	M. Reef	
	Rand Victoria Mines	French Rand			Cason	Van Ryn	
	Simmer & Jack East	Henry Nourse			East Rand Explor.	Violet	
	Simmer & Jack West	Jumpers			Clipfontein Estate	West Rand	
	South Geldenhuis Dp	New Heriot			New Blue Sky	Aurora West	
	South Rose Deep	New Modderfontein			Rand Klipfontein		
	Sub. Nigel	Robinson					
		Village Main Reef					

A.Goerz & Co.
Representative - Mr G.J.Hoffmann

Producing mines	Non-producing mines
Balmoral	Geduld Proprietary
Ginsberg	Tudor
Glencairn	Modderfontein Dp
New Croesus	Randfontein Dp
New Primrose	
New Rietfontein	
New Spes Bona	
New Unified	
Rietfontein 'A'	
Rietfontein 'B'	
Roodepoort	
Witwatersrand	

Consolidated Investment Co.
Representative - Mr J.H.Johns

Producing mines	Non-producing mines
	Langlaagte Royal

S.Neumann & Co.
Representative - Mr S.C.Thomson

Producing mines	Non-producing mines
Consol. Main Reef	Bantjes Consol.
Treasury	Knight Central
Witwatersrand Dp	Main Reef Deeps
Wolhuter	Vogelstruis Con. Dp
	West Roodepoort Dp
	South Randfontein Deep

Lewis & Marks
Representative - Dr F.H.Hatch

Coal mines

Rand Mines Limited
Representative - Mr G.E.Webber

Producing mines	Non-producing mines
Crown Deep	South Nourse
Durban Roodepoort Dp	
Ferreira Deep	
Geldenhuis Deep	
Glen Deep	
Jumpers Deep	
Langlaagte Deep	
Nourse Deep	
Paarl Central	
Rose Deep	

J.B.Robinson
Representative - Mr Pope Yeatman

Producing mines	Non-producing mines
Block 'B' Langlaagte	Block 'A' Randfontein
Langlaagte Estate	East Randfontein
Langlaagte Star Estate	Ferguson Randfontein
North Randfontein	Johnson Randfontein
Porges Randfontein	Mynpacht Randfontein
Robinson Randfontein	Randfontein Estates
South Randfontein	Stubbs Randfontein
	Van Hulsteyn Randfontein
	West Randfontein

Sundry

Producing mines	Representatives	Non-producing mines
Durban Roodepoort	Mr H.R.Skinner	Vogelstruis Estate
Champ D'Or	Mr S.J.Jennings	
Jubilee Gold Mines	Mr W.L.Honnold	
Salisbury	Mr W.L.Honnold	
Windsor	Mr R.N.Kotze	
Geldenhuis Estate	Mr G.J.Hoffmann	
Nigel	Mr S.J.Jennings	
Wemmer	Mr J.H.Johns	
Worcester	Mr J.H.Johns	
York	Mr S.C.Thomson	

Appendix 2

Labour resources of Africa
(Source: 'WNLA Annual Report 1902')

District	1896-1898 Rand Native Labour Association, Limited			March, 1901-December, 1902 Witwatersrand Native Labour Assoc., Ltd	
	Number	%		Number	%
East Coast and Mozambique	32,271	60.3	-	39,135	53.5
Northern Transvaal	12,535	23.4	-	17,570	24.
Southern Transvaal	-	-	-	10	
Western Transvaal	-	-	-	170	0.2
Zululand and Swaziland	511	0.9			
Basutoland and Cape Colony	5,963	11.2	-	3,548	4.9
Bechuanaland	2,068	3.7	-	357	0.5
Rhodesia	263	0.5			
I.M.Railway	-	-	-	5,554	7.6
Army Labour Department	-	-	-	1,597	2.2
Local	-	-	-	5,171	7.1
Total	53,611	100	-	73,112	100

NOTE. Rand Native Labour Association supplied only a
small proportion of the 'fields' requirements.
The W.N.L. Assoc., Ltd., was started in Sept.,
1901, and supplies all natives to the Rand.

Appendix 3

Chart showing numbers employed by WNLA, 1901-6
(Source: 'WNLA Annual Report 1906')

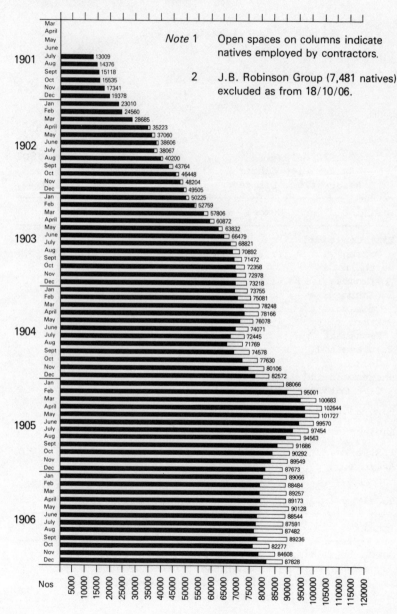

Note 1   Open spaces on columns indicate natives employed by contractors.

2   J.B. Robinson Group (7,481 natives) excluded as from 18/10/06.

Appendix 4

Modus Vivendi 1897; 1901

AGREEMENT FOR A 'MODUS VIVENDI'
Made between His Excellency The High Commissioner
for South Africa and
His Excellency the Governor-General of Mozambique.
December 18th, 1901.

The undersigned, Lord Milner, His Britannic Majesty's High
Commissioner for South Africa, etc., represented by His
Britannic Majesty's Consul-General at Lourenco Marques,
Captain F.H.E.Crowe, Royal Navy, and Manoel Raphael
Gorjâo, Privy Counsellor to His Most Faithful Majesty,
The King of Portugal, Brigadier-General, Governor-
General of the Province of Mozambique, etc., etc.,
having recognised that, pending the conclusion of an
agreement relative to the Province of Mozambique and
the neighbouring British Territories, it is indispensable that the terms of a *modus vivendi* should be
established: and in particular that the *status quo
ante bellum* should be as far as possible re-established
between the Province of Mozambique and the Transvaal,
have together arranged the following:

Article 1. The engagement of native labourers from the
Province of Mozambique for the Transvaal and Rhodesia
shall be established from now, and shall be allowed by the
Government-General of the said Province while the present
modus vivendi is in force or until the said *modus vivendi*
shall be denounced by one of the parties in conformity
with the terms of Article 13.

Article 2. The said engagement of native labourers
shall be made in conformity with the procedure set forth
in the Provincial Regulation of the Eighteenth of November, One Thousand Eight Hundred and Ninety-seven, subject
to such modifications as may be agreed on between the
parties now or hereafter: The collectors of labour to be

accepted by both parties and to be subject as regards the collecting of labourers in Portuguese Territory, not only to the laws and regulations in force in the Province of Mozambique, but also to those that may be promulgated in the future. It is understood that the guarantee deposit and licence which the collectors have to pay will not be higher than those set forth in the said Regulation of the Eighteenth of November, One Thousand Eight Hundred and Ninety-seven.

Article 3. The Curator's Office for natives from the Province of Mozambique is re-established in Johannesburg in the terms of the Regulation of the Eighteenth of November, One Thousand Eight Hundred and Ninety-seven, save for the modifications which may be adopted by agreement between the two parties. It is understood that the powers and duties of the Curator are only similar to those of a Consular officer.

The Transvaal Government will give to the Curator every facility and assistance in its power and in particular facilities will be given to ensure as far as possible that the names of all natives immigrating from Portuguese Territory and their places of employment are registered in the Curator's Office.

Article 4. The combined tariffs and classification of goods on the Lourenco Marques-Ressano Garcia and Ressano Garcia-Johannesburg lines, which were in force before the war, shall be re-established, and shall be in force as long as this *modus vivendi* shall exist, save for the modifications which may be made by agreement between the two parties. It is understood that should the tariffs or classification of goods be modified on the lines from Durban, East London, Port Elizabeth and Capetown to the Transvaal, during the existence of the *modus vivendi,* the classification and tariffs on the Lourenco Marques-Johannesburg line shall be equally modified in proportion and in such a manner as to preserve the relation which existed between the tariffs prior to the war.

Article 5. Upon the commencement of immigration the civil traffic from the Portuguese frontier into the Transvaal will be allotted such a number of trucks as the Director of the Imperial Military Railways is able to allot to the said civil traffic without prejudice to the indispensable military traffic. It is also understood that the civil traffic above-mentioned will be regulated on the same principles, and in equally favourable manner, as the civil traffic coming from the Cape and Natal.

Article 6. For the expenses of fiscalization, passports, contracts, registration, etc., etc., the Government-General shall receive during the period of the *modus*

vivendi for every immigrated native who is passed by a
Transvaal Government official at the border, or at such
place as may be agreed on between the parties, the sum
of thirteen shillings (13s). This sum will cover all expenses, and no other amount will be charged, with the exception of a fee on re-engagement, as specified in
Article 9.

Article 7. It is agreed that the Government-General of
the Province of Mozambique and the Directorate of the
Lourenco Marques Railway will grant to the Imperial
Military Railways equal treatment, in all respects, and
will concede the same privileges, as were conceded to the
Netherlands Railway Company, with the exception of the
military and hospital trains, to which there will be given
a special rebate, according to the arrangement made on
December the 11th, one thousand nine hundred and one, with
the Director of the Imperial Military Railways, which is
hereby sanctioned during the continuance of the *modus
vivendi*.

Article 8. The railway charges for immigrated natives
returning to the Portuguese frontier shall be equally
favourable with the railway charges made for the convey-
ance of immigrating natives from the Portuguese frontier
into the Transvaal.

Article 9. The contracts of employment of immigrating
natives shall be made in the first place for not more than
one year. The Transvaal Government undertakes that
natives will be given their discharge at the expiration of
the period of contract and that no pressure shall be put
on them to renew their contracts. Should a native renew
his contract voluntarily at the end of the year either
with the same or with another employer, the Portuguese
Authorities shall be entitled to receive a further fee
at the rate of sixpence (6d.) per month for the period
of the new contract.

Article 10. The provisions of the Treaty of the 11th
of December, One thousand eight hundred and seventy-five,
will be observed by the Transvaal Colony and reciprocally
by the Portuguese Authorities.

But notwithstanding anything to the contrary in the
aforesaid provisions, alcoholic liquors manufactured in
the Province of Mozambique may be subjected on entering
the Transvaal to the same duties as, but no greater than,
the duties imposed on similar alcoholic liquors manufactured in the Cape Colony and Natal.

Reciprocally alcoholic liquors manufactured in the
Transvaal may be subjected to the same duties on entering
the Province of Mozambique.

It is also to be understood that nothing in the above-mentioned Treaty shall be held to prevent the entry of the Transvaal or of the Province of Mozambique or of both into the South African Customs Union, should such entry take place during the continuance of the *modus vivendi*.

Article 11. During the existence of the *modus vivendi*, goods sent in transit from Lourenco Marques on entering the Transvaal shall have equal treatment with, and shall pay no higher customs duties than, the same class of goods sent in transit from Durban, East London, Port Elizabeth, and Cape Town.

Article 12. The Transvaal Government will use its best endeavours to discourage and prevent the clandestine immigration of natives from Portuguese Territory.

Article 13. The present *modus vivendi* shall be in force until the conclusion of a definite Convention. It can, however, be determined by either of the parties by means of one year's notice. As soon as the *modus vivendi* is denounced by either of the parties, the engagement of natives in the Province of Mozambique will be *ipso facto* suspended.

Done at Lourenco Marques this Eighteenth day of December, in the year of Our Lord one thousand nine hundred and one.

(Sgd.) Manoel R.Gorjao, G.G.,

(Sgd.) Fritz H.E.Crowe,

For and on behalf of His Excellency the High Commissioner for South Africa.

Appendix 5

Gold production of the Transvaal, 1884-1905,
in fine ounces and comparisons with world production
(Source: Government Mining Engineer's Annual Report,
1905-6)

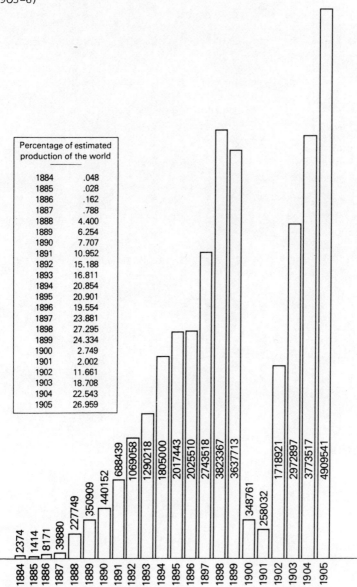

Percentage of estimated production of the world	
1884	.048
1885	.028
1886	.162
1887	.788
1888	4.400
1889	6.254
1890	7.707
1891	10.952
1892	15.188
1893	16.811
1894	20.854
1895	20.901
1896	19.554
1897	23.881
1898	27.295
1899	24.334
1900	2.749
1901	2.002
1902	11.661
1903	18.708
1904	22.543
1905	26.959

Bar chart values:

Year	Fine ounces
1884	2374
1885	1414
1886	8171
1887	39880
1888	227749
1889	350909
1890	440152
1891	688439
1892	1069058
1893	1290218
1894	1805000
1895	2017443
1896	2025510
1897	2743518
1898	3823367
1899	3637713
1900	348761
1901	258032
1902	1718921
1903	2972897
1904	3773517
1905	4909541

Appendix 6

Items of cost in the total working cost in the year 1898
(Source: 'TCM 13th Annual Report 1902')

Group		No. of co.s	Salaries and wages, whites	Native wages	Native food	Cost of procuring native labour	Explosives	Fuel	Mining timber, deals, etc.	Iron, steel, tools, ropes, shoes, dies, lubricants, candles, paraffin	Chemicals	Animal food	Sundries	Total
Consolidated Goldfields	Producing mines	2	27.52	16.69	4.51	2.32	13.70	9.39	1.20	5.30	1.64	.22	17.61	100
	Non-producing mines	5	29.54	23.82	5.87	.40	9.13	5.13	12.48	7.30	-	.23	6.10	100
H.Eckstein & Co.	Producing mines	11	31.03	15.71	3.42	1.79	9.20	7.36	1.54	6.50	2.45	.37	20.63	100
	Non-producing mines	2	9.52	4.48	1.02	1.66	.95	.31	8.48	2.89	-	.04	70.65	100
Farrar & Anglo-French	Producing mines	3	23.08	17.61	5.14	3.88	12.48	4.69	1.51	10.30	2.18	.27	18.86	100
	Non-producing mines	2	23.86	14.34	2.72	0.48	8.35	4.55	2.58	6.08	0.13	.35	36.56	100
General Mining & Finance	Producing mines	3	31.58	21.89	3.57	-	8.54	8.35	1.72	10.34	4.25	.33	9.43	100
	Non-producing mines	-	-	-	-	-	-	-	-	-	-	-	-	-
A.Goerz & Co.	Producing mines	3	24.14	19.18	4.41	1.35	12.65	8.30	0.69	11.87	1.34	.22	15.85	100
	Non-producing mines	1	30.70	23.10	4.40	-	12.40	7.70	5.30	-	-	-	16.40	100
J'burg Con. Invest.Co.	Producing mines	9	24.75	21.33	4.30	2.46	10.21	9.42	4.32	3.71	1.32	.21	17.97	100
	Non-producing mines	-	-	-	-	-	-	-	-	-	-	-	-	-

S.Neumann & Co.	Producing mines	3	26.92	21.04	3.55	1.64	11.91	8.67	.54	7.09	3.07	.42	15.15	100
	Non-producing mines	4	34.35	20.28	3.48	0.81	9.06	11.02	7.76	5.91	.06	.52	6.75	100
Rand Mines	Producing mines	8	35.26	14.12	3.36	4.08	12.64	8.37	1.15	4.58	3.94	.30	12.20	100
	Non-producing mines	1	24.48	8.68	2.05	1.09	3.79	3.78	10.79	3.21	.09	.25	41.79	100
J.B.Robinson	Producing mines	7	31.11	14.45	3.80	5.85	7.22	8.45	1.91	9.17	4.11	.50	13.43	100
	Non-producing mines	–	–	–	–	–	–	–	–	–	–	–	–	–
Sundry	Producing mines	9	28.47	23.52	4.46	0.90	10.93	9.29	1.33	9.45	2.39	.40	8.86	100
	Non-producing mines	2	42.08	16.73	3.33	1.07	6.97	17.38	.74	7.11	.11	.07	4.41	100

Average percentage for all groups

Producing mines	58	28.39	18.56	4.06	2.43	10.95	8.23	1.59	7.83	2.66	0.32	14.98	100
Non-producing mines	17	27.79	15.92	3.27	.79	7.23	7.12	6.88	4.64	.06	.21	26.09	100

Appendix 7

Abstract of ordinance to regulate the introduction into the Transvaal of unskilled non-European
labourers

    3. The Superintendent or any Inspector may at any time
enter upon the premises on which labourers are employed
and inspect the condition and general treatment of such
labourers and the condition of their housing accommodation
and hospital accommodation and may enquire into any complaint which an employer may have against a labourer or
which a labourer may have against his employer or any
person placed in authority over him by such employer and
may require any labourer to be brought before him on any
such visit and may either before or after such enquiry as
aforesaid make a complaint or lay an information in his
own name on behalf of a labourer against the employer or
against any other person before the Magistrate of the
District.
    4. (1) The Superintendent or Inspector may summon any
person as a witness whose evidence he considers necessary
for the proper determination of any enquiry held by him;
such summons shall be served by the person to whom it is
directed in the same manner as a summons issued by a
Magistrate is required to be served.
    (2) Every person on whom such summons has been duly
served who without any reasonable excuse refuses or
neglects to attend at the time and place mentioned in such
summons shall be liable to a penalty not exceeding ten
pounds and in default of payment to imprisonment for a
period not exceeding one month.
    (3) The Superintendent or Inspector shall require
every statement given by any person at an enquiry held by
him to be given upon oath and for such purpose he is
hereby authorised to administer an oath to every such
person.
    (4) Every person who refuses to be so sworn when
thereto required shall be deemed to have hindered the officer holding the enquiry in the execution of his duty and
shall be liable to be punished accordingly.

(5)   Every person who after being so sworn wilfully
makes a false statement as to anything material to the
proper determination of the matter then in question shall
be deemed guilty of perjury and shall be liable to be
dealt with and punished accordingly.

INTRODUCTION OF LABOURERS.

5.   It shall not be lawful for any labourer to enter
be or reside in or to be introduced into this Colony
unless he shall previously have entered into the contract
referred to in section *eight* and until such contract has
been registered in the Office of the Superintendent.

6.   No person shall introduce labourers into this
Colony or employ such labourers unless he has obtained a
licence to do so from the Lieutenant-Governor under the
next succeeding section nor contrary to the terms of such
licence;   any person contravening this section shall be
liable to a penalty of one hundred pounds for every such
labourer introduced or employed by him and shall further
be bound to refund to the Superintent any expenses incurred by him in returning such person to his country of
origin.

7.   (1) The Lieutenant-Governor may subject to the
provisions of this Ordinance grant a licence to any person
to introduce labourers into this Colony to perform unskilled labour only in the exploitation of minerals within
the Witwatersrand District.

Appendix 8

SCHEDULE I.

Amalgamator

Assayer

Banksman

Blacksmith

Boilermaker

Brass-finisher

Brassmoulder

Bricklayer

Brickmaker overseer

Carpenter

Clerk

Coppersmith

Cyanide shiftsman

Drill sharpener

Driver of air or steam winch

Driver of mechanical or electrical machinery

Electrician

Engine-driver

Engineer

Fireman overseer

Fitter

Ganger

Ironmoulder

Joiner

Machine rock driller

Machine sawyer

Machinist

Mason

Mechanic

Miller

Millwright

Mine carpenter

Mine storeman

Miner overseer

Onsetter

Overseer, in any capacity other than the management and control of labourers

Painter

Patternmaker

Pipeman

Plasterer

264

Platelayer

Plumber

Pumpman

Quarryman overseer

Rigger

Sampler

Signaller

Skipman

Stonecutter

Timberman

Time keeper

Tinsmith

Turner

Wire splicer

Woodworking machinist

Appendix 9

Chart showing gross wastage for each month
comprising discharges, desertions, deaths since June 1901
(Source: 'WNLA Annual Report 1906')

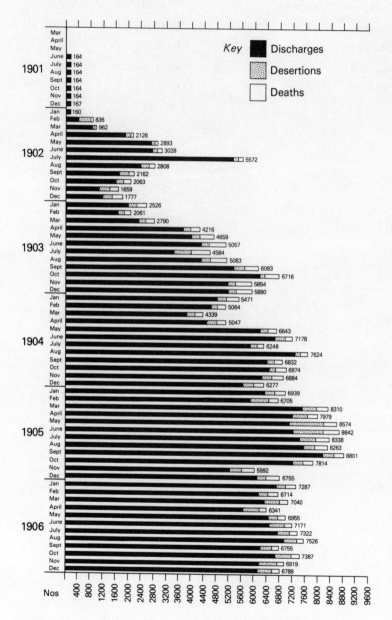

Appendix 10

A. ANNEXURE TO PASS REGULATIONS

            NATIVE LABOUR DISTRICT PASS,   ) Schedule A

Regstd. No. .....   ) of Regulations under

               For the Labour District of ....) Art. 88 of Gold Law.

Issued this ..... day of ...., 189...   Expires the ..... day of .... 189...

Name of Native.	No. of Badge.	Name of Chief.	Tribe and District.	Stature and Marks

Authority is hereby granted to the above-described Native to circulate within this Labour District for the purpose of employing himself as a Labourer, for a term of ... months from date, subject to the provisions and regulations of this Act.

FEES AND FINES DUE, AND HOW IMPOSED.   WHEN AND BY WHOM PAID.

How Arising.	Amount.	Signature of Officer imposing same.	Date.	By whom Paid.	Date.	Amount.	Signature of Officer who received same.	Remarks.

In terms of Art. 6a extended to seek employment from ..... to ..... 8 days. .... Signature of Pass Officer.

Name of Employer.	Nature of Employment.	Term of Service From	To	Rate of Wages.	Date of Disch'rge	Reasons for Discharge.	Signature of Employer.
1*							
2							
3							
4							
5							
6							

* Employers of this Native are bound, under penalties, to fill in this form as occasion may arise, and generally to see that this Pass is renewed on expiry of term, and that all provisions and regulations of this Law are carried out in so far as they relate to the Employer.

Appendix 11

B. ANNEXURE TO PASS REGULATIONS

SCHEDULE B.

Labour District ...... REGISTER.

Date.	No.	Name	Tribe	Chief	Country or District	Stature	Marks	Fees due	Fees paid	When paid	Date Paid.	Date when em-ploy'd	First Em-ployer	Date when First District Pass Renewed.	Fees paid	District Pass	Date when Renewed 2nd time.	Fees paid	District Pass	Date when Renewed 3rd time.

| Totals | | | | | | | | | | | | | | £ | | | £ | | | |

Fees paid.	Agent or Contractor	Travelling Pass.	Date of Issue. Exit or Travelling Pass.	No.	To.	Fees paid.	Period.	Remarks.

268

Appendix 12

<u>C.   ANNEXURE TO PASS REGULATIONS</u>

SCHEDULE C.
of Regulations under
Art 88 of Gold Law.

No.....

       NATIVE LABOUR EXIT PASS.

       For the Native ....

       From the Labour District ....

       To ....

       He has with him ....

       and handed in his Badge No......

       and 'District Pass' No.........

                    ....
                       Pass Officer.

SCHEDULE D.
of Regulations under
Gold Law Art. 88.

NATIVE LABOUR EMPLOYEES PASS

for the Labour District of ......

and for the month ending ... 189

NO. BADGE	NO. DIST.PASS	NATIVE'S NAME	CHIEF.	TRIBE-DISTRICT.

---

engaged by .... on the ... . day of ....

for a period of .... in terms of Law ....

his 'District Pass' as above being in $\frac{my}{our}$ possession.

                    Signature of Employer ....

                    Address of Employer ....

Date of issue ....

Notes

CHAPTER 1   CALCULATING THE WAGE RATE

1   A.P.Cartwright, 'The Gold Miners', Purcell, London,
    1963, pp.220 and 223 (emphasis added). For the de-
    termination of the cash wage in the early industrial
    economy of Britain, by way of comparison, see E.J.
    Hobsbawm, 'Labouring Men, Studies in the History of
    Labour', Weidenfeld & Nicolson, London, 1974, pp.
    345-6. For the wages of the migratory miners in the
    early British coal-mining industry, see Keith Burgess,
    'The Origins of British Industrial Relations', Croom
    Helm, London, 1975, p.161.
2   Report of the Committee of the Mine Managers Associ-
    ation on the Native Labour Question, cited in the
    'Witwatersrand Chamber of Mines 5th Annual Report,
    1893', p.44. (Hereafter cited as 'WCM Ann. Rep.')
3   Evidence, H.Jennings to Industrial Commission of
    Enquiry, 1897, p.219. All subsequent references to
    the Industrial Commission are taken from 'Evidence and
    Report of the Industrial Commission of Enquiry', com-
    piled and published by WCM, Johannesburg, Times
    Printing and Publishing Works, 1897.
4   See E.J.Dyer, The South African Labour Question,
    'Contemporary Review', March 1903, p.441. See also
    H.C.Thomson, Kaffir Labour and Kaffir Marriage,
    'Monthly Review', May 1903.
5   See especially Chapters 7,11,12 and 15, below.
6   See C.Bundy, 'The Rise and Fall of the South African
    Peasantry', Heinemann, London, 1979, p.204 and passim.
7   On the implications of this point see M.Legassick,
    South Africa: Forced Labour, Industrialization and
    Racial Differentiation, in R.Harris (ed.), 1975;   S.
    Gervasi, 'Industrialization, Foreign Capital and
    Forced Labour in South Africa' (United Nations, New

York, 1970); H.Wolpe, Capitalism and Cheap Labour
Power in South Africa: from Segregation to Apartheid,
'Economy and Society', vol.1, 1972, who properly
characterized the system as basic to the present South
African economy.

8 See C.Perrings, The production process, industrial
labour strategies and worker responses in the Southern
African gold mining industry, 'Journal of African
History', vol.XVIII, no.1, 1977, pp.130-4.

9 On the geological nature of the ore and the constraints upon mining techniques see Owen Letcher,
'The Gold Mines of Southern Africa', Waterlow & Sons,
London, 1936; S.J.Truscott, 'The Witwatersrand Gold
Fields, Banket and Mining Practice', London, Mac-
millan, 1898, esp. pp.357-61; L.V.Praagh (ed.), 'The
Transvaal and its Mines', Praagh & Lloyd, London,
1906, p.580 and passim. On the constraint on working
costs generally, see P.Richardson, 'The Provision of
Chinese Indentured Labour for the Transvaal Gold Mines
1903-1908', unpublished PhD thesis, University of
London, 1977.

10 The Rand system was less concerned with theft than
worker-discipline, coercion and cost-redemption. See
Ch.2.

11 Letcher, op.cit., p.130. For some of the very early
difficulties in relation to water, fuel, labour and
gold recovery by the amalgamation process, see C.W.
Biccard Jeppe, 'Gold Mining in South Africa', Todd
Publishing Group, London, 1948, pp.32,33, and
Letcher, op.cit., p.106.

12 See below, pp. 14-16. For a succinct account of the
technological problems associated with gold extraction
in the Transvaal, see 'Transvaal Chamber of Mines 17th
Ann. Rep. 1906', pp.83-6. (Hereafter cited as 'TCM
Ann. Rep.')

13 Truscott, op.cit., pp.6,7,18,190. Letcher, op.cit.,
pp.5,6,7. The most important early developments were
confined to the 27-mile strip between Randfontein and
Modderfontein. It was here that almost the whole
output from the banket was being obtained. Cf.
Truscott, op.cit., p.1.

14 Perrings, op.cit., p.132. See below, p.26.

15 'T.C.M. Gold in South Africa', Transvaal Chamber of
Mines, Johannesburg, 1969, p.11, cited by F.Wilson,
'Labour in the South African Gold Mines 1911-69',
Cambridge University Press, 1972, p.16.

16 Truscott, op.cit., p.151; Letcher, op.cit., p.357.

17 Truscott, op.cit., p.151.

18 On this point see F.Wilson, op.cit., p.16.

19 See below, Ch.11(i). The consulting engineer, John
    Hays Hammond, estimated that in the case of a deep-
    level mine of 250 claims with two shafts (2,500 feet
    deep) the extra capitalization (by comparison with the
    first-row deeps) which would be required to pay for
    the sinking and equipment of such shafts would be
    about £800 per claim. The extra capitalization re-
    quired on the third row would have been proportionate-
    ly greater. Cf. Letcher, op.cit., p.358.

20 Truscott, op.cit., p.3.

21 The average area of a deep-level mine of the first row
    was approximately 220 claims. A single claim as de-
    fined by the Gold Law of the South African Republic
    was 150 feet in length along the direction of the reef
    and 400 feet in breadth. The depth is indefinite.
    See Truscott, op.cit., pp.357,2.

22 Truscott, op.cit., p.190. Praagh, op.cit., p.581, ap-
    propriately notes the difficulty of estimating the
    cost and time of sinking any particular shaft, owing
    to discrepancies in the class of ground and the amount
    of water encountered.

23 Truscott, op.cit., p.190.

24 Ibid.

25 'Tramming' was the underground term for moving the
    ore. 'Transport' referred to surface movements.

26 See F.Wilson, op.cit., p.16. See also p. 14 below;
    'TCM 17th Ann. Rep. 1906', p.84.

27 Truscott, op.cit., p.357.

28 Letcher, op.cit., pp.108,109. Truscott, op.cit., p.
    360. According to the former (p.130) the cost per
    foot by means of hand drilling was £1 less than the
    average cost of machine stoping.

29 Truscott, op.cit., p.360.

30 Ibid., p.361. See note on capital and working costs
    below, p.19.

31 Letcher, op.cit., p.131, notes that the Little Giant
    'proved to be better adapted' than the larger drills
    used, but does not comment on the paradox that their
    general introduction was at first delayed because of
    the relatively higher cost of explosives used in
    machine drilling compared with hand labour.

32 On this see F.Wilson, op.cit., p.18.

33 Perrings, op.cit., p.132. See also 'TCM 17th Ann.
    Rep. 1906', p.85.

34 Truscott, op.cit., p.364, notes the elaborate plans
    established to survey the stope work over monthly or
    longer intervals. By means of a planimeter, more ac-
    curate figures of the tonnage mined from any one stope
    could be determined than by taking a physical count of
    the number of trucks filled from any particular stope.

35 Screening the broken rock was conducted on the head-
    gear, and the remaining two operations of sorting and
    crushing were carried out at the so-called crusher
    stations. For the description of the process, see
    'TCM 17th Ann. Rep. 1906', pp.85,86. Truscott, op.
    cit., pp.406-12, and Praagh, op.cit., pp.588-9.
36 Truscott, op.cit., p.408.
37 With the adoption of the tube mill, the cost of ore
    reduction was substantially reduced.
38 See below, p. 18. According to Praagh, op.cit., p.
    580, the average working cost per ton of ore milled
    in 1906 was 22s. 6d. See also Truscott, op.cit.,
    pp.442-3.
39 On the fixed price of gold, see below, pp. 17-19. For
    details of the wage rate, see Chs 3,7,8,11. On the
    migrant character of the workforce, see Ch.1(iii).
    These factors affected not only the above matters but
    the organization of the financial, technical and ad-
    ministrative sectors of the industry, as well as the
    political strategies followed by the Chamber to sup-
    port a permanent low-cost labour system.
40 'Ev. of the Gold Producers' Committee of the TCM',
    Statement No.5, p.12. See also ibid., Annexure 'B',
    Effect of Increases in the Cost of Mining, pp.20,21.
41 See Table 1.2, below. See also Pierre Villar, 'A
    History of Gold and Money 1450-1920', New Left Books,
    London, 1976, p.320. According to Villar it is a
    historical phenomenon that a fall in general prices
    expressed in terms of precious metals indicates a re-
    valuation of the metal and an incentive to explore it.
    The explorations in California, Australia, Canada and
    South Africa to some extent confirm this (ibid., p.
    328). Further theories concerning the relationship
    between gold, prices and business movements are more
    problematical and are not here explored.
42 Villar, op.cit., p.320.
43 Ibid., pp.351,352. Whilst Villar is advancing a con-
    nection between the relative quantity of gold and
    world prices, there is no such intention in the
    present study.
44 The principal stores at this time included dynamite,
    nitro-glycerine, blasting gelatine, fuses, cyanide of
    potassium, zinc, mining timber, drill steel, candles,
    iron, galvanized iron and piping. See Truscott, op.
    cit., pp.457-8.
45 See P.Richardson, 'The Provision of Chinese Indentured
    Labour for the Transvaal Gold Mines, 1903-8', p.20.
46 For the downward movement in the average grade of ore
    see p.17 above, and Ch.9(ii) below. For the crisis of
    1903, see Chs 11 and 12.

47   Richardson, op.cit., p.23.
48   On recruitment and labour strategies see Chs 11 and
     15, below. On the calculation of working costs see
     Richardson, op.cit., p.23. The calculation of working
     costs depended very much on whether the cost of equip-
     ment or depreciation was included. Hence Hennen
     Jennings in his evidence before the 1897 Industrial
     Commission noted that from the annual reports of
     twenty-nine of the principal companies working in
     1896, the total working cost without depreciation was
     27s. 4d. per ton, and with depreciation 31s. 0.44d.
     per ton. See Truscott, op.cit., p.442. Alternative
     figures to that of Richardson for so-called 'working
     costs' during the early period in respect of the
     twenty-nine principal companies referred to by
     Truscott are therefore:

     1894 - 38s. 10d.   1895 - 33s. 5.25d.
     1896 - 31s. 6.90d.   1897 - 19s. 6.70d.

49   These 'more flexible' costs might include such items
     as recruiting costs, wages, certain stores and
     housing, feeding and medical costs for the labour
     force. For a more specific discussion on the in-
     ternal reorganization to reduce costs, see pp.42,46
     below.
50   On this see Richardson, op.cit., p.26; Perrings, op.
     cit., p.132. Richardson, op.cit., p.27, notes the
     important impact of the post-war Profits Tax and
     certain indirect taxes (Transfer duties, African Pass
     charges and municipal rates on mine properties on the
     Chamber's labour strategies. In particular they 'ac-
     centuated the need for cheap labour policies' (ibid.).
51   Claude Meillassoux, From Reproduction to Production,
     'Economy and Society', vol.1, no.1, 1972, p.102 (em-
     phasis added). On the migrant labour system, see also
     H.Wolpe, Capitalism and Cheap Labour Power in South
     Africa, pp.437-8; F.Wilson, 'Migrant Labour in South
     Africa', SACC & SPRO-CAS, Johannesburg, 1972, p.48,
     and Wilson, 'Labour in the South African Gold Mines',
     p.135.
52   Perrings, op.cit., p.132, possibly too inflexibly con-
     trasts the difficulties of Witwatersrand mines with
     the copper industry when he notes that, in the former,
     geological and technical inflexibilities 'meant that
     mining capital could not respond relative to the other
     factors by an adjustment of the method' while, in the
     latter, mining and metallurgical techniques were ad-

justed 'regularly to meet shifts in relative factor prices'.

53   Burgess, op.cit., p.155, explains that the high level of labour-intensive techniques in the English coal-mining industry was partly due to unfavourable geo-logical conditions (particularly faulting and steeply pitching seams), but the more substantial reason for the tardiness in introducing mechanization was due to an abundance of labour and the high price of coal. Hence the industry persuaded investors that 'the cost of machinery was not a paying proposition compared with other investment opportunities'.

54   The exercise on the Rand was on the whole more ex-tensive and systematic. See Chs 2(ii) and 7(i)(b) below.

55   For a contrasting description of the migrant labour system in California, see Michael Burawoy, The Func-tions of Migrant Labour: Comparative Material from Southern Africa and the United States, 'American Journal of Sociology', no.81, 1976.

56   Wilson, 'Migrant Labour in South Africa', p.148.

57   Wolpe, Capitalism and Cheap Labour Power in South Africa, p.435.

58   Ibid. See also below.

59   Ibid. On this point see H.Wolpe, The Theory of Internal Colonialism, 'Bulletin of the Conference of Socialist Economists', no.9, Autumn 1974, pp.9,10. See also the reply to Wolpe by Michael Williams, An Analysis of South African Capitalism, 'Bulletin of the Conference of Social Economists', vol.IV, no.1, 1975, pp.5-10. Williams's contention is that migrant labour 'loses its significance in relation to capital's growing ability to reproduce on its own basis ... labour power' (op.cit., p.10); however, it is not possible to deal with this conflict of views in the present study. On migrant labour and the role of the state in the maintenance and renewal of the labour force, see Burawoy, op.cit., p.1051 and passim. For discussion on this theme, see below, pp.22-6.

60   Cartwright, 'The Gold Miners', p.234 (emphasis added). See also L.V.Praagh, op.cit., p.580. It should be noted that the converse of the citation is also true. With a relatively small decrease in working costs 'a quantity of ore unpayable under existing conditions would be brought within the range of profitable mining that the available tonnage would be more than doubled' (Praagh, op.cit., p.580).

61   Economic and Wage Commission, 'Evidence of the Gold Producers' Committee of the TCM', Annexure B to Statement No.5, p.21.

62 Williams, op.cit., p.6.
63 Wolpe, The Theory of Internal Colonialism, pp.8 and 9.
64 The citation is from Marx, 'Capital', iii, Lawrence &
    Wishart, London, 1962, pp.349-50.
65 Williams's contention is that Wolpe has explained the
    depression of wages not by the migrant's being paid at
    less than his value but by the subsidization of the
    mine-owners by the migrant worker's family who produce
    part of their means of subsistence in the Reserves.
    Wolpe's argument, however (The Theory of Internal
    Colonialism, p.8), is 'that subsistence necessary for
    the production of labour power must *include* the means
    necessary for the labourers substitute, that is, his
    children' (emphasis added).
66 See A.Hepple, 'South Africa: A Political and Economic
    History', Pall Mall Press, London, 1966, p.204.
    Hepple does not note that the comment is an extreme
    one. 'Survival' was relative to changes in the cost
    of production and frequently a euphemism for greater
    or lesser profitability. Hence L.V.Praagh, op.cit.,
    p.580, noted in 1906 that (with a reduction of working
    costs by 7s. 6d. per ton) 'many properties now neg-
    lected as unprofitable would pay handsomely, and some
    of the lower grade banket-beds ... could also be
    worked to pay'.
67 Burawoy, op.cit., p.1056. For a discussion of 'cheap'
    labour in the nineteenth-century British context see
    Hobsbawm's essay Custom, Wages and Workload in
    'Labouring Men', p.355. The coincidence of the rise
    and fall of the supply-price with the dearth or abun-
    dance of labour is very marked with the Witwatersrand
    gold industry. See below, pp.59-60.
68 Burawoy, op.cit., p.1056.
69 For a useful contrast with Rhodesia see C.Arrighi,
    Labour Supplies in Historical Perspective: A Study
    of the Proletarianization of the African Peasantry
    in Rhodesia, in G.Arrighi and J.S.Saul, 'Essays on
    the Political Economy of Africa', Monthly Review
    Press, London, 1973, pp.184,187,191. Arrighi's empha-
    sis on the 'effort-price' of labouring in the capital-
    ist sector tends, however, to undermine his earlier
    argument.
70 The various institutions are discussed separately
    below, especially in Chs 2(ii); 6(i); 7(i)(b).
71 Burawoy, op.cit., p.1056.
72 See Chs 6; 10(ii).
73 On the latter point see Cartwright, 'The Gold Miners',
    p.221. For the geographical separation of the pro-
    cesses, see Meillassoux, op.cit., p.102; Burawoy,
    op.cit., p.1056.

74 See also 'TCM 13th Ann. Rep. 1902', pp.74-7, for the handling of remittances.

75 Meillassoux, op.cit., p.103, notes that 'because of this process of absorption within the capitalist economy the agricultural communities, maintained as reserves of cheap labour, are both being undermined and perpetuated at the same time, undergoing a prolonged crisis and not a smooth transition to Capitalism'. On this point see also Wolpe, Capitalism and Cheap Labour Power, pp.432,434.

76 See below, Ch.12(vii).

77 Burawoy, op.cit., p.1056.

78 Perrings, op.cit., p.312.

79 See below, Ch.6.

80 S.H.Frankel, 'Capital Investment in Africa', Oxford University Press, London, 1938, p.95. For the size of the labour force see 'WCM 7th Ann. Rep. 1895', p.180.

81 See Letcher, op.cit., p.114. For an analysis of the Rand output for the first six years of mining (from 1887 to 1892) see T.Reunert, 'Diamonds and Gold in South Africa', Juta, Cape Town, 1893, p.223 and Appendix xxvii. The total yearly output for 1892 was registered at 1,210,869 oz, an increase of 66 per cent on the previous year. Output during the first year of mining was 23,155 oz.

82 Letcher, op.cit., p.114. According to R.R.Mabson, 'Mines of the Transvaal', The Statist, London, 1900, p.5, the approximate value of gold mined between 1887 and 1895 was £2,250,000 and £7,840,779 respectively. Dividends paid in 1887-9 are unavailable, but the amount in 1895 was £2,198,943. (Frankel's figures, op.cit., p.95, are lower.)

83 The organization extended its representation and became the Transvaal Chamber of Mines in 1901. The early Chamber was described by Harry Oppenheimer as a 'mighty empire-minded body'. Its deliberations were held in secret and had the aura of a parliamentary cabinet. The Chamber, however, despite its consolidated structure, was careful to avoid dictating to individual companies. On the above see T.Green, 'The World of Gold', Michael Joseph, London, 1968, p.58.

84 For full details of the Chamber's functions up to the end of the period covered by this work, see Constitution of the Transvaal Chamber of Mines as amended in 1902 and 1906 respectively in 'TCM 17th Ann. Rep.' for the year 1906.

85 Ibid., p.v.

86 Letcher, op.cit., p.106; see especially below, Chs 4(i),(ii); 10(iii).

87   It was no secret to Kruger's government that the
      principals of this firm were implacably opposed to
      his regime. T.Pakenham, 'The Boer War', Weidenfeld
      & Nicolson, London, 1979, p.89, does not acknowledge
      this when he notes that Beit, Wernher and Fitzpatrick,
      'unbeknown to the press and public, encouraged
      Milner's belligerence'.
88   See below, Ch.10(ii).
89   For early internecine rivalry of the various compa-
      nies, see below, pp.30-1.
90   See below, Ch.13.
91   The groups were both investment companies and issue
      houses. On this point see F.A.Johnstone, 'Class,
      Race and Gold', Routledge & Kegan Paul, London, p.15,
      who notes that the groups invested the bulk of their
      investment capital in the goldmines and were able to
      provide amounts of capital and a continuity of in-
      vestment 'beyond the resources of the average, single
      gold mining company'. For details of the various
      groups see Appendix 1, below.
92   Letcher, op.cit., p.412. The mining and financial
      corporations which constituted the parental organ-
      ization were termed 'Controlling Houses' or 'Groups'.
      The Controlling Group need not necessarily hold the
      'dominating preponderance of shares' in the mining
      companies under its control, but as the 'Report of
      the Witwatersrand Mine Natives Wage Commission 1944',
      p.3, noted, 'real power is vested in the hands of
      that Group which has sufficiently large shareholding
      to permit of its assuming control of the Company".
93   For further details of the Group System as a 'working
      model of a "rationalized" industry', see Frankel, op.
      cit., p.82. J.Martin, H.Clay, 'Group Administration
      in the Gold Mining Industry on the Witwatersrand',
      Econ. section of the British Association for the
      Advancement of Science, Johannesburg, August 1929.
      For some of the managerial defects of this central-
      ized system of control see Correspondence L.Phillips
      to I.Wernher, 5.3.1906, HE 152, p.153, in M.Fraser
      and A.Jeeves, 'All that Glittered, Selected Corre-
      spondence of Lionel Phillips 1890-1924', Oxford
      University Press, Cape Town, 1977.
94   'WCM 8th Ann. Rep., 1896', p.22.
95   See F.Wilson, 'Migrant Labour in South Africa', pp.
      138-9, 151, and Wilson, 'Labour in the South African
      Gold Mines', p.153.
96   For a detailed analysis of the deficiencies of the
      system, see F.Wilson, 'Migrant Labour in South
      Africa', pp.174-90.

97   Cf. D.Hobart Houghton, 'The South African Economy',
     Oxford University Press, Cape Town, 1964, pp.87-96.
     Considering the human waste, he concludes that the
     migrant practice 'condemns the workers to being in
     perpetuity merely undifferentiated units of unskilled
     labour' (ibid., p.88). See also F.Wilson, 'Labour in
     the South African Gold Mines', p.98. According to
     Wilson, the estimated cost in the turnover of migrant
     labour in 1969 was between 3 and 4 million Rand
     (+ £1.5m and £2 million). There are no estimates for
     the early period.
98   See Chs 3; 7(i); 8; 11(iii). The wage rate was
     reduced three times in the decade before 1900.
99   'WCM 1st Ann. Rep.', 31.12.1889.
100 Cf. Statement by Chairman of Chamber of Mines, cited
     in ibid.
101 'WCM 1st Ann. Rep.', 31.12.1889.
102 Ibid. For a more systematic discussion on the sub-
     ject of migrant labour, see below, pp.149-50.
103 Ibid.
104 Ibid., p.9.
105 Ibid. The *retention of wages* was practised in the
     Kimberley diamond fields, where the men living in
     closed compounds were afforded the opportunity of
     'saving their earnings'. In essence, it served to
     control the labour supply, prevent desertions and in-
     hibit theft (F.Wilson, 'Migrant Labour in South
     Africa', p.2). Wilson suggests that the Kimberley
     system was popular to the extent that employers who
     practised the scheme seldom had to recruit as
     vigorously as others. See also Charles van Onselen,
     'Chibaro', Pluto Press, London, 1976, pp.130,131, on
     the Kimberley compound system. He disputes Wilson's
     contention that Kimberley employers did not have to
     recruit as vigorously as others (ibid., p.131). For
     the discussion on the Rand compound system see Ch.2
     below.
106 'WCM 1st Ann. Rep. 1889', p.10.
107 A pass system had been in existence from the in-
     ception of the Rand goldmines, having its origins in
     the Cape Proclamations of 1809. It concerned itself
     largely with the registration of labour contracts but
     was unequal to the complex problem of controlling the
     movement of Africans to and from the mines. The
     Chamber estimated an African population in 1889 of
     15,000 on the Witwatersrand, but the statistics of
     Von Brandis (the Landrost - Magistrate) bore little
     relation to reality. According to this official the
     number of passes issued monthly was 7,966 into the

city and 2,360 per month out of the city. As a result, the mining managements generally had little confidence in the efficacy of the system then in operation.

108 Ibid.

109 Interesting contemporary detail of 'the free and easy administration of Boer penal rule' may be found in The Transvaal and its Gold Fields, Impressions of a recent visit, 'Blackwood's Magazine', April 1890, p.541.

CHAPTER 2 THE BLACK LABOUR SUPPLY: EARLY RECRUITMENT AND REGULATION

1 On the early assessment of the potential labour supply, see J.Robinson, South Africa as it is, 'Contemporary Review', June 1887, and F.H.P.Creswell, The Transvaal Labour Problem, 'National Review', 1902, p.448. Total African population south of the Zambezi was estimated at 6 million at the turn of the century.

2 'WCM 4th Ann. Rep. 1892', p.45.

3 Demand, however, has to be related to cost. See S. van der Horst, 'Native Labour in South Africa', F. Cass, London, 1971, p.168, and Arrighi and Saul, 'Essays on the Political Economy of Africa', 1973.

4 'WCM 5th Ann. Rep. 1893', p.52.

5 'WCM 3rd Ann. Rep. 1891', p.50.

6 Ibid.

7 Ibid.

8 Contract for the erection of 'Kafir-compound' 29.5.1891 cited 'WCM 3rd Ann. Rep. 1891', p.52. Approximately five months after the signing of the Concession, the Chamber discovered that the concessionaires had applied for a concession on the supply of African labour to the mines, but the government carefully denied these allegations.

9 Ibid., p.52.

10 Ibid., p.54.

11 See Correspondence Chamber of Mines and T.W.Beckett & Co., 18.11.1891, cited 'WCM 3rd Ann. Rep. 1891'.

12 Correspondence Secretary, Chamber of Mines to Johannesburg Chamber of Commerce, 19.8.1892, cited 'WCM 4th Ann. Rep. 1892'. As a result of pressure a Government Act of 1892 allowed concessionaires holding licences to trade along the Reef, to grant 'anyone permission to have a stand licence on the claims'.

13 S.B.Spies, 'The Origins of the Anglo-Boer War', Edward Arnold, London, 1972, p.20.
14 R.E.Robinson, J.Gallagher, and Denny, 'Africa and the Victorians', Macmillan, London, 1961, p.211.
15 Cited A.Jeeves, The Control of Migratory Labour on the South African Gold Mines in the Era of Kruger and Milner, 'Journal of Southern African Studies', vol.2, no.1, October 1975. But see also 'WCM 2nd Ann. Rep. 1890', p.61.
16 W.B.Worsfold, 'South Africa: a Study in Colonial Administration and Development', Methuen, London, 1895, p.150. For further contemporary details of Kimberley compounds in 1906 see F.Wilson and D.Perrot (eds), 'Outlook on a Century: 1870-1970', SPRO-CAS, Lovedale Press, Johannesburg, 1973, pp.297,298.
17 S.Moroney, 'Industrial Conflict in a Labour Repressive Economy: Black Labour in the Transvaal Gold Mines, 1901-12', BA Hons thesis, University of the Witwatersrand, 1976, p.49.
18 Cartwright, 'The Gold Miners', p.215.
19 Ibid.
20 Moroney, op.cit., p.45. For duties of mine police and their abuses see 'WCM 5th Ann. Rep. 1894', pp.66,75.
21 Cartwright, 'The Gold Miners', pp.215,221,222. On worker control and manipulation in the mine compounds, see Moroney, op.cit., pp.40-9. See also C. van Onselen, 'Chibaro', pp.34 ff. on conditions in Rhodesian compounds, and p.133 for reference to the 'closed compounds' on the Rand, and p.157 for a general commentary on the compound system as a means of control. For abuses within the compounds and the official conception of the system, see 'Report of Native Grievances Inquiry 1913-14, U.G. 37-14', especially Part III, pp.64-9. Though the system had been tightened up between the 1890s and 1913 (especially after 1903), the structure appears to have seen little change since its inception.
22 Cf. 'Report of Native Grievances Inquiry', pp.19-20, para. 149.
23 Cf. Mining Industrial Commission, Minutes of Evidence, H.M.Taberer, 14 October 1907, p.1315, cited Moroney, op.cit., p.42.
24 Moroney, op.cit., p.42. Many mines were named after the mine managers by the members of the African workforce, e.g. the Primrose mine was dubbed *Singaungau* ('Fierce Temper') and the Mayer-Charlton mine *Mahleka* ('One who laughs'). See Moroney, op.cit., p.42, cited from Secretary of Native Affairs (hereafter cited as SNA) 8/858/02.

25   'Report of Native Grievances Inquiry', p.19, para.
     143. For the section concerning labour control in
     the compounds, see ibid., Part III, pp.64-9.
26   Ibid., p.19, para. 143.
27   Ibid., p.20, para. 154.
28   Ibid., p.64, Part III (Control), para. 476/7.
29   Johnstone, op.cit., p.53. See also van Onselen,
     'Chibaro', p.133.
30   'Report of Native Grievances Inquiry', p.66, para.
     499.
31   Ibid., p.67, para. 501 (4).
32   Ibid.
33   Report by Pieterson, departmental inspector, 1902:
     SNA 9/1200/02/23/7/190. See also SNA 13/1761/02,
     cited Moroney, op.cit., p.63.
34   SNA 76/1616/08.
35   Ibid.
36   For details of the Coloured Labour Compound Com-
     mission, see 'TCM 15th Ann. Rep. 1904', pp.396-411.
     See also Moroney, op.cit., pp.64-5, for a vivid
     description of compound conditions.
37   'Report of Native Grievances Inquiry', p.17, para.
     126. The food costs per black worker between 1903
     and 1904 were 10s. 1.2d. per month (Moroney, op.cit.,
     p.54). The price fluctuated from year to year,
     reaching an unusually low rate of 6.94d. per month
     in 1904/5 (ibid., p.54, cited SNA 19/1314/05).
38   Cf. Cartwright, 'The Gold Miners', p.222.
39   Moroney, op.cit., p.72.
40   SNA 3868/05 Boksburg Controller to Windham 15/12/05,
     cited Moroney, op.cit., p.76.
41   For a detailed description see Moroney, op.cit., pp.
     71-80.
42   H.J.Simons, Death in the South African Mines, 'Africa
     South', vol.5, no.4, July-September 1961, p.44.
43   R.Horwitz, 'Political Economy of South Africa',
     Weidenfeld & Nicolson, London, 1967. See also Simons
     and Simons, 'Class, Race and Conflict', and H.J.
     Simons, Death in the South African Mines, for more
     extensive treatment of this theme. According to the
     'Star' (20.8.1892), 'Africans had no value in the com-
     munity except as the equivalent of so much horse-
     power'.
44   Cf. the 'Standard and Transvaal Mining Chronicle',
     Johannesburg, Transvaal, 9.5.1890. At a special
     meeting of the Chamber to discuss African wages,
     Eckstein, the Chairman, stated: 'We must have labour,
     but it is necessary that we have it as cheaply as
     possible. We must work in unity.'

45 According to a contemporary witness, 'it is almost a
    canon among investors that gold shares should be
    bought between April and August, and sold during the
    intervening months'. The Transvaal and its Gold
    Fields, 'Blackwood's Magazine', April 1890, p.550.
46 Correspondence Secretary of Chamber of Mines to State
    Secretary at Pretoria, 23.1.1890; cited 'WCM 2nd Ann.
    Rep. 1890', p.61. The question of the profitability
    of the smaller and poorer companies was frequently
    brought under review in the context of the white-black
    labour ratio, and during periods when the Chamber took
    major steps to cut the cost of production.
47 See Cartwright, 'The Gold Miners', p.215.
48 Ibid.
49 'WCM 2nd Ann. Rep. 1890', p.61. This was considered
    only as a partial remedy.
50 Ibid. (emphasis added).
51 Ibid., p.62. Cf. also 'WCM 3rd Ann. Rep. 1891', p.51.
    This was a *general* response to increase the flow of
    farm and mine labour. The Minister clearly had in
    mind the coercive tax measures being mooted in the
    Orange Free State and Cape Colony at the time to force
    up the supply of African labour. The far-reaching
    Glen Grey Act was subsequently introduced in the Cape
    Colony by Rhodes in 1894. (See below.) A year later,
    in 1895, African taxation in the South African Repub-
    lic was *revised*.
52 'WCM 2nd Ann. Rep. 1890', pp.66-7, and 'WCM 3rd Ann.
    Rep. 1891', p.51.
53 'WCM 4th Ann. Rep. 1892', p.11.

CHAPTER 3   THE WAGE BILL: THE AGREEMENT OF 1890

1 The next step was the creation of a recruiting agency.
   See Ch.7 (i)(b) below.
2 Variants of this wage and work structure characterized
   the non-mining sector during the late 1920s and subsequently. For the reasoning behind the earlier
   structure see pp.158-9 below.
3 'WCM 2nd Ann. Rep. 1890', pp.12 and 66. The Chamber
   estimated that for the first six months of 1890, its
   monthly wage bill would be £45,000. This would represent an overall African workforce of 15,000. It accordingly circulated its constituent companies in
   April of that year suggesting a reduction of wages to
   a maximum 'fair rate of pay' approximately of 40s. per
   month of 28 days.
4 'WCM 2nd Ann. Rep. 1890', pp.68-9. 'An Ordinary

Kaffir' represented an African who did not fall under
any of the classifications concerning 'specially
skilled' Africans, i.e. shaft developers, station men,
surface stokers, police and office workers. Wages
many years later (1967) was £8. 10. 0 (R17.00) with
some additional payments in kind. A white miner
earned £142 per month (R283) on average. See S.
Gervasi, 'Industrialization, Foreign Capital and
Forced Labour in South Africa', United Nations, New
York, 1970, p.3, para. 15.

5   See Correspondence Secretary of Chamber of Mines to
Mine Managers 18.10.1890, cited 'WCM 2nd Ann. Rep.
1890', p.70 (emphasis added).

6   'WCM 2nd Ann. Rep. 1890', p.12.

7   Cf. Correspondence Chamber of Mines to Head of Mining
Department, 22.10.1890, cited ibid., p.66.

8   Ibid., p.64. See also M.H. De Kock, 'Selected
Subjects in the Economic History of South Africa',
Juta, Cape Town, 1924, p.248. According to De Kock
it was not only wages that were resolved. Most of
the mines were placed on a sound working basis by 1891
and substantial dividends paid. In 1892 'an amount of
£1,000,000 was distributed in dividends, which meant
the general restoration of confidence amongst investors'. The market price of shares also rose substantially. (Ibid.)

9   'WCM 3rd Ann. Rep. 1891', p.13.

10 Ibid., p.51.

11 S. van der Horst, op.cit., p.130, suggests that the
rate did not rise above 1889 levels. However, see
also 'Annual Report of the Chamber of Mines, 1889',
p.10. Wage-returns of 53 companies analysed indicated
an average of 15s. per week made up of underground
workers at 14s. 11d.; surface workers 14s. 2d.; contractors 17s.

12 'WCM 7th Ann. Rep. 1895', p.52, cited from letter to
the Cape government labour agent; cf. also S. van der
Horst, op.cit., p.251. During this time average
earnings varied 'from two to three pounds per month'
although skilful drillers might earn up to 70s. One
year before the Chamber established a uniform wage
policy, the rates had reached a peak of 63s. 6d. for
30 completed shifts.

13 The Chamber soon became aware of other alternatives
to direct wage changes. These included the placing
of artificial pressure on the population to seek wage-
earning employment by taxation, restricting possession
and occupation of land; enforcing vagrancy laws and
curtailing mobility through Pass Laws. Most of these

measures were subsequently adopted and were the
subject of debate at the International Labour Organ-
isation Conferences in 1926/53/57. See 'Forced Labour
in South Africa' (Memo No.6), The Joint Council of
Europeans and Natives, Johannesburg, 1930. Also
Gervasi, op.cit., pp.25-7.

CHAPTER 4   QUASI-OFFICIAL CONTROL: THE STATE AND THE
CHAMBER OF MINES

1 Report of Executive Committee on Native Labour,
   8.12.1892, cited 'WCM 4th Ann. Rep. 1892', pp.43-4.
2 'WCM 4th Ann. Rep. 1892', p.41. The Assistant Commissioner at the Cape allowed a special reduced rate
   of a halfpenny a head when 25 or more were forwarded
   in one batch.
3 Ibid., p.42. Correspondence H.C.Shepstone, Secretary
   for Native Affairs to Chamber of Mines, 29.10.1892.
4 'WCM 4th Ann. Rep. 1892', p.43. The agreed wage rate
   was in some instances 20s. below the current 'market'
   rate.
5 'WCM 5th Ann. Rep. 1893', p.3.
6 Ibid., pp.4,29. The total addition to the labour
   force from this source was 800. In fact only 100 had
   been expected, but 'several hundred' arrived - without
   any food. Altogether 1,000 Africans were forwarded to
   the Chamber for distribution among the various companies.
7 Ibid., p.43.
8 A Cartwright, South African Labour Question, 'Westminster Review', July 1893, p.48.
9 See Correspondence Witwatersrand Chamber of Mines and
   Mining Companies, 12.12.1892, cited 'WCM 4th Ann. Rep.
   1892'. The office of the Commissioner was to be
   funded by a contribution by each of the mining companies of 3d. per month for each labourer employed.
10 'WCM 5th Ann. Rep. 1893', pp.30-1.
11 Report of the Commission of First Volksraad, 22.8.
   1893, cited 'WCM 5th Ann. Rep. 1893', pp.40-1.
12 Report of the Commission of First Volksraad, 22.8.
   1893, cited 'WCM 5th Ann. Rep. 1893', p.40. The im-
   putation that Africans were idle was effectively re-
   futed by Sir H.H.Johnston soon after the turn of the
   century: 'The proportion of *able-bodied* (between the
   Zambesi and the Antarctic) willing to labour apart
   from the work required in their homes is perhaps at
   the outside not more than 500,000.... I think it will
   be found on inquiry that lazy as the South African

Negro is reputed to be, these 500,000 are already
fully engaged as farm labourers, herdsmen, domestic
servants, police, transport riders, railway employees,
gardeners, plantation workers, miners, bricklayers and
so forth' (The Native Labour Question in South Africa,
'National Review', November 1902, p.726. The comment
also throws much light on the extent at the time of
the migratory labour system. Sir H.H.Johnston envisaged the importation of a million migrant workers
at one-third of the local cost (ibid., p.730).

13 Report of Committee of Mine Managers Association on
the Native Labour Question, quoted 'WCM 5th Ann. Rep.
1893', pp.43-4.

14 Ibid., p.43.

15 The effect of this measure would be to coerce African
tribesmen into taking up contractual obligations with
the mines in order to derive sufficient revenue to
render their taxes to the government. The matter is
discussed more fully below.

16 Ibid., p.48.

17 See Correspondence Witwatersrand Chamber of Mines to
Mine Managers Assoc. 3.11.1893, cited 'WCM 5th Ann.
Rep. 1893', p.19. Penal clauses subsequently became
a common feature in nearly all inter-company Agreements. The signatories saw their action as an attempt
to secure the united action of mine managers towards
reducing the rate of wages. The priority of unity was
so urgent that the Chamber's Native Labour Committee
specifically addressed itself to mining companies who
were not members of the Mine Managers Association to
join that body.

18 Report of the Chairman of the Witwatersrand Chamber
of Mines, cited 'WCM 5th Ann. Rep. 1893', p.19.

19 'WCM 5th Ann. Rep. 1893', p.19.

CHAPTER 5   THE EAST COAST LABOUR SUPPLY: AN ALTERNATIVE
LABOUR SUPPLY

1 P.Harries, Labour Migration from the Delagoa Bay
Hinterland to South Africa, 1852-1895, 'University of
London Institute of Commonwealth Studies, Collected
Seminar Papers No.21, The Societies of Southern Africa
in the Nineteenth and Twentieth Centuries', vol.7,
p.62.

2 This was so because of the revenue the Portuguese
received from this source. See below, pp.69-70.

3 Early in 1893 arrangements were made for the entry of
a further 7,000 East Coast Africans under differential

wage rates of 52s. 6d. for men and 40s. for boys -
but this did not materialize ('WCM 5th Ann. Rep.
1893', p.4).

4   Report of the Chairman, 'WCM 6th Ann. Rep. 1894',
    p.19. The point was made in the Johannesburg 'Star',
    2.2.1895: 'The one great fact that must never be lost
    sight of is that labour in the raw is superabundant
    throughout South Africa. The Natives in the Transvaal
    alone are probably more than sufficient to meet the
    wants ... of the Industry.'
5   See below, pp.68-9.
6   'WCM 5th Ann. Rep. 1893', pp.4 and 16.
7   E.Roux, 'Time Longer Than Rope', Gollancz, London,
    1948, p.76. See Wilson and Thompson (eds), 'The
    Oxford History of South Africa', pp.65-6. See also
    S.Marks, 'Reluctant Rebellion: The 1906-1908 Dis-
    turbances in Natal', The Clarendon Press, Oxford,
    1970, who notes that 'the efficiency of taxation in
    ensuring a constant labour supply for the white man
    was well recognised in Natal' (p.132). S. van der
    Horst, op.cit., pp.152-3, has helpful insights on
    taxation in the South African Republic.
8   See S. van der Horst, op.cit., p.149, quoted from
    Cape Hansard, 1894, pp.362-9.
9   In the following year the South African government
    introduced Law No.24 of 1895 which made it compulsory
    for all males over twenty-one years of age to pay a
    hut tax of 10s. See S. van der Horst, op.cit., p.152,
    and A.Hepple, 'South Africa', p.196. However, the
    urgency of the Chamber's needs in 1894 led them to
    divert their attention to Mocambique.
10 'Star', 29.2.1896.
11 See Correspondence Native Labour Commissioner to
    R.Bennington, Recruiting Agent, January-March 1894,
    quoted 'WCM 6th Ann. Rep. 1894', pp.28-30. The rates
    were to be 52s. 6d. per month for men and 40s. for
    boys.
12 Ibid., p.27.
13 Ibid., p.34. The initial charge per head of each
    foreign labourer was 110s., which was described as
    the lowest cost if labourers were to be *legally*
    acquired. See correspondence R.Bennington and W.
    Grant, Native Labour Commissioner, 1.3.1894, quoted
    'WCM 6th Ann. Rep. 1894', p.27.
14 The list of offers closed with firm proposals from
    three firms: Messrs Benningfield, Wilhelm F. Hexting,
    and Best and Williams. None was taken up.
15 See Correspondence Messrs Best and Williams and L.
    Phillips, September 1894, cited 'WCM 6th Ann. Rep.
    1894', p.34.

16 'WCM 6th Ann. Rep. 1894', p.34.
17 For problems of communication see p.36 above, and for
the impact of rural poverty see below.
In fact it was only after 1904 that the supply situation turned wholly in favour of the Chamber. See
below, p.238.
18 'WCM 6th Ann. Rep. 1894', p.34. Poverty was one of
the most promising indicators of an uninterrupted flow
of labour - but unless the 'right' strategy was followed, this could by no means be assured.
19 Ibid., p.39.
20 Ibid., p.29. The words 'fostering' and 'protective'
were used to underline the rationale that the existing
treatment of Africans was 'unjust, irritating and de-
structive of the supply'.
21 Ibid., p.39 (Report of the Native Labour Commissioner
10.5.1894). See also M.Legassick, South Africa,
Capital Accumulation and Violence in 'Economy and
Society', vol.3, no.3, 1974, for some penetrating
insights into the role of the gold mining industry in
the Transvaal Republic and later.
22 This conflict escalated and became known as the
Malaboch War.
23 See Instructions to Special Commissioner Samuel Duncombe, cited 'WCM 6th Ann. Rep. 1894', p.43.
24 Ibid., p.43.
25 Ibid. It was, in fact, from this area that substantial supplies of labour had already been drawn and
whence the labourers had personally undertaken the
long journey to the Rand mines.
26 However, if a recruit chose to defray the entire cost
of his journey (which might be deducted from his
wages) he need not be bound to complete the twelve
months contractual labour. See 'Report of Special
Commissioner', 12.9.1894; also 'WCM 6th Ann. Rep.
1894', p.43.
27 See below.
28 'WCM 6th Ann. Rep. 1894', p.44. The Portuguese
normally levied a fine of £3 per head for each tribes-
man leaving their territory without a passport.
29 Ibid., p.47. The first depot was established at
Makan's Poort.
30 The total number of African employees in 1890 was
14,000 as against 40,000 in 1894 (ibid.).
31 Ibid.
32 Ibid.
33 'Star', 19.1.1898.
34 'WCM 6th Ann. Rep. 1894', p.51. This document was
drafted as Article 88 of the Gold Law.

35   For an analysis of the Regulations see below, pp.
     74-5.
36   The Chamber believed that the supply would be doubled
     if its pass regulations were adopted by central
     government. See above, p.65.

CHAPTER 6   PASS REGULATIONS AND THE CONTROL OF MOBILITY

1   The full impact of tne gold industry upon the South
    African state is still the subject of historical
    debate.
2   See Yves Guyot, 'Boer Politics', John Murray, London,
    1900: 'The Boers have created a democracy among them-
    selves [but] with regard to Natives and Uitlanders
    they are an oligarchy' (p.49).
3   In 1903 the Native Pass Law was extended. The Pass
    Regulations were to be applied not only to the public
    diggings, but throughout the Transvaal Colony.
    Special rules for labour districts were, however,
    still enforced. 'TCM 14th Rep. 1903', p.47.
4   See the Gold Law of the South African Republic as
    amended 1886, cited in D. Hobart Houghton and J.Dagut
    (eds), 'Source Material on the South African Economy,
    1860-1970', Oxford University Press, Cape Town, 1972,
    vol.III. Article 76 of this law, pp.11-12, stipu-
    lated: 'No coloured person, Coolie or Chinese, can
    hold a licence or be in any capacity engaged in
    working the goldfields, otherwise than in the service
    of white men.'
5   The Regulations were promulgated after prolonged delay
    approximately eighteen months after the submission of
    the draft by the Chamber. See the 'Star', 21.12.1896.
6   'WCM 6th Ann. Rep. 1894', p.51. See also A.Hepple,
    op.cit., p.199, who quite properly relates the Pass
    Laws to the attempt to reduce wages 'to a reasonable
    level' and to more adequate employer combinations.
    See also Chamber of Mines Memorial to the Raad, cited
    in the 'Star', 6.4.1895: In their petition to the
    Volksraad, the Chamber blamed the existing inadequate
    Pass Laws (and regulations for controlling African
    labour) for the mining companies' failure to secure
    combinations that would enable wages to be reduced.
7   There is no contemporary written record of the African
    reaction to the badge. Some years later (1898), how-
    ever, one of the members of the Transvaal Volksraad,
    A.D.Wolmarans, noted that 'pass officials were of the
    opinion that the badge should be abolished as it was
    no check on the natives. There were many Kaffirs who

were partly civilized and who objected to the wearing
of the badge.' The Volksraad agreed to draft an
amendment to the law. Cf. the 'Transvaal Advertiser'
cited C.O. 879/51 end. 4, no.184.

8   'WCM 6th Ann. Rep. 1894', p.53.
9   Reports of Native Labour Commissioner for the year
    1895, cited 'WCM 7th Ann. Rep. 1895', p.38 (emphasis
    added).
10 See 'WCM 7th Ann. Rep. 1895', p.29.
11 The 'Star', 5.1.1895, referred to Delagoa Bay 'as the
    sick man of Africa ... engaged in a hard struggle with
    its Native subjects'. Leading article in the same
    issue criticized the East Coast administration -
    'which is on the one hand, so lamentably incapable of
    maintaining public order among its white subjects, and
    on the other is unable to suppress a Kafir rising
    which any other South African government would have
    stamped out in three months'. However, the war esca-
    lated throughout 1895, making the deficiency in supply
    more serious.
12 'WCM 8th Ann. Rep. 1896', p.26.
13 Ibid., p.105.
14 Ibid., p.22.
15 Ibid., p.6. Fines for a first offence were not to
    exceed 10s. or one week's imprisonment, and 20s. for
    a second offence with the alternative of two weeks'
    detention with hard labour and lashes. Subsequent to
    the outbreak of the war, in defending itself against
    'unspecified' accusations of forced labour, the
    Chamber claimed that in the draft law the punishments
    to be inflicted for evasion were left in blank. 'They
    were filled in by the government officials.' On ac-
    count of laxity the Chamber asked for a more stringent
    application. Cf. 'TCM 12th Ann. Rep. 1900-1901',
    p.xl.
16 Ibid., p.7. In a petition submitted to the State
    President the Chamber referred to the 'ineffectual
    administration of the Pass Law', claiming that the
    legislation 'lends itself to touts and others who
    induce Natives to desert their employers and enter
    their service by reason of their being able to bail
    the Natives out for the sum of 10/-'. Cf. 'WCM 8th
    Ann. Rep. 1896', p.104.
17 D.J.N.Denoon, 'A Grand Illusion: The Failure of
    Imperial Policy in the Transvaal Colony During the
    Period of Reconstruction, 1900-1905', Longman, London,
    1973, p.4, noted that 'when the British troops arrived
    in Johannesburg and Pretoria during 1900, there were
    mass burnings of pass-books in the belief that these

oppressive documents would not be required'. See also
L.S.Amery (ed.), 'The Times History of the War in
South Africa 1899-1902', vol.VI, London, 1909. The
authors noted: 'Many Kaffirs, in the belief that the
British would not enforce the Pass Law, destroyed
their passes, and it took some time for them to
realise that the military authorities intended to
continue the old system of registration.... Many of
the Kaffirs looked for the millennium with the arrival
of the British' (p.595).

18 'WCM 8th Ann. Rep. 1896'.
19 Ibid., pp.104-5.
20 'Evidence of the Witwatersrand Chamber of Mines to the
Industrial Commission of Inquiry', 1897, cited 'WCM
9th Ann. Rep. 1897', pp.44-5. Another witness to this
Commission provided a different dimension of the problem when he said that in his district (of Boksburg)
'the gaol had been overcrowded with deserters who had
failed to produce a £3 fine; and as there was no
further prison accommodation the Landdrost was obliged
to reduce the fine from £3 to 3d'. (cited in 'The
Natives of South Africa', ed. The South African Races
Committee, London, 1901, p.167).
21 F.H.P.Creswell, The Transvaal Labour Problem,
'National Review', November 1902, p.445.

CHAPTER 7   THE FORMATION OF A CENTRAL RECRUITING ORGAN-
IZATION

1 This pattern may be discerned from the inter-company
rivalry already outlined above, p.52.
2 'WCM 7th Ann. Rep. 1895', p.42. The mine managers
felt the loss acutely as the departing men from the
East Coast were prized as 'the best available labour
for underground purposes'. On the Northern Transvaal
front the Commissioner, Grant, complained (June 1895)
that rumours regarding the Republic's contemplated
attack on the Chief Magato 'had had a most damaging
and mischievous effect' ('Star', 8.6.1895).
3 'WCM 8th Ann. Rep. 1896', p.4.
4 Ibid. The plea that lack of labour relief would lead
to the suspension of mining operations was on this occasion not merely an attempt to coerce the executive
into rapid action, but reflected serious conditions in
the industry: e.g. The Roodepoort Deep Level Gold
Mining Co. complained to the 'Superintendent of
Natives' at Pretoria that only 15 stamps out of 50
were in operation owing to lack of adequate labour

supplies despite desperate attempts to obtain manpower. See ibid., p.140.

5 Cf. Correspondence Government Commissioner to Witwatersrand Chamber of Mines, dated 25.2.1896. See
also the 'Star', 14.3.1896. The Chamber appealed to
the authorities to be more co-operative in dealing
with the industry's recruiting agents on the East
Coast. It claimed that the state had been deliberately obstructive and had 'alienated Portuguese sympathy'
by instructing Portuguese officials to enforce rigidly
the Portuguese administrative orders which prohibited
Africans from leaving Gazaland for service on the
Rand. It drew the attention of the government,
through its press, to the misdemeanours of their
Consul at Delagoa Bay - who 'received a handsome
salary besides his emoluments emanating from the
position he holds', and instead of graft and ob-
struction asked that the government co-operate with
the industry.

6 'WCM 8th Ann. Rep. 1896', p.140 (emphasis added).

7 Ibid., p.143. This officer was subsequently removed
from his post after charges of 'theft, extortion, em-
bezzlement and assault'. See the 'Star', 14.12.1895.

8 'WCM 8th Ann. Rep. 1896', p.145. He also noted that
a large number of companies' agents were trying to
get labour and told the Executive Committee of the
Chamber that if this competition ceased Africans could
be procured without payment of premiums and at a lower
rate of wages. Report of Meeting of Executive Committee, cited in the 'Star', 14.3.1896.

9 See Correspondence P.J.Joubert to Commissioner of
Natives, 'WCM 8th Ann. Rep. 1896', p.145.

10 'Star', 2.2.1895.

11 Statement made by the Chamber's Native Commissioner,
cited 'WCM 7th Ann. Rep. 1895', p.43.

12 Ibid.

13 'Star', 30.3.1895.

14 'WCM 8th Ann. Rep. 1896', p.157.

15 Food was apportioned at a maximum allowance of 2½ lb
of mealie meal (maize) per person per day and a
maximum of 2 lb of meat per 'boy' per week. Cf.
ibid., p.161.

16 For 'Classification of Maximum Rates of Native Wages',
cf. chart in ibid., p.162.

17 Cf. Correspondence Witwatersrand Chamber of Mines and
The State Secretary, Pretoria, dated 30.7.1896.

18 'WCM 8th Ann. Rep. 1896', p.166.

19 Ibid., p.154.

20 Subscription amounted, initially, to 3s. for each

African labourer employed during an average of four
months of each year. See Aims and Objects of the
Native Labour Supply Association, quoted 'WCM 8th Ann.
Rep. 1896', pp.158-9.

21 See Aims and Objects of the Native Labour Supply Association, cited 'WCM 8th Ann. Rep. 1896', p.159.

22 Foul play by mining managements was to be avoided by
the elaborate procedure of supplying each labourer
with the badge, which was to accompany each labourer
to the mine at which he agreed to work, and which was
to be returned to the Association by each particular
mine manager - together with the necessary statistical
returns of the labour so employed.

23 It reserved the right to act as a pressure group upon
the republican Legislature and 'interview, intercede,
pray and petition the State President and Executive
... to assist by proper measures the carrying out of
the work of the Association'. Art.15: Aims and
Objects of the Native Labour Supply Association. See
'WCM 8th Ann. Rep. 1896', p.159.

24 Art.14: The Native Labour Supply Association. 'WCM
8th Ann. Rep. 1896', p.159.

25 'WCM 8th Ann. Rep. 1896', p.161.

26 Art.15: Aims and Objects of the Native Labour Supply
Association. See 'WCM 8th Ann. Rep. 1896', p.159.

27 'WCM 8th Ann. Rep. 1896', p.160. According to the
Annual Report of the Chamber in 1896, the Native
Labour Association undertook the work of supply but
the regulation of wages and laws affecting the performance of engagements were 'closely and earnestly'
scrutinized by the Chamber. See ibid., p.4.

28 Ibid., p.164. These concessions, it was hoped, would
facilitate the supply and end the frequent reports of
molestation that reached the Chamber. See ibid.,
p.198.

29 See Ch.3(i).

30 This aspect is discussed at greater length in the
previous chapter.

CHAPTER 8   MANIPULATING THE WAGE RATE

1 See 'WCM 9th Ann. Rep. 1897', pp.4 and 107. In fact
the Chamber was informed that the supply exceeded the
demand.

2 See Resolution of combined meeting of the Chamber and
the Association of Mines, 1897. The new schedule was
to be brought into operation in June of that year.

3 'WCM 9th Ann. Rep. 1897', p.5. The Chamber actually

made contingency preparations for 'a temporary disturbance of labour conditions' which might result from
the departure of 'boys' unwilling to accept the lower
wage. Despite the far-reaching nature of the changes,
there was little serious interruption of the working
of the mines despite *a considerable exodus* in May
1897, when notice of the change in the wage rate was
given (emphasis added).

4   The impact of the disease is discussed comprehensive-
ly by C. van Onselen, Reaction to Rinderpest in
Southern Africa 1896-97, 'Journal of African History',
vol.XIII, no.3, 1972, pp.473-86. Van Onselen notes
(p.486) that, despite the reduction of 90 per cent of
the cattle herds in the Transvaal (plus 43 per cent
of the cattle in the Cape as a whole), 'it was only
with extreme reluctance that Africans from the Cape
and elsewhere would proceed to the Transvaal Goldfields'. Harsh mining conditions were described as
the cause of this reluctance to travel to the Transvaal. However, despite the immediate reaction, the
large-scale ravages of the rinderpest disease must in
the long term have worked in the interest of the gold
industry. For further evidence of the extent of the
disease see also M.Wilson and L.Thompson (eds), 'The
Oxford History of South Africa', vol.II, p.116.

5   See Revised Schedule of Native Wages, May 1897, 'WCM
9th Ann. Rep. 1897', pp.238-42 and 113. See Ch.11
(iii) below for a discussion on the significance of
'special rates'. At the time of the 1897 wage reduction, the white miners almost had their wages reduced
by 10s. in the £1 per week but struck work and won
their contest so that the white wage rates remained
unaltered.

6   'WCM 10th Ann. Rep. 1898', p.56.

7   Ibid., pp.56-7.

8   'WCM 9th Ann. Rep. 1897', p.120. See also M.Harris,
Labour Emigration among the Mocambique Thonga: Cultural and Political Factors, 'Africa', vol.XXIX,
January 1959, p.52, and R.First, The Gold of Migrant
Labour, 'Africa South', vol.5, no.3, April-June 1961,
pp.13-14, for early, and more specific, subsequent
agreements with the Portuguese.

9   'WCM 9th Ann. Rep. 1897', p.120. The cost of imported
labour had progressively increased. Eighteen months
previously (1895/6) labourers were acquired at 35s. to
40s. per head, but could not be obtained in 1897 for
under 70s. per head. Part of the reason for this increase was the 'Privilege licence' which the Portuguese government now imposed at a cost of £500, plus

a charge of £1. 7s. 6d. per labourer leaving Mocambique for the South African Republic. Complex labour-
exporting regulations were published by the Portuguese
authorities to this effect.

10 J.Duffy, 'Portugal in Africa', Penguin, Harmondsworth,
1962, pp.132-3. See also Report of Commissioner for
the Colony of the Transvaal Native Affairs Department,
Transvaal Administration Report for 1902. According
to this source 68,000 out of 98,000 miners from Portuguese territory were in the Transvaal *before the war*.
Cited by Hobart Houghton and Dagut, op.cit., pp.30-1.
There seems to be some doubt about the precise percentage of the Portuguese contingent of the labour
force. See M.Harris, op.cit., pp.51-2. According
to Harris three-quarters (80,000) of the total African
labour force *before* the Boer War were from Mocambique.
The mortality rate was 67.6 per 1,000. See Duffy,
op.cit., p.138.

11 The Chairman of the Chamber noted significantly for
the year 1897: 'Taking into consideration the increased demand owing to the deep level companies
entering the list of gold producers, the supply must,
on the whole, be regarded as very satisfactory, more
especially as concurrently ... a large reduction in
the scale of native wages had been successfully
carried through' (Chairman, 'TCM 9th Ann. Rep. 1897',
p.129.

12 See Ch.10(ii) below. See also J.A.Marais, 'The Fall
of Kruger's Republic', The Clarendon Press, Oxford,
1951, for a systematic treatment of the political
causes of the war and some of the manipulations of
the Kruger administration.

13 The formation of the recruiting organization did much
to promote this. The Supply Association underwent
some structural change although no alteration in
principle. In 1900 its name was changed to the Witwatersrand Native Labour Association (WNLA). In 1912
the Chamber established the Native Recruiting Corporation (NRC) to organize recruitment within South
Africa and the British Protectorates. WNLA confined
itself to Mocambique. See F.Wilson, 'Labour in the
South African Gold Mines', pp.4-5, and S.T. van der
Horst, op.cit., p.63.

14 See below, Ch.10(ii).

15 See Chapter 7.

CHAPTER 9   THE NEEDS OF DEEP-LEVEL MINING: THE GOLD
INDUSTRY AND THE STATE

1   See above. The labour force multiplied itself seven
    times in seven years between 1890 and 1897.
2   Report of the Industrial Commission, 5.4.1897, cited
    'WCM 9th Ann. Rep. 1897', p.75. In this respect the
    Commission's projections are generally accurate. Ac-
    cording to the Chamber, 96,704 African labourers were
    employed in 1899 ('WCM 13th Ann. Rep. 1902', p.7).
    See also D.J.N.Denoon, The Transvaal Labour Crisis,
    1901-1906, 'Journal of African History', vol.VIII,
    no.3, 1967, pp.481-2. According to Denoon, ibid.,
    p.482, there were 107,482 Africans and 12,350 whites
    (a ratio of 8.6 to 1) in 1899. Afterwards the diffi-
    culties of recruiting Africans was so great that the
    ratio fell to 5.7 to 1 (70,608 Africans and 12,414
    whites). Reasons given for the scarcity included
    'deplorable' physical conditions of living and work-
    ing, and the demand of other sectors.
3   B.Rose, 'The Truth about the Transvaal', Morning
    Leader Publications Department, London, 1902, p.70.
4   Speech by Rouliot, Chairman of the Chamber, to annual
    meeting of the TCM, January 1899, cited 'Standard and
    Diggers News', Johannesburg, 27.1.1899. The average
    number of companies at work (outcrop and deep-level)
    per month in 1899 was 63.5. Total number of stamps
    was 4,765, of which 864 were from the deep-levels.
5   Source: 'Annual Reports of Witwatersrand Chamber of
    Mines 1902 and 1912', pp.7 and 72. The pre-war Afri-
    can labour force was 96,709, which rapidly declined
    in numbers as war proceeded. See Colony of the Tvl.
    Native Affairs Dept, Report of Commissioner for Native
    Affairs for 1902, cited Hobart Houghton and Dagut
    (eds), op.cit., pp.28-9. For monthly details of Afri-
    can recruitment between 1901 and 1906 see Appendix 3,
    below.
6   Richardson, 'The Provision of Chinese Indentured
    Labour for the Transvaal Gold Mines', pp.18,388.
7   See Ch.7, above.
8   'WCM 9th Ann. Rep. 1897', p.408. See also 'Debates
    of Transvaal Legislative Council', 30.12.1903, speech
    by Loveday, cols. 300,301, pp.150,151. Quoting the
    Report of the Chamber for 1897, he noted that the im-
    provement in supply conditions had become so favour-
    able that wages were reduced 'on an average of 30%'.
9   See S.H.Frankel, 'Gold and International Equity In-
    vestment', Institute of Economic Affairs, London,
    1969, p.17. The position was, however, complicated

by the depression (1896-9) which the government accused the mine-owners of engineering in order to
strengthen their position vis-à-vis the Bewaarplaatsen
- their mining claims at the potentially wealthy deep-
level properties. See 'Standard and Diggers News',
31.3.1898. According to this source the depression
'engineered by the industry' was severe. The shrink-
ing in the cash held by the banking institutions in
the Republic amounted to no less than £1,852,000.
The figures showed 'that not only has no great capital
come into the country, but that much has actually been
withdrawn'. The result had been that mining claims
(unfavourable to the mine-owners) had been dropped
'and merchants forced to draw upon their resources at
the banks'. See also C.O. 879/55 No.260 on the subject of the Bewaarplaatsen and the 'Transvaal Leader',
21.4.1899, for address by G.Rouliot, Chairman of the
Chamber of Mines, on this subject. Despite the depression, labour needs were high.

10 Frankel, 'Gold and International Equity Investment',
    p.19.
11 Ibid., p.20.
12 For some of the deficiencies of early investment de-
    cisions see Jeeves, op.cit., p.9. On production, cf.
    B.Rose, op.cit., p.70. The Rand mines contributed
    25 per cent of the world gold output by 1895. In
    this respect, see also the 'Star', 12.1.1895.
13 According to G.Blainey, The Lost Causes of the Jameson
    Raid, in 'Economic History Review', 2nd Series, vol.
    XVIII, no.2, 1965, p.352, the outcrop companies 'pro-
    duced all the gold on the Rand as late as 1895'.
    Hence all the dividends paid in June 1895 came from
    42 of the outcrop companies (p.352).
14 J.A.Hobson, 'The War in South Africa', James Nisbet,
    London, 1900, p.4. For early predictions (on the
    potential of the deep-level mines) by engineers
    Hamilton Smith, Hays Hammond, et al., see below,
    pp.105-6.
15 See Jeeves, op.cit., p.9, who notes that 'in the
    aftermath of the war, the mining houses confronted
    the consequences of their earlier optimism'.
16 'Transvaal Leader', 22.4.1904, Report of the Meeting
    of West Rand Mines Ltd, F.W.Hatch and J.A.Chalmers,
    'The Gold Mines of the Rand', Macmillan, London, 1895,
    pp.47-8, confirm the uniformity of the Main Reef
    Series of gold-bearing ore on the Witwatersrand. How-
    ever, although this series was unparalleled in the
    world, the grade of ore varied significantly along the
    Reef as a whole.

17   J. Hays Hammond, in preface to Hatch and Chalmers,
     op.cit., p.vii.
18   For both Smith and Schmeisser's estimates, see Cart-
     wright, 'The Gold Miners', p.103. For further details
     of Hamilton Smith's report see W.B.Worsfold, 'South
     Africa: a Study in Colonial Administration and
     Development', Methuen, London, 1895, pp.160-1.
19   Phillips, the firm's Johannesburg representative,
     wrote to his principals: 'deep-levels are getting
     fashionable ... I am gradually acquiring as much as
     possible without making a stir' (Phillips to Messrs
     Wernher, Beit & Co. H.E. 149, 3.10.1891, in Fraser
     and Jeeves, op.cit., p.50.
20   R.V.Kubicek, The Randlords in 1895: A Reassessment,
     'Journal of British Studies', vol.XI, 1972, p.96.
21   Ibid., pp.90-1. See also A.P.Cartwright, 'Gold Paved
     the Way', Macmillan, London, 1967, pp.68-9, and Con-
     solidated Goldfields of South Africa Ltd, 'The Gold
     Fields, 1887-1937', London, 1937, pp.38-9. Percy
     Tarbutt and his engineer associate, S.Boucher of the
     African Gold Share Investment Co., the South African
     Gold Trust and the Agency Company, respectively,
     actually pioneered deep-level mining on the Rand,
     starting in 1890. Their companies were bought out
     by Consolidated Goldfields when the company was re-
     constituted and Tarbutt joined the board. See 'The
     Gold Fields', p.38.
22   Hatch and Chalmers, op.cit., p.89.
23   Kubicek, The Randlords, p.99. The other groups, the
     German-financed Goerz & Co. (est. 1893) and the
     General Mining & Finance Co. (est. 1895), acquired
     deep-level claims (ibid., p.100).
24   On Farrar's activities see Ch.13, below. For details
     of Chinese employment see Richardson, 'The Provision
     of Chinese Indentured Labour', pp.379,380, Appendix 2.
25   Blainey, op.cit., pp.355-6.
26   Rouliot to Chamber, cited 'Standard and Diggers News',
     27.1.1899. The appearance of these items as capital
     charges is discussed by Richardson, 'The Provision of
     Chinese Indentured Labour', p.28.
27   See Blainey, op.cit., p.355. According to Hatch and
     Chalmers, op.cit., p.106, the total cost was nearer
     £350,000. The 'Standard and Diggers News', 18.1.1896,
     notes that the Geldenhuis Deep mine 'virtually stood
     sponsor for the rest' - although not a true deep-level
     in the strictest application of the term. When the
     mine failed to make profits 'the economic environment
     of Kruger's land' was blamed.
28   Hatch and Chalmers, op.cit., p.106. Hays Hammond saw

no reason why the mines should not be worked to a
depth of 5,000 feet, and calculated that the value of
the annual output of gold would exceed £20 million
around the year 1900. Cited Cartwright, 'The Gold
Miners', p.104.

29 Cartwright, 'The Gold Miners', p.104.
30 Blainey, op.cit., p.355.
31 Hatch and Chalmers, op.cit., p.107.
32 Ibid., pp.259-70. See also Blainey, op.cit., p.356.
33 Blainey, op.cit., p.356.
34 See Cartwright, 'The Gold Miners', p.122. In the five
    years preceding the war, 1,002,060 dynamite cases of
    50 lb each were sold to the industry. The profit on
    these cases was £2 per case or over £2,000,000 (ibid.,
    p.122, citing the Report of the Post War Commission
    that was appointed to inquire into the concessions
    granted by the Republic).
35 Blainey, op.cit., p.359.
36 On the Jameson Raid see especially ibid.; and R.
    Mendelsohn, Blainey and the Jameson Raid: The Debate
    Renewed, 'University of London Institute of Common-
    wealth Studies Collected Seminar Papers: The Societies
    of Southern Africa in the Nineteenth and Twentieth
    Centuries', 1976. Blainey, op.cit., pp.361-3, spe-
    cifically differentiates the fraction of mine-owners
    involved in the Raid, and attributes Jameson's attempt
    to topple the Kruger regime in 1895-6 to the needs of
    the deep-level companies for cuts in the cost of pro-
    duction. Cecil Rhodes, who inspired the revolt, was
    Managing Director of Consolidated Goldfields of South
    Africa, and Alfred Beit, the other plotter, was one
    of the partners in the private London company of
    Wernher, Beit & Co., which held half the shares in
    Rand Mines. George Farrar of the Anglo-French Ex-
    ploration Company was also a conspirator. His main
    mines - the East Rand Proprietory Mines - controlled
    both large outcrop mines and adjacent deep-levels.
    Farrar subsequently played a vital role in defending
    the labour structure of the industry. See Chs 12 and
    14, below. Kubicek, The Randlords, pp.97,98, also
    discusses the matter of the Raid. According to
    Kubicek, Beit's support of Rhodes was emotional and
    not financial (ibid., p.99). Mendelsohn disputes
    this, op.cit., p.6.
37 See Hobson, 'The War in South Africa', p.87. For
    comments on the Gold Law see below, pp.132,307.
38 Ibid.
39 Praagh (ed.), 'The Transvaal and its Mines', p.517.
40 See Ch.7(i), above.

41   See Ch.10(i), below, p.123.
42   C.O. 879/55 No.249. Chamberlain to Milner 10.5.1899.
     Chamberlain went further than the mine-owners in this
     respect: they did not oppose the legislation on the
     whole. See below, p.137.
43   Mrs L.Phillips, 'Some South African Recollections',
     Longmans, Green & Co., London, 1899, p.33. On the
     subject of liquor and the capitalists see C. van
     Onselen, The Randlords and Rotgut, 1886-1903, 'Uni-
     versity of London Institute of Commonwealth Studies
     Collected Seminar Papers: The Societies of Southern
     Africa in the Nineteenth and Twentieth Centuries',
     May 1975, p.4.
44   C.O. 879/51 No.313.
45   'Standard and Diggers News', 6.4.1899.
46   The introduction to this work, entitled 'Een Eauw van
     Onrecht', was written by J.C.Smuts. According to van
     Jaarsveld it was designed for overseas consumption and
     showed the 'injustice' inflicted on a small 'op-
     pressed' nation compelled to struggle for its freedom
     against a world power. See F.A. van Jaarsveld, 'The
     Afrikaner's Interpretation of South African History',
     Simondium Publishers, Cape Town, 1964, p.126.
47   Hobson, 'The War in South Africa', pp.73-4 (emphasis
     added).
48   Ibid., p.36. There were 3,000 men in government em-
     ployment, including police. They looked to Holland
     to assist them. 'The Hollander taught the government
     of the country the art of red tape qualified by cor-
     ruption' (ibid., p.75).
49   Simons and Simons, op.cit., p.62.
50   Ibid.
51   J.P.Fitzpatrick, 'The Transvaal from Within: A Private
     Record of Public Affairs', Heinemann, London, 1900,
     pp.80-1. See also Y.Guyot, op.cit., p.260, and
     Hobson, 'The War in South Africa', pp.84-6.
52   Hobson, 'The War in South Africa', p.84.
53   C.W. De Kiewiet, 'A History of South Africa - Social
     and Economic', Oxford, The Clarendon Press, 1942,
     p.119. See also the Report of the State Mining
     Engineer cited in the 13.7.1895 edition of the 'Star'.
     This official noted that the mining industry contri-
     buted 43.1/4 per cent of the entire revenue of the
     state during the year (1894). Four years previously
     the President's salary had been increased from £2,000
     to £8,000.
54   Guyot, op.cit., p.57. A new tax system was adopted
     but not implemented (cf. p.133 below).
55   Cited by Hobson, Capitalism, Imperialism and South

Africa, 'Contemporary Review', 1900, p.9. See also
C.O. 879/55, No.42, Chamberlain to W.F.Butler, 13.1.
1899, for a succinct review of the question of explosives manufactured in the Transvaal under state
monopoly. On the subject of concessions, the
'Standard and Diggers News', 2.2.1899, rather significantly pointed out the illogicality of the mine-
owners' argument: 'We would ask if the Chamber really
means to sustain as a principle its objection to "all
concessions". We think not. If it does, then the
mining industry should undergo a process of national-
ization for it is founded on the bedrock of concession, monopoly and protection.' The mine-owners
did not see the situation in this light, however.
56 There were numerous items of expenditure which the
Chamber disputed. Foreign representation alone
amounted to £17,500 in 1898. After an 'animated
debate' in the Volksraad (4.3.1898) the amount was
reduced by £2,500. See C.O. 879/51, No.175.
57 Fitzpatrick, op.cit., p.256. See also Imperial South
African Association, 'Handy Notes on South Africa',
London, 1901, p.36, in Hobart Houghton and Dagut
(eds), op.cit., pp.340-1.
58 Fitzpatrick, op.cit., p.256. The republican government seems to have accepted some of the complaints
that the Estimates Committee of the South African
Republic had 'investigated the causes of the dispro-
portion of official salaries and [recommended] certain
changes'. The salaries of several head officials were
to be revised in order to make their remuneration more
proportionate 'to that of head officials ... who draw
one or more fixed grants above their salaries'. See
Transvaal State Revenue and Expenditure for 1898 and
the 1899 Estimates, C.O. 879/55, No.145.
59 Guyot, op.cit., p.260. See also Hobson, 'The War in
South Africa', p.26. According to Hobson, 'Enemies
boldly cast in [Kruger's] teeth personal corruption,
insisting that he has taken large sums of money, not
merely for dynamite, but for other concessions and
dealings' (p.26).
60 The Concessions Commission which was created by the
imperial government in 1901 to consider dynamite,
railways and other indirect tax 'burdens' on the gold-
mines provided considerable evidence of bribes in connection with the dynamite concessions. See 'TCM 12th
Ann. Rep. 1900-1901', p.xlv. Between 1897 and 1899,
£39,000 was 'transmitted to Pretoria for corrupt expenditure ... especially in the bribery of members of
the Raad' (ibid.). There was continual suspicion as

to the honesty of republican officials. Conyngham
Green wrote to Milner on 16.3.1898 in connection with
a loan the Transvaal government wished to make: 'I
have heard it stated ... that as much as 2½% on the
six millions (or £150,000) was to have been divided
among the members of the Transvaal Executive Council
as "commission" and that one of the reasons why the
proposal was so strongly opposed in the Rand was because the members of the House had not been sufficiently "squared"' (C.O. 879/51, No.182 (secret)).
See also C.O. 879/51, No.210, and 879/55, No.186,
21.3.99.

61 The Chairman of the Chamber, with the 'English'
victory fresh in his mind, expressed this view quite
clearly in 1903: 'It is my hope and belief that we
shall obtain from this continent ... sufficient
[labour] to enable us to develop our industry and the
collateral industries *to the extent which we have
heretofore* anticipated' ('TCM 13th Ann. Rep. 1902',
p.xlvi, emphasis added).

62 Morning Leader leaflet No.2, 1900, reprinted in S.
Koss (ed.), 'The Pro-Boers', University of Chicago
Press, 1973, p.60. See also the extracts of articles
by J.Kier Hardie and Edward Carpenter respectively in
ibid., pp.54-7.

63 Hobson, Capitalism, Imperialism and South Africa (emphasis added). Eckstein's and Rand Mines had separate
managements but both were controlled from London by
Wernher, Beit & Co. On the distinctions between Rand
Mines and Eckstein's, see Mawby, Capital, Government
and Politics in the Transvaal 1900-1907, 'Historical
Journal', vol.XVII, no.2, 1974, p.392.

64 'Standard and Diggers News', 1.2.1899.

CHAPTER 10 THE TRANSITION FROM BOER TO BRITISH ADMINIS-
TRATION: THE IMPACT OF STATE INTERVENTION

1 Report of the Chairman in 'TCM 12th Ann. Rep. 1900-1',
pp.xlix ff.

2 Ibid.

3 Ibid. In the following year, the President of the
Chamber told the 13th Annual Meeting: 'I cannot see
one single point in the conditions of this place which
is to our disadvantage as compared with our position
before the war. In almost every respect - indeed I
can think of no solitary exception - the conditions
are intrinsically better' ('TCM 13th Ann. Rep. 1902',
p.lxiv).

4   G.H. Le May, 'British Supremacy in South Africa
    1899-1907', The Clarendon Press, Oxford, 1965.
5   Ibid., p.30. Lord Salisbury said in 1899: 'We seek
    no goldfields. We seek no territory. What we desire
    is equal rights for men of all races' (cited Le May,
    op.cit., p.30). The author reveals the hypocrisy and
    conflicting statements in war aims made at the time,
    not least those of Milner. See also J.A.Spender,
    'The Life of the Rt. Hon. Sir H.Campbell-Bannerman',
    Hodder & Stoughton, London, 1923, vol.II, pp.37,38:
    'To Lord Roseberry, Mr. Asquith and Sir Edward Grey
    the South African war was a dangerous emergency for
    the Empire.'
6   J.A.Marais, 'The Fall of Kruger's Republic', The
    Clarendon Press, Oxford, 1961, p.189.
7   Le May, op.cit., p.36.
8   C.W. De Kiewiet, 'A History of South Africa - Social
    and Economic', The Clarendon Press, Oxford, 1942.
9   Ibid., p.139.
10 Ibid., pp.138,139.
11 Ibid., p.129. Marais, op.cit., p.326, rejects De
    Kiewiet's thesis that 'unification' for economic
    reasons was 'inevitable'.
12 For varying views of the causes and aims of the war,
    cf. Le May, op.cit., ch.1, Sir Alfred Milner's War,
    pp.29-37.
13 R.E.Robinson and J.Gallagher, 'Africa and the
    Victorians', Macmillan, London, 1961.
14 Ibid., p.468.
15 Ibid.
16 E.A.Walker, 'A History of Southern Africa', Longman,
    London, 1964; L.Marquard, 'The Story of South
    Africa', Faber & Faber, London, 1954.
17 Although recent scholarship pays greater attention to
    the covert intervention of the mine-owners, especially
    the principals of Wernher, Beit & Co., Marais's work
    is still an important study. For the role of Alfred
    Beit in the pre-war period, see T.Pakenham, 'The Boer
    War', Weidenfeld & Nicolson, London, 1979, ch.9.
18 Marais, op.cit., p.189.
19 Marais, op.cit., pp.324-5. The imperial government
    itself was not unanimous. Chamberlain, Lord Salisbury
    and the Cabinet were all divided, and when Milner and
    the Colonial Secretary were agreed upon a provocative
    course of negotiations, Lord Salisbury was opposed:
    'We have to act upon a moral field prepared for us by
    [Milner] and his jingo supporters ... and all for
    people we despise and for that which will bring no
    profit and no power to England' (see ibid., p.318).

Eventually Chamberlain's view prevailed in the Cabinet
and war followed (ibid., p.319).

20 Ibid., p.325.
21 Ibid.
22 Cf. Blainey, op.cit. Of the twenty-six deep-level
    companies in 1895 Consolidated Goldfields held a
    dominant interest in twelve, and ten were dominated
    by Rand Mines Ltd.
23 Eckstein's was originally an outcrop company which
    formed the Rand Mines in the early 1890s to co-ordi-
    nate its deep-level operations. The two companies -
    Eckstein's and Rand Mines - were administered sepa-
    rately but controlled by the same partners. See
    A.A.Mawby, Capital, government and politics in the
    Transvaal 1900-1907, 'Historical Journal', vol.XVII,
    no.2, 1974, p.392.
24 See 'Standard and Diggers News', 30.3.1899.
25 Ibid., 31.1.1899.
26 The government attitude towards Bewaarplatzen spe-
    cifically angered the deep-level concerns, as did the
    high cost of transport, coal, dynamite, food and
    labour. See Ch.9(ii).
27 See Ch.9(ii).
28 For the intervention of Wernher, Beit & Co. see
    Marais, op.cit., pp.324,325, and Pakenham, op.cit.,
    ch.9.
29 On the latter point see Kubicek, The Randlords, p.102.
    See also Mawby, op.cit., p.392.
30 See Blainey, op.cit., p.364. According to Blainey the
    Jameson Raid at the end of 1895 was the revolt of the
    two large deep-level companies. More mine-owners
    joined the Reform Committee or promised support 'in
    order to be on the winning side, i.e. to control the
    mining laws and shape the economic environment of the
    Rand'.
31 'Standard and Diggers News', 30.3.1899.
32 Ibid., 16.3.1899.
33 Ibid. As late as March 1899 the official view was
    that this section of the mine-owners would not attack
    with another Jameson Raid but win a constitutional
    victory through political pressure.
34 Ibid.
35 Marais, op.cit., p.188 (emphasis added).
36 Ibid., p.189. Kruger allegedly opposed the opening
    of certain new goldfields on the ground that it re-
    quired '1,000 more police to cope with the resulting
    increase in population'.
37 According to Fitzpatrick, local representative of
    Wernher, Beit & Co: 'the President and people are

dead against any reforms ... reform by voluntary
action - is out of it'. Correspondence Fitzpatrick
to J.Wernher, 8.5.1896, in A.H.Duminy and W.R.Guest,
'Fitzpatrick, South African politician, Selected
Papers 1888-1906', McGraw Hill, Johannesburg, 1976,
p.102.

38 Ibid., p.324.
39 See below, Ch.10(ii). See also citation from
    Legassick below, p.136.
40 H.J.Simons and R.E.Simons, 'Class and Colour in South
    Africa, 1850-1950', Penguin, Harmondsworth, 1969.
41 Ibid., p.62.
42 Ibid.
43 Ibid.
44 Ibid., p.63.
45 Ibid.
46 M.Wilson and L.Thompson, 'The Oxford History of South
    Africa', The Clarendon Press, Oxford, vol.II, 1971.
47 Ibid., p.320.
48 Ibid., p.322.
49 'TCM 12th Ann. Rep. 1900-1901', p.xxv.
50 Ibid., pp.xiv,xv,x,viii. See also 'TCM 13th Ann. Rep.
    1902', p.xxv.
51 The supply of African labour was still far below par
    at the end of 1903, when the number of Africans
    available for work on the mines was only 60 per cent
    of the pre-war supply and 45 per cent of actual re-
    quirements. See Consolidated Goldfields of South
    Africa Ltd, 'The Gold Fields, 1887-1937', London,
    p.77.
52 Report of Government Mining Engineer for the statisti-
    cal year ended 30.6.1902.
53 See below, pp.156-7.
54 This agreement with the Portuguese, the modus vivendi,
    is discussed below, pp.151-2. See Appendix 4.
55 'TCM 12th Ann. Rep. 1900-1901', p.xxxii.
56 'TCM 13th Ann. Rep. 1902', p.lviii.
57 On this point see D.J.N.Denoon, 'Capitalist Influence'
    and the Transvaal Government during the Crown Colony
    Period, 1900-1906, 'Historical Journal', vol.XI, no.2,
    1968, p.307.
58 'TCM 13th Ann. Rep. 1902', p.lviii.
59 Interview between High Commissioner and Chamber of
    Mines, 25.4.1901, cited 'TCM 12th Ann. Rep. 1900-
    1901', p.74. Denoon, 'Capitalist Influence', p.304,
    notes that Milner had attempted to re-open the mines
    during the guerrilla phase of the war but had met with
    resistance from the Uitlander troops who suspected
    that the mine managers (whom Milner had sent back to
    the Rand) would replace the old (white) mineworkers.

60   'TCM 12th Ann. Rep. 1900-1901', p.75.
61   On average wages for 1901-2, see Report of Government
     Mining Engineer 30.6.1902. On constitution of WNLA
     see Cartwright, 'The Gold Miners', p.216. See also
     'TCM 12th Ann. Rep. 1900-1901', pp.112-13.
62   The wage rate, WNLA and the market situation are dis-
     cussed below on pp.145-6,153-5.
63   The literature on this theme has become increasingly
     rich. See, for example, Denoon, 'Capitalist Influ-
     ence', p.307; S.Moroney, 'Industrial Conflict in a
     Labour Repressive Economy: Black Labour in the Trans-
     vaal Gold Mines 1901-1912', unpublished University of
     the Witwatersrand BA Hons thesis, 1976; P.Warwick,
     African Labour during the South African War 1899-1902,
     'University of London Institute of Commonwealth
     Studies Collected Seminar Papers: The Societies of
     Southern Africa in the Nineteenth and Twentieth Cen-
     turies', 30.10.1975, p.11; Jeeves, op.cit., p.19;
     D.Tiktin, 'White Labour's Attitude, 1902-1904, Towards
     the Importation of Indentured Chinese Labourers by the
     Transvaal Chamber of Mines', unpublished paper pre-
     sented to the University of Cape Town, Africa Research
     Seminar Group, April 1974.
64   C.O. 417/326. 42283. Milner to Chamberlain, 8 Novem-
     ber 1901, cited Denoon, 'Capitalist Influence', p.306.
65   'TCM 13th Ann. Rep. 1902', p.lxii.
66   Ibid.
67   Ibid., p.lxiii.
68   Speech by Hays Hammond, 13.11.1899, reprinted in
     'Morning Leader Leaflet' No.2 in S.Koss (ed.), 'The
     Pro-Boers', University of Chicago Press, 1973, p.61
     (original emphasis).
69   Le May, op.cit., p.30.
70   'TCM 12th Ann. Rep. 1900-1901', pp.xix,69.
71   The difference between the prices charged by the
     monopoly and that at which dynamite could have been
     imported was 35s. per case. Annual consumption was
     300,000 cases. The industry thus had to pay £525,000
     more for dynamite annually. The Chamber viewed this
     as 'a direct annual tax on the mines for which the
     State received no benefit' ('TCM 12th Ann. Rep. 1900-
     1901', p.69).
72   'TCM 14th Ann. Rep. 1903', p.xlv.
73   F.A.Johnstone, Class Conflict and Colour Bars in the
     South African Gold Mining Industry, 1910-1926, in
     'University of London Institute of Commonwealth
     Studies Collected Seminar Papers', vol.I, p.116.
74   In opposing the liquor concession held by the
     Hatherley Distillery Company, the Chamber argued

that the liquor sold seriously impaired the health of
the Africans as well as their general efficiency ('TCM
12th Ann. Rep. 1900-1901', p.72). See also C. van
Onselen, The Randlords and Rotgut 1886-1903. By 1903
the Milner administration allowed the mines to brew
their own beer, which was subsequently to be issued
to African miners as a 'supplement to their diet....
It would make the natives more contented and help to
prolong their stay on the Rand' (cited S.N.A.
14/185802 by Moroney, op.cit., p.61).

75 See below, pp.206-7.

76 'TCM 12th Ann. Rep. 1900-1901', p.72.

77 Cited Marais, op.cit., p.3.

78 Solomon to Milner 12.1.1902, cited Denoon, 'Capitalist
Influence', p.311.

79 Denoon, 'Capitalist Influence', p.311.

80 Ibid. Milner was in fact very lethargic in finding a
suitable formulation. For a detailed description of
the Gold Law, see L.V.Praagh (ed.), 'The Transvaal and
its Mines', p.518. As promulgated in 1898, 'the right
of mining for, and of all precious metals [belonged]
to the State' (ibid.).

81 'TCM 12th Ann. Rep. 1900-1901', p.xx.

82 Ibid., p.291.

83 'TCM 14th Ann. Rep. 1903', p.xlv.

84 See Denoon, 'Capitalist Influence', pp.307,308.

85 Ibid., p.307. According to Mawby, op.cit., p.400, the
new tax was a re-introduction of a *basic* scheme introduced in 1898-9 but never effectively administered,
owing to the outbreak of the war. The main innovation
was the increase from 5 per cent to 10 per cent of the
profits tax under which the Chamber estimated it would
be paying as much as it would have done under the
republican scheme and 'far more than under any system
ever in force' (ibid.). This, however, was the
Chamber's perception. Denoon, 'Capitalist Influence',
p.308, notes that the industry as a whole paid *less*
to the state than it had done before the war.

86 Mawby, op.cit., p.401.

87 'TCM 14th Ann. Rep. 1903', p.xlv.

88 Ibid., pp.xliv-xlv.

89 'TCM 13th Ann. Rep. 1902', pp.xxv,467. See also
Cd.1895, 1904, p.187.

90 Tiktin, op.cit., p.2, cites the comment of the Liberal
MP T.J.Macnamara that it was 'monstrous that a great
public office like that held by Lord Milner should be
prostituted by so undisguised a partisanship' (with
the Chamber of Mines). See also Moroney, op.cit.,
p.32, on the assistance rendered by Milner at all

levels of worker control and manipulation. See also
Jeeves, The Control of Migratory Labour on the South
African Gold Mines in the era of Kruger and Milner,
'Journal of Southern African Studies', 1975, p.14,
who is on the whole more cautious, and Denoon,
'Capitalist Influence', pp.312,315,317, on the
alliance between the Chamber and administration and
the flow of personnel between the mining industry and
government departments.

91   On the above points see below, pp. 137-9. On govern-
ment encouragement of mine labour see Jeeves, op.
cit., p.19; P.Warwick, African Labour during the
South African War 1899-1902, 'University of London
Institute of Commonwealth Studies Collected Seminar
Papers No.21: The Societies of Southern Africa in the
Nineteenth and Twentieth Centuries'. Moroney, op.
cit., pp.32,33. On the Master and Servant Laws see
F.A.Johnstone, 'Class, Race and Gold', pp.48,49. On
direct negotiations for labour recruitment in British
Africa, see below, pp. 168-9.

92   Cited by Denoon, 'Capitalist Influence', p.305.

93   'Milner Papers', ed. C.G.Headlam, vol.II, London,
1933, p.419; Walker, op.cit., pp.501-7. See also
S. van der Horst, op.cit., p.259.

94   Chairman's Report, in 'TCM 12th Ann. Rep. 1900-1901',
p.xlviii.

95   Ibid., p.lv.

96   Correspondence Lord Salisbury to the Secretary of
State for War, Lord Lansdowne, 30.8.1899, quoted in
'Lord Newton, Lord Lansdowne; a Biography', Mac-
millan, London, 1929, p.157.

97   Chairman's Report in 'TCM 12th Ann. Rep. 1900-1901',
p.xlviii.

98   D.J.N.Denoon, The Transvaal Labour Crisis 1901-6,
'Journal of African History', vol.III, no.3, 1967,
p.481. There were approximately 140,000 Boers.
Milner noted in 1900, 'If ten years hence there are
three men of British race to two of Dutch, the country will be safe and prosperous' (Milner to Hanbury
Williams, 27.12.1900, 'Milner Papers').

99   Denoon, 'Capitalist Influence', p.306. Mawby, op.
cit., p.398, takes a different view. He (a) places
the emphasis on Milner's population plans as being
part of the means to end the struggle between the two
white nationalities and (b) rejects the view that
Milner followed a financial policy 'conciliatory to
the leaders of the mining industry' in order to
achieve his plans for an expansion of population.
There seems to be some evidence that this was

Milner's approach to the former but the latter is a
curious formulation of his relationship with the
Capitalists.

100   'TCM 12th Ann. Rep. 1900-1901', p.xxxviii.

101   See below, pp.

102   'TCM 14th Ann. Rep. 1903', p.xlv. The Chamber's
Executive was at the same time told, 'What is of the
utmost importance to us as members of the Mining Industry, is that we now know that any representations
that we may make ... will at least be carefully considered' (ibid.). In the post-war Transvaal Legislative Council, with its predominance of nominated
members, the Chamber received twenty-two of the
twenty-six votes for its crucial legislation on
Chinese labour. See 'Debates of Transvaal Legislative Council', cols 312/3, pp.156,157.

103   M.Legassick, South Africa: Capital Accumulation and
Violence, 'Economy and Society', vol.3, no.3, 1974.

104   Ibid., pp.260-1.

105   See below, p.310 n.118 for comments on 'Milner's
Kindergarten' and the personnel involved.

106   See Praagh (ed.), op.cit., pp.517,518, for list of
important legislation favourable to the gold mining
industry between 1897 and 1906. See also E.N.Katz,
'A Trade Union Aristocracy', African Studies Institute, University of the Witwatersrand, 1976, for
comments on the re-introduction of the colour bar in
the Mines, Works and Machinery Regulations in 1903.

107   'TCM 13th Ann. Rep. 1902', p.xl.

108   Jeeves, op.cit., p.15. Moroney, op.cit., p.62, notes
that Lagden did pressurize mine managements for improvements to the unhealthy compounds but 'seldom
sought confrontation when improvements were not
adequately done'.

109   Jeeves, op.cit., p.15, citing SNA: H.Strange to
Lagden, 8.1.1902.

110   Jeeves, op.cit., p.15.

111   For the active encouragement of African mine recruits
by NAD officials see Moroney, op.cit., p.34, and
Jeeves, op.cit., p.15. According to Moroney (p.34),
Native Commissioners aided recruiting efforts by ig-
noring malpractices, issuing passes and approving
contracts without ensuring that Africans understood
the contents thereof.

112   Praagh (ed.), op.cit., pp.517-18, lists seventeen
laws that were important to the gold industry in
1906. The list included legislation carried over
(either unaltered or amended) from the old state.
The record is incomplete as it does not include tax

and pass laws, or the Master and Servant legislation
enacted in the previous period. Nor does it include
the various regulations enacted under these laws. It
is none the less an impressive list.

113   Sir Godfrey Lagden to Milner, Cd.904 of 1901. This
sentiment was echoed in the High Commissioner's
correspondence with the Colonial Secretary: 'it was
not so much bad laws which were to blame ... as very
bad administration' (Milner to Chamberlain, Cd.904,
p.27).

114   The Pass Regulations became Proclamation Transvaal
No.37 of 1901. By the end of 1902, 2,644 convictions
were reported. Desertions and failure to report
within six days accounted for nearly half the cases.
(See 'Tvl. Admin. Rep. 1902', p.A33.) In 1903 the
regulations were extended so as to apply not only to
the public diggings but throughout the Transvaal
Colony. Special rules for labour districts were
still enforced. See 'TCM 14th Ann. Rep. 1903', p.47.
In their effect and control over the African population, they were described as causing 'pressure and
hardship' and had the effect of '[forcing] men into
obtaining [rapid] employment ... at rates unfavourable to themselves' (Minutes of Evidence, South
African Native Affairs Commission, 1903-5, Evidence
B.Mama).

115   On the implications of the Master and Servant Laws
see Johnstone, 'Class, Race and Gold', pp.24,34 and
35.

116   For Lagden's emphasis on reform of the compound conditions - which the Chamber was happy to underwrite -
see Jeeves, op.cit., p.17. For a helpful and comprehensive discussion on compound conditions, see
Moroney, op.cit., pp.45-8.

117   'TCM 12th Ann. Rep. 1900-1901', p.xx.

118   On this point see W.Nimocks, 'Milner's Young Men',
Hodder & Stoughton, London, 1970: '[Milner] was determined to enlist the very best brains ... the
greatest possible energy [and] ... to secure ripe
experience as well' (p.21). The nucleus of 'the
Kindergarten' included Perry, Curtis, Duncan, Robinson and Wyndham. But Denoon, 'Capitalist Influence',
p.304, notes that Milner abandoned the policy of appointing men with any previous association with Rand
politics to administrative posts in the new administration, because of the charges against him of being
under the influence of the capitalists. Jeeves, op.
cit., p.15, makes the same point.

119   Denoon, 'Capitalist Influence', pp.316,312.

120   Jeeves, op.cit., p.5. For a contrary view, see
      Mawby, op.cit., pp.387-415. According to the latter,
      Milner essentially made use of the mining industry to
      foster his political objectives.
121   'TCM 13th Ann. Rep. 1902', p.lxi.
122   Ibid. On the newly centralized railways 6,200 men,
      English and Africans, were employed. The Chairman
      of the Chamber noted: '[these men] were employed not
      from foreign countries, as in the past, taught and
      expected for political reasons to oppose all that is
      British' (ibid.).
123   Harris of Consolidated Goldfields considered the con-
      tribution to be 'very excessive', and Fitzpatrick of
      Eckstein's opposed payment of more than £15 million,
      adding that whatever sum was loaned should be spent
      on the development of the Transvaal. See Mawby, op.
      cit., p.401. On the loan, see Tiktin, op.cit., p.5,
      and Denoon, 'Capitalist Influence', p.313.
124   Cartwright, 'The Gold Miners', pp.141,142. The five
      predominantly deep-level firms - Wernher, Beit & Co.,
      S.Neumann & Co., Barnato Bros, Consolidated Gold-
      fields, G. & L.Albu, and A.Goerz & Co. - each under-
      wrote £1 million. The remaining £5 million of the
      loan was underwritten by fourteen other firms in
      varying denominations from £500,000 to £100,000
      (ibid., p.142).
125   Ibid. According to Cartwright, 'the war and recon-
      struction of the defeated republics had cost the
      British Government ten times more than the estimate
      prepared in 1899' (ibid.).
126   Chairman's Report in 'TCM 13th Ann. Rep. 1902',
      p.Lvii (emphasis added). Subsequently the Transvaal
      Boers opposed the war contribution and asked that it
      should not be implemented until it could be agreed
      to 'in a constitutional manner under self governing
      institutions' (Cd.1894, 1903, p.53). The substance
      of the protest was that there should be no taxation
      without representation.
127   On this point see Tiktin, op.cit., p.5; Denoon,
      'Capitalist Influence', p.313. For Chamberlain's
      'flirtation' with the mine-owners see A.P.Cartwright,
      'The First South Africans - the Life and Times of Sir
      Percy Fitzpatrick', Purcell, London, 1971, p.125.
128   On the mine-owners' resistance to the loan, see
      Mawby, op.cit., p.401, and on Chamberlain's need to
      persuade the magnates see Cartwright, 'The Gold
      Miners', p.142.
129   Denoon, 'Capitalist Influence', pp.313,314.

CHAPTER 11   THE POST-WAR LABOUR MARKET

1   See 'Report of Transvaal Labour Commission', 1904,
    p.74. Immediately after the war no fewer than 299
    new mining companies were established.
2   In January 1904 the number of Africans employed in
    government departments was 28,232, of which 19,193
    were employed on the Central South African Railways.
    See 'TCM 15th Ann. Rep. 1904', p.17.
3   President, 'TCM 13th Ann. Rep. 1902', p.xxxv.
4   'Report of Special Committee of the Chamber', 1902,
    p.56. This committee reported on the reasons for the
    resistance to African recruitment in 1901-2 and con-
    cluded, inter alia, that in view of the reduced
    schedule of wages 'old boys, who have attained a con-
    siderable degree of skill, will not come except at
    higher pay' (ibid.). Little attention has been paid
    to this aspect of the labour force which indicates a
    certain permanence, training and degree of stratifi-
    cation. See also Cd.1895, p.30. Statement by F.
    Perry.
5   Cd.1895, 1904, p.23. Statement by F.Perry, April
    1903, 1st AGM of WNLA. The WNLA defended the measure
    as 'a bold experiment, one that is justified to the
    public by success' (ibid., p.29).
6   See below, pp.152-3. The Chamber's research into the
    reasons for the frequent shortages in the labour
    supply seldom did more than scratch the surface of the
    problem. This 'inaction' may have been deliberate in
    order to conceal shortages caused by strategies to
    reduce labour costs and other costs of production.
7   It may be stretching the evidence too far to suggest
    (as Raitt, the Chamber's opponent on the Chinese issue
    on the Transvaal Legislative Council, has hinted) that
    African wage rates were lowered with an expectation of
    a loss in the supply, to enable the mine-owners to
    make out a case for Chinese indentured labourers. See
    'Debates of the Transvaal Legislative Council', 220,
    p.110, 29.12.1903.
8   For further details of the post-war wage reduction and
    the modus vivendi respectively, see below, pp.145,152.
9   See below, pp.153-4. Not until one year after the
    indenture of Chinese labour was the Chamber - for a
    time - able to employ African labour at heavily re-
    duced rates and on conditions highly advantageous to
    the mines. See also Ch.15, pp.238-9.
10 'TCM 13th Ann. Rep. 1902', p.xxxvii. The President
    of the Chamber noted that 'whatever rate of wages paid
    by the mines might be the employees in the town and

neighbourhood would be bound to outbid them. The
small employers ... rely entirely on higher wages to
attract natives' (ibid., p.xxxvi).

11 'TCM 13th Ann. Rep. 1902', p.xli.

12 Town wages were between 60s. and 100s. as against 35s.
on the mines (ibid., p.xxxii).

13 On this point, see Moroney, op.cit., p.13, who notes
that Africans learnt how to 'work' the WNLA system,
how to take advantage of agents, and 'when and how'
to desert: all were 'stepping stones' to more desirable job opportunities (ibid.).

14 The Chairman of the Chamber noted for the year 1902
that 'there was a wastage during the year of 28,399
[Africans] some of whom returned to their homes and
some sought other employment' ('TCM 13th Ann. Rep.
1902', p.xxxv).

15 Ibid., p.xxxvi. In 1902 the General Manager of the
East Rand Proprietary Mines advised the Chamber that
'the rates paid by the railways constitute a serious
obstacle to recruiting of natives for the mines'. He
asked the railways to reduce their rate to that paid
by the mines.

16 Cd.1895, p.23. Cf. also 'Tvl. Admin. Rep. 1902'.
There had been no systematic collection of taxes in
the Transvaal since 1899. It was proposed to make
the collection of taxes coincidental with the receipt
of compensation after April 1903 (ibid., p.A3).

17 'Tvl. Admin. Rep. 1902', p.A12.

18 Ibid., p.A4. Report of Sir G.Lagden, Commissioner for
Native Affairs, 1903.

19 'Tvl. Admin. Rep. 1902', p.PA1. See also S.Marks,
op.cit., pp.129,130,134-5, for the impact of rural
poverty in Natal after the South African War. Whilst
the labour shortage in that colony was extremely
severe, 'the number of Natal Africans seeking work in
the Transvaal exceeded the number of any pre-war
years' (ibid., p.135). In 1894 the number of Natal
work-seekers numbered 10,500, in 1903 and 1904 23,000,
and in 1905, 26,000 (ibid.).

20 See 'Tvl. Admin. Rep. 1902', p.A2. Under the Terms of
Surrender the Boers could not be disturbed in their
possession of stock, no matter how this was acquired.
On the land question the Secretary for Native Affairs
reported, 'The country formerly occupied by native
clans had been at intervals absorbed for sale or occupation by white people with or without consent of
the natives.' The white persons concerned could like-
wise not be dispossessed of the land they had earlier
acquired either by (illegal) outright occupation or
by purchase from a third party.

21 Ibid.
22 Milner to Chamberlain, 21.7.1902, cited D.J.N.Denoon,
    Participation in the Boer War, in B.A.Ogot (ed.), 'War
    and Society in Africa', F.Cass, London, 1972, p.116
    (emphasis added).
23 Denoon, Participation in the Boer War, p.116. See
    also 'Tvl. Admin. Rep. 1902', p.A22.
24 Cd.1895, p.23.
25 Ibid. According to Denoon, Participation in the Boer
    War, p.116, compensation payments were not released
    until 1904.
26 'Tvl. Admin. Rep. 1902', p.23.
27 Ibid., p.A3.
28 According to one of the (Waterberg District) Native
    Commissioners, 'The natives generally thought that
    after the war it was the intention of our Government
    ... to divide the Boer farms among them, at least in-
    sofar that each native would receive the holding that
    he then rented from his landlord' ('Tvl. Admin. Rep.
    1902', p.A17). A similar theme occurs in the vastly
    populated Zoutpansberg District of an estimated
    400,000 people. Here, according to the Native Com-
    missioner for the area, 'Sufficient [military opera-
    tions] occurred to give the native quite a mistaken
    idea that the land would revert to the original native
    occupiers' (ibid., p.A24).
29 Ibid., p.K51.
30 Ibid.
31 Ibid. Cd.1895, p.23. Statement by F.Perry, April
    1903. There were various explanations for the labour
    shortage. H.Houghton and Dagut, op.cit., p.21, at-
    tribute the labour dearth to 'the disturbance of
    tribal life, the dislocation of transport and the de-
    moralization of the civilian population.' See also
    'Tvl. Admin. Rep. 1902', Part I, Administration, pp.
    A2 ff., and Ch.12(v) (b) below.
32 'Tvl. Admin. Rep. 1902', p.A19. On the whole there
    was general acknowledgment of African poverty and
    loss. In some instances the Native Commissioner made
    a virtue out of poverty: 'Generally speaking, the re-
    settlement of the Native has been carried out most
    successfully, and this success is due to the native
    characteristic of easily adapting themselves to
    changes in conditions and to a large extent to the
    happy hand to mouth existence which they enjoy. With
    few cares and no wants and a general absence of any
    desire to improve his social status, the little the
    native lost during the war has had a proportionate
    effect upon them, especially as they ... have applied

for compensation for all their losses' ('Tvl. Admin.
Rep. 1902', Report of Native Commissioner for Pretoria
and Heidelberg Districts, p.A19).

33 See Wolpe, Capitalism and Cheap Labour Power, pp.
434-6, for the general argument in this connection.

34 See Milner's correspondence with Chamberlain, 28.12.
1901, Cd.904 No.20, p.21: 'I agree ... that Native
institutions should not be unnecessarily interfered
with; that their existing system of communal tenure
and of tribal government, and their traditional customs ... should be respected.'

35 'Tvl. Admin. Rep. 1902' (Pretoria, 1903), Part I,
Administration, pp.A1. 2.

36 See 'WCM 10th Ann. Rep. 1898', p.458. According to
this source 60.2 per cent of the total came from East
Coast territories.

37 'TCM 12th Ann. Rep. 1900-1901', p.108. See also
ibid., pp.xxxix,111,112, and Cd.1895, p.26.

38 'TCM 12th Ann. Rep. 1900-1901', p.108. (All members
of WNLA were shareholders and parties to the agreed
wage. Breach of agreement resulted in the shareholders' exclusion from the institution and disbarment
from personal engagement or a share in the distribution of the workforce.) According to the Objects of
the Association the body was formed 'to substitute co-
operation for competition ... and to secure that even
distribution of the available supply which is impossible without such cooperation' (cited 'TCM 17th Ann.
Rep. 1906', p.xx).

39 'TCM 12th Ann. Rep. 1900-1901', pp.116-18.

40 'TCM 12th Ann. Rep. 1900-1901', p.106. See also
Cd.1895.

41 'TCM 12th Ann. Rep. 1900-1901', p.106. See Appendix
4, below, for details of the re-activated modus
vivendi of 1897.

42 'TCM 12th Ann. Rep. 1900-1901', p.125. See also
Denoon, 'A Grand Illusion', p.130, for further details
on this point. Portugal was offered a larger share of
the railway traffic as a consequence of this agreement. Milner conceded this because of the pressure
for mine labour.

43 Denoon, 'A Grand Illusion', p.125.

44 'TCM 13th Ann. Rep. 1902', p.xviii.

45 See Denoon, The Transvaal Labour Crisis, p.484.

46 See 'TCM 13th Ann. Rep. 1902', pp.xxxvi-xxxviii.

47 On this point, see p.   below.

48 'Tvl. Admin. Rep. 1902', p.A16.

49 'Transvaal Labour Commission, 1903' (hereafter cited
as 'Tvl. Lab. Comm.'): Evidence of Grant, p.478,
Majority Report.

50   'Tvl. Lab. Comm. Minority Report', (1903) para. 68.
51   See 'Tvl. Admin. Rep. 1902', p.A18. The official re-
     ports could only have encouraged the Chamber to await
     the effects of rural poverty. For instance in the
     Waterberg District, the Native Commissioner for the
     area believed that 'the labour supply [was] intimately
     connected with the cattle question'. He was referring
     to the appreciation of the value of cattle and the in-
     ability of African farmers to buy cattle at prices
     equivalent to that which the military had paid for
     the cattle commandeered or stolen during the war. The
     matter was further exacerbated by the fact that im-
     ported cattle would probably not withstand the climate
     and it would therefore be 'practically impossible for
     [an African] to buy'. The sums of money thus received
     from the military enabled him temporarily to resist
     the recruiting agents of the Chamber. But only for a
     time.
52   See above, p.145. Cf. 'TCM 12th Ann. Rep. 1900-1901',
     pp.xli,26, for comments on discussions between the
     Governor General of the Province and F.Perry on this
     topic. Child labour was employed at 6d. per day or
     15s. per month.
53   'TCM 12th Ann. Rep. 1900-1901', p.121.
54   Ibid.
55   On this point see Denoon, The Transvaal Labour Crisis,
     p.482.
56   'TCM 13th Ann. Rep. 1902', p.xviii.
57   Ibid. Inquiries had been made on the miners' behalf
     by Chamberlain, Secretary of State for the Colonies,
     regarding recruiting possibilities in the Congo Free
     State (ibid.). Similarly Milner 'supported the Cham-
     ber by urging on the authorities at Home that facili-
     ties [in British East Africa] be given for recruiting'
     (ibid., p.13).
58   Ibid., p.xix.
59   Ibid., p.13. He was overoptimistic. Ugandan peasants
     were diverted into cash crop production and Nyasa
     labour was exported to Southern Rhodesia. On this
     point see Denoon, 'A Grand Illusion', p.131.
60   Report of Special Committee 1902, cited 'TCM 13th Ann.
     Rep. 1902', p.55.
61   Questions Affecting the Natives and Coloured People
     Resident in British South Africa, statement by the
     Executive of the South African Native Congress 1903
     to the Rt Hon. J.C.Chamberlain, cited T.Karis and G.
     Carter (eds), 'From Protest to Challenge: A Docu-
     mentary History of African Politics in South Africa,
     1882-1964', vol.1, Hoover Institution Press, Stanford
     University, 1972, p.24.

62   'TCM 13th Ann. Rep. 1902', p.55.
63   See Ch.13(iii) (b). On the criticism of the Chamber's
     claim for an absolute restoration of its pre-war work-
     force, see the interview of the African Labour League
     with Milner, 14.3.1903, Ch.13(ii), below.
64   See 'Tvl. Lab. Comm. (1903) Minority Report', para.
     48 (2) (a). It is significant that these jobs later
     fell into Schedule I of the Transvaal Labour Ord.
     1904, for whites exclusively.
65   Ibid., para. 48 (2) (b). See also Ch.12(iv), below.
66   Ibid., para. 48 (2) (b).
67   Tvl. Mines Dept, Reports of Govt Mining Engineer 1901,
     1901/2, 1908/9, cited R.Davis, Mining Capital and
     Unskilled White Workers in South Africa 1901-13,
     'Journal of Southern African Studies', vol.3, no.1,
     October 1976, p.67.
68   Ibid., table II, p.69.
69   Although the Chamber as a body rejected the general
     principle that unskilled white labourers should re-
     place African workers there were important differences
     of opinion between the local and London representa-
     tives of Wernher, Beit & Co. on the short-term use of
     white unskilled labour. Cf. Correspondence Fitz-
     patrick to J.Wernher, Q2 A/LB xvii 5.7.1902, and
     Q2 A/LB xvii 23.8.1902, in Duminy and Guest, op.cit.,
     pp.154,159.
70   On this point see Mawby, op.cit., p.394.
71   Ibid.
72   Ibid. The chief spokesman for the group was in fact
     Fitzpatrick, who advised his London principal: 'One
     thing is quite certain and that is that if Chinese
     immigration should be advocated by the Chamber of
     Mines before it is convincingly shown to be essential,
     there will be a frightful row here' (Fitzpatrick to
     J.Wernher, Q2 A/LB xvii 25.7.1902, cited Duminy and
     Guest, op.cit.).
73   Denoon, 'Capitalist Influence', pp.314,315; Mawby,
     op.cit., p.395.
74   Rep. of Special Committee, 1902, p.56, cited 'TCM 13th
     Ann. Rep. 1902'.
75   See Moroney, op.cit., p.13.
76   Special Committee of the TCM, 1902, cited 'TCM 13th
     Ann. Rep. 1902', pp.56,57.
77   'TCM 14th Ann. Rep. 1903', p.xxvii. See also Scale
     of Native Pay adopted by TCM 28.4.1903, ibid., p.112.
     Labourers were paid an 'inducement' to re-engage if
     their time had expired. If they had not yet reached
     the maximum of 60s. they could receive this on re-
     engagement. Companies were also permitted to pay a

bonus of £3 for twelve months and half that for six months. The important constraint was that no mine could exceed the fixed average of 50s. per thirty shifts and therefore the number of men to receive this differential was always severely limited.

78 'TCM 13th Ann. Rep. 1902', p.xix. Report of Special Committee, ibid., pp.56-7. The importance of this arrangement in maintaining the labour structure is considered below, p.159.

79 Ibid., pp.56-7.

80 Ibid., p.xx.

81 See below, pp.206-7, for a full discussion on this matter.

82 See Ch.13(iii), below.

83 Denoon, The Transvaal Labour Crisis, p.489. The Consolidated Goldfields Group had undertaken a cost benefit analysis to illustrate the prevailing (uneconomic) cost structure. See n.84, below.

84 Ibid. Denoon reproduces the following *cost benefit analysis* of major costs of production (shown as percentages of costs)

White salaries	34.5%
African wages	24.5%
Explosives	12.0%
Coal	8.6%
Sundries	20.4%

85 Ibid. A small number of Africans did in fact work in some of the so-called skilled mining occupations until 1903, but this was not so much a revision of policy as part of the Chamber's 'flexible' African wage arrangements. See p.159 below.

86 On this point see H.Simson, The Myth of the White Working Class in South Africa, 'African Review', vol.4, no.2, 1974, pp.194-5. For the unionization of early white mining immigrants see Simons and Simons, op.cit., pp.52,53.

87 This matter has become the subject of considerable debate. See H.Wolpe, The 'White Working Class' in South Africa, 'Economy and Society', vol.5, no.2, 1976, p.211 and Davis, op.cit., pp.45-6. See also the more general study of G.Carchedi, On the Economic Identification of the New Middle Class, 'Economy and Society', vol.4, no.1, 1975, p.379; H.Simson, op. cit., pp.194-7.

88 See speech by Farrar below, p.161.

89 See Statement of F.Perry to 1st AGM to the WNLA, April 1903, Cd.1895, p.24. In 1905 Selbourne told the Colonial Secretary, 'Very many, if not most of the "boys" have worked on the mines before, and have re-

turned there a second or third or even fourth time as
skilled and competent workmen' (C.O.879/90, No.44.
Selbourne to Littleton.   26.8.1905).

90 Cd.1895, p.30.

91 Ibid. Carried away by his enthusiasm for East Coast
labour, Perry predicted that 'as long as the mines
rely on black labour, they stand or fall by the supply
of Portuguese natives' (ibid.). Fortunately for the
Chamber this presumption was not accurate as (i) skill
was a function of time and training not inherent
qualities; (ii) local labour and migrants from north
of latitude 22 degrees were to contract for longer
periods than hitherto on the mines. See also 'TCM
13th Ann. Rep. 1902', p.56, Report of Spec. Comm.

92 See above, p.157.

93 On the employment of Africans in certain skilled jobs
up to the year 1903, see Davis, op.cit., p.69.

94 See F.Wilson, 'Migrant Labour', pp.138,139.

95 Sir George Farrar, 'Debates of the Transvaal Legislative Council', 28.12.1903, col.150, implied that a
migrant structure, as opposed to white unskilled
labour, obviated trade union combinations and made
the strike action either less likely or more control-
lable.

96 See Ch.2, above, pp.40-1.

97 See above, p.157.

98 Speech by President of the Chamber of Mines, March
1908, cited Johnstone, 'Class, Race and Gold', p.85.

CHAPTER 12   THE FIRST DEFENCE OF THE LABOUR STRUCTURE:
THE TRANSVAAL LABOUR COMMISSION AND THE UNSKILLED LABOUR
SUPPLY

1 'TCM 13th Ann. Rep. 1902', p.xli. Statement by
Chairman of the Chamber of Mines on the occasion of
Chamberlain's visit to the Transvaal, December 1902.

2 See P.Richardson, The Recruiting of Chinese Indentured
Labour for the South African Gold Mines, 1903-1908,
'Journal of African History', vol.XVIII, no.1, 1977,
p.87.

3 Cf. Jeeves, op.cit., p.9. See also Ch.9, p.105,
above.

4 'TCM 13th Ann. Rep. 1902', p.xli.

5 Ibid., p.xxii.

6 For details of these experiments see Section iv, pp.
183-5.   See also Davis, op.cit., pp.52-5, and Katz,
op.cit., pp.78-81.

7 An alternative formulation of this problem would be

that African labour was acquired *below its value* and
for this and other reasons was cheaper than white
labour. For an elaboration of this view see H.Wolpe,
The Theory of Internal Colonialism, pp.8-9, and (for
a reply to Wolpe), M.Williams, op.cit., pp.5,6. See
also p. 21 below.

8   See Katz, op.cit., p.122. See also below, pp.209-12.
9   'TCM 13th Ann. Rep. 1902', p.11.
10 Ibid., p.xliv.
11 Cd. 1905, 1904, p.37. According to Katz, op.cit.,
    p.83: 'The imported navvies proved expensive. Their
    work was unsatisfactory, and the cost to the British
    administration proved so great that their contracts
    for a year were terminated after only seven months,
    and the men were "packed home in disgrace".'
12 'TCM 13th Ann. Rep. 1902', p.xlvi.
13 Draft Contract cited ibid., p.92. The contract, of
    course, was never taken up.
14 See Ch.10(ii) above.
15 'TCM 13th Ann. Rep. 1902', p.xxxvii.
16 'Debates of the Transvaal Legislative Council',
    29.12.03, col.219, p.110.
17 Ibid., cols 219,220, p.110. Raitt's statement was
    prompted by a speech made by Fricker on 28.3.1903
    cited in the appendix to the 'Transvaal Labour Com-
    mission Minority Report, 1903'. According to
    Richardson, 'The Provision of Chinese Indentured
    Labour for the Gold Mines 1903-8', p.65, the princi-
    ples of the subsequent Transvaal Labour Ordinance were
    outlined at the Chamber's Special Committee in July
    1902 and drafted in February 1903, ten months before
    the legislation was requested in the Transvaal Legis-
    lative Council.
18 'Debates of the Tvl. Leg. Coun.', 29.12.03, col.219,
    p.110.
19 'TCM 13th Ann. Rep. 1902', p.xlii.
20 Ibid.
21 Ibid., p.xxxiv. WNLA was fortified by a salaried
    Chairman and Managing Director, Mr Perry, the former
    Imperial Secretary.
22 Ibid., p.xlii.
23 See below, p.169.
24 'Debates of the Tvl. Leg. Coun.', 29.12.03, col.221,
    p.111.
25 Ibid.
26 Ibid. According to Raitt free passages for the trans-
    port of African labour to the mines might improve re-
    cruiting. He also thought recruiting should be under
    the aegis of the government (ibid., cols 221,222).

27 Cd.1895, 1904, p.33 (WNLA 1st Annual General Meeting, April 1903).
28 'TCM 13th Ann. Rep. 1902', p.xlvi.
29 Ibid.
30 'TCM 14th Ann. Rep. 1903', p.xxv.
31 Ibid., p.xxiii. The WNLA attributed this loss to two factors: (i) 'the inherent restless spirit of the native himself' and (ii) his reluctance to remain for a continuous lengthened period in the service of one employer or in one district (ibid., p.xxvii). For a more cogent explanation, cf. the Chamber's assessment below, p.170.
32 See Table 15.3 below for total recruitment during 1903. See also Richardson, 'Journal of African History', 1977, p.91. According to Richardson the total proportion of Portuguese East African labourers that were recruited declined by 14.65 per cent (from 67.35 in 1902 to 58.71 in 1903).
33 Cf. 'TCM 14th Ann. Rep. 1903', p.xxiv. The Charters concerned the Nyasa Company and the Companhis da Zambesia.
34 Ibid.
35 Richardson, 'The Provision of Chinese Indentured Labour', p.34.
36 See Ch.15, p.242 below.
37 Cf. 'TCM 13th Ann. Rep. 1902', p.xviii.
38 See Ch.15, p.243 below.
39 Cf. 'Tvl. Labour Commission (1903) Minority Report', para. 25. (Hereafter cited as 'Tvl. Lab. Comm. (1903) Min. Rep.')
40 Cited 'Tvl. Lab. Commission (1903) Majority Report', para. 21. (Hereafter cited as 'Tvl. Lab. Comm. (1903) Maj. Rep.')
41 Milner to Chamberlain, 6.4.1903, cited in Headlam (ed.), 'Milner Papers', vol.II, p.460.
42 For Chamberlain's views on Asian labour see Cartwright, 'Gold Paved the Way', p.107. According to this account Chamberlain, who had travelled home from South Africa with Ross Skinner and Noyce, 'was strongly in favour of continued efforts being made to obtain labour in Africa without importing Asiatics' (ibid.). See below, pp.197,214. Generally, Chamberlain considered it essential that the mine-owners should show consensus of the Transvaal population on the subject of indentured labour.
43 'Debates of Tvl. Leg. Coun.', 28.12.1903, col. 162, p.81.
44 Ibid.
45 Ibid., p.81.

46 Ibid., 30.12.1903, col. 300, p.150.
47 Cited 'TCM 14th Ann. Rep. 1903', p.xxvi. The subse-
    quent South African Native Affairs Commission dealt
    inter alia with the labour problem of British South
    Africa. For allegations of the influence of the
    Chamber's evidence on the Commission, see 'Tvl. Lab.
    Comm. (1903) Min. Rep.', para. 59 (a).
48 'Debates of Tvl. Leg. Coun.', 30.12.03, col. 300,
    p.150.
49 A Minority Report was issued, signed by two of the
    twelve-man Commission. The two Minority commission-
    ers, Quinn and Whiteside, led the subsequent political
    campaign against indentured labour.
50 Katz, op.cit., p.122.
51 'Tvl. Lab. Comm. (1903) Maj. Rep.', Historical Intro-
    duction.
52 'TCM 14th Ann. Rep. 1903', p.xxvi. According to the
    Chamber, the existing spheres of recruitment were
    'almost, if not quite, exhausted'.
53 'Tvl. Lab. Comm. (1903) Maj. Rep.', Conclusions:
    para. IV. These conclusions were totally consistent
    with those of the Chamber's in its statement of evi-
    dence in chief to the Commission. See below, pp.
    187-8.
54 'Tvl. Lab. Comm. (1903) Maj. Rep.', para. 68 (i).
55 Ibid., para. 68 (2) (a).
56 Ibid., para. 68 (2) (b). The total number of men
    employed before the war varied in the estimates be-
    tween 96,000 and 110,000.
57 Ibid.
58 Ibid., para. 69.
59 Ibid., para. 70. In making this assessment, the Com-
    mission felt guided by the Labour Commission of the
    Cape Government, 1894, which said: 'The mere neces-
    saries are few and obtainable with little exertion in
    this new sunny country' (cited 'Tvl. Lab. Comm. (1903)
    Maj. Rep.', para. 70).
60 Ibid., para. 71.
61 Ibid. Cf. also Evidence of Grant, Taberer, Moorcroft,
    Edwards, Maxwell et al. See especially the comments
    of Meillassoux on this point, below.
62 'Tvl. Lab. Comm. (1903) Maj. Rep.', para. 75.
63 See above.
64 Meillassoux, op.cit., p.103.
65 Ibid.
66 See above, p.174 (emphasis added).
67 'Tvl. Lab. Comm. (1903) Maj. Rep.', para. 72. See
    also below, pp.191-2.
68 Ibid., para. 73.

69   Ibid. (emphasis added).
70   Ibid., para. 76. (1) Estimated value of goods im-
     ported into the Colony of Natal for Kaffir trade
     1894-1902, (2) Value of dutiable goods imported into
     Basutoland during the period 1893-99 with relation to
     extracts from the Resident Commissioner's Annual
     Reports.
71   For Milner and Lagden's views on this point respec-
     tively, see above, p.149, and below, p.192.
72   Ibid., para. 79.
73   See Moroney, op.cit., pp.4-18. Moroney's argument is
     on the whole a convincing one, that there was 'an
     acute awareness [by Africans] of market forces,
     [their] bargaining position and the disadvantages of
     the contract system' (ibid., p.4).
74   Formulated differently, this might be stated as the
     problems arising from the continued access of Africans
     to the land. For further discussion on this point,
     see below, p.192.
75   'Tvl. Lab. Comm. (1903) Maj. Rep.', para. 80.
76   See below, pp.178-9.
77   'Tvl. Lab. Comm. (1903) Min. Rep.', para. 9. For the
     Commission's undue reliance on the Chamber's evidence,
     see Tiktin, op.cit., p.10; Jeeves, op.cit., p.7.
78   'Tvl. Lab. Comm. (1903) Min. Rep.', para. 11. The
     'White Labour' view could best be summed up in the
     words of the subsequent 1907-8 'Report of the Mining
     Industry Commission 1908, TG2', para. 24: 'The aim
     should in fact be to make the working of the mines de-
     creasingly dependent on coloured labour and increas-
     ingly dependent on the labour of white men in all
     classes of work'. The 1907 Commission rejected this
     view, cf. para. 275, p.35.
79   Ibid., para. 31 (c). They considered the evidence of
     the Chamber to be misleading and to 'cast grave re-
     sponsibility on those who submitted this evidence
     under oath' (ibid., para. 50). They reserved their
     most scathing comments for the Chamber's conclusion
     that the country was losing the benefits that might
     have been desired 'had labour been forthcoming to work
     the ... 3420 stamps that are now idle'. To this the
     'Minority Report' responded that the 3420 stamps in
     question were on mines that 'were more notorious for
     refloatations than profits' (ibid.).
80   Ibid., para. 31 (c).
81   Ibid., para. 32 (3).
82   Ibid., para. 19. The implication of the latter state-
     ment is that reductions in the wage scale would not
     have been effected unless the labour demand had been
     satisfied.

83   'Tvl. Lab. Comm. (1903) Maj. Rep.', para. 18.
84   'Tvl. Lab. Comm. (1903) Min. Rep.', para. 25.
85   Ibid.
86   On the employment of whites outside the customary
     range of white employment see Davis, op.cit., pp.43,
     52,55,67.
87   'Tvl. Lab. Comm. (1903) Min. Rep.', para. 36. For
     the complete evidence to the 1903 Commission by the
     Chamber see Statement to Tvl. Lab. Comm., Appendix,
     'TCM 14th Ann. Rep. 1903', p.vi.
88   Statement to Tvl. Lab. Comm., 'TCM 14th Ann. Rep.
     1903', p.vii.
89   Ibid.
90   Ibid.
91   'Tvl. Lab. Comm. (1903) Min. Rep.', para. 36, citing
     evidence on pp.242,243 and 245 of the 'Report of the
     Industrial Commission 1897'.
92   In 1903 on the Rand 10 to 12 Africans were used with
     a contingent of 3 or 4 white miners per stamp. In
     the Sierra Butes and Plumas Eureka mines, 'which
     might with all fairness be compared with the mines
     on the Rand', only 6 to 7.5 white labourers per stamp
     were employed as against 20 coloured and 2 white
     labourers on the Rand ('Tvl. Lab. Comm. (1903) Min.
     Rep.', para. 37).
93   Ibid., para. 36, citing evidence given to Industrial
     Commission 1897.
94   'TCM 14th Ann. Rep. 1903', Appendix, p.xxvii. State-
     ment of Evidence of Chamber to Tvl. Lab. Comm. 1903.
95   See Ch.11, pp.39-41.
96   See below, p.185.
97   'Tvl. Lab. Comm. (1903) Min. Rep.', para. 45. The
     witness implied that he had been subjected to
     'political pressure' by the Chamber to present his
     evidence in a way that was favourable to them.
98   Cited by ibid., para. 48 (i) from Report of the
     Special Committee of Chamber of Mines, 1902.
99   'Tvl. Lab. Comm. (1903) Min. Rep.', para. 48 (b).
     The phrasing of this report reflects to some degree
     the conflict of views within the Chamber on this
     issue. Cf. Correspondence Fitzpatrick to A.Beit,
     16.6.1902 A/LBI, and Fitzpatrick to J.Wernher,
     5.7.1902 QZ A/LB xvii, in Duminy and Guest, op.cit.,
     Nos 152,154. In the correspondence, Fitzpatrick told
     his London principals: 'we may be able to use [white
     labour] instead of black on the surface ... and free
     natives to increase the output. The idea is Cres-
     well's and I have only backed him.'
100 A second reason for the Chamber's experimentation was

to placate Milner. Despite the latter's vision of a
predominantly British White South Africa he rapidly
'changed his mind' when pressed by the mine-owners -
who had never been impressed by his immigration proposals - and decided on a 'crash policy of allowing
imported labour to fill the gap'. Milner's regime,
it seems, insisted on a period of experimentation
before acceding to the request for Chinese labour.
In fact the final decision had to be made in London -
and it was possibly on Chamberlain's (rather than
Milner's) insistence that the mine-owners were required to make out a convincing case, outlining
their reasons for rejecting the extended use of
white unskilled labour on the Rand. See Cartwright,
'The Gold Miners', p.135; and Davis, op.cit., p.53.

101 See below, p.184.
102 For cost of ore mined by Creswell's men see Evidence
     to Tvl. Lab. Comm., pp.574-95. For helpful commenta-
     ries on Creswell's experiments see Katz, op.cit.,
     pp.78-81, and especially Davis, op.cit., pp.53-4.
103 Cf. Davis, op.cit., p.53.
104 See Evidence in 'TCM 14th Ann. Rep. 1904', p.lxxiv.
     The sum of 9s. 10d. per day per African clearly in-
     cluded non-cash items such as, inter alia, food and
     quarters.
105 See below, p.184.
106 'Tvl. Lab. Comm. (1903) Maj. Rep.', para. 96 (iii)
     (emphasis added).
107 Cf. Simons and Simons, op.cit., p.79; Katz, op.cit.,
     pp.79-81. To offset the costs of board and lodging,
     Creswell made each skilled miner 'supervise six men
     on three drills instead of four men on two drills for
     no extra remuneration' (Katz, op.cit., p.80). The
     result was a strike in September 1902 of supervisors,
     rockdrillers and their helpers on the Village Main
     reef.
108 Davis, op.cit., p.54.
109 Ibid. The Chamber estimated that all the experi-
     menting companies lost a combined total of £20,380
     (10.49d.) per ton (ibid.).
110 Evidence of TCM to Tvl. Lab. Comm. 1903, cited 'TCM
     14th Ann. Rep. 1903', p.lxxiv.
111 Cf. Katz, op.cit., p.84; Davis, op.cit., p.52.
112 Up to 30 per cent were incapacitated by drink ('TCM
     12th Ann. Rep. 1900-1901', p.xli).
113 For full citation, see above, p.182.
114 See below, p.186.
115 Cf. 'Tvl. Lab. Comm. (1903) Min. Rep.', para. 48 (2)
     (b).

116   See Davis, op.cit., p.53.
117   See above, pp.155,182.
118   'Tvl. Lab. Comm. (1903) Min. Rep.', para. 48 (2) (a).
119   Ibid., para. 48 (2) (b).
120   Ibid. This part of the plan was implemented. See above, p.185.
121   Ibid., para. 48 (2) (b).
122   The number considered in 1903 was 7,000. Cf. Davis, op.cit., p.55.
123   'Tvl. Lab. Comm. (1903) Min. Rep.', para. 55.
124   Ibid., para. 59 (a).
125   Conclusions, 'Tvl. Lab. Comm. (1903) Min. Rep.'
126   For the three points see 'Tvl. Lab. Comm. Maj. Rep.' para. 96.
127   On this point see Davis, op.cit., p.43, who shows that 'a considerable proportion of the total number of whites ... were employed outside the range of job around which white employment later [after the Transvaal Labour Ordinance] tended to be concentrated').
128   For full citation of this point, see above, p.184.
129   'Tvl. Lab. Comm. (1903) Maj. Rep.', Conclusions, para. 11.
130   Ibid., para. iv.
131   See Conclusions to Statement presented by the Chamber of Mines to Tvl. Lab. Comm. 1903, cited 'TCM 14th Ann. Rep. 1903', Appendix, p.ix.
132   Cf. Tabular Statement to Tvl. Lab. Comm., cited 'TCM 14th Ann. Rep. 1903', p.v. In the event the number of recruits five years after the Commission was 140,304. See Table 15.6, below.
133   See Ch.13, pp. 196-7, below.
134   Selected from 'Tvl. Lab. Comm. (1903) Min. Rep.', para. 60.
135   See 'TCM 14th Ann. Rep. 1903', Appendix, p.iv. The significance of extra-legal measures to secure this labour force are discussed below, pp.191-3.
136   Ibid. For the improvement in the supply position after 1904, see Ch.15 below.
137   See Arrighi and Saul, op.cit., pp.184,194,195.
138   'Tvl. Lab. Comm. (1903) Maj. Rep.', para. 88.
139   Ibid., para. 89.
140   Two significant existing taxes were (i) the Glen Grey Act, which imposed 10s. per head; (ii) The Plakkers Wet (or Squatters' Law) No.24 of 1895 - Art. 3 (b), which imposed a tax of £2 per head. Each imposed a labour tax on those who had not worked for a white employer in any year.
141   'Tvl. Lab. Comm. (1903) Maj. Rep.', para. 91.

142 Ibid.
143 Ibid.
144 See Arrighi and Saul, op.cit., p.194. See also
     Wolpe, Capitalism and Cheap Labour Power in South
     Africa, p.438, who notes the importance for the mi-
     grant system of means of subsistence being distri-
     buted among all the families in the Reserves, in
     particular those with which migrant workers are con-
     nected.
145 'Tvl. Lab. Comm. (1903) Maj. Rep.', para. 92.
146 Ibid.
147 See below, pp.193-4.
148 Ibid., para. 93. The Commission considered the
     desirability of modifying the African tribal system
     through the abolition of African locations and re-
     serves like Basutoland, Swaziland, etc. No decision
     was arrived at.
149 See C.Meillassoux, p.102. Wolpe, Capitalism and
     Cheap Labour Power in South Africa, pp.434-5. See
     also Wolpe's remarks on the preservation of social
     relations of the familial community and the retention
     of the pre-Capitalist mode of production, ibid., p.
     436.
150 'Tvl. Lab. Comm. (1903) Maj. Rep.', para. 93.
151 On Lagden's policy for conserving the African areas
     see 'Tvl. Admin. Rep. for 1902', Part I, Admin.,
     pp.A1-2.
152 'Tvl. Lab. Comm. (1903) Maj. Rep.', para. 93.
153 Ibid. (emphasis added).
154 Wolpe, Capitalism and Cheap Labour Power in South
     Africa, p.437.
155 'Tvl. Lab. Comm. Maj. Rep.', para. 95.
156 Act 27 of 1913. This was supplemented by provisions
     of the Native Trust and Land Act of 1936.
157 Wolpe, Capitalism and Cheap Labour Power in South
     Africa, p.440.
158 For example, the adoption of a land policy that al-
     lowed each man only a single plot of land. For a
     discussion on the Native Land Act of 1913 see,
     ibid., pp.436-43; Simons and Simons, op.cit., pp.
     130-7; Legassick, South Africa, Capital Accumulation
     and Violence, pp.264-5.
159 See above, p.191. The unification of South Africa
     took place in 1910 - seven years after the Labour
     Commission reported.

CHAPTER 13 THE ASIAN LABOUR ALTERNATIVE

1 Cf. 'TCM 13th Ann. Rep. 1902', p.xxxv. For the increases in wages see Ch.11(iii), above.
2 Hobart Houghton and Dagut, op.cit., p.2 (emphasis
   added).
3 Van der Horst, op.cit., p.168. Arrighi and Saul, op.
   cit., p.184, makes the same point in connection with
   the Rhodesian mining industry: 'Like British capitalists in earlier times, Rhodesian employers, "when they
   spoke of plenty in connection with supply, [they] had
   in mind not only quantity but also price".'
4 See above, p.156.
5 Cf. Richardson, 'The Provision of Chinese Indentured
   Labour for the Transvaal Gold Mines 1903-1908', pp.
   30-44.
6 This view seemed to have been held strongly *prior* to
   the introduction of Chinese labour but the capital
   intensity of the industry did vary soon after Chinese
   labour arrived. For a discussion on technological innovation on the Rand see below, p.205.
7 Cf. Williams, op.cit., p.6, citing Marx, 'Capital',
   vol.III, Lawrence & Wishart, London, 1972, pp.349-50,
   on the incapacity of the gold industry to produce
   relative surplus value and the tendency of the producer of gold to 'depress the wages of labour below
   ... its minimum'. See also above, p.21.
8 This is elaborated in Ch.11(ii), above. See also
   Denoon, 'Capitalist Influence', pp.314,315.
9 See 'WCM 8th Ann. Rep. 1896', p.167. The question
   seems to have been discussed more formally in 1898
   and explicitly rejected on grounds of cost and 'un-
   desirability'. See 'WCM 10th Ann. Rep. 1898', pp.4,
   79.
10 See above, p.156.
11 See Ch.11(ii), above.
12 Mawby, op.cit., p.394.
13 Ibid.; Tiktin, op.cit., p.3. The latter view was
    most prominently held by Fitzpatrick (in opposition
    to his principals). According to Fitzpatrick two
    solutions might be attempted: 'first, of course,
    development of African native labour and second, cheap
    white labour' (Fitzpatrick to J.Wernher, 25.7.02,
    cited in Duminy and Guest, op.cit., Q2 A/LB xvii, No.
    157).
14 See Ch.11(iii) and Ch.12(ii) above.
15 'Debates of the Tvl. Leg. Coun.', 29.12.1903, col.
    220, p.110. See above, p.166.
16 See Ch.12(iii) above.

17 Apart from extensive indentures into British Natal in
    the previous two decades, Indian labour had been suc-
    cessfully imported into Uganda for railway construc-
    tion work in the 1890s, and Chinese labourers used by
    Germans for plantation work in Samoa. See Richardson,
    'Journal of African History', vol.XVIII, no.1, 1977,
    p.85. See also C.Newbury, Labour Migration in the
    Imperial Phase: an Essay in Interpretation, 'Journal
    of Imperial and Commonwealth History', vol.III, no.2,
    January 1975.
18 See Norman Levy, Problems of Acquisition of Labour for
    the South African Gold Mining Industry: The Asian
    Labour Alternative and the Defence of the Wage Struc-
    ture, 'Southern African Research in Progress, Col-
    lected Papers in Progress No.3', Papers given at the
    Centre for Southern African Studies, University of
    York, 1978, pp.58-63.
19 Initially it would seem that the Chamber hoped to
    employ Chinese labour at lower rates pro-rata than
    African wages. In its Statement to the Tvl. Lab.
    Comm. it stated: 'The Chinese would work in the
    country for 1/- per day plus their food.... Let it
    be assumed that the Chinaman would receive a total
    wage of 2/- per day. He is at once the most efficient
    and most persistent of workmen' (cited 'TCM 14th Ann.
    Rep. 1903', Appendix, p.xli).
20 According to P.Richardson, Coolies, Peasants and
    Proletarians: The Origins of Chinese Labour in South
    Africa 1904-7, 'Southern African Research in Progress,
    Collected Papers in Progress No.3', Papers given at
    the Centre for Southern African Studies, University
    of York, 1978, p.80, 'the recruits were most likely
    drawn from members of poor peasant families ... from
    rural wage labourers ... from urban casual labourers
    ... and from the entirely destitute.' See also below,
    pp.199-200.
21 'TCM 13th Ann. Rep. 1902', p.xlviii.
22 Ibid. See also Statement to Tvl. Lab. Comm. 1903,
    cited 'TCM 14th Ann. Rep. 1903', Appendix, p.xcvi.
    In its Statement to the Commission the Chamber listed
    thirty skilled occupations 'in and about the mines'
    from which the new migrants should be debarred (ibid.,
    p.xlvii). The matter is discussed more fully below,
    pp.223-5.
23 'TCM 14th Ann. Rep. 1903', p.xxx. For the legisla-
    tion, see Transvaal Labour Ordinance No.17 of 1904.
24 Richardson, 'Journal of African History', vol.xviii,
    no.1, 1977, p.90.
25 Various proposals were also received from India,

China, Japan, Syria, Egypt, Morocco and the United
States. Cf. 'TCM 14th Ann. Rep. 1903', p.xxx.

26   Ibid., pp.xxxi,155,169. On the scale of wages see
pp. 227-8. For a comprehensive discussion on the
recruitment of Chinese labourers see the luminous
work of P.Richardson, 'The Provision of Chinese Indentured Labour for the Transvaal Gold Mines 1903-
1908', part II, p.112 and passim.

27   T.W.Pearce, Chinese Labour: A China View, October
1904, in F.Wilson and D.Perrot (eds), op.cit., p.295.

28   See Katz, op.cit., p.122.

29   Le May, op.cit., p.163, notes that the Colonial
Secretary, Lyttleton, 'was impressed' by the strong
opposition of 'representative Boers' to the scheme.
Botha was 'emphatically opposed to the measure', and
six of the foremost Boer leaders, including Schalk
Burger (whose 'moderation' was noted by the Chamber
at the time of the Industrial Commission) hoped that
the Colonial Secretary would not remain under the
mistaken idea that the Boer people is in favour of a
measure which it looks upon as a public calamity.
(Ibid., p.152.) The 'Boers' held mass meetings, supporting the holding of a referendum on the matter.
The National Democratic Federation, founded in August
1903, was opposed to indentured labour but had a
broader purpose and called for Responsible government
based on adult white suffrage. See Tiktin, op.cit.,
p.11.

30   The Chairman of the Association was G.H.Goch, a listed
representative of the Chamber. The members of the
Association included some of the most prominent representatives of commerce on the Rand: Messrs Stewarts
& Lloyds Ltd; Reunert & Lenz; Hunt Leuchars & Hep-
burn. See Cd.1895, 1904, p.59. Thus the commercial
element was divided in its attitude to Asian labour.
The African Labour League more specifically represented the majority of the Chamber of Commerce. See
also below, pp.209-10.

31   Cd.1895, 1904, p.15. Extract of speech made in Boksburg, 1.4.1903, by Sir G.Farrar. The terms of the
restrictions then adumbrated were virtually repeated
in the Transvaal Labour Ordinance No.17 of 1904.

32   Cd.1895, 1904, p.14. The Chamber exaggerated the
claim although by 31.12.1904 the Witwatersrand area
employed 14,346 whites as opposed to 12,044 twelve
months earlier ('TCM 15th Ann. Rep. 1904'). In 1905
the number of skilled whites on the mines increased
to 18,159. Cf. 'TCM 16th Ann. Rep. 1905', p.ix.

33   See Annexure A to Statement of Evidence to Tvl. Lab.

Comm., cited 'TCM 14th Ann. Rep. 1903', Appendix, p.
xv.

34 Tiktin, op.cit., p.10, attributes this particular
fear to the founders of the White League (see below,
p.213), but it is not unlikely that Asian business
competition was a general fear. Most of the aims of
the two leagues overlapped anyway. It was the emphasis that differed.

35 Cd.1895, 1904, pp.47,48.

36 Cd.1895, 1904, p.48. Cf. also the 'Star', 1.7.1903.

37 See above, p.45.

38 See Ch.1, above.

39 See Praagh (ed.), op.cit., p.589.

40 Cd.1895, 1904, p.50.

41 Cartwright, 'The Gold Miners', p.149. Richardson,
'The Provision of Chinese Indentured Labour for the
Transvaal Gold Mines', p.23, notes the reduction in
working costs between 1895 and 1899 as 6s. 8d. (from
24s. 9d. per ton to 18s. 1d.). In November 1901 the
costs had risen to 23s. 8.047d. per ton (ibid.).
Cartwright's calculations for 1904 should therefore
be seen as a reflection of the post-war developments
in reducing working costs. Praagh (ed.), op.cit.,
p.580, puts average working costs for 1906 at approximately 22s. 6d.

42 Cartwright, 'The Gold Miners', p.149.

43 'TCM 15th Ann. Rep. 1904', p.lix.

44 A rock drill was introduced in 1903 but the significance of this innovation was marred by the increased
stoping width that this machine required. Consequently it caused a rise in working costs. On this see
Consolidated Goldfields of South Africa, 'The Gold
Fields 1887-1937', pp.77,78.

45 'TCM 15th Ann. Rep. 1904', p.lix. The main periods
of innovation were 1890-8, 1910-20, and in the 1920s
when the hand-drill was replaced by the jack-hammer.
See for the effects of these, Evidence of the Gold
Producers' Committee to the Low Grade Ore Commission,
1930, p.31.

46 For problems of mechanical invention see C.Perrings,
The Production Process, Industrial Labour Strategies
and Worker Responses in the Southern African Gold
Mining Industry, 'Journal of African History', vol.
XVIII, no.1, 1977, pp.131-2.

47 African Labour League, Manifesto Cd.1895, p.50.

48 Cf. Richardson, 'The Provision of Chinese Indentured
Labour for the Transvaal Mines', pp.24,25. Only
marginal gains in liquidity and profitability were to
be made, because of the system by which capital

charges were included in working costs. See ibid.
Where working costs (which in 1896 consisted of
materials and stores on the one hand, and labour costs
on the other - in the ratio of roughly 6:4) were high,
they adversely affected the balance on the year-end
profit and loss account. For a discussion on the effects of an increasing cost see also Economic and Wage
Comm. 1925, Evidence of the Gold Producers' Committee
of the TCM Statement No.5, Annexure B, p.20.

49 See Consolidated Goldfields of South Africa, 'The Gold
Fields 1887-1937', pp.77,78. The Government Mining
Engineer for 1905-6 assessed the white-black ratio as
5:383 in June 1903 and 4:343 in June 1902. The Consolidated Goldfields calculation cited above clearly
reflects a statistical year of January to December.
See Table 15.9, below.

50 Cf. ibid., p.78, for the Consolidated Goldfields reduction of average costs, and p.79 for the improvements in the Robinson mine.

51 Ibid., p.79. The application of this technology
created new problems in regard to the skilled/un-
skilled division of labour on the mines especially
after 1918.

52 See 'TCM 17th Ann. Rep. 1906', pp.83-4. For the
benefits of Chinese labour in this context see
Richardson, 'The Provision of Chinese Indentured
Labour for the Transvaal Gold Mines', p.95.

53 Cd.1895, p.48.

54 Ibid. Milner to Chamberlain 14.3.1903.

55 Ibid., p.48. The shortfall in labour was estimated by
the 'Tvl. Lab. Comm. (1903) Maj. Rep.' at 129,000.
The Minority commissioners estimated the shortage to
be in the range of 75,000. See Ch.12, above.

56 Cd.1895, 1904, p.48.

57 Ibid., p.28.

58 Ibid., p.49.

59 'Star', 14.5.1904.

60 Ibid., 13.5.1903. See also Manifesto of the League,
Cd.1895, 1904, p.49.

61 On this point, see WNLA's defence, below, p.209.

62 Cd.1895, 1904, p.49.

63 Ibid.

64 Cd.1895, 1903, p.57. Ministers to Governor.

65 Sir H.H.Johnson, 'The Times', 13.2.1903, cited
Cd.1895, p.50.

66 Speech by Dr Jameson, Grahamstown, 1903. Cd.1895,
p.50.

67 Sir Godfrey Lagden, cited. Cd.1895, p.50.

68 In this respect it took a historical (and somewhat

philosophical) approach and observed that twenty-five
years previously fewer than 20,000 Africans were employed on the mines and public works. 'Today it may
be estimated that the number is something like ten
times as great' (Manifesto of The League, cited Cd.
1895, p.50).

69 Ibid. The Cape Prime Minister equally referred to 'a
fair wage' and 'considerate' treatment in respect of
housing and food (ibid., p.57).

70 Tiktin, op.cit., p.10; see also P.C.Campbell,
'Chinese Coolie Emigration to Countries within the
British Empire', P.S.King, London, 1923, p.173; Katz,
op.cit., p.122, who describes the LIA as 'an organization which supported the importation of the Chinese
and which was financed by the Chamber of Mines'. For
the composition of the LIA see also p.330 n.30.

71 Cd.1895, July 1903, p.57. Manifesto of the LIA.

72 Cd.1895, 1903. 1st AGM, WNLA, April 1903, p.30.

73 Ibid. Statement to 1st AGM by Perry, Chairman of the
WNLA, April 1903.

74 Cd.1895, p.57.

75 Ibid., p.58.

76 Ibid.

77 Ibid.

78 Cd.1895, 1903, p.74. On the eve of the Transvaal
Labour Commission report, the Colonial Secretary
cabled the Lieutenant Governor: 'If the Commission
finds that the supply of labour in South Africa is
insufficient it will be necessary for me, before arriving at a decision, to know the feeling as to
Asiatic labour in the Colony ...' (ibid.). (Lyttleton
succeeded Chamberlain as Colonial Secretary in September 1903.)

79 Cf. R.V.Kubicek, 'French Capitalism and British
Imperialism: the Case of South African Gold Mining
before 1914', University of London Institute of
Commonwealth Studies, unpublished postgraduate seminar
paper, p.3.

80 Ibid., cited by Kubicek from the Rand Mines Johannesburg Archives, Alfred Beit to Eckstein & Co. 4.12.
1903.

81 Ibid., p.58. Cf. Manifesto, Labour Importation Association.

82 For the coercion of mining employees see Tiktin, op.
cit., pp.17,18. For the various meetings see Cd.1895,
pp.60-3. After a meeting held in August 1903 at
Krugersdorp under the auspices of the LIA the Chairman
sent the resolution to the Lieutenant Governor of the
Transvaal and asked if His Excellency 'would favour

the meeting by forwarding the resolution to the Secretary of State for the Colonies' (ibid., p.63).

83   Ibid. G.Farrar, the Chief mining spokesman on Asian
labour, was a member of the Tvl. Lab. Comm., and
G.H.Goch, the Chairman of the LIA, gave substantial
evidence to the Commission.

84   Merriman Papers, No.202 of 1903, 29.11.1903, cited
Tiktin, op.cit., p.12. See also the speech of Hull,
'Debates of the Tvl. Leg. Coun.', 28.12.03, cols
161-2. Hull commented: 'immediately the names of
the Commissioners were published the public of
Johannesburg ... indicated that a vast majority of
the Commissioners were in favour of ... importation'.

85   Cd.1895, p.17. See also 'Transvaal Leader', 2.3.1903.

86   Cd.1895, p.17. See also 'Transvaal Leader', 2.4.1903.

87   Cd.1895, p.55.

88   Ibid., p.69.

89   Ibid. For a detailed discussion on the Trade Union
movement's opposition to Chinese labour see Katz, op.
cit., pp.122-37.

90   Cf. Tiktin, op.cit., pp.15,16 (emphasis added). According to Katz, op.cit., p.123, 'Unorganized white
workers ... did not share the trade unions' fears of
encroachment by the Chinese and were convinced that
their jobs were dependent on the employment of unskilled Chinese labourers' (emphasis added). For
further discussion on this point see below, pp.218-19.

91   Katz, op.cit., p.121, citing F.Hellman, Consulting
Engineer, East Rand Proprietary Mines.

92   See the League's interview with Milner below, p.214.

93   Cd.1895, p.15. See also 'Transvaal Leader', 2.4.1903.
The pledge was adopted at a mass meeting of 5,000
white employees in April 1903. Much of this opposition was neutralized by the Chamber towards the close
of the agitation. In August of that year the Witwatersrand Trade and Labour Council complained 'that
undue pressure is being exercised by the leading officials on the mines to induce employees to sign
papers favouring the importation of Asiatics' (Cd.
1895, p.55). For evidence of coercion see below,
p.219.

94   Cd.1895, 1904. Report of the Deputation of the White
League, 2.6.1903, p.37.

95   Cd.1895, 1904, p.37.

96   Ibid.

97   Ibid., p.41. Nonetheless Milner threw his full support into the Chamber's case and did his utmost to
influence opinion - despite his comments to Chamberlain: 'Following your wise precept, that we should

treat the Transvaal ... as if it were self-governing
... I should say [this] is just one of the questions
which the people might fight out for themselves'
(Milner to Chamberlain, 6.4.1903). Cf. C.Headlam
(ed.), 'Milner Papers', vol.II, p.461.

98   Cd.1895, 1904, p.41.
99   Ibid.
100 Ibid.
101 Ibid. For Milner's comments on improvements in the
     labour force, see above, p.206.
102 Ibid., Milner to Chamberlain.
103 Ibid., p.44. He did not accept the other less men-
     tioned strategy for a migratory labour supply, i.e.
     forced labour. He saw 'no objection to [forced
     labour] in principle, but the practical difficulties
     are immense and the relief it could afford ... would
     be so trifling that it is not worthwhile wasting time
     over it'. Cf. Cd.1895. In Natal it did little 'to
     solve their labour problem'. Moreover, 'public
     opinion in England would never tolerate it'. Least
     of all would it produce 'an abundant and an efficient
     supply of native labour'. (Ibid., p.44). 'A Migrant
     labour system was most likely to achieve these aims.'
104 Ibid., p.42. Before the war, Milner had written:
     'One thing is quite evident. The *ultimate* end is a
     self-governing white community, supported by well-
     treated and justly governed black labour from Cape
     Town to Zambesi' (Milner to Fitzpatrick, 19 November
     1899, Headlam (ed.), 'Milner Papers', vol.II, pp.
     35-6).
105 Cd.1895, p.42.
106 On the latter point see Ch.11 above. See also R.
     Davis, op.cit., p.66, and Wolpe, The 'White Working
     Class' in South Africa, p.206 and passim; Howard
     Simson, op.cit., pp.194-5 also discusses the subject.
107 Cd.1895, 1904, p.42 (emphasis added).
108 Two weeks prior to the official publication of the
     Report on 27 November 1903, the Lieutenant Governor
     (in Milner's absence) supplied the Colonial Secretary
     with the terms of *a draft ordinance* to regulate the
     introduction into the Transvaal of unskilled non-
     white labourers. This ordinance was confirmed by the
     Colonial Secretary, who cabled confirmation immedi-
     ately the Report was made public and urged the
     tabling of the resolution (outlined below) before the
     Transvaal Legislative Council. Cf. Cd.1895, p.117.
     On the history of the Transvaal Labour Ordinance see
     Richardson, 'The Provision of Chinese Indentured
     Labour for the Transvaal Gold Mines, pp.64-5.

109   Cd.1895, p.143. 'Transvaal Leader', 3.12.03.
      Special Meeting of the Chamber.
110   Cf. Chaplin on the Chamber of Mines Special Meeting,
      1.12.1903, Cd.1895, pp.143-56.
111   See Richardson, 'The Provision of Chinese Indentured
      Labour for the Transvaal Gold Mines', pp.62-6.
112   Cd.1895, p.155.
113   Ibid., p.176. For details of the lengthy debate see
      Cd.1895, p.246, and 'Debates of the Tvl. Leg. Coun.',
      28-30 December 1903, pp.71-151. The motion was
      passed in the 26-man legislature on 30 December 1903
      with 4 against. A draft ordinance was hastily pub-
      lished in a Gazette Extraordinary on 6 January 1904,
      after Milner had cabled the Colonial Secretary on
      31 January 1904 stating that the government ought
      without unnecessary delay to introduce legislation
      on the lines laid down on the motion. Cd.1895, p.
      176.
114   Ibid., p.177.
115   Ibid. Milner to Lyttleton. Within the Legislative
      Council Hull, Raitt, Loveday (and Bourke to a lesser
      extent) mounted a valiant campaign of opposition to
      Chinese labour against equal odds. See 'Debates of
      the Tvl. Leg. Coun.', 28.12.03, pp.80,81; 29.12.03,
      pp.110,111; 30.12.03, pp.150,151. For debates on
      the Labour Importation Ordinance held in committee
      stage, see 'Debates of the Tvl. Leg. Coun.', 26.1.
      1904, pp.204-6. For the support (outside the Trans-
      vaal Legislative Council) of certain professionals,
      commercial men and Australian radicals, see Tiktin,
      op.cit., p.26.
116   Prior to the formal adoption of the Ordinance, the
      High Commissioner was presented with a petition
      signed by 3,735 white residents on the Witwatersrand
      who favoured the scheme (Cd.1895, p.181). Although
      the method of collection of these signatures was much
      criticized at the time, there was clearly consider-
      able support especially (as Katz, op.cit., p.123
      notes) by the unorganized workforce who constituted
      the majority of the working class.
117   Cf. Tiktin, op.cit., pp.16,17.
118   Katz, op.cit., pp.110,111; Tiktin, op.cit., p.16.
119   Cited by Katz, op.cit., p.122.
120   Ibid., p.123. For further evidence of coercion, see
      Tiktin, op.cit., p.17, and below, p.220.
121   'Debates of the Tvl. Leg. Coun.', 29.12.1903, col.
      220, p.110.
122   For Milner's remarks see Cd.1895, p.177. See also
      Tiktin, op.cit., p.21, who sees the commercial de-

pression as 'the main cause' of the 'swing of public opinion on the Rand'.

123 'Star', 15.12.1903.

124 Annexure A to Statement of Evidence submitted to the Tvl. Labour Commission, cited 'TCM 14th Ann. Rep. 1903', Appendix, p.xv.

125 Cd.1895, p.187. The actual statement of the African Labour League was quite explicit: 'It was not right to rush the matter before the Legislative Council before the people had a chance of voting on it.... The people should see that they were accorded their rights and that the nominated Legislative Council should not legislate to the detriment of their interests' (ibid.).

126 Ibid., p.177. For details of the 'fiasco' see n.128, below. Milner equally dismissed the Cape agitation against Asian labour as an electioneering stunt on the part of the Bond who hoped to capture the African vote in the Cape by fanning fears 'of Asiatics sweeping all over S.A. and supplanting them in their own country'. Cf. ibid., p.178.

127 Cf. 'Star', 15.12.1903.

128 Cf. ibid., 14.12.1903; Cd.1895, pp.184-5. According to the 'Star', 'A penny trumpet sounded at intervals above a medley of indescribable noise and Mr. Quinn was unable to get beyond the initial word "Gentlemen".' Cf. 'Star', 15.12.1903; Cd.1895, pp.184-5.

129 Milner (quite accurately) noted that 'as far as the Boers were concerned it would not be a vote for or against the Referendum but a vote against the present form of government' (Milner to Lyttleton, 11.2.1904, No.2, cited Le May, op.cit., p.163). Milner's objection to the proposal was similar to the Chamber's: the 'serious' consequences of delay - there were no rural voting lists and the referendum would take six months to prepare (ibid., p.163).

130 The motion read: 'This meeting affirms the principle of the Government of the people by the people for the people; and in the absence of representative government calls upon the Legislative Council as the only present means of legislation, to pass a law permitting a Referendum to introduce indentured unskilled coloured labour under restrictions as to employment and repatriation' (Cd.1895, p.187). The Chamber's objections to the proposal were (i) that it was unreasonable to put the question unless the alternative question could be put: 'were they to remain stagnant or develop the natural resources of the country?'; and (ii) a Referendum would take 'a year or two' and

delay would mean that 'incalculable harm would be
done' ('Star', 15.12.1903).
131 Ibid.

CHAPTER 14   RACIST LEGISLATION AND THE INTRODUCTION OF
CHINESE LABOUR

1 Apart from formal authorization of colonial legislation the imperial government were required under
   treaty with China (made in 1860) to provide that
   'regulations ... be framed by the two powers for the
   common advantage of both' (Cd.357, 1903). It is
   noteworthy that the Chinese Legation in Britain approved the highly discriminatory Ordinance before it
   became law: 'I have given the draft ordinance my
   careful consideration, and I am glad to be able to
   inform your Lordship that I do not find anything in
   it which is likely to conflict with anything I shall
   have to propose when we come to negotiate the
   "Reglement"' (Cd.1945, 1904).
2 For the co-operation of the state in respect of
   sanctions, cf. sections 31 and 32 of Offences in
   order to Regulate the Introduction into the Transvaal
   of unskilled non-European Labourers (cited 'TCM 14th
   Ann. Rep. 1903', Appendix, p.ccxliii). For state co-
   operation generally, see Richardson, 'The Provision
   of Chinese Indentured Labour for the Transvaal Gold
   Mines', pp.67-70 and passim. For the cost of Chinese
   labour, see below, p.226.
3 The Chamber's compromises amounted to the terms of
   white incorporation. For these see above, p.199.
4 Cf. Cd.1895, 1904, p.41.
5 It was an irony that these restrictions actually
   raised the unit costs of Chinese labour. Firstly,
   state intervention had a direct effect on costs
   through government fees and restrictions on 'management flexibility' in relation to the deployment of
   the indentured labourers in certain occupations.
   Secondly, the enforcement of the Truck Act of 1896,
   which excluded the mine stores from trading with
   Chinese on the mines, plus the absence of a closed
   compound system, meant that unit costs could not be
   recovered through direct trading. Nor could any
   saving on food be made in view of omission of a compulsory allotment scheme from the terms of contract.
   Attempts to reduce unit costs were therefore made by
   increasing productivity through piece rates, work
   discipline and coercion. On these points see

Richardson, 'The Provision of Chinese Indentured
Labour in the Transvaal Gold Mines', pp.62,74,84, and
(for increased productivity and coercion) below,
p.229.

6 'TCM 14th Ann. Rep. 1903', p.xlv.

7 Ibid., p.xlvi.

8 Ibid. Milner was impatient with the opposition to
the immigration of Asian labour. On this point see
Nimocks, op.cit., p.38, who cites the correspondence
between Milner and the Rt Rev. A. Hamilton Hayes, the
Bishop of Natal. Milner wrote: 'There is an immense
amount of cant about the "moral" evils attending
Chinese immigration.... Without a substratum of
Coloured people, white labour cannot exist here, and
when the very rich mines are worked out, the country
will return to its primitive barrenness - and the
Boer.'

9 Milner to Chamberlain 13.7.1903, cited by Richardson,
'The Provision of Chinese Indentured Labour for the
Transvaal Gold Mines', p.64, from Milner Papers,
vol.41, Pt 4, p.24.

10 Tvl. Lab. Importation Ordinance No.17 of 1904, para.
9 (a).

11 According to the Mines, Works and Machinery Act 1903,
which reintroduced the republican occupational colour
bar in which the job of winding engine-driver was reserved for white drivers, the new regulations required
all drivers of locomotive engines (and of winding
engines) used for hauling men, to be white. They
were also required to hold a certificate of competency
according to the conditions of the Mining Certificates
Ordinance of 1903. See Katz, op.cit., p.140, who
cites the Chamber as stating that 'there were practically no coloured drivers' in 1903.

12 See Schedule I to Ord. 17 of 1904.

13 On this point, see 'Debates of the Leg. Coun.',
January 1904, for the debate on the renewal of contracts of service.

14 'Rand Daily Mail', 1.4.03. Extract of speech by Sir
G.Farrar cited Cd.1895, p.1.

15 According to the oral evidence of C.Gazides, a Medical
Officer on the West Rand until 1964, iron bars are
still to be found in the former mining hospitals and
compounds that were set aside for Chinese occupation.

16 Cf. Ord. No. 17 of 1904, paras 18,19.

17 Ord. No. 54 of 1903.

18 Laws 11 and 12 of 1897 and 1898 respectively.

19 In terms of constitutional settlement with the Transvaal in 1902, legislation was subject to external
scrutiny by the Secretary of State in Whitehall.

20 For instance, the regulations regarding the importa-
    tion of Chinese to the Transvaal had not been laid
    before the Commons by April 1904. Cf. report in the
    'Transvaal Leader', 19.4.1904, p.7. The matter had
    been raised by a Liberal member on 18.4.1904. The
    British and Foreign Anti-Slavery Society, the
    Aborigines Protection Society, and the Native Races
    Committee were prominent among those who scrutinized
    the policy in the new British possessions of the
    Transvaal and Orange River Colonies. They had little
    to say about the Mines Works and Machinery Ordinance,
    although they protested vigorously against the Cham-
    ber's treatment of the Chinese.
21 A series of amendments consolidated the situation in
    1906 under Government Notices 173, 176 and 1232 of
    that year.
22 See Katz, op.cit., pp.141,142.
23 Ibid., p.142.
24 Cf. H.Wolpe, The Theory of Internal Colonialism: The
    South African Case, in I.Oxaal et al. (eds), 'Beyond
    the Sociology of Development', Routledge & Kegan Paul,
    London, 1975.
25 Cf. S.Trapido, South Africa in a Comparative Study of
    Industrialization, 'University of London Institute of
    Commonwealth Studies, Collected Seminar Papers: The
    Societies of Southern Africa in the Nineteenth and
    Twentieth Centuries', October 1970 - June 1971, p.55.
    See also Moroney, op.cit., p.116; Richardson,
    'Journal of African History', vol.XVIII, no.1, 1977,
    p.100. See also Ch.15 below.
26 'TCM 15th Ann. Rep. 1904', p.xxvii. For a detailed
    account of the functions and structure of the CMLIA
    see Richardson, 'The Provision of Chinese Indentured
    Labour for the Transvaal Gold Mines', p.112.
27 'TCM 15th Ann. Rep. 1904'. According to Richardson,
    'Journal of African History', vol.XVIII, no.1, 1977,
    p.93, capitation charges for the whole exercise
    amounted to £17. 5s. 2d. per man and were actually
    higher if capital costs and advances are included.
    The difference between the two types of recruitment
    (African and Chinese) was £7. 17s. Od. per man, i.e.
    £9. 12s. for Africans as against £17. 10s. for Chinese
    (cited, ibid., from W.L.Bagot, 'Chinese Labour on the
    Witwatersrand', unpublished MS dd 1906 Archives Trans-
    vaal Chamber of Mines, ch.26).
28 Richardson, 'Journal of African History', vol.XVIII,
    no.1, 1977, p.93.
29 'TCM 15th Ann. Rep. 1904', p.xxvii.
30 Ibid. A further shipload of 6,112 was on the water

at that date. The average number imported from June
1904 to January 1905 was 3,500 per month (ibid.,
p.xlix). They were recruited largely from the
northern provinces of Shantung, Chili and Honan.

31 Ibid., p.xxvii.
32 'TCM 17th Ann. Rep. 1906', p.xxv. Figures vary. According to Richardson, 'Journal of African History',
vol.XVIII, no.1, 1977, p.86, 63,296 men were shipped
between February 1904 and November 1906. According
to 'TCM 17th Ann. Rep. 1906', p.xxv, 63,568 arrived;
and of those who arrived, 1,922 *died* and 6,532 were
repatriated. The industry soon began to develop a
dependence upon the Chinese. In 1905 it was estimated
by the Chamber that if the pressure for the withdrawal
of Chinese labour continued 3,135 stamps would be hung
up and 6,405 skilled Europeans dismissed. Gold output
would be reduced by 40 per cent (cf. 'TCM 16th Ann.
Rep. 1905', p.lxvi). Unimpressed by this response,
the Colonial Secretary (under pressure to end the
Asian expedient) charged the Chamber with not attempting to introduce labour-saving devices or to improve its organization or to 'develop all those expedients to which ... an industry would have to resort
in other countries where mining is conducted with a
limited labour supply' (cited ibid.).
33 For details of the distribution see Richardson,
'Journal of African History', vol.XVIII, no.1, 1977,
p.101.
34 Ibid.
35 'TCM 15th Ann. Rep. 1904', p.xxviii. About 15 per
cent signed on as married men.
36 Ibid., p.xxx. The death rate in 1905 was 18.386 per
thousand. According to the Coloured Labour Compound
Commission (1904/5), 'The Chinese, if he has a mat and
a blanket, cares little about what is underneath, so
that it is impossible in these compound huts to make
these floors sanitary and impervious and provide wood
bunks with iron frames which can be cleansed frequently.' The report made little of the lack of hygiene of
the huts but noted that the limitation of 200 cu.ft of
air space per person was approximately 50 cu.ft below
the side of safety. Cited 'TCM 16th Ann. Rep. 1905',
p.58.
37 'TCM 16th Ann. Rep. 1905', pp.lviii, liv.
38 Cf. Report of Economic Commission 1914, p.37, para.
54; Simons and Simons, op.cit., p.83; 'TCM 16th Ann.
Rep. 1905', p.xxxi. See also Denoon, The Transvaal
Labour Crisis, pp.492-3, who notes that Milner turned
a blind eye to payments by the Chamber that fell below

contract levels. He also notes (Denoon, 'A Grand
Illusion') that at the end of six months the labourers
were receiving substantially less wages than the contracts appeared to guarantee. In computing the
average wage, the employers considered only the best
80 per cent of the labourers. The remaining 20 per
cent were excluded from the calculations to eradicate
the inefficient and the sick. Richardson, 'Journal
of African History', vol.XVIII, no.1, 1977, p.100,
notes that African wages declined from 55s. in June
1903, to 51s. 11d. in December-January 1905-1906.
See below, p.242.

39   Denoon, The Transvaal Labour Crisis, p.492.
40   See Consolidated Goldfields of South Africa (1937),
p.78: 'The experiment was an immediate success....
The Chinese proved apt learners, and by 1907 the
average cost ... had been reduced by 4/6 per ton.'
For the general benefits of Chinese labour cf. 'TCM
17th Ann. Rep. 1906', pp.xxvii, lx.
41   See Moroney, op.cit., p.126.
42   Cd.1786 of 1905, p.9. Selbourne to Lyttleton. See
also C.O. 879/90, No.4, 21.7.1905, and 879/90, No.44,
of 26.8.1905, for details of Chinese Resistance. See
also Richardson, 'The Provision of Chinese Indentured
Labour for the Transvaal Gold Mines', pp.96-7, who
notes that 'coercive legal machinery', notably the
Labour Importation Amendment Ordinance of 1905,
worsened industrial relations but improved control and
raised productivity so that 26 per cent of all profits
in 1906 emanated from Chinese labour.
43   Cf. Cd.2786 of 1905, pp.30-1. Statement by British
and Foreign Anti-Slavery Society, 7.10.1905. The
statement considered that the contract made by the
labourer was 'contrary to the principles of English
law, as allowing him to incorporate into his contract
the ingredients of slavery'. The Society further considered the conditions of employment degrading and inconsistent with 'British traditions of freedom'. See
also 'TCM 16th Ann. Rep. 1905', p.lx. The conditions
of the Chinese provoked much comment and two commissions: the Secret Commission of the TCM, and the
Special Committee of the Lieutenant Governor.
44   Cf. 'TCM 17th Ann. Rep. 1906', p.xxvii.
45   See below, pp.239-40.
46   This is not to suggest that the industry lightly accepted the British government's refusal to grant
further licences. A great dependence on Chinese
labour had been established and large benefits obtained through Chinese industrial efficiency. See
ibid., pp.76-8,xxvii,80-1.

47   Ibid., p.lv. According to Richardson, 'Journal of
     African History', vol.XVIII, no.1, 1977, p.93, the
     cost per unit was £17. 5s. 2d. and not £16 as stated
     by the Chamber.

CHAPTER 15   THE RESTORATION OF THE LABOUR SUPPLY

1   'TCM 15th Ann. Rep. 1904', p.xxiii. For the areas of
     recruitment cf. Tables 15.2 and 15.3 below. See also
     Denoon, 'A Grand Illusion', p.130, on new areas of
     recruitment.
2   'TCM 16th Ann. Rep. 1905', p.xxiii.
3   'TCM 15th Ann. Rep. 1904', p.2; 'TCM 16th Ann. Rep.
     1905', p.11. For details of geographical areas of
     recruitment see Tables 15.2, 15.3 and 15.4 below.
4   'TCM 16th Ann. Rep. 1905', p.xxiv.
5   For details on the withdrawal of labour in 1905 and
     1906 see Moroney, op.cit., p.98. The increasing ef-
     fectiveness of the Pass Laws in recovering labourers
     was confirmed by the 1907 Report of the Mining Indus-
     try Commission, which noted the recovery of deserting
     labourers as 23.8 per cent for 1905 and 29.1 per cent
     for 1906. Moroney, op.cit., p.98 cited from the
     Report of the Mining Industry Commission 1907,
     Annexure E, p.1535. For the liquor laws and Kaffir
     Beer legislation of 1903 and comments on productivity,
     see 'TCM 15th Ann. Rep. 1904', p.xxv.
6   Ibid., p.xxii. See also Tables 15.1 - 15.4 below.
7   For further comments on the Portuguese East Africa
     supply, see below.
8   'TCM 15th Ann. Rep. 1904', p.49.
9   'TCM 16th Ann. Rep. 1905', p.xxv.
10   See R.Kubicek, Finance Capital and South African Gold
     Mining, 1886-1914, 'Journal of Imperial and Common-
     wealth History', vol.III, no.3, 1975. Cost inflation
     (largely in labour, transport and stores) and de-
     clining output were seen to be contributing factors.
     The steady decline in the value of gold, relative to
     other commodities, persistently raised the cost of
     stores. On this see S.H.Frankel, 'Gold and Inter-
     national Equity Investment', pp.27,28.
11   According to Amery (ed.), 'The Times History of the
     War in South Africa 1899-1902', vol.VI, pp.100-1, the
     harvest failure was severe on all groups of the popu-
     lation.
12   'TCM 16th Ann. Rep. 1905', p.xxiv.
13   'TCM 15th Ann. Rep. 1904', p.xxvi, 394, 83, 89, 91.
     Statistics vary. After 1904, the mortality rate de-

344 Notes to chapter 15

creased to 46.8 per cent per thousand per annum in
1905 to 33.11 in 1906 per thousand per annum. Cf.
'TCM 16th Ann. Rep. 1905', p.21; 'TCM 17th Ann. Rep.
1906', p.xxiii. Individually, e.g. Portuguese Africans, the rate is still very high. See below, p.236.

14 See 'TCM 15th Ann. Rep. 1904', p.xxiii, and 'TCM 16th
Ann. Rep. 1905', p.xxv. See also Tables 15.2, 15.4
and 15.5, below.

15 For comments on recruitment from the Cape, see below,
p.243.

16 The Chinese comprised 35.46 per cent of the total unskilled labour force in 1906 as compared with 30.80
per cent from Portuguese East Africa. See Richardson,
'Journal of African History', vol.XVIII, no.1, 1977,
p.100. In 1907 the Chinese accounted for 34.44 per
cent comprising 53,856 labourers (ibid.).

17 'TCM 15th Ann. Rep. 1904', p.292.

18 Ibid., p.337. See also WNLA Table of Distribution,
Appendix 3 below. Though the numbers recruited in the
'non-traditional districts of Quilimane, Tete and
Mocambique were on the increase, they did not rise in
August and were in any case insignificant, yielding
between January and August 1904 less than 100 labourers each.

19 Ibid., p.325. These reasons were seen by the Chamber
to absolve WNLA from charges of inadequate recruiting
(ibid.).

20 The figures refer to the units *recruited* rather than
distributed to the various mines. In 1904, for instance, the numbers distributed were 782 fewer than
those recruited. Those from the Quilimane and Tete
districts had the most 'wastage'.

21 See Table 15.5. For details of rural poverty see
citation on p.236.

22 'A short account of the Recruiting Work by the WNLA
Ltd. in Portuguese East Africa, South of Lat.22º'.
Pamphlet cited 'TCM 17th Ann. Rep. 1906', p.4.

23 Ibid., pp.5,6,7. 'TCM 15th Ann. Rep. 1904', p.xxiii.

24 'TCM 15th Ann. Rep. 1904', p.xxvi.

25 Ibid. (emphasis added). The phrase was something of
a euphemism. In four months 5,849 men were detained
before proceeding to work. The average period of detention was fourteen days (ibid.). (Chances of
mortality were lessened only one month after recruitment when the recruit became acclimatized. Cf. 'TCM
15th Ann. Rep. 1904', p.62.)

26 Cf. Correspondence Medical Officer, WNLA, to TCM,
20.5.04. The content of the correspondence reveals
harrowing poverty in Portuguese East Africa. Cf.
'TCM 15th Ann. Rep. 1904', p.57.

27   'TCM 17th Ann. Rep. 1906', p.xxi.
28   Ibid.
29   Ibid.
30   'TCM 15th Ann. Rep. 1904', p.xxiv. During 1904, 941
     men were recruited from this source and in 1905 a
     further 2,068 ('TCM 16th Ann. Rep. 1905', p.xxv).
31   'TCM 15th Ann. Rep. 1904', p.xxiv. This Rhodesian
     contingent was provided after the Rhodesian Labour
     Bureau agreed to supply the WNLA with labour obtained
     but not currently required in Rhodesia. They were not
     available in the summer. (Ibid., 'TCM 16th Ann. Rep.
     1905', p.xxv.)
32   Harvest failure, nevertheless, made these workers more
     dependent on the mines. See below, p.241.
33   'TCM 15th Ann. Rep. 1904', p.xxiv. 'TCM 16th Ann.
     Rep. 1905', p.xxvi.
34   'TCM 17th Ann. Rep. 1906', p.xxvi. See Tables 15.3
     and 15.4 below.
35   Report of the General Manager, WNLA, for the Year
     1906, cited 'TCM 17th Ann. Rep. 1906', p.583. One of
     the advantages of local recruitment was that Africans
     could be employed on a monthly basis and the mining
     companies would not be obliged to hold them for longer
     than they needed them. That the Chamber accepted this
     was an indicator of the improving supply situation.
     See ibid., pp.648-9.
36   Correspondence Vereeniging Estates Ltd to TCM, 28.9.
     1904, cited 'TCM 15th Ann. Rep. 1904', pp.68-70.
37   See note against Table 15.6 below in respect of this
     calculation.
38   There were various projections ranging from 250,000
     to 368,637 unskilled labourers required by 1908.
     Cf. Exhibit 2, Annexure D, Tvl. Lab. Comm. See also
     'TCM 16th Ann. Rep. 1905', p.lxiv. The Chamber's
     figures were much disputed by the Colonial Secretary,
     who reduced the Chamber's estimate by approximately
     one-third. The Chamber did not concede this. (Ibid.,
     p.lxv.)
39   SNA 56/12 82/05 cited by Moroney, op.cit., p.124. See
     also Report of WNLA for 1905, p.362.
40   SNA 56/12 82/05, cited Moroney, op.cit., p.124.
41   Ibid.
42   Denoon, The Transvaal Labour Crisis, p.493.
43   Average wage rates decreased from 55s. per month in
     June 1904 to 50s. 11d. in December 1905 and January
     1906, rallying only slightly at the end of that year.
     On this see Richardson, 'Journal of African History',
     vol.XVIII, no.1, 1977, p.100. For wage rates between
     1905 and 1908 cf. Annual Reports of the Govt. Mining

Engineer 1905/6; 06/7; 07/8. The wage rate for 1907-8
is recorded at 49s. 1d. per month as opposed to 52s.
52s. 3d. at the end of 1906.

44 See Moroney, op.cit., p.102, citing SNA 71/3 588/05.
In 1905 and 1906 there were 10,233 and 11,973 cases
respectively of men who broke their contracts. In
addition, 3,585 complaints were registered at Pass
Offices along the Reef for shortfalls in wages. Of
these cases, £10,332 was recovered in wages improperly
held. (Ibid.)

45 'TCM 17th Ann. Rep. 1906', p.xlix (emphasis added).
The fluctuations were 3 per cent and considered insignificant (ibid.).

46 See Tables 15.8 and 15.9 and Appendix 3 below.
Reasons given for the decrease in the recruitment of
Africans in the 1906 Report were the refusal of the
imperial government to permit the resumption of recruiting in the British Central African Protectorate
and N.E. Rhodesia for underground work on the mines
('TCM 17th Ann. Rep. 1906', p.583). However, as noted
above, Table 15.7, the Chinese component increased by
9,161 between July 1905 and June 1906 and their efficiency was constantly increasing. This may have influenced the African supply for 1906.

47 This is not to suggest that there was no worker
protest, but the flow of labour was sufficient for
the Chamber to withstand a substantial turnover of
migrants. Hence the high turnover of labour in 1905
and 1906 was more than likely a response to new contract conditions, and the best (and most literal)
indicator that dissatisfied African recruits voted
with their feet. 'Desertions' for the year 1905 were
7,941 out of a total employed of 94,696, and 6,652
out of a total recruited of 85,696 for the year 1906.
Cf. 'TCM 16th Ann. Rep. 1905', p.13, and 'TCM 17th
Ann. Rep. 1906', pp.xxiii, 3.

48 On this point see Bundy, 'Passing through a Period of
Stress: The Transkei Peasantry 1890-1914', paper pre-
sented to Workshop on Social and Economic History of
South Africa, Oxford, September 1974, p.12; and
Moroney, op.cit., p.130.

49 'TCM 16th Ann. Rep. 1905', p.4.

50 'TCM 17th Ann. Rep. 1906', p.34.

51 On this point see SNA 63/665/06, cited by Moroney,
op.cit., pp.127,130. Moroney notes that by November
1905 WNLA retreated to allow certain recruiters to
engage labour on four-monthly contracts. By March
1906, 225 Cape workers were recruited on these terms,
the Secretary for Native Affairs claiming 'there was
no real shortage'. (Ibid., p.130.)

52 WNLA Report of General Manager for the year 1905 in 'TCM 16th Ann. Rep. 1905', Appendix, p.362.

53 'TCM 17th Ann. Rep. 1906', p.xxviii. Cf. Table of White Employment on Gold Mines of the Witwatersrand, ibid., p.xxviii.

54 See Table of White Employment, 'TCM 17th Ann. Rep. 1906', p.lx and 'TCM 16th Ann. Rep. 1905', p.lxviii.

55 'TCM 17th Ann. Rep. 1906', pp.xviii, 482,483.

56 Phillips to J.Wernher, 26.2.1905, in Fraser and Jeeves, op.cit., p.124 (emphasis added). In a subsequent 'private' communication to F.Eckstein on 5.3.1905, Phillips noted that a number of white rock drill men 'of a very inferior class' have been openly discharged, including 18 from the Robinson Deep Mine. Albu had also 'discharged a lot of men ... without any heed of consequences, simply on the ground of cheapness'. (Ibid., p.129.) See also 'TCM 15th Ann. Rep. 1905', pp.xxiv and lxviii for new capital expenditure 'justified' by the satisfactory labour supply.

57 'TCM 15th Ann. Rep. 1905', p.lxviii.

58 Cf. WNLA, Table of African Recruitment for 1905, in 'TCM 16th Ann. Rep. 1905', Appendix, p.4.

59 Phillips to Wernher, 26.2.1905, in Fraser and Jeeves, op.cit., p.124. Phillips's contention was that white miners would probably leave of their own accord if diverted to different work.

60 'TCM 17th Ann. Rep. 1906', pp.lx, lxi.

61 Jeeves, The Control of Migratory Labour on the South African Gold Mines in the Era of Kruger and Milner, 'Journal of Southern African Studies', vol.2, no.1, 1975, pp.19-20.

62 See ibid., p.28, and Moroney, op.cit., p.131.

63 The worst offender in this respect was J.B.Robinson's group. See below.

64 SNA 71/3721/06, cited by Moroney, op.cit., p.132.

65 Ibid.

66 Richardson, 'Journal of African History', vol.XVIII, no.1, 1977, p.107.

67 SNA Minute by Lagden, 29.11.06, cited Jeeves, op.cit., p.28. The major issue was the independent recruitment of labour by the Robinson Group in Portuguese East Africa. For the Chamber's statement on the withdrawal of this group and their comments on the consequences of this action see 'TCM 17th Ann. Rep. 1906', pp.7, 646.

68 President of TCM, cited 'TCM 17th Ann. Rep. 1906', p.lxiii. L.M.Thompson, 'The Unification of South Africa 1902-1910', Oxford, The Clarendon Press, 1960, p.14, notes that 'with the help of Chinese labour,

output of the Rand mines rose from £12,628,057 in
1903 to £27,400,992 in 1907'.   Thompson also notes,
significantly, that 'without Chinese labour the
recovery and expansion of the gold mining industry
would have been much less rapid *and it might have
become necessary to modify the labour structure:* with
it, the industry, became the sheet-anchor of the
entire South African economy ... re-established on the
pre-war basis of ... highly paid White men and a relatively large number of non-whites ... confined to unskilled tasks and paid low wages' (emphasis added).

Bibliography

OFFICIAL DOCUMENTS

Colonial Office, Secret Despatches (abbreviated as C.O.)

879/55   No.249
879/55   No.314 (1)
879/51   No.226
879/51   No.184 encl. (4)
879/55   No.145
879/55   No.42
879/55   No.186
879/90   No.44
879/90   No.44   encl. (2)
879/90   No.40
879/55   No.260 and 260 encl. (2)
879/51   No.313
879/51   No.182
879/51   No.210

Cd Papers

Cd.904,   1901
Cd.1895, 1904
Cd.2786, 1905
Cd.714,   1898

Debates of the Transvaal Legislative Council

28.12.1903
29.12.1903
30.12.1903

18.1.1904
26.1.1904

ORDINANCES

Mines, Works and Machinery Ordinance No.54 of 1903
Transvaal Labour Importation Ordinance No.17 of 1904

REPORTS AND GOVERNMENT COMMISSIONS

1897 Industrial Commission
1904 Transvaal Labour Commission
1905 South African Native Affairs Commission 1905
1908 T.G.2 Mining Industry Commission
1914 U.G.37 The Native Grievances Inquiry
1920 U.G.34 Low Grade Ore Mines Commission
1926 U.G.14 Economic and Wage Commission
1944 U.G.21 Witwatersrand Mine Native Wages Commission
Reports of Government Mining Engineer 1901-6
Transvaal Administration Reports 1902-6
Witwatersrand Chamber of Mines/Transvaal Chamber of Mines
Annual Reports 1890-1912
Witwatersrand Native Labour Association 1903-6 Annual
Reports

NEWSPAPERS

'Morning Leader'
'Rand Daily Mail', Johannesburg
'Standard and Diggers News', Johannesburg S.A.R.
'Standard and Transvaal Mining Chronicle', Johannesburg,
Transvaal, 1890
'Star', Johannesburg
'Transvaal Advertiser'
'Transvaal Leader'

BOOKS, ARTICLES AND THESES

AMERY, L.S. (ed.) (1909), 'The Times History of the War
in South Africa 1889-1902', vol.VI, London.
ARRIGHI, G. and SAUL, J.S. (1973), 'Essays on the
Political Economy of Africa', Monthly Review Press,
London.
ATMORE, A. and MARKS, S. (1974), The Imperial Factor in
South Africa in the Nineteenth Century: Towards a Reas-

sessment, 'Journal of Imperial and Commonwealth History',
vol.III, no.1.
BICCARD JEPPE, C.W. (1948), 'Gold Mining in South Africa',
Todd Publishing Group, London.
BLAINEY, G. (1965), The Lost Causes of the Jameson Raid,
'Economic History Review', second series, vol.XVIII, no.2.
BURAWOY, M. (1976), The Functions of Migrant Labour:
Comparative Material from Southern Africa and the United
States, 'American Journal of Sociology', no.81.
BUNDY, C. (1971), The Responses of African Peasants in
the Cape to Economic Changes, 1870-1910: A Study of Growth
and Decay, 'University of London Institute of Commonwealth
Studies, Collected Seminar Papers: The Societies of
Southern Africa in the Nineteenth and Twentieth Centu-
ries', vol.3.
BUNDY, C. (1974), 'Passing through a Period of Stress:
The Transkei Peasantry 1890-1914'. Paper presented to
Workshop on Social and Economic History of South Africa,
Oxford.
BUNDY, C. (1979), 'The Rise and Fall of the South African
Peasantry', Heinemann, London.
BURGESS, K. (1975), 'The Origins of British Industrial
Relations, Croom Helm, London.
CAMPBELL, P.C. (1923), 'Chinese Coolie Emigration to
Countries within the British Empire', P.C.King, London.
CARCHEDI, G. (1975), On the Economic Identification of
the New Middle Class, 'Economy and Society', vol.4, no.1.
CARTWRIGHT, A. (1893), South African Labour Question,
'Westminster Review', July.
CARTWRIGHT, A.P. (1963), 'The Gold Miners', Purcell,
London.
CARTWRIGHT, A.P. (1967), 'Gold Paved the Way', Macmillan,
London.
CARTWRIGHT, A.P. (1971), 'The First South Africans - The
Life and Times of Sir Percy Fitzpatrick', Purcell, London.
CONSOLIDATED GOLDFIELDS OF SOUTH AFRICA LTD (1937), 'The
Gold Fields, 1887-1937', London.
CRESWELL, F.H.P. (1902), The Transvaal Labour Problem,
'National Review', November.
DAVIS, R. (1976), Mining Capital and Unskilled White
Workers in South Africa 1901-13, 'Journal of Southern
African Studies', vol.3, no.1, October.
DE KIEWIET, C.W. (1942), 'A History of South Africa -
Social and Economic', The Clarendon Press, Oxford.
DE KOCK, M.H. (1924), 'Selected Subjects in the Economic
History of South Africa', Juta, Cape Town.
DENOON, D.J.N. (1967), The Transvaal Labour Crisis 1901-6,
'Journal of African History', vol.III, no.3.
DENOON, D.J.N. (1968), 'Capitalist Influence' and the

Transvaal Government during the Crown Colony Period,
1900-1906, 'Historical Journal', vol.XI, no.2, p.307.
DENOON, D.J.N. (1972), Participation in the Boer War,
People's War, People's Non-War, or Non-People's War?, in
B.A.Ogot (ed.), 'War and Society in Africa', F.Cass,
London.
DENOON, D.J.N. (1973), 'A Grand Illusion: The Failure of
Imperial Policy in the Transvaal Colony during the Period
of Reconstruction, 1900-1905', Longman, London.
DUFFY, J. (1962), 'Portugal in Africa', Penguin, Harmonds-
worth.
DUMINY, A.H. and GUEST, W.R. (1976), 'Fitzpatrick, South
African Politician, Selected Papers 1888-1906', McGraw-
Hill, Johannesburg.
DYER, E.J. (1903), The South African Labour Question,
'Contemporary Review', March.
FITZPATRICK, J.P. (1900), 'The Transvaal from Within: A
Private Record of Public Affairs', Heinemann, London.
FRANKEL, S.H. (1938), 'Capital Investment in Africa',
Oxford University Press, London.
FRANKEL, S.H. (1969), 'Gold and International Equity
Investment', Institute of Economic Affairs, London.
FRASER, M. and JEEVES, A. (1977), 'All That Glittered,
Selected Correspondence of Lionel Phillips 1890-1924',
Oxford University Press, Cape Town.
GERVASI, S. (1970), 'Industrialization, Foreign Capital
and Forced Labour in South Africa', United Nations, New
York.
GREEN, T. (1968), 'The World of Gold', Michael Joseph,
London.
GUYOT, Y. (1900), 'Boer Politics', John Murray, London.
HARRIES, P. (1977), Labour Migration from the Delagoa Bay
Hinterland to South Africa, 1852-1895, 'University of
London Institute of Commonwealth Studies, Collected
Seminar Papers No.21, The Societies of Southern Africa in
the Nineteenth and Twentieth Centuries', vol.7.
HATCH, F.H. and CHALMERS, J.A. (1895), The Gold Mines of
the Rand', Macmillan, London.
HEADLAM, C.G. (ed.) (1933), 'Milner Papers (South Africa)
1899-1905', vol.II, London.
HEPPLE, A. (1966), 'South Africa: A Political and Economic
History', Pall Mall Press, London.
HOBART HOUGHTON, D. (1964), 'The South African Economy',
Oxford University Press, Cape Town.
HOBART HOUGHTON, D. and DAGUT, J. (eds) (1972), 'Source
Material on the South African Economy, 1860-1970', vols II
and III, Oxford University Press, Cape Town.
HOBSBAWM, E.J. (1974), 'Labouring Men, Studies in the
History of Labour', Weidenfeld & Nicolson, London.

HOBSON, J.A. (1900), Capitalism, Imperialism and South Africa, 'Contemporary Review'.

HOBSON, J.A. (1900), 'The War in South Africa', James Nisbet, London.

HORWITZ, R. (1967), 'The Political Economy of South Africa', Weidenfeld & Nicolson, London.

JEEVES, A. (1975), The Control of Migratory Labour on the South African Gold Mines in the Era of Kruger and Milner, 'Journal of Southern African Studies', vol.2, no.1, October.

JOHNSTONE, F.A. (1976), 'Class, Race and Gold: A Study of Class Relations and Racial Discrimination in South Africa', Routledge & Kegan Paul, London.

JOHNSTONE, F.A. (1970), Class Conflict and Colour Bars in the South African Gold Mining Industry, 1910-1926, in 'University of London Institute of Commonwealth Studies Collected Seminar Papers', vol.I

KARIS, T. and CARTER, G. (eds) (1972), 'From Protest to Challenge: A Documentary History of African Politics in South Africa 1882-1964', Hoover Institution Press, Stanford University.

KATZ, E.N. (1976), 'A Trade Union Aristocracy', African Studies Institute, University of the Witwatersrand.

KOSS, S. (ed.) (1973), 'The Pro-Boers', University of Chicago Press.

KUBICEK, R.V. (1972), The Randlords in 1895: A Reassessment, 'Journal of British Studies', vol.XI.

KUBICEK, R.V. (1974), 'French Capitalism and British Imperialism: The Case of South African Gold Mining before 1914'. Unpublished postgraduate seminar paper, University of London Institute of Commonwealth Studies.

KUBICEK, R. (1975), Finance Capital and South African Gold Mining, 1886-1914, 'Journal of Imperial and Commonwealth History', vol.III, no.3.

LEGASSICK, M. (1971), 'Development and Underdevelopment in South Africa'. Unpublished seminar paper for the Southern Africa Group, Institute of International Affairs, London.

LEGASSICK, M. (1974), South Africa, Capital Accumulation and Violence, 'Economy and Society', vol.3, no.3.

LEGASSICK, M. (1975), South Africa: Forced Labour, Industrialization and Racial Differentiation, in Harris, R. (ed.), 'The Political Economy of South Africa', John Wiley and Sons, London.

Le MAY, G.H. (1965), 'British Supremacy in South Africa 1899-1907', The Clarendon Press, Oxford.

LETCHER, O. (1936), 'The Gold Mines of Southern Africa', Waterlow & Sons, London.

LEVY, N. (1978), Problems of Acquisition of Labour for the South African Gold Mining Industry: The Asian Labour

Alternative and the Defence of the Wage Structure,
'Southern African Research in Progress, Collected Papers
in Progress No.3'. Paper given at the Centre for
Southern African Studies, University of York.
MACMILLAN, W.M. (1930), 'Complex South Africa: An Economic
Footnote to History', Faber & Faber, London.
MARAIS, J.A. (1951), 'The Fall of Kruger's Republic', The
Clarendon Press, Oxford.
MARKS, S. (1970), 'Reluctant Rebellion: The 1906-1908
Disturbances in Natal', The Clarendon Press, Oxford.
MARQUARD, L. (1954), 'The Story of South Africa', Faber &
Faber, London.
MARX, K. (1972), 'Capital', vol.III, Lawrence & Wishart,
London.
MAWBY, A.A. (1974), Capital, Government and Politics in
the Transvaal 1900-1907: A Revision and a Reversion,
'Historical Journal', vol.XVII, no.2.
MEILLASSOUX, C. (1972), From Reproduction to Production,
'Economy and Society', vol.1, no.1.
MENDELSOHN, R. (1976), Blainey and the Jameson Raid: The
Debate Renewed, 'University of London Institute of
Commonwealth Studies Collected Seminar Papers: The
Societies of Southern Africa in the Nineteenth and
Twentieth Centuries'.
MOFFAT, J.S. (1901), South African Natives, 'Contemporary
Review', May.
MORONEY, S. (1976), 'Industrial Conflict in a Labour
Repressive Economy: Black Labour in the Transvaal Gold
Mines, 1901-12'. BA Hons thesis, University of the
Witwatersrand.
NEWBURY, C. (1975), Labour Migration in the Imperial
Phase: An Essay in Interpretation, 'Journal of Imperial
and Commonwealth History', vol.III, no.2, January.
NIMOCKS, W. (1970), 'Milner's Young Men', Hodder &
Stoughton, London.
PAKENHAM, T. (1979), 'The Boer War', Weidenfeld &
Nicolson, London.
PERRINGS, C. (1977), The Production Process, Industrial
Labour Strategies and Worker Responses in the Southern
African Gold Mining Industry, 'Journal of African
History', vol.XVIII, no.1.
PHILLIPS, MRS LIONEL (1899), 'Some South African Recol-
lections', Longmans Green & Co., London.
PHIMESTER, I.R. (1974), Rhodes, Rhodesia and the Rand,
'Journal of Southern African Studies', vol.1, no.1,
October.
PRAAGH, L.V. (ed.) (1906), 'The Transvaal and its Mines',
Praagh & Lloyd, London.
RICHARDSON, P. (1976), Coolies and Randlords: The North

Randfontein Chinese Miners' Strike of 1905, 'Journal of
Southern African Studies', vol.2, no.2, April.
RICHARDSON, P. (1977), The Recruiting of Chinese
Indentured Labour for the South African Gold Mines,
1903-1908, 'Journal of African History', vol.XVIII, no.l.
RICHARDSON, P. (1977), 'The Provision of Chinese
Indentured Labour for the Transvaal Gold Mines 1903-1908'.
Unpublished PhD thesis, University of London.
RICHARDSON, P. (1978), Coolies, Peasants and Proletarians:
The Origins of Chinese Labour in South Africa 1904-07,
'Southern African Research in Progress, Collected Papers
in Progress No.3'. Papers given at the Centre for
Southern African Studies, University of York.
ROBINSON, J. (1887), South Africa As It Is, 'Contemporary
Review', June.
ROBINSON, R.E., GALLAGHER, J. and DENNY (1961), 'Africa
and the Victorians', Macmillan, London.
ROSE, E.G. (1902), 'The Truth about the Transvaal',
Morning Leader Publications Dept, London.
ROUX, E. (1948), 'Time Longer than Rope', Gollancz,
London.
SCHAPERA, I. (1947), 'Migrant Labour and Tribal Life',
Oxford University Press, London.
SIMONS, H.J. (1961), Death in the South African Mines,
'Africa South', vol.5, no.4, July-September.
SIMONS, H.J. and SIMONS, R.E. (1969), 'Class and Colour
in South Africa 1850-1950', Penguin, Harmondsworth.
SIMSON, H. (1974), The Myth of the White Working Class in
South Africa, 'African Review', vol.4, no.2.
SOUTH AFRICAN NATIVES RACES COMMITTEE (ed.) (1901), 'The
Native Races of South Africa', John Murray, London.
SPENDER, J.A. (1923), 'The Life of the Rt. Hon. Sir H.
Campbell-Bannerman', Hodder & Stoughton, London.
SPIES, S.B. (1972), 'The Origins of the Anglo-Boer War',
Edward Arnold, London.
THOMPSON, L.M. (1960), 'The Unification of South Africa
1902-1910', The Clarendon Press, Oxford.
THOMSON, H.C. (1903), Kaffir Labour and Kaffir Marriage,
'Monthly Review', May.
TIKTIN, D. (1974), 'White Labour's Attitude, 1902-1904,
Towards the Importation of Indentured Chinese Labourers
by the Transvaal Chamber of Mines'. Paper presented to
the University of Cape Town Africa Research Seminar Group,
April.
TRANSVAAL CHAMBER OF MINES (1969), 'Gold in South Africa',
Transvaal Chamber of Mines, Johannesburg.
TRAPIDO, S. (1971), South Africa in a Comparative Study
of Industrialization, 'University of London Institute of
Commonwealth Studies Collected Seminar Papers: The

Societies of Southern Africa in the Nineteenth and
Twentieth Centuries', October 1970 - June 1971.
TRUSCOTT, S.J. (1898), 'The Witwatersrand Gold Fields,
Banket and Mining Practice', Macmillan, London.
VAN DER HORST, S. (1971), 'Native Labour in South Africa',
F.Cass, London.
VAN DER POEL, T. (1951), 'The Jameson Raid', Oxford
University Press, London.
VAN JAARSVELD, F.A. (1964), 'The Afrikaner's Interpreta-
tion of South African History', Simondium Publishers
(Pty), Cape Town.
VAN ONSELEN, C. (1972), Reaction to Rinderpest in Southern
Africa 1896-97, 'Journal of African History', vol.XIII,
no.3.
VAN ONSELEN, C. (1975), The Randlords and Rotgut
1886-1903, 'University of London Institute of Commonwealth
Studies Collected Seminar Papers: The Societies of
Southern Africa in the Nineteenth and Twentieth Centu-
ries', May.
VAN ONSELEN, C. (1976), 'Chibaro', Pluto Press, London.
VILLAR, P. (1976), 'A History of Gold and Money
1450-1920', New Left Books, London.
WALKER, E.A. (1964), 'A History of Southern Africa',
Longman, London.
WARWICK, P. (1975), African Labour during the South
African War 1899-1902, 'University of London Institute
of Commonwealth Studies Collected Seminar Papers: The
Societies of Southern Africa in the Nineteenth and
Twentieth Centuries', vol.7.
WILLIAMS, M. (1975), An Analysis of South African
Capitalism: Neo Ricardianism or Marxism, 'Bulletin of the
Conference of Socialist Economists', vol.IV, no.1.
WILSON, F. (1972), 'Migrant Labour in South Africa',
SACC & SPRO-CAS, Johannesburg.
WILSON, F. (1972), 'Labour in the South African Gold
Mines, 1911-69', Cambridge University Press.
WILSON, F. and PERROT, D. (eds) (1973), 'Outlook on a
Century: 1870-1970', SPRO-CAS, Lovedale Press, Johannes-
burg.
WILSON, M. and THOMPSON, L. (eds) (1971), 'The Oxford
History of South Africa', vol.II, The Clarendon Press,
Oxford.
WOLPE, H. (1972), Capitalism and Cheap Labour Power in
South Africa: from Segregation to Apartheid, 'Economy and
Society', vol.1.
WOLPE, H. (1975), The Theory of Internal Colonialism:
The South African Case, in I.Oxaal et al. (eds), 'Beyond
the Sociology of Development', Routledge & Kegan Paul,
London.

WOLPE, H. (1976), The 'White Working Class' in South
Africa, 'Economy and Society', vol.4, no.2.
WORSFOLD, W.B. (1895), 'South Africa: a Study in Colonial
Administration and Development', Methuen, London.

Index

accidents, 232
Acts: Glen Grey (1894),
   63,65,168;   Gold Law,
   75-6,100,109,111,132,
   289n;   Native Lands
   (1913), 35,63,193;
   Master and Servants Law
   (1889), 5,134,137,138;
   New Pass Law (1896), see
   Pass Law
African Labour League,
   201-4,206-13,215,220-1
'agitation' debates, see
   labour supply, Chinese
agriculture, African, 4,
   34-5,92;   post-war, 144,
   147-50,314-16n;   as in
   Transvaal Labour Com-
   mission, 174-7
Albu, G., 6-7,23,62-3,72,
   121
Albu Group, 210
Amalgamated Society of
   Engineers, 218-19
amortization, 133
Anglo-Boer War, 89,94,112;
   aims of, 102,115-16,126;
   causes of, 117-19;
   historiography of,
   118-27;   land settlement
   of, 313-14
Anglo French Exploration,
   106
apprenticeship system, 155,
   185-6

Arrighi, G., 190,196,205,
   328n
Asian labour, see labour
   supply, Chinese
Association of Mine
   Managers, see Mine
   Managers, Association of
Association of Mines, 81,
   84,88,91,120

Barnato, B., 106,120
Beit, A., 106
Beit, O., 106
Blainey, G., 107-8,299n
bribery, of Volksraad, 74
bride price, 68
Bundy, C., 35,144
Burawoy, M., 22,25

Campbell-Bannerman, Sir H.,
   229
capital, 26-7,104-5,107;
   agricultural fraction of,
   107;   deep-level fraction
   of, 102,104-6,122-5
capitalists: mining section
   of, 117,119,121-2,124-6,
   136;   non-mining section
   of, 109,111,125
Cartwright, A.P., 1,21,39,
   107,139,204
central recruiting organ-
   ization: formation of,

Routledge Social Science Series

Routledge & Kegan Paul   London, Henley and Boston

39 Store Street,
London WC1E 7DD
Broadway House,
Newtown Road,
Henley-on-Thames,
Oxon RG9 1EN
9 Park Street,
Boston, Mass. 02108

Contents

*Authors wishing to submit manuscripts for any series
in this catalogue should send them to the Social Science Editor,
Routledge & Kegan Paul Ltd, 39 Store Street,
London WC1E 7DD.*
● *Books so marked are available in paperback.*
○ *Books so marked are available in paperback only.*
*All books are in metric Demy 8vo format (216 × 138mm approx.)
unless otherwise stated.*

International Library of Sociology
General Editor John Rex

GENERAL SOCIOLOGY

Barnsley, J. H. The Social Reality of Ethics. *464 pp.*

Brown, Robert. Explanation in Social Science. *208 pp.*

● Rules and Laws in Sociology. *192 pp.*

Bruford, W. H. Chekhov and His Russia. *A Sociological Study. 244 pp.*

Burton, F. and **Carlen, P.** Official Discourse. *On Discourse Analysis, Government Publications, Ideology. About 140 pp.*

Cain, Maureen E. Society and the Policeman's Role. *326 pp.*

● **Fletcher, Colin.** Beneath the Surface. *An Account of Three Styles of Sociological Research. 221 pp.*

Gibson, Quentin. The Logic of Social Enquiry. *240 pp.*

Glassner, B. Essential Interactionism. *208 pp.*

Glucksmann, M. Structuralist Analysis in Contemporary Social Thought. *212 pp.*

Gurvitch, Georges. Sociology of Law. *Foreword by Roscoe Pound. 264 pp.*

Hinkle, R. Founding Theory of American Sociology 1881–1913. *About 350 pp.*

Homans, George C. Sentiments and Activities. *336 pp.*

Johnson, Harry M. Sociology: *A Systematic Introduction. Foreword by Robert K. Merton. 710 pp.*

● **Keat, Russell** and **Urry, John.** Social Theory as Science. *278 pp.*

Mannheim, Karl. Essays on Sociology and Social Psychology. *Edited by Paul Kecskemeti. With Editorial Note by Adolph Lowe. 344 pp.*

Martindale, Don. The Nature and Types of Sociological Theory. *292 pp.*

● **Maus, Heinz.** A Short History of Sociology. *234 pp.*

Myrdal, Gunnar. Value in Social Theory: *A Collection of Essays on Methodology. Edited by Paul Streeten. 332 pp.*

Ogburn, William F. and **Nimkoff, Meyer F.** A Handbook of Sociology. *Preface by Karl Mannheim. 656 pp. 46 figures. 35 tables.*

Parsons, Talcott and **Smelser, Neil J.** Economy and Society: *A Study in the Integration of Economic and Social Theory. 362 pp.*

Payne, G., Dingwall, R., Payne, J. and **Carter, M.** Sociology and Social Research. *About 250 pp.*

Podgórecki, A. Practical Social Sciences. *About 200 pp.*

Podgórecki, A. and **Łos, M.** Multidimensional Sociology. *268 pp.*

Raffel, S. Matters of Fact. *A Sociological Inquiry. 152 pp.*

● **Rex, John.** Key Problems of Sociological Theory. *220 pp.*

Sociology and the Demystification of the Modern World. *282 pp.*

● **Rex, John.** (Ed.) Approaches to Sociology. *Contributions by Peter Abell, Frank Bechhofer, Basil Bernstein, Ronald Fletcher, David Frisby, Miriam Glucksmann, Peter Lassman, Herminio Martins, John Rex, Roland Robertson, John Westergaard and Jock Young. 302 pp.*

Rigby, A. Alternative Realities. *352 pp.*

Roche, M. Phenomenology, Language and the Social Sciences. *374 pp.*

Sahay, A. Sociological Analysis. *220 pp.*

Strasser, Hermann. The Normative Structure of Sociology. *Conservative and Emancipatory Themes in Social Thought. About 340 pp.*

Strong, P. Ceremonial Order of the Clinic. *267 pp.*

Urry, John. Reference Groups and the Theory of Revolution. *244 pp.*

Weinberg, E. Development of Sociology in the Soviet Union. *173 pp.*

FOREIGN CLASSICS OF SOCIOLOGY

● **Gerth, H. H.** and **Mills, C. Wright.** From Max Weber: *Essays in Sociology. 502 pp.*

● **Tönnies, Ferdinand.** Community and Association *(Gemeinschaft und Gesell-schaft).\Translated and Supplemented by Charles P. Loomis. Foreword by Pitirim A. Sorokin. 334 pp.*

SOCIAL STRUCTURE

Andreski, Stanislav. Military Organization and Society. *Foreword by Professor A. R. Radcliffe-Brown. 226 pp. 1 folder.*

Broom, L., Lancaster Jones, F., McDonnell, P. and **Williams, T.** The Inheritance of Inequality. *About 180 pp.*

Carlton, Eric. Ideology and Social Order. *Foreword by Professor Philip Abrahams. About 320 pp.*

Clegg, S. and **Dunkerley, D.** Organization, Class and Control. *614 pp.*

Coontz, Sydney H. Population Theories and the Economic Interpretation. *202 pp.*

Coser, Lewis. The Functions of Social Conflict. *204 pp.*

Crook, I. and **D.** The First Years of the Yangyi Commune. *304 pp., illustrated.*

Dickie-Clark, H. F. Marginal Situation: *A Sociological Study of a Coloured Group. 240 pp. 11 tables.*

Giner, S. and **Archer, M. S.** (Eds) Contemporary Europe: *Social Structures and Cultural Patterns, 336 pp.*

● **Glaser, Barney** and **Strauss, Anselm L.** Status Passage: *A Formal Theory. 212 pp.*

Glass, D. V. (Ed.) Social Mobility in Britain. *Contributions by J. Berent, T. Bottomore, R. C. Chambers, J. Floud, D. V. Glass, J. R. Hall, H. T. Himmelweit, R. K. Kelsall, F. M. Martin, C. A. Moser, R. Mukherjee and W. Ziegel. 420 pp.*

Kelsall, R. K. Higher Civil Servants in Britain: *From 1870 to the Present Day. 268 pp. 31 tables.*

● **Lawton, Denis.** Social Class, Language and Education. *192 pp.*

McLeish, John. The Theory of Social Change: *Four Views Considered. 128 pp.*

● **Marsh, David C.** The Changing Social Structure of England and Wales, 1871–1961. *Revised edition. 288 pp.*

Menzies, Ken. Talcott Parsons and the Social Image of Man. *About 208 pp.*

● **Mouzelis, Nicos.** Organization and Bureaucracy. *An Analysis of Modern Theories. 240 pp.*

● **Ossowski, Stanislaw.** Class Structure in the Social Consciousness. *210 pp.*

● **Podgórecki, Adam.** Law and Society. *302 pp.*

Renner, Karl. Institutions of Private Law and Their Social Functions. *Edited, with an Introduction and Notes, by O. Kahn-Freud. Translated by Agnes Schwarzschild. 316 pp.*

Rex, J. and **Tomlinson, S.** Colonial Immigrants in a British City. *A Class Analysis. 368 pp.*

Smooha, S. Israel: Pluralism and Conflict. *472 pp.*

Wesolowski, W. Class, Strata and Power. *Trans. and with Introduction by G. Kolankiewicz. 160 pp.*

Zureik, E. Palestinians in Israel. *A Study in Internal Colonialism. 264 pp.*

SOCIOLOGY AND POLITICS

Acton, T. A. Gypsy Politics and Social Change. *316 pp.*

Burton, F. Politics of Legitimacy. *Struggles in a Belfast Community. 250 pp.*

Crook, I. and **D.** Revolution in a Chinese Village. *Ten Mile Inn. 216 pp., illustrated.*

Etzioni-Halevy, E. Political Manipulation and Administrative Power. *A Comparative Study. About 200 pp.*

Fielding, N. The National Front. *About 250 pp.*

● **Hechter, Michael.** Internal Colonialism. *The Celtic Fringe in British National Development, 1536–1966. 380 pp.*

Kornhauser, William. The Politics of Mass Society. *272 pp. 20 tables.*

4

Korpi, W. The Working Class in Welfare Capitalism. *Work, Unions and Politics in Sweden. 472 pp.*

Kroes, R. Soldiers and Students. *A Study of Right- and Left-wing Students. 174 pp.*

Martin, Roderick. Sociology of Power. *About 272 pp.*

Merquior, J. G. Rousseau and Weber. *A Study in the Theory of Legitimacy. About 288 pp.*

Myrdal, Gunnar. The Political Element in the Development of Economic Theory. *Translated from the German by Paul Streeten. 282 pp.*

Varma, B. N. The Sociology and Politics of Development. *A Theoretical Study. 236 pp.*

Wong, S.-L. Sociology and Socialism in Contemporary China. *160 pp.*

Wootton, Graham. Workers, Unions and the State. *188 pp.*

CRIMINOLOGY

Ancel, Marc. Social Defence: *A Modern Approach to Criminal Problems. Foreword by Leon Radzinowicz. 240 pp.*

Athens, L. Violent Criminal Acts and Actors. *104 pp.*

Cain, Maureen E. Society and the Policeman's Role. *326 pp.*

Cloward, Richard A. and Ohlin, Lloyd E. Delinquency and Opportunity: *A Theory of Delinquent Gangs. 248 pp.*

Downes, David M. The Delinquent Solution. *A Study in Subcultural Theory. 296 pp.*

Friedlander, Kate. The Psycho-Analytical Approach to Juvenile Delinquency: *Theory, Case Studies, Treatment. 320 pp.*

Gleuck, Sheldon and Eleanor. Family Environment and Delinquency. *With the statistical assistance of Rose W. Kneznek. 340 pp.*

Lopez-Rey, Manuel. Crime. *An Analytical Appraisal. 288 pp.*

Mannheim, Hermann. Comparative Criminology: *A Text Book. Two volumes. 442 pp. and 380 pp.*

Morris, Terence. The Criminal Area: *A Study in Social Ecology. Foreword by Hermann Mannheim. 232 pp. 25 tables. 4 maps.*

Rock, Paul. Making People Pay. *338 pp.*

● Taylor, Ian, Walton, Paul and Young, Jock. The New Criminology. *For a Social Theory of Deviance. 325 pp.*

● Taylor, Ian, Walton, Paul and Young, Jock. (Eds) Critical Criminology. *268 pp.*

SOCIAL PSYCHOLOGY

Bagley, Christopher. The Social Psychology of the Epileptic Child. *320 pp.*

Brittan, Arthur. Meanings and Situations. *224 pp.*

Carroll, J. Break-Out from the Crystal Palace. *200 pp.*

● Fleming, C. M. Adolescence: Its Social Psychology. *With an Introduction to recent findings from the fields of Anthropology, Physiology, Medicine, Psychometrics and Sociometry. 288 pp.*

● The Social Psychology of Education: *An Introduction and Guide to Its Study. 136 pp.*

Linton, Ralph. The Cultural Background of Personality. *132 pp.*

● Mayo, Elton. The Social Problems of an Industrial Civilization. *With an Appendix on the Political Problem. 180 pp.*

Ottaway, A. K. C. Learning Through Group Experience. *176 pp.*

Plummer, Ken. Sexual Stigma. *An Interactionist Account. 254 pp.*

● Rose, Arnold M. (Ed.) Human Behaviour and Social Processes: *an Interactionist Approach. Contributions by Arnold M. Rose, Ralph H. Turner, Anselm Strauss, Everett C. Hughes, E. Franklin Frazier, Howard S. Becker et al. 696 pp.*

Smelser, Neil J. Theory of Collective Behaviour. *448 pp.*

Stephenson, Geoffrey M. The Development of Conscience. *128 pp.*

Young, Kimball. Handbook of Social Psychology. *658 pp. 16 figures. 10 tables.*

SOCIOLOGY OF THE FAMILY

Bell, Colin R. Middle Class Families: *Social and Geographical Mobility. 224 pp.*
Burton, Lindy. Vulnerable Children. *272 pp.*
Gavron, Hannah. The Captive Wife: *Conflicts of Household Mothers. 190 pp.*
George, Victor and **Wilding, Paul.** Motherless Families. *248 pp.*
Klein, Josephine. Samples from English Cultures.
    1. Three Preliminary Studies and Aspects of Adult Life in England. *447 pp.*
    2. Child-Rearing Practices and Index. *247 pp.*
Klein, Viola. The Feminine Character. *History of an Ideology. 244 pp.*
McWhinnie, Alexina M. Adopted Children. *How They Grow Up. 304 pp.*
● **Morgan, D. H. J.** Social Theory and the Family. *About 320 pp.*
● **Myrdal, Alva** and **Klein, Viola.** Women's Two Roles: *Home and Work. 238 pp.*
    27 tables.
Parsons, Talcott and **Bales, Robert F.** Family: Socialization and Interaction Process.
    In collaboration with James Olds, Morris Zelditch and Philip E. Slater. 456 pp.
    50 figures and tables.

SOCIAL SERVICES

Bastide, Roger. The Sociology of Mental Disorder. *Translated from the French by*
    Jean McNeil. 260 pp.
Carlebach, Julius. Caring For Children in Trouble. *266 pp.*
George, Victor. Foster Care. *Theory and Practice. 234 pp.*
    Social Security: *Beveridge and After. 258 pp.*
George, V. and **Wilding, P.** Motherless Families. *248 pp.*
● **Goetschius, George W.** Working with Community Groups. *256 pp.*
Goetschius, George W. and **Tash, Joan.** Working with Unattached Youth. *416 pp.*
Heywood, Jean S. Children in Care. *The Development of the Service for the Deprived*
    Child. Third revised edition. 284 pp.
King, Roy D., Ranes, Norma V. and **Tizard, Jack.** Patterns of Residential Care.
    356 pp.
Leigh, John. Young People and Leisure. *256 pp.*
● **Mays, John.** (Ed.) Penelope Hall's Social Services of England and Wales.
    368 pp.
Morris, Mary. Voluntary Work and the Welfare State. *300 pp.*
Nokes, P. L. The Professional Task in Welfare Practice. *152 pp.*
Timms, Noel. Psychiatric Social Work in Great Britain (1939–1962). *280 pp.*
●   Social Casework: *Principles and Practice. 256 pp.*

SOCIOLOGY OF EDUCATION

Banks, Olive. Parity and Prestige in English Secondary Education: a Study in
    Educational Sociology. *272 pp.*
● **Blyth, W. A. L.** English Primary Education. *A Sociological Description.*
    2. Background. *168 pp.*
Collier, K. G. The Social Purposes of Education: *Personal and Social Values in*
    Education. 268 pp.
Evans, K. M. Sociometry and Education. *158 pp.*
● **Ford, Julienne.** Social Class and the Comprehensive School. *192 pp.*
Foster, P. J. Education and Social Change in Ghana. *336 pp. 3 maps.*
Fraser, W. R. Education and Society in Modern France. *150 pp.*
Grace, Gerald R. Role Conflict and the Teacher. *150 pp.*
Hans, Nicholas. New Trends in Education in the Eighteenth Century. *278 pp.*
    19 tables.
●   Comparative Education: *A Study of Educational Factors and Traditions. 360 pp.*
● **Hargreaves, David.** Interpersonal Relations and Education. *432 pp.*
●   Social Relations in a Secondary School. *240 pp.*
    School Organization and Pupil Involvement. *A Study of Secondary Schools.*

● **Mannheim, Karl** and **Stewart, W. A. C.** An Introduction to the Sociology of Education. *206 pp.*
● **Musgrove, F.** Youth and the Social Order. *176 pp.*
● **Ottaway, A. K. C.** Education and Society: An Introduction to the Sociology of Education. *With an Introduction by W. O. Lester Smith. 212 pp.*
Peers, Robert. Adult Education: *A Comparative Study. Revised edition. 398 pp.*
Stratta, Erica. The Education of Borstal Boys. *A Study of their Educational Experiences prior to, and during, Borstal Training. 256 pp.*
● **Taylor, P. H., Reid, W. A.** and **Holley, B. J.** The English Sixth Form. *A Case Study in Curriculum Research. 198 pp.*

SOCIOLOGY OF CULTURE

Eppel, E. M. and **M.** Adolescents and Morality: *A Study of some Moral Values and Dilemmas of Working Adolescents in the Context of a changing Climate of Opinion. Foreword by W. J. H. Sprott. 268 pp. 39 tables.*
● **Fromm, Erich.** The Fear of Freedom. *286 pp.*
● The Sane Society. *400 pp.*
Johnson, L. The Cultural Critics. *From Matthew Arnold to Raymond Williams. 233 pp.*
Mannheim, Karl. Essays on the Sociology of Culture. *Edited by Ernst Mannheim in co-operation with Paul Kecskemeti. Editorial Note by Adolph Lowe. 280 pp.*
Merquior, J. G. The Veil and the Mask. *Essays on Culture and Ideology. Foreword by Ernest Gellner. 140 pp.*
Zijderfeld, A. C. On Clichés. *The Supersedure of Meaning by Function in Modernity. 150 pp.*

SOCIOLOGY OF RELIGION

Argyle, Michael and **Beit-Hallahmi, Benjamin.** The Social Psychology of Religion. *256 pp.*
Glasner, Peter E. The Sociology of Secularisation. *A Critique of a Concept. 146 pp.*
Hall, J. R. The Ways Out. *Utopian Communal Groups in an Age of Babylon. 280 pp.*
Ranson, S., Hinings, B. and **Bryman, A.** Clergy, Ministers and Priests. *216 pp.*
Stark, Werner. The Sociology of Religion. *A Study of Christendom.*
  Volume II. *Sectarian Religion. 368 pp.*
  Volume III. *The Universal Church. 464 pp.*
  Volume IV. *Types of Religious Man. 352 pp.*
  Volume V. *Types of Religious Culture. 464 pp.*
Turner, B. S. Weber and Islam. *216 pp.*
Watt, W. Montgomery. Islam and the Integration of Society. *320 pp.*

SOCIOLOGY OF ART AND LITERATURE

Jarvie, Ian C. Towards a Sociology of the Cinema. *A Comparative Essay on the Structure and Functioning of a Major Entertainment Industry. 405 pp.*
Rust, Frances S. Dance in Society. *An Analysis of the Relationships between the Social Dance and Society in England from the Middle Ages to the Present Day. 256 pp. 8 pp. of plates.*
Schücking, L. L. The Sociology of Literary Taste. *112 pp.*
Wolff, Janet. Hermeneutic Philosophy and the Sociology of Art. *150 pp.*

SOCIOLOGY OF KNOWLEDGE

Diesing, P. Patterns of Discovery in the Social Sciences. *262 pp.*

● **Douglas, J. D.** (Ed.) Understanding Everyday Life. *370 pp.*
● **Hamilton, P.** Knowledge and Social Structure. *174 pp.*
  Jarvie, I. C. Concepts and Society. *232 pp.*
  Mannheim, Karl. Essays on the Sociology of Knowledge. *Edited by Paul Kecskemeti. Editorial Note by Adolph Lowe. 353 pp.*
  Remmling, Gunter W. The Sociology of Karl Mannheim. *With a Bibliographical Guide to the Sociology of Knowledge, Ideological Analysis, and Social Planning. 255 pp.*
  Remmling, Gunter W. (Ed.) Towards the Sociology of Knowledge. *Origin and Development of a Sociological Thought Style. 463 pp.*
  Scheler, M. Problems of a Sociology of Knowledge. *Trans. by M. S. Frings. Edited and with an Introduction by K. Stikkers. 232 pp.*

URBAN SOCIOLOGY

  Aldridge, M. The British New Towns. *A Programme Without a Policy. 232 pp.*
  Ashworth, William. The Genesis of Modern British Town Planning: *A Study in Economic and Social History of the Nineteenth and Twentieth Centuries. 288 pp.*
  Brittan, A. The Privatised World. *196 pp.*
  Cullingworth, J. B. Housing Needs and Planning Policy: *A Restatement of the Problems of Housing Need and 'Overspill' in England and Wales. 232 pp. 44 tables. 8 maps.*
  Dickinson, Robert E. City and Region: *A Geographical Interpretation. 608 pp. 125 figures.*
    The West European City: *A Geographical Interpretation. 600 pp. 129 maps. 29 plates.*
  Humphreys, Alexander J. New Dubliners: *Urbanization and the Irish Family. Foreword by George C. Homans. 304 pp.*
  Jackson, Brian. Working Class Community: *Some General Notions raised by a Series of Studies in Northern England. 192 pp.*
● **Mann, P. H.** An Approach to Urban Sociology. *240 pp.*
  Mellor, J. R. Urban Sociology in an Urbanized Society. *326 pp.*
  Morris, R. N. and **Mogey, J.** The Sociology of Housing. *Studies at Berinsfield. 232 pp. 4 pp. plates.*
  Mullan, R. Stevenage Ltd. *About 250 pp.*
  Rex, J. and **Tomlinson, S.** Colonial Immigrants in a British City. *A Class Analysis. 368 pp.*
  Rosser, C. and **Harris, C.** The Family and Social Change. *A Study of Family and Kinship in a South Wales Town. 352 pp. 8 maps.*
● **Stacey, Margaret, Batsone, Eric, Bell, Colin** and **Thurcott, Anne.** Power, Persistence and Change. *A Second Study of Banbury. 196 pp.*

RURAL SOCIOLOGY

  Mayer, Adrian C. Peasants in the Pacific. *A Study of Fiji Indian Rural Society. 248 pp. 20 plates.*
  Williams, W. M. The Sociology of an English Village: *Gosforth. 272 pp. 12 figures. 13 tables.*

SOCIOLOGY OF INDUSTRY AND DISTRIBUTION

  Dunkerley, David. The Foreman. *Aspects of Task and Structure. 192 pp.*
  Eldridge, J. E. T. Industrial Disputes. *Essays in the Sociology of Industrial Relations. 288 pp.*
  Hollowell, Peter G. The Lorry Driver. *272 pp.*
● **Oxaal, I., Barnett, T.** and **Booth, D.** (Eds) Beyond the Sociology of Development.

8

Economy and Society in Latin America and Africa. 295 pp.

Smelser, Neil J. Social Change in the Industrial Revolution: *An Application of Theory to the Lancashire Cotton Industry, 1770–1840. 468 pp. 12 figures. 14 tables.*

Watson, T. J. The Personnel Managers. *A Study in the Sociology of Work and Employment, 262 pp.*

ANTHROPOLOGY

Brandel-Syrier, Mia. Reeftown Elite. *A Study of Social Mobility in a Modern African Community on the Reef. 376 pp.*

Dickie-Clark, H. F. The Marginal Situation. *A Sociological Study of a Coloured Group. 236 pp.*

Dube, S. C. Indian Village. *Foreword by Morris Edward Opler. 276 pp. 4 plates.*
  India's Changing Villages: *Human Factors in Community Development. 260 pp. 8 plates. 1 map.*

Fei, H.-T. Peasant Life in China. *A Field Study of Country Life in the Yangtze Valley. With a foreword by Bronislaw Malinowski. 328 pp. 16 pp. plates.*

Firth, Raymond. Malay Fishermen. *Their Peasant Economy. 420 pp. 17 pp. plates.*

Gulliver, P. H. Social Control in an African Society: a Study of the Arusha, Agricultural Masai of Northern Tanganyika. *320 pp. 8 plates. 10 figures.*
  Family Herds. *288 pp.*

Jarvie, Ian C. The Revolution in Anthropology. *268 pp.*

Little, Kenneth L. Mende of Sierra Leone. *308 pp. and folder.*
  Negroes in Britain. *With a New Introduction and Contemporary Study by Leonard Bloom. 320 pp.*

Tambs-Lyche, H. London Patidars. *About 180 pp.*

Madan, G. R. Western Sociologists on Indian Society. *Marx, Spencer, Weber, Durkheim, Pareto. 384 pp.*

Mayer, A. C. Peasants in the Pacific. *A Study of Fiji Indian Rural Society. 248 pp.*

Meer, Fatima. Race and Suicide in South Africa. *325 pp.*

Smith, Raymond T. The Negro Family in British Guiana: *Family Structure and Social Status in the Villages. With a Foreword by Meyer Fortes. 314 pp. 8 plates. 1 figure. 4 maps.*

SOCIOLOGY AND PHILOSOPHY

Adriaansens, H. Talcott Parsons and the Conceptual Dilemma. *About 224 pp.*

Barnsley, John H. The Social Reality of Ethics. *A Comparative Analysis of Moral Codes. 448 pp.*

Diesing, Paul. Patterns of Discovery in the Social Sciences. *362 pp.*

● **Douglas, Jack D.** (Ed.) Understanding Everyday Life. *Toward the Reconstruction of Sociological Knowledge. Contributions by Alan F. Blum, Aaron W. Cicourel, Norman K. Denzin, Jack D. Douglas, John Heeren, Peter McHugh, Peter K. Manning, Melvin Power, Matthew Speier, Roy Turner, D. Lawrence Wieder, Thomas P. Wilson and Don H. Zimmerman. 370 pp.*

Gorman, Robert A. The Dual Vision. *Alfred Schutz and the Myth of Phenomenological Social Science. 240 pp.*

Jarvie, Ian C. Concepts and Society. *216 pp.*

Kilminster, R. Praxis and Method. *A Sociological Dialogue with Lukács, Gramsci and the Early Frankfurt School. 334 pp.*

● **Pelz, Werner.** The Scope of Understanding in Sociology. *Towards a More Radical Reorientation in the Social Humanistic Sciences. 283 pp.*

Roche, Maurice. Phenomenology, Language and the Social Sciences. *371 pp.*

Sahay, Arun. Sociological Analysis. *212 pp.*

● **Slater, P.** Origin and Significance of the Frankfurt School. *A Marxist Perspective. 185 pp.*

Spurling, L. Phenomenology and the Social World. *The Philosophy of Merleau-Ponty and its Relation to the Social Sciences. 222 pp.*

Wilson, H. T. The American Ideology. *Science, Technology and Organization as Modes of Rationality. 368 pp.*

International Library of Anthropology
General Editor Adam Kuper

● Ahmed, A. S. Millennium and Charisma Among Pathans. *A Critical Essay in Social Anthropology. 192 pp.*
Pukhtun Economy and Society. *Traditional Structure and Economic Development. About 360 pp.*

Barth, F. Selected Essays. *Volume I. About 250 pp.* Selected Essays. *Volume II. About 250 pp.*

Brown, Paula. The Chimbu. *A Study of Change in the New Guinea Highlands. 151 pp.*

Foner, N. Jamaica Farewell. *200 pp.*

Gudeman, Stephen. Relationships, Residence and the Individual. *A Rural Panamanian Community. 288 pp. 11 plates, 5 figures, 2 maps, 10 tables.*
The Demise of a Rural Economy. *From Subsistence to Capitalism in a Latin American Village. 160 pp.*

Hamnett, Ian. Chieftainship and Legitimacy. *An Anthropological Study of Executive Law in Lesotho. 163 pp.*

Hanson, F. Allan. Meaning in Culture. *127 pp.*

Hazan, H. The Limbo People. *A Study of the Constitution of the Time Universe Among the Aged. About 192 pp.*

Humphreys, S. C. Anthropology and the Greeks. *288 pp.*

Karp, I. Fields of Change Among the Iteso of Kenya. *140 pp.*

Lloyd, P. C. Power and Independence. *Urban Africans' Perception of Social Inequality. 264 pp.*

Parry, J. P. Caste and Kinship in Kangra. *352 pp. Illustrated.*

Pettigrew, Joyce. Robber Noblemen. *A Study of the Political System of the Sikh Jats. 284 pp.*

Street, Brian V. The Savage in Literature. *Representations of 'Primitive' Society in English Fiction, 1858–1920. 207 pp.*

Van Den Berghe, Pierre L. Power and Privilege at an African University. *278 pp.*

International Library of Phenomenology and Moral Sciences
General Editor John O'Neill

Apel, K.-O. Towards a Transformation of Philosophy. *308 pp.*

Bologh, R. W. Dialectical Phenomenology. *Marx's Method. 287 pp.*

Fekete, J. The Critical Twilight. *Explorations in the Ideology of Anglo-American Literary Theory from Eliot to McLuhan. 300 pp.*

Medina, A. Reflection, Time and the Novel. *Towards a Communicative Theory of Literature. 143 pp.*

International Library of Social Policy
General Editor Kathleen Jones

Bayley, M. Mental Handicap and Community Care. *426 pp.*

Bottoms, A. E. and McClean, J. D. Defendants in the Criminal Process. *284 pp.*

Bradshaw, J. The Family Fund. *An Initiative in Social Policy. About 224 pp.*

Butler, J. R. Family Doctors and Public Policy. *208 pp.*
Davies, Martin. Prisoners of Society. *Attitudes and Aftercare. 204 pp.*
Gittus, Elizabeth. Flats, Families and the Under-Fives. *285 pp.*
Holman, Robert. Trading in Children. *A Study of Private Fostering. 355 pp.*
Jeffs, A. Young People and the Youth Service. *160 pp.*
Jones, Howard and Cornes, Paul. Open Prisons. *288 pp.*
Jones, Kathleen. History of the Mental Health Service. *428 pp.*
Jones, Kathleen with **Brown, John, Cunningham, W. J., Roberts, Julian** and
   Williams, Peter. Opening the Door. *A Study of New Policies for the Mentally
   Handicapped. 278 pp.*
Karn, Valerie. Retiring to the Seaside. *400 pp. 2 maps. Numerous tables.*
King, R. D. and **Elliot, K. W.** Albany: Birth of a Prison—End of an Era. *394 pp.*
Thomas, J. E. The English Prison Officer since 1850: *A Study in Conflict. 258 pp.*
Walton, R. G. Women in Social Work. *303 pp.*
● **Woodward, J.** To Do the Sick No Harm. *A Study of the British Voluntary Hospital
   System to 1875. 234 pp.*

International Library of Welfare and Philosophy
General Editors   Noel Timms and David Watson

● **McDermott, F. E.** (Ed.) Self-Determination in Social Work. *A Collection of Essays
   on Self-determination and Related Concepts by Philosophers and Social Work
   Theorists. Contributors: F. P. Biestek, S. Bernstein, A. Keith-Lucas, D. Sayer,
   H. H. Perelman, C. Whittington, R. F. Stalley, F. E. McDermott, I. Berlin, H. J.
   McCloskey, H. L. A. Hart, J. Wilson, A. I. Melden, S. I. Benn. 254 pp.*
● **Plant, Raymond.** Community and Ideology. *104 pp.*
Ragg, Nicholas M. People Not Cases. *A Philosophical Approach to Social Work.
   168 pp.*
● **Timms, Noel** and **Watson, David.** (Eds) Talking About Welfare. *Readings in
   Philosophy and Social Policy. Contributors: T. H. Marshall, R. B. Brandt, G. H.
   von Wright, K. Nielsen, M. Cranston, R. M. Titmuss, R. S. Downie, E. Telfer, D.
   Donnison, J. Benson, P. Leonard, A. Keith-Lucas, D. Walsh, I. T. Ramsey.
   320 pp.*
● Philosophy in Social Work. *250 pp.*
● **Weale, A.** Equality and Social Policy. *164 pp.*

Library of Social Work
General Editor   Noel Timms

● **Baldock, Peter.** Community Work and Social Work. *140 pp.*
○ **Beedell, Christopher.** Residential Life with Children. *210 pp. Crown 8vo.*
● **Berry, Juliet.** Daily Experience in Residential Life. *A Study of Children and their
   Care-givers. 202 pp.*
○ Social Work with Children. *190 pp. Crown 8vo.*
● **Brearley, C. Paul.** Residential Work with the Elderly. *116 pp.*
● Social Work, Ageing and Society. *126 pp.*
● **Cheetham, Juliet.** Social Work with Immigrants. *240 pp. Crown 8vo.*
● **Cross, Crispin P.** (Ed.) Interviewing and Communication in Social Work.
   *Contributions by C. P. Cross, D. Laurenson, B. Strutt, S. Raven. 192 pp. Crown
   8vo.*

- **Curnock, Kathleen** and **Hardiker, Pauline.** Towards Practice Theory. *Skills and Methods in Social Assessments. 208 pp.*
- **Davies, Bernard.** The Use of Groups in Social Work Practice. *158 pp.*
- **Davies, Martin.** Support Systems in Social Work. *144 pp.*
- **Ellis, June.** (Ed.) West African Families in Britain. *A Meeting of Two Cultures. Contributions by Pat Stapleton, Vivien Biggs. 150 pp. 1 Map.*
- **Hart, John.** Social Work and Sexual Conduct. *230 pp.*
- **Hutten, Joan M.** Short-Term Contracts in Social Work. *Contributions by Stella M. Hall, Elsie Osborne, Mannie Sher, Eva Sternberg, Elizabeth Tuters. 134 pp.*
- **Jackson, Michael P.** and **Valencia, B. Michael.** Financial Aid Through Social Work. *140 pp.*
- **Jones, Howard.** The Residential Community. *A Setting for Social Work. 150 pp.*
- (Ed.) Towards a New Social Work. *Contributions by Howard Jones, D. A. Fowler, J. R. Cypher, R. G. Walton, Geoffrey Mungham, Philip Priestley, Ian Shaw, M. Bartley, R. Deacon, Irwin Epstein, Geoffrey Pearson. 184 pp.*
- **Jones, Ray** and **Pritchard, Colin.** (Eds) Social Work With Adolescents. *Contributions by Ray Jones, Colin Pritchard, Jack Dunham, Florence Rossetti, Andrew Kerslake, John Burns, William Gregory, Graham Templeman, Kenneth E. Reid, Audrey Taylor. About 170 pp.*
- ○ **Jordon, William.** The Social Worker in Family Situations. *160 pp. Crown 8vo.*
- **Laycock, A. L.** Adolescents and Social Work. *128 pp. Crown 8vo.*
- **Lees, Ray.** Politics and Social Work. *128 pp. Crown 8vo.*
- Research Strategies for Social Welfare. *112 pp. Tables.*
- ○ **McCullough, M. K.** and **Ely, Peter J.** Social Work with Groups. *127 pp. Crown 8vo.*
- **Moffett, Jonathan.** Concepts in Casework Treatment. *128 pp. Crown 8vo.*
- **Parsloe, Phyllida.** Juvenile Justice in Britain and the United States. *The Balance of Needs and Rights. 336 pp.*
- **Plant, Raymond.** Social and Moral Theory in Casework. *112 pp. Crown 8vo.*
- **Priestley, Philip, Fears, Denise** and **Fuller, Roger.** Justice for Juveniles. *The 1969 Children and Young Persons Act: A Case for Reform? 128 pp.*
- **Pritchard, Colin** and **Taylor, Richard.** Social Work: Reform or Revolution? *170 pp.*
- ○ **Pugh, Elisabeth.** Social Work in Child Care. *128 pp. Crown 8vo.*
- **Robinson, Margaret.** Schools and Social Work. *282 pp.*
- ○ **Ruddock, Ralph.** Roles and Relationships. *128 pp. Crown 8vo.*
- **Sainsbury, Eric.** Social Diagnosis in Casework. *118 pp. Crown 8vo.*
- Social Work with Families. *Perceptions of Social Casework among Clients of a Family Service. 188 pp.*
- **Seed, Philip.** The Expansion of Social Work in Britain. *128 pp. Crown 8vo.*
- **Shaw, John.** The Self in Social Work. *124 pp.*
- **Smale, Gerald G.** Prophecy, Behaviour and Change. *An Examination of Self-fulfilling Prophecies in Helping Relationships. 116 pp. Crown 8vo.*
- **Smith, Gilbert.** Social Need. *Policy, Practice and Research. 155 pp.*
- Social Work and the Sociology of Organisations. *124 pp. Revised edition.*
- **Sutton, Carole.** Psychology for Social Workers and Counsellors. *An Introduction. 248 pp.*
- **Timms, Noel.** Language of Social Casework. *122 pp. Crown 8vo.*
- Recording in Social Work. *124 pp. Crown 8vo.*
- **Todd, F. Joan.** Social Work with the Mentally Subnormal. *96 pp. Crown 8vo.*
- **Walrond-Skinner, Sue.** Family Therapy. *The Treatment of Natural Systems. 172 pp.*
- **Warham, Joyce.** An Introduction to Administration for Social Workers. *Revised edition. 112 pp.*
- An Open Case. *The Organisational Context of Social Work. 172 pp.*
- ○ **Wittenberg, Isca Salzberger.** Psycho-Analytic Insight and Relationships. *A Kleinian Approach. 196 pp. Crown 8vo.*

Primary Socialization, Language and Education
General Editor   Basil Bernstein

Adlam, Diana S., *with the assistance of Geoffrey Turner and Lesley Lineker.* Code in *Context. 272 pp.*

Bernstein, Basil. Class, Codes and Control. *3 volumes.*
● 1. *Theoretical Studies Towards a Sociology of Language. 254 pp.*
 2. *Applied Studies Towards a Sociology of Language. 377 pp.*
● 3. *Towards a Theory of Educational Transmission. 167 pp.*

Brandis, W. and **Bernstein, B.** Selection and Control. *176 pp.*

Brandis, Walter and **Henderson, Dorothy.** Social Class, Language and Communi-cation. *288 pp.*

Cook-Gumperz, Jenny. Social Control and Socialization. *A Study of Class Differences in the Language of Maternal Control. 290 pp.*

● **Gahagan, D. M.** and **G. A.** Talk Reform. *Exploration in Language for Infant School Children. 160 pp.*

Hawkins, P. R. Social Class, the Nominal Group and Verbal Strategies. *About 220 pp.*

Robinson, W. P. and **Rackstraw, Susan D. A.** A Question of Answers. *2 volumes. 192 pp. and 180 pp.*

Turner, Geoffrey J. and **Mohan, Bernard A.** A Linguistic Description and Computer Programme for Children's Speech. *208 pp.*

Reports of the Institute of Community Studies

Baker, J. The Neighbourhood Advice Centre. A Community Project in Camden. *320 pp.*

● **Cartwright, Ann.** Patients and their Doctors. *A Study of General Practice. 304 pp.*

Dench, Geoff. Maltese in London. *A Case-study in the Erosion of Ethnic Conscious-ness. 302 pp.*

Jackson, Brian and **Marsden, Dennis.** Education and the Working Class: *Some General Themes Raised by a Study of 88 Working-class Children in a Northern Industrial City. 268 pp. 2 folders.*

Marris, Peter. The Experience of Higher Education. *232 pp. 27 tables.*
● Loss and Change. *192 pp.*

Marris, Peter and **Rein, Martin.** Dilemmas of Social Reform. *Poverty and Com-munity Action in the United States. 256 pp.*

Marris, Peter and **Somerset, Anthony.** African Businessmen. *A Study of Entre-preneurship and Development in Kenya. 256 pp.*

Mills, Richard. Young Outsiders: *a Study in Alternative Communities. 216 pp.*

Runciman, W. G. Relative Deprivation and Social Justice. *A Study of Attitudes to Social Inequality in Twentieth-Century England. 352 pp.*

Willmott, Peter. Adolescent Boys in East London. *230 pp.*

Willmott, Peter and **Young, Michael.** Family and Class in a London Suburb. *202 pp. 47 tables.*

Young, Michael and **McGeeney, Patrick.** Learning Begins at Home. *A Study of a Junior School and its Parents. 128 pp.*

Young, Michael and **Willmott, Peter.** Family and Kinship in East London. *Foreword by Richard M. Titmuss. 252 pp. 39 tables.*
The Symmetrical Family. *410 pp.*

Reports of the Institute for Social Studies in Medical Care

Cartwright, Ann, Hockey, Lisbeth and **Anderson, John J.** Life Before Death. *310 pp.*
Dunnell, Karen and **Cartwright, Ann.** Medicine Takers, Prescribers and Hoarders. *190 pp.*
Farrell, C. My Mother Said. . . *A Study of the Way Young People Learned About Sex and Birth Control. 288 pp.*

Medicine, Illness and Society
General Editor W. M. Williams

Hall, David J. Social Relations & Innovation. *Changing the State of Play in Hospitals. 232 pp.*
Hall, David J. and **Stacey, M.** (Eds) Beyond Separation. *234 pp.*
Robinson, David. The Process of Becoming Ill. *142 pp.*
Stacey, Margaret *et al.* Hospitals, Children and Their Families. *The Report of a Pilot Study. 202 pp.*
Stimson, G. V. and **Webb, B.** Going to See the Doctor. *The Consultation Process in General Practice. 155 pp.*

Monographs in Social Theory
General Editor Arthur Brittan

● **Barnes, B.** Scientific Knowledge and Sociological Theory. *192 pp.*
Bauman, Zygmunt. Culture as Praxis. *204 pp.*
● **Dixon, Keith.** Sociological Theory. *Pretence and Possibility. 142 pp.*
The Sociology of Belief. *Fallacy and Foundation. About 160 pp.*
Goff, T. W. Marx and Mead. *Contributions to a Sociology of Knowledge. 176 pp.*
Meltzer, B. N., Petras, J. W. and **Reynolds, L. T.** Symbolic Interactionism. *Genesis, Varieties and Criticisms. 144 pp.*
● **Smith, Anthony D.** The Concept of Social Change. *A Critique of the Functionalist Theory of Social Change. 208 pp.*

Routledge Social Science Journals

The British Journal of Sociology. *Editor – Angus Stewart; Associate Editor – Leslie Sklair. Vol. 1, No. 1 – March 1950 and Quarterly. Roy. 8vo. All back issues available. An international journal publishing original papers in the field of sociology and related areas.*
Community Work. *Edited by David Jones and Marjorie Mayo. 1973. Published annually.*
Economy and Society. *Vol. 1, No. 1. February 1972 and Quarterly. Metric Roy. 8vo. A journal for all social scientists covering sociology, philosophy, anthropology, economics and history. All back numbers available.*

Ethnic and Racial Studies. *Editor – John Stone. Vol. 1 – 1978. Published quarterly.*
Religion. Journal of Religion and Religions. *Chairman of Editorial Board, Ninian Smart. Vol. 1, No. 1, Spring 1971. A journal with an inter-disciplinary approach to the study of the phenomena of religion. All back numbers available.*
Sociology of Health and Illness. *A Journal of Medical Sociology. Editor – Alan Davies; Associate Editor – Ray Jobling. Vol. 1, Spring 1979. Published 3 times per annum.*
Year Book of Social Policy in Britain. *Edited by Kathleen Jones. 1971. Published annually.*

Social and Psychological Aspects of Medical Practice
Editor   Trevor Silverstone

Lader, Malcolm. Psychophysiology of Mental Illness. *280 pp.*
● **Silverstone, Trevor** and **Turner, Paul.** Drug Treatment in Psychiatry. *Revised edition. 256 pp.*
Whiteley, J. S. and **Gordon, J.** Group Approaches in Psychiatry. *240 pp.*

Printed and bound in Great Britain by
Redwood Burn Limited, Trowbridge & Esher